THE LONG PRESIDENCY

The Long Presidency

France in
the Mitterrand Years,
1981–1995

Julius W. Friend

Westview Press
A Member of the Perseus Books Group

Copyright © 1998 by Westview Press, A Member of the Perseus Books Group

Published in 1998 in the United States of America by Westview Press, 5500 Central Avenue, Boulder, Colorado 80301-2877, and in the United Kingdom by Westview Press, 12 Hid's Copse Road, Cumnor Hill, Oxford OX2 9JJ

Library of Congress Cataloging-in-Publication Data
Friend, Julius Weis.
  The long presidency : France in the Mitterrand years, 1981–1995 /
Julius W. Friend.
     p.   cm.
  Includes bibliographical references and index.
  ISBN 0-8133-2850-0 (hc.) — ISBN 0-8133-2851-9 (pb.)
  1. Mitterrand, François, 1916–   —Influence. 2. France—Politics
and government—1981–1995. 3. Socialism—France—History—20th
century. 4. Europe—Politics and government—1945–   I. Title.
DC423.F748   1998
944.083'8'092—dc21
                                                                    97-31017
                                                                       CIP

The paper used in this publication meets the requirements of the American National Standard for Permanence of Paper for Printed Library Materials Z39.48-1984.

10   9   8   7   6   5   4   3   2   1

Contents

Acknowledgments

This book is in part the result of more than 300 interviews conducted between 1983 and 1996, often followups with the same people over the years. I should like to thank Philippe Alexandre, Gilles Andréani, Jean Audibert, Robert Badinter, Raymond Barre, Jean-Louis Bemer, Maurice Benassayag, the late Pierre Bérégovoy, Suzanne Berger, Yannick Bodin, Didier Borotra, Jean-Michel Boucheron, Bernard Brizay, Daniel Boy, Elisabeth Burg, Guy Carcassonne, Christophe Caresche, André Carmon, Jean-Claude Casanova, Roland Cayrol, Bernard Cazes, Christian Chapman, Paul Chauvat, Michel Charzat, Pierre Cherruau, Élie Cohen, Samy Cohen, Lyne Cohen-Solal, Laurent Cohen-Tanugi, Jean-Claude Colliard, Gerard Collomb, Jean-Marc de Comarmond, Stephane Courtois, Michel Crépeau, Joseph Daniel, Ian Davidson, Yves Delahaye, Bertrand Delanoë, Gérard Delfau, Jacques Delors, Jacques Douffiagues, René Drouin, Claude Dubillot, Michel Dubreuil, Jean-Claude Duchalard, Gérard Dumas, Elisabeth Dupoirier, Joelle Dussaut, Henri Emmanuelli, Paul Fabra, Jean-Pierre Faugère, Christine Fauvet-Mycia, Nicole and Jean Feidt, the late Henri Fiszbin, Jean-Pierre Foubert, Pierre Frappat, Michel Garicoix, Roland Garrigue, Marcel Garrouste, Jean-Dominique Giuliani, Michel Gonelle, Christian Goux, Gilbert Gouze, Catherine and Pierre Gremion, Alfred Grosser, Gérard Grunberg, Jean-Marie Guéhenno, Yves Guéna, Pierre Guidoni, Elisabeth Guigou, Henri Guillaume, Régis Guyotat, Arthur Hartmann, Pierre Hassner, the late Charles Hernu, Philippe Herzog, Pierre Heurtin, Francois Hincker, Jacques Huntzinger, Serge Hurtig, Gérard Jacquet, Patrick Jarreau, Jean-Noël Jeanneney, Jacques Jessel, Jacques Julliard, Alain Juppé, Jean-François Kahn, Riva Kastoryano, the late Annie Kriegel, Denis Lacorne, Pascal Lamy, the late Georges Lavau, Branko Lazitch, Jean-Yves Le Déaut, Gerard LeGall, Anne-Marie LeGloannec, Gerard Lesprit, Max Levita, Raymond Lory, Marcel Lucotte, Henri Madelin, Patrick Martinat, Gilles Martinet, René Mathevet, Pierre Mauroy, Pierre Méhaignerie, Yves Mény, Denis Mercier, Didier Migaud, Alain Minc, Dominique Moisi, Bernard Montergnole, Philippe Moreau-Defarges, Didier Motchane, Louis Moulinet, Jean-Louis Moynot, Jean Musitelli, Henry Nau, Frédéric Niedielski, Michel Noir, Charles Pasqua, André Pautard, Guy Penne, Pascal Perrineau, Thierry Pfister, François Platonne, Diana Pinto, the late Jean Pronteau, Antoine Prost, Nicole Questiaux, Roger Quilliot, Jean Ranger, Jean-Marie Rausch, Guy Revellat, Dominique Richard, Philippe Robrieux, Michel Rocard, Lucien Rolland, Pierre Rosanvallon, Patricia Roubillet, Joseph Rovan, Michel Sainte-Marie, André

Salomon, Jacques Santrot, Claude Saunier, Christian Sautter, Elisabeth Schemla, Philippe Séguin, Jean Serisé, Brigitte Stoffaës, Christian Stoffaës, Dominique Strauss-Kahn, Françoise Subillot, Paul Thibaud, the late Marie-France Thoinet, Georges Touchard, Claire Tréan, Christian Tual, Philippe Tugas, Jean-Claude Vajou, Hubert Védrine, Jean Verlhac, Jean-Yves Vif, Jérôme Vignon, Henri Weber, Pierre-André Wilzer, Jean-Pierre Worms, Colette Ysmal, and Martha Zuber. To my friends John and Nancy Condon and Marina, Dmitri, and Eugène Savostianoff go my thanks for much hospitality and advice.

Anton Deporte, Harvey Feigenbaum, and Steven Philip Kramer, who read drafts of several chapters of this book, are not responsible for my errors, but are responsible for much improvement. My thanks go to them also.

I am grateful to the editors of *French Politics and Society* for permission to use materials that have appeared in a number of articles I contributed to that remarkable journal.

My greatest debt is to Louise Friend: gentle but severe critic and editor. This book is dedicated to her.

Julius W. Friend
Chevy Chase, Maryland

Abbreviations and Acronyms

CDS	Centre des Démocrates Sociaux
CDU	Christian Democratic Union (Germany)
CERES	Centre d'Etudes, de Recherches, et d'Education Socialistes
CFDT	Conféderation Française Démocratique du Travail
CGE	Compagnie Générale d'Electricité
CGT	Confédération Générale du Travail
CIP	*contrat d'insertion professionelle*
CIR	Convention des Institutions Républicaines
CJTF	combined joint task forces
CNAL	Centre National d'Action Laïque
CNCL	Conseil National des Communications et des Libertés
DGSE	Direction Générale de Sécurité Exteriéure
EC	European Community
EMS	European Monetary System
EMU	economic and monetary union
ENA	Ecole Nationale d'Administration
EU	European Union
FAR	Force Armée Rwandaise
FAR	Force d'Action Rapide
FCC	Federal Communications Commission (U.S.)
FEN	Fédération de l'Education Nationale
FGDS	Fédération de la Gauche Démocratique et Socialiste
FIS	Front Islamique de Salut (Algeria)
FLN	Front de Libération Nationale (Algeria)
FLNKS	Front de Libération National Kanak Socialiste
FN	Front National
FNSEA	Fédération Nationale des Syndicats d'Exploitants Agricoles
FO	Force Ouvrière
FPR	Front Patriotique Rwandais
GATT	General Agreement on Tariffs and Trade
GDP	gross domestic product
GIA	Groupe Islamique Armée (Algeria)
GNP	gross national product
IGC	intergovernmental conference

IMF	International Monetary Fund
INSEE	Institut National de la Statistique et des Etudes Economiques
MNPDG	Mouvement National de Prisonniers et Deportés de Guerre
MRG	Mouvement des Radicaux de Gauche
MRP	Mouvement Républicain Populaire
NATO	North Atlantic Treaty Organization
OECD	Organization for European Cooperation and Development
ORA	Organisation de Résistance de l'Armée
PCF	Parti Communiste Français
PLO	Palestine Liberation Organization
PR	Parti Républicain
PRS	Parti Radical-Socialiste
PS	Parti Socialiste
PSU	Parti Socialiste Unifié
RMI	*revenue minimum d'insertion*
RPR	Rassemblement pour la République
SED	Socialist Unity Party (East Germany)
SFIO	Section Française de l'Internationale Ouvriére
SMIC	*salaire minimum de croissance*
SPD	Social Democratic Party (Germany)
SDI	Strategic Defense Initiative (U.S.)
TUC	*travail d'utilité collective*
UDC	Union Démocratique du Centre
UDF	Union pour la Démocratie Française
UDSR	Union Démocratique et Socialiste de la Résistance
VAT	value-added tax
WEU	Western European Union

Introduction

The story of François Mitterrand's two seven-year terms is one of rapid reversals of fortune, beginning with the triumphant and unexpected elections of the president and a Socialist parliamentary majority, then a brief honeymoon spent in intoxicated self-assurance. There followed economic difficulties, which forced retreat from original Socialist party principles. Unacknowledged at first, then admitted, retreat undermined popular confidence in the president and government, engendering confusion about their real policy and doubts of their competence.

Entering into power after twenty-three years of Gaullist and post-Gaullist rule in the Fifth Republic, the Left had believed, in the rhetoric of Culture Minister Jack Lang, that it had crossed "the frontier that separates the light from darkness." For the French Socialists and the adherents of the Left in general, a new age had begun. For the defeated Right, an age had ended. Said former interior minister Michel Poniatowski: "The trouble-makers of 1968 are in power."

It is easy enough, years after a political event, to scoff at the rhetoric of winners and losers. At the difficult end of the twentieth century it is harder to transport ourselves back to the time of unprecedented growth and understand the mind-set and the assumptions of both Right and Left in 1981. The period in France improperly baptized the "Trente Glorieuses"—the Thirty Glorious Years—had ended with the oil shock of 1974. Both Left and Right denied that anything but a short interruption of prosperity had occurred. They could not know that enormous changes in the economic nature of society were nearly upon them, changes that would strip the nation-state dear to all the French of much of its economic sovereignty and would impose revision of a welfare state built up since World War II by Left and Right.

In 1981, both camps intended to continue on the course on which the events of May 1968 had launched them. The Right wished to pursue a *dirigiste* capitalism, tempered by a need for social policy. The Left demonized the Right, denied its social achievements, and promised great results from a radical policy of mixed Keynesianism and socialist nationalization.

Did the years 1981–1983 see the end of socialism *à la française*? The failures in those years were of the inflated hopes and ill-adapted policies that carried the Socialists into office. The rhetoric of *rupture*—a break with capitalism—vanished

1

with the collapse of the neo-Keynesian policy of reflation and hopes of stemming unemployment. Nationalization of industry and of the banking system provided no medicines for a rapid cure of the ailing economy. Socialist legislative reforms failed to sway voters more concerned with unemployment and other economic worries. Amid a general impression of administrative muddle, Socialist ratings in polls and interim elections slipped badly.

But the legislation of those years was responsible for changes both deliberate and unintended that have affected many aspects of French life. The first Socialist government and parliamentary majority produced a flood of legislation. Laws on nationalization, decentralization, labor relations, legal reform, restructuring of radio and television, educational reform, and much else tumbled from the National Assembly.

The change in policies and leaders in 1983–1984 permitted a slow recovery in late 1985 and early 1986, but that was not enough to save Socialist fortunes; the election of 1986 was lost because of the mistakes of 1981–1983. The 1986 defeat was expected, even discounted in advance. Still, by winning 31 percent of the vote, the Socialist party confirmed to itself that the Left electorate had accepted the sober notion that the desirable is not always the possible.

Socialist retrenchment might have benefited a Communist party that had not hesitated to criticize the Socialist shift when it was still in office and that had left the government to resume embittered opposition in 1984. Throughout the 1960s and 1970s the Communist vote had remained at a level slightly above 20 percent of the electorate. From 1981 through the presidential elections of 1988, the percentage went down at every election, recovering in the legislative elections of 1988 to a point roughly half its level of the 1970s, sinking again in 1993. As the Communist vote dropped, the Socialists concluded that voters of the Left had rejected the PCF as a valid critic of Mitterrand's performance. A high Communist vote would have encouraged fissile tendencies within the Socialist party. A low one allowed the Socialists to follow a gradualist course that abandoned the leftist rhetoric of a few years earlier. Mitterrand could not take the entire credit for the demolition of the Communist party, which has largely self-destructed. It is, however, fair to ask whether the decline would have been as swift or as great if Mitterrand had not in 1971 adopted the dangerous but effective tactic of alliance with the PCF.

The Socialist party had entered office under the illusion that a generous spirit and vigorous policy could remove all obstacles, a belief that had found mean-spirited and shortsighted capitalists responsible for almost all the faults of the French economy. The congress of Toulouse in 1985 saw all party factions agreeing that the equitable distribution desired by socialism could take place only where imaginative enterprise has created profitable production. But the economy failed to produce the growth that might have permitted more redistribution. Instead, rising unemployment and the shoving of more elements of society to the margins produced a rise in inequality.

Although the collapse of communism in Central and Eastern Europe, then in the Soviet Union, perhaps should not have affected democratic socialists, the French Socialists had believed firmly in *le sens de l'histoire,* a phrase that in French encompasses the ideas of the meaning and the direction of history, which they knew moved inexorably to the left. By 1991, when a Socialist congress adopted in its program the phrase "capitalism limits our theoretical horizon," French Socialists had become uncertain about both history's meaning and its direction. French socialism, which had in the 1970s boasted that it was and would be quite distinct from social democracy, even the Swedish version, by the early 1990s had accepted for itself the description of social democratic, at a time when the meaning and content of even that term were increasingly in question. French Socialists still knew they were on and of the Left, not the Right, but beyond that, they were unsure where the boundaries lay.

Since 1945 the French Right had taken it almost as an axiom that the state should have the leading role in the economy. After 1981 it found itself in opposition to a more thoroughgoing Socialist version of this same doctrine. The Right's response was to look westward to Ronald Reagan's America for a newfound belief in free enterprise capitalism. In 1986, the Right won back a parliamentary majority. A conservative prime minister ruled France while the president reigned in so-called cohabitation with him—above the melee but still the guarantor of the constitution. RPR and UDF ministers returned to power singing the praises of less government, more and more free enterprise. They proposed an extensive list of privatizations, which they continued to work on when they returned to power in 1993. Social policies—except on immigration—remained, however, little different, and fiscal policy continued much the same. Indeed, post-1981 politics have been de-ideologized on both sides.

By 1988 Mitterrand had won the game of cohabitation. His popularity renewed, he easily won a second term, dissolved the National Assembly, as he had done in 1981—and failed to win a stable majority. In the following five years the president had three prime ministers: one whom he disliked and finally dismissed, the second, France's first female prime minister, who proved not up to the job, and a third, who committed suicide in despair shortly after disastrous parliamentary elections. Economic downturn, rising unemployment, and scandal, which tarnished both the president and his party, had reduced the Socialist delegation in the National Assembly by more than three-quarters. Mitterrand, diminished by illness and continuing unpopularity, ended his second term in another cohabitation with the Right.

Mitterrand both amended and adhered to Gaullist foreign policy. By abandoning what had become a mythical "special relationship" with the Soviet Union for a somewhat closer tie to the United States, at least in North Atlantic affairs, Mitterrand amended Gaullist policy. France followed Gaullist traditions in seeking to improve its nuclear deterrent and in moving closer to Germany. After 1983, Mitterrand replaced his goal of socialism with European integration, and the prospect of German unification caused him to step up the pace. The policy of close cooperation with Germany became and, despite many tensions, remains the central tenet of French foreign policy.

Outside Europe, Socialist policies first challenged the United States on Central America, then retreated. The tyranny of the real that the Socialists faced in domestic affairs was reflected also in the frustration of early attempts to change traditional

Gaullist policies on Africa. Despite early Socialist declarations, Mitterrand's policies there became largely consonant with the Gaullist tradition. The years of cohabitation saw no real disagreement on foreign policy between president and prime ministers. Many Gaullist positions had been rendered obsolete by the end of the Cold War. Mitterrand's successor, Jacques Chirac, encountered little opposition in taking his country nearly all the way back into the North Atlantic Treaty Organization (NATO)—a step from which the paradoxically more Gaullist Mitterrand had shrunk.

The election of a Socialist president in 1981 appeared at first to present a major discontinuity in French politics. In later perspective, the original Socialist economic policies can be seen as another variation on postwar *dirigiste* policies, whereas the return to a more orthodox policy after 1983, continuing toward the end of the century, was closer to the policies of Giscard's prime minister Raymond Barre than to earlier Gaullism. Both Socialist Pierre Bérégovoy and conservative Edouard Balladur as economics and finance ministers or prime ministers throughout the period 1984–1995 pursued a tight fiscal and deflationary policy, which kept the franc strong in relation to the deutsche mark but permitted the inexorable rise of unemployment.

The Mitterrand years occupy a period in French history longer than the First, Second, and Fourth French Republics and nearly as long as the preeminence of Napoleon I. Their significance is clearest on the institutional level, where they marked an end to the exclusively conservative legitimism of the Fifth Republic. Mitterrand's victory in 1981, his party's defeat in 1986, and his reelection confirmed the legitimation of the Socialists as a governing party. Two periods of cohabitation of a Socialist president and a conservative prime minister demonstrated the strength and flexibility of the constitution of the Fifth Republic.

The Socialists elected in 1981 had been talking of a break with capitalism; instead they came to terms with it. The processes of change that the Socialists began, or occasioned, or underwent made up, in their entirety, an unintended revolution, which must be set beside the continuities described above. At the end of his fourteen years in office, François Mitterrand left behind him a changed France—but not altered in the ways he had originally intended. A Socialist president had made France safe for capitalism. France was less divided politically than before 1981. But it was little less unequal economically, although in different ways than in 1981. Unemployment and racial tension had become the nightmares of French society.

When thus briefly summarized, the fourteen years of this long presidency strike a melancholy and declining note. No one could describe them as triumphant, despite real accomplishments. Very possibly, however, a longer perspective will show the achievements of the Mitterrand era in domestic and foreign policy in a more positive light than that thrown by the twilight of the twentieth century. An era is often judged by what its successors do or do not do.

This account of the years 1981–1995 does not seek to compete with books of specialist essays describing in detail particular aspects of this period. References to a number of those will be found in my notes and bibliography. My principal concern is to accomplish what scholarly compendia cannot easily do—to give a single, balanced, and coherent description of an important period in recent history.

My ambition is to bring a historian's approach to a recent and very important period of French history. The chronological technique has its defects, but politics in action is such a confused battleground that political analysis runs the risk of overclarification. Confusion was not lacking in French politics between 1981 and 1995, and I have thought it useful to describe the manner in which events occurred before attempting to sort out their meaning. All translations are my own unless otherwise specified, and French official statistics are cited from INSEE, the Institut National de la Statistique et des Etudes Economiques.

This book builds on a predecessor volume on Mitterrand's first term, *Seven Years in France.* I have used parts of that book, extensively revised and reconsidered in the light of later information, before continuing with the history of France in Mitterrand's second term. I am acutely aware that a historical account written soon after the events it describes can be no more than a beginning. But a great many documents on the period are already available, to say nothing of personal and journalistic accounts. Judgments on the significance of these events is a greater problem, but I take comfort in the implicit lesson in Chou En-lai's response to a visitor asking his opinion of the significance of the French Revolution, "It's too soon to tell."

1

Genesis

Prologue: The Pantheon

On May 21, 1981, François Mitterrand, the newly elected president of the Fifth French Republic, entered the Elysée palace, seat of the presidency, to assume his office. Eleven days earlier this Socialist politician had won his third presidential campaign, having lost to Charles de Gaulle in 1965, then to Valéry Giscard d'Estaing in 1974. Mitterrand was briefed on state secrets for a few minutes in private by his predecessor. Then, once the president of the Constitutional Council had officially proclaimed the results of the election and the grand chancellor of the Legion of Honor had invested him with the rank of grand master of the order, François Mitterrand became president.

In a brief speech, he struck two contradictory notes: "The political majority of the French people has just found its identity with its social majority," and "President of all the French, I want to bring them together for the great causes that await us, and to create in all ways the conditions for a true national community."[1] Riding up the avenue des Champs-Elysées, Mitterrand placed a wreath by the flame under the Arc de Triomphe commemorating the Unknown Soldier. This was the ceremony incumbent on a new leader; the young president Giscard, seven years earlier, had marked it by striding up the grand avenue leading to the arch.

Mitterrand would mark his entry into office with an additional ceremony. After a luncheon at the Elysée for 200 guests, he entered his automobile to proceed to the Left Bank, descending at the corner of the boulevard Saint-Michel and the rue Soufflot. Before him rose the great domed Pantheon, planned before the Revolution to be the new church of Paris's patron saint, Sainte Geneviève, then converted into the last resting place of the secular saints of the French Republic. As an immense crowd applauded, and the Orchestre de Paris sounded out Beethoven's "Ode to Joy," Mitterrand marched up the street and entered the Pantheon alone, a red rose in his hand. Television viewers could see him moving in the shadows of the crypt, placing roses on the tombs of three symbolic figures. Two were martyrs: Jean Jaurès, the Socialist leader assassinated by a fanatic just as World War I was breaking out, and Jean Moulin, de Gaulle's chief representative to the internal Resistance in World War II, who died under torture when he was betrayed to the Gestapo. The third, Victor Schoelcher, had championed the cause that abolished slavery in the French colonies in the 1840s. (The television coverage did not show the aide who signaled the way to Mitterrand in the gloom of the crypt or the helpers who handed him fresh roses.) Mitterrand emerged on the portico of the Pantheon into a pouring rain, to the strains of the "Marseillaise" and the joyful shouts of his supporters.

This republican rite was designed by Jack Lang, Mitterrand's new minister for culture, who had first made his mark as a theatrical producer. Many thought it triumphal and very beautiful. It honored, not the country's patriots who had fallen in war—the wreath at the Arc de Triomphe took care of that—but a Socialist hero, a Gaullist Resistance hero, and a (very obscure) early civil rights hero. Later, critics would increasingly find it pompous and in bad taste, more imperial than republican.

At the same time Mitterrand's new prime minister, Pierre Mauroy, had left rue Soufflot to spend his first hours at the Hôtel Matignon, seat of the government. He was joined by Jacques Delors, the new minister of economics and finance, and the governor of the Bank of France. They could glance at the end of the ceremony on a television screen, but they had more urgent business. The French franc, overvalued but protected by the previous government, was under heavy attack, as panicky investors took their money out of the country and speculators hovered. Some advisers urged Mitterrand to proclaim an instant devaluation on entering office, like that adopted by de Gaulle in 1958 and his successor, Georges Pompidou, in 1969. But Mitterrand had already told Mauroy that the Left could not begin its work with a devaluation. During the next two years, he would have to accede to three devaluations. The new era had thus begun with a display of republican triumphalism and an important monetary decision taken for political, not economic, reasons.

History and Mythology

François Mitterrand was the new leader of an old party with a complex history. His Parti Socialiste (PS) had descended from socialist parties founded as early as 1882, which in 1905 had merged into the Section Française de l'Internationale Ouvrière (SFIO). The SFIO split in 1920. A majority followed left-wing leaders who wished to affiliate French socialism with Lenin's new revolutionary workers' international, creating the new Parti Communiste Français (PCF).

Except for a World War I coalition, the SFIO participated in only one government in the Third Republic, when its leader Léon Blum became prime minister of the Popular Front government in 1936. The failures and the successes of Blum's Popular Front government entered the mythology of the French Left. The Socialists of the 1970s saw in it important milestones—the forty-hour week and paid vacations for workers. Yet Blum's ministry lasted only thirteen months; its rapid loss of momentum, defeat in a key Senate vote, and fall in June 1937 also became part of Socialist mythology. Blum had battered in vain against "the wall of money."

World War II saw the defeat of the French armies and the dissolution of the republic, which became Marshal Philippe Pétain's authoritarian "French state." Political parties were dissolved.

After Hitler's attack on the Soviet Union, the Communist party played a major role in a Resistance that was still in its earliest phases when they joined it. The PCF's new weight became apparent in the first postwar elections in October 1945, when the party took 26.2 percent of the vote (and 28.3 percent the next year), with the SFIO getting only 23.4 percent—its high point for the next thirty-six years.

In the Fourth Republic, the SFIO under its new leader, Guy Mollet, found itself backing repression in Madagascar, Vietnam, and then in Algeria. Its vote diminished steadily and splits appeared, notably the Parti Socialiste Unifié (PSU). One of the PSU's leaders was a young technocrat named Michel Rocard.

When de Gaulle returned to power in May 1958, Mollet backed him and did not break with him until 1962. Many disgusted voters regarded the SFIO as a party of opportunist bureaucrats.

The presidential election of 1965 was the first held under universal suffrage. Gaston Defferre, the moderate Socialist mayor of Marseilles, tried to re-federate the French Center-Left and non-Communist Left. To win, he needed a Communist vote he was unwilling to bargain for. Defferre was trying to reach too far right and not far enough left, and his candidacy collapsed. After Defferre's failure, no one in France supposed that any candidate could defeat Charles de Gaulle. In this unpromising situation one farsighted and adventurous politician glimpsed real opportunity. His name was François Mitterrand.[2]

The New Leader of the Left

The Mitterrand who ran for president in 1965 was very far from being the Socialist leader of 1981. To many of the French on the Left he was an improbable standard-bearer. At forty-nine, he was a veteran of eleven coalition cabinets of the Fourth Republic, in which he had represented the small, mildly leftist Union Démocratique et Socialiste de la Résistance (UDSR). Leftists knew that he came from the well-to-do middle class, that his background was Catholic, and that his education until university level was entirely in Catholic schools. They wanted to know whether Mitterrand really belonged to the Left or was merely an opportunist. If he was now genuinely on their side, how had he arrived there?

François Mitterrand was born on October 26, 1916, in the small town of Jarnac, in southwestern France. His father, Joseph Mitterrand, was a station master who later took over his father-in-law's vinegar distillery. The Mitterrands were proud, conservative, and intensely Catholic. A university comrade visiting the Mitterrand family noted that they all felt intellectually superior to the snobbish brandy makers of Cognac, six miles distant, who looked down on them as vinegar merchants. "François held them in deep contempt . . . and it was at that time that he conceived his attitude toward money, which he never lacked—characterized by contempt for those who have it and show it."3

Mitterrand framed it differently: "My family was revolted by [the idea that] money could be more important than the values they held important: country, religion, liberty, dignity. It was the enemy, the corrupter."4 This suspicion of capitalism had its origin in medieval Catholicism but gained force among the conservative Catholic bourgeoisie of the nineteenth century; it owed nothing to the ideas of the Left.

Arriving in Paris at the age of eighteen in October 1934, Mitterrand attended classes at the Sorbonne and the Ecole des Sciences Politiques and was caught up in the politics of that tumultuous era—very much on the Right. The story of Mitterrand's political attitudes in his youth has been complicated by Mitterrand's own versions and distortions of it.5 In his 1969 book, *Ma part de verité,* Mitterrand omitted the fact that he had joined the youth wing of the semi-Fascist Croix de Feu. He gave his earlier biographers to understand that he had defended an unpopular law professor who was Haile Selassie's lawyer, when in fact he had participated in noisy and anti-Semitic student demonstrations against him. Mitterrand also went to Belgium to visit the Bourbon pretender.

When war broke out in 1939, Mitterrand was a sergeant in a regiment of colonial infantry. Wounded just before the armistice, he was hospitalized, then made prisoner. In POW camp he met, not only the fortunate youth of the middle classes he had always known, but also workers and Communists. The experience put a slight dent into young Mitterrand's elitist view of life and society—but did not change his politics.

As soon as he had recovered from his wound, he began to plot escape, and on the third try he succeeded. His home in Jarnac was in occupied France, where he could not stay without false papers. Family friends helped him find a job in Vichy. In 1969, Mitterrand described his passage from POW camp to Vichy to the Resistance rather too simply: "Once returned to France, I became a resister, without any great problem."6

A biographer wrote in 1977 of the then–first secretary of the PS that as a young functionary in Vichy in 1942, he was "not, properly speaking, anti-Pétainist." Again: "Another complaint against him . . . Mitterrand is supposed to have been vaguely tempted by the theses of the National Revolution. All his friends from the time of the Occupation . . . say the contrary."7 The new information on his early opinions, which was published in 1994, however, documents in great detail the continuation of Mitterrand's right-wing views after his student and POW days. Clearly he was at first a great admirer of Marshal Pétain.

The fact is that François Mitterrand carefully retouched the history of his early youth and Vichy period and apparently encouraged his close friends to back his story. The confirmation in 1994 of this systematic retouching obviously threw fresh doubt on the veracity of everything Mitterrand had recounted about his youthful opinions and activities—and not that period alone.

In Vichy, Mitterrand worked at the Commission for the Rehabilitation of War Prisoners. (As many as 1.5 million French soldiers remained in German POW camps.) When his chief at the prisoners' commission was replaced in early 1943 by a man thought close to Pierre Laval, Mitterrand and his friends decided to use their organization as a Resistance net.

Rapidly, ex-sergeant Mitterrand showed himself to be a leader. While working against the Germans, Mitterrand tried to appear a loyal Vichy official. He allowed friends with credit on Marshal Pétain's staff to propose him for a Vichyite decoration, the *francisque*. Later in his career enemies among both the Gaullists and the Communists charged that his receipt of it proved that he had played an opportunist role in Vichy. Mitterrand's active Resistance work began in the early winter of 1943. His group aided prisoners, gleaned intelligence from them, and re-formed escapees into Resistance units. Later it became known as the Mouvement National de Prisonniers et Deportés de Guerre (MNPDG).

Mitterrand's group was supported by the ORA (Organisation de Résistance de l'Armée)—the Resistance group set up by former general staff officers after November 1942, whose links were with General Henri Giraud. Giraud believed himself in line with Pétain's secret intentions, intentions that Pétain was unable to apply. Giraud was still a believer in the Marshal when he arrived in North Africa under American auspices in November 1942 and did not break until September 1943. The officers of the ORA respected Giraud as a military leader and were doubtful of de Gaulle as an overly political one.

Mitterrand was in close touch with senior ORA officers, and his work was financed by them (with funds from London). When his double life as Vichy official and member of the Resistance became too dangerous, he went underground. The prisoner of war movement needed a contact with the French National Liberation Committee, then still coheaded by General Henri Giraud and de Gaulle and headquartered in Algiers. Mitterrand proposed himself. A British Lysander picked him up at a clandestine airfield and flew him to London.

From there the twenty-seven-year-old emissary, now "Captain Morland" of the Resistance, flew to Algiers—still using the ORA-Giraudist connection—for another of the formative events of his life, a meeting with de Gaulle. It went badly. Mitterrand was known to sympathize with de Gaulle's rival Giraud. Worse, he refused to merge his Resistance network with one led by de Gaulle's nephew Michel Cailliau and place himself under the latter's orders.

Mitterrand was from the first suspect to de Gaulle and the Gaullists, not so much because he was a latecomer to the Resistance who had first believed in Marshal Pétain, but because he was a Giraudist. Giraud was the link with Pétainism for those who had believed in the marshal—and for de Gaulle (and still more for his zealots), Giraudists were still believers in Vichy.

Nevertheless, Mitterrand was able to return to Britain and then to France in February 1944. Merging his organization with the network organized by Cailliau and with another led by the Communists, Mitterrand emerged as the leader of the new group. Mitterrand's Resistance record has been disparaged by his enemies, but those in a good position to judge thought it distinguished. De Gaulle in his *Mémoires de guerre* included Mitterrand in a short list of resisters who gave significant aid to the overall Resistance effort in 1944.[8] The accusation that Mitterrand was a resister of the last minute is unjust—his activities began in early-to-mid-1943—at which time the number of active resisters in occupied France was still tiny.

After the Allied landings, Mitterrand, as a leader of the MNPDG, was named secretary-general of the provisional government's ministerial department for prisoners, until the government could be formed. In this capacity young Mitterrand felt himself slighted by de Gaulle and then disappointed at being denied the post of minister for prisoners. Another encounter with the general took place in June 1945 when Mitterrand went along with a Communist-organized mass protest on the slowness of repatriation of POWs and other griefs. Receiving the leaders, de Gaulle violently criticized Mitterrand and rebuked him sharply for criticizing the government. The tone, if not the rebuke, seems to have permanently alienated Mitterrand from the general.[9]

In late 1944 Mitterrand married Danielle Gouze, the sister of a Resistance friend. Her family could not have differed more from the Mitterrands: atheist schoolteachers and freemasons, the very stereotype of everything passionately distrusted by conservative Catholic France. Sometime during the war, Mitterrand's religious faith had slipped its moorings.[10] He did not cease at once to practice his religion—witness the church marriage—but he gradually moved toward a deism strongly marked by suspicion of the social role of the Catholic church. In 1973 he told an interviewer: "I was born a Catholic and will doubtless die as one. . . . [He did.] But I also have an irreconcilable argument with a certain attitude of the Church, as the accomplice across the centuries of an established order that I abhor."[11]

Young Mitterrand did not join the new Catholic party, the Mouvement Républicain Populaire (MRP), preferring the forces emerging from the Resistance. His choice, the UDSR, combined left-wing Gaullists, socialists, and moderates. Mitterrand in 1945 belonged to the last category. He had discovered that he could be a leader. To fill a political role he needed to be a deputy. His first try failed, but in October 1946, after the approval of the constitution for the Fourth Republic, Mitterrand was offered a difficult constituency in the department of the Nièvre and won.

Thirty years old, the new deputy became in 1947 the youngest minister in France, in charge of veterans' affairs in Paul Ramadier's cabinet. He would number among those most frequently holding office in the Fourth Republic, named to eleven of its twenty-four brief and sometimes stillborn governments. No one in the early years would have called him a leftist.

In the Fourth Republic Mitterrand was a centrist moving toward the left under the whips of his enemies. He made a number of them in 1951 as minister for Overseas France when he negotiated with African leaders who were near rebellion and satisfied their immediate grievances. Several of those leaders were deputies, and their small group sat in parliament with the Communist party. Mitterrand's dealings with them and his success in bringing them over from the PCF alliance to one with his own UDSR outraged diehard defenders of colonialism, who thought he was opening the gates of respectability to a pack of African Reds. The African deputies included Félix Houphouet-Boigny, later president of the Ivory Coast.

Mitterrand's next crisis was the notorious *affaire des fuites* (leaks) in 1954. Interior minister at that time, he had fired the Paris police prefect for advocating action against the PCF using evidence fabricated by the police themselves. The prefect's PCF expert responded with an accusation that Mitterrand was a PCF informant, leaking material from the National Defense Council.[12]

The initial investigations were sabotaged by the police, but the real leakers were eventually discovered. In the meantime Mitterrand had been suspected of being a traitor, his name dragged in the mud by gossip and the denunciations of right-wing deputies. If the mud did not stick, the memory that there had been mud was not entirely effaced.

Mitterrand went on to be minister of justice in the disastrous Mollet government of 1956, which sent draftees to Algeria and covered up for torture. He disapproved, but he went along. In 1958, the Fourth Republic collapsed amid military disobedience that frightened the politicians into supporting the providential return of Charles de Gaulle. This time Mitterrand did not go along.

Was the fact that he disliked de Gaulle and had little credit with him solely responsible for Mitterrand's decision to join a handful of Fourth Republic notables in rejecting the general? His hatred for some of the Gaullists was certainly a factor. Among them were men who had attacked his honor in the *affaire des fuites*. Leaders who had rallied to de Gaulle during the war, like Pierre Mendès-France, now opposed the general. Some men of the Left, notably Guy Mollet, now backed him. To refuse support to de Gaulle in 1958 meant a move to the left and a long political exile—although Mitterrand may not have known quite how long it would be.

By 1958 Mitterrand clearly wanted to be seen as a man of the Left. He had criticized the reigning Algerian policy after the fall of the Mollet government (and, more quietly, before the fall) and had become more and more critical of the colonial lobby, which in turn attacked him as one of those ready to sell out the French empire.[13] The collapse of the Fourth Republic meant the defeat of his hopes to lead France, but it also provided him the chance finally to break with the compromises his ambition had urged him to accept.

In 1959 Mitterrand was the victim of another provocation. When a suspicious character claiming to be an unwilling conspirator against his life asked him to collude in a fake shooting, Mitterrand foolishly did not inform the police. The apparent assassination attempt (staged at the place de l'Observatoire) at first won him sympathy. Then his "co-conspirator" denounced him as the instigator of the plot.

Sneered at by his enemies and doubted by many he had thought his friends, Mitterrand faced the charge that he had not informed the police and saw his parliamentary immunity lifted by the Gaullist assembly majority. The charge was then dropped. After this attempt to frame him, Mitterrand had every reason to dislike the Gaullist regime.

By 1965, however, Mitterrand had emerged from the obloquy that had threatened to destroy him, from a period when "his fingers sufficed to count his friends."[14] He had become one of the strongest opponents of Gaullism among the old politicians of the Fourth Republic, had won back his seat in the National Assembly, and published a much discussed attack on Gaullist rule, *Le Coup d'état permanent*. Consistent opposition to a Gaullist regime inconsistently opposed by the SFIO gave him new credentials as a man of the Left.

Mitterrand had always been anti-Communist. But in 1962, when a referendum changed the constitution to allow direct election of the president, he gained two cardinal insights into the new politics. First, an elected president would be the most important man in France. Second, de Gaulle's hold on the centrist vote was too strong and the non-Communist Left too weak for any anti-Gaullist leftist to succeed without the active support of the Communist party.

In the 1965 presidential elections, after the collapse of Defferre's candidacy, that support was available even (perhaps especially) for so newly fledged a leftist as Mitterrand. Under its new secretary-general Waldeck Rochet, the PCF was trying cautiously to move away from its public role as Moscow's agent in France. Maneuvering rapidly, Mitterrand won support for his candidacy from both the SFIO and the Communists. No one believed he would achieve even relative success.

The disparate forces of the Left in splinter parties and unions backed Mitterrand, but without enthusiasm. Another candidate, MRP leader Jean Lecanuet competed for centrist votes. Mitterrand had no illusions of victory. At the least he wanted political rehabilitation, but his real goal was the leadership of the Left. The campaign was remarkable for its vagueness of program, but many French voters were weary of de Gaulle and still more of the arrogant and all-powerful Gaullists.

In the first round the general fell short of a decisive majority. Forced into a second round by his pygmy opponents, the great man lost something of his prestige. He was decisively reelected in the second round with 55 percent, but Mitterrand, with 44.8 percent, had in this "brilliant defeat" made himself the most prominent leader of the opposition.

Mitterrand proceeded to craft an electoral coalition called the Fédération de la Gauche Démocratique et Socialiste (FGDS), which included the SFIO, the Radicals, and his own minuscule organization, the Convention des Institutions Républicaines (CIR). Mitterrand became president of the FGDS.

The turmoil of May 1968 smashed the FGDS and Mitterrand's prospects. Like the other politicians, he was booed and spat at by the excited young people in the streets. After twenty-five days of street fighting, de Gaulle tried and failed to calm the situation with his old device of a referendum. The general's departure seemed inevitable, and Mitterrand proposed a provisional government to be headed by Mendès-France and declared his candidacy in the presidential election, which would be called immediately thereafter.

The canny tactician had blundered. Two days later de Gaulle disappeared from Paris to seek the support of the army and, after a day of panic for the Gaullists, reappeared with the assurance that it would back him in the event of more street violence. But to avoid violence he dissolved the National Assembly and called new elections.

The wave of leftism was followed by a strong backlash. The conservatives were returned in force; the FGDS lost half of its deputies, and the Communists more than half of theirs. Mitterrand appeared to the man in the street as an adventurer, a clumsy opportunist who had grabbed for power that was not for the seizing; the FGDS speedily collapsed.

The French Right had nonetheless suffered a traumatic shock in the troubles of 1968. The Gaullist regime, which had brought France back from the brink of civil war in 1958 and gone on to witness an amazing prosperity, had been shaken by street riots and strikes. Despite the new right-wing majority, de Gaulle considered himself disavowed, and when he sought relegitimation in a referendum in 1969, he was defeated and resigned. There followed five years of renewed prosperity under Georges Pompidou. For three years a conservative president and his moderate prime minister, Jacques Chaban-Delmas, tried out a "new society" that would offer more to those excited by 1968 and dissatisfied by the redistribution of the fruits of the prosperous years.

The Making of a New Socialist Party

In the presidential election of 1969, Socialist candidate Gaston Defferre took only 5 percent of the vote, while the notorious Stalinist Jacques Duclos had over 21 percent. A shocked SFIO determined that it had to do better. It changed its name, becoming the Parti Socialiste (PS), chose new leaders, and took in splinter groups that had left the SFIO in earlier years. In the wake of the 1969 results, the new PS also concluded that it must change the anti-Communist tactic it had pursued from 1945 on. But the new leadership negotiated very slowly. A coup mounted at the 1971 PS congress of Epinay by the most leftist SFIO group, the Centre d'Etudes, de Recherches, et d'Education Socialistes (CERES), led by Jean-Pierre Chevènement; a more centrist one led by Pierre Mauroy; and the outsider François Mitterrand's CIR led to the takeover of the party by Mitterrand. Mitterrand, never a member of the SFIO, became on the same day a member of the PS and its first secretary.

Mitterrand and his allies had won the leadership of the PS by backroom maneuver in order to conduct a bold new policy. Mitterrand rejected the idea of an ideological debate with the Communists to clarify the terms of an alliance. "The dialogue with the Communist party," said Mitterrand, "will concern the concrete problems of a government with the mission of beginning the socialist transformation of society."[15]

The Dangerous Ally

In 1971–1972 the French Communist party was the largest party in France and by far the best organized.[16] It exerted complete control over the Confédération Général du Travail (CGT), the country's largest trade union organization—with over 2 million members. Communist mayors administered forty-five of the largest cities; Socialists controlled only thirty.[17]

The Communist party was monolithic and centrally governed, and internal dissent was impossible. Most of the French considered the PCF to be fundamentally undemocratic, giving too much weight to Soviet interests in its decisions.[18]

The PS, a freshly united coalition of factions, was still imperfectly controlled by a newcomer and outsider who had yet to prove his leadership qualities and assert complete authority. Mitterrand's PS had at most 80,000 members, few of them real militants.

If a Communist-Socialist alliance should somehow attain power, how many Communist ministers would sit in the government, and what portfolios might they have? Even if the most sensitive posts were not given to Communists, could the PCF be prevented from seeding the civil service, nationalized industry, and radio-television with its servants, along the lines followed in 1944–1945?

Mitterrand was undeterred by these questions. After his takeover of the PS in June 1971, he moved rapidly forward. Following intensive negotiations, a Common Program of Government was announced in June 1972 and signed in July by the PCF, the PS, and a junior partner, the Mouvement des Radicaux de Gauche (MRG).

The Common Program was the product of great hopes—and of mutual bad faith. Mitterrand was quite frank about it. Two days after the final agreement of June 26 he flew off to Vienna, where he told a meeting of the overwhelmingly social democratic Socialist International (deeply disturbed by his infringement of the Cold War injunction against alliances with Communists) that 3 million out of 5 million voters for the French Communist party were potential Socialist voters and that he intended to win them over. Next day PCF secretary-general Georges Marchais told his Central Committee that he fully recognized that the PS was an untrustworthy partner and admitted that the PCF had made compromises to reach an agreement. But he added that "the development of independent party activity in the masses" would parallel the parliamentary path to power. (Marchais's speech was not made public until the PCF-PS quarrel of 1974–1975.)[19]

The PCF in 1972 was an undemocratic party with vestiges of revolutionary rhetoric but no firm revolutionary intent. Its strategy aimed at a reprise of the Popular Front of 1936, with the immediate aim of "advanced democracy," which meant a larger measure of Communist power in a system that would still be nominally pluralist and democratic.

Mitterrand had few illusions about the PCF. He believed that although Communist leaders could not be compelled to act as he desired, their voters might desert them if the party reacted evasively and insincerely to his policy.[20] Postwar Europe's experience in Socialist alliances with Communist parties suggested that the Communists—always better organized—always won out. Mitterrand's task was to prove that France could be an exception to the rule.

Mitterrand's Socialist Party

The PS in 1971 was weak, still discouraged, split into several factions. Party rules, which had been changed at Epinay to elect officials by proportional representation, had in fact raised factionalism to a principle of government. Mitterrand, who owed his election to this change of rules, would show how skillfully he could manipulate them. His first task, however, was to assert his leadership and overcome the doubts of older Socialists about this upstart leader, who in the scornful phrase of Guy Mollet had not become a socialist, only learned to "speak socialist."[21]

Wary old militants at first nicknamed their new first secretary "the foreign prince," but Mitterrand charmed his opposition even as he outmaneuvered it. His success in uniting the PS behind him and leading it to victory in 1981 was achieved by his idiosyncratic methods of rule, which even as they succeeded, led to new problems for the future. Having always been a leader of small groups—the UDSR and later the CIR—he depended on an inner clan of close associates even when he became the leader of a large party. In order to control the factionalized PS, he allied himself with first one faction, then another. The CERES, the most leftist group, was part of his coalition until 1975, then banished from it until he needed the group to face a challenge from Michel Rocard and Pierre Mauroy in 1979. But the CERES was not the only leftist faction in the party. Among Mitterrand's new partisans were the followers of Jean Poperen, an ex-Communist and independent socialist more anti-Communist than the CERES, who was anticlerical in the old SFIO manner. (Thirty to 40 percent of CERES members came from the new Catholic Left.)

A generalized aspiration for social justice united Socialist and Communist voters and militants, convinced that the government and economy of France had been monopolized and dominated by a narrow class of big capitalists who they thought were intellectually no better than the common people and morally much worse. Although conservative governments had introduced social measures (and France by the 1970s was a thoroughgoing welfare state), they got little credit for them from the Left. The Left found such measures both approximate and incomplete, sops to the working class to keep it quiet.

This leftist mentality was profoundly and voluntarily ignorant of economic reality. When an economist or politician spoke of the fragility of the French economy, the Left immediately recognized the language of the enemy. Leftists were possessed by an intense and moralistic voluntarism, the notion that ill will had created intolerable conditions, which good will would suffice to change, what the French call the "all you have to do is . . ." spirit—all you have to do is raise minimum wages, nationalize industry, introduce equalized salaries, soak the rich, forbid capital flight, and so on.

Illusion entered the scene with the hope that all who joined in the mutual aspirations of the Left could work harmoniously together. This had not been possible in the Fourth Republic after the demise of the left-oriented coalition of late 1944 to early 1947. (That period saw enactment of some of the most radical social measures of the twentieth century, but as the period was largely presided over by de Gaulle, it did not enter into the mythology of the Left.)

If the expression *"la gauche"* was synonymous with what Mitterrand liked to call *"le peuple de gauche,"* it easily included the voters of the Communist party. If it meant the parties of the Left, then there was an irreconcilable difference between them and a common ambition: Each wished to eat the other up. Some members of the PS might not formulate the Socialist design this way; Mitterrand did. But he had realized by the mid-1960s that the only way to reach and then seduce Communist voters was by entering into an extended alliance with their leaders; appeals from without were useless.

Mitterrand recognized that the needed language, both to appeal to the Communist voter and to tell the Socialist voter that the PS was not the old SFIO, had a leftist vocabulary ringing with echoes of Marxism. In 1972 he told an interviewer: "I have acquired the conviction that the economic structure of capitalism is a dictatorship, and in my eyes it represents a danger for that taste for liberty that is at the depths of my being."[22] He talked of "breaking with capitalism" and denounced multinational corporations as the quintessence of evil. Reminiscing on the Mitterrand of those years, the veteran Socialist Gilles Martinet remarked, "When he happened in the 1970s to talk about 'the exploitation of man by man,' I used to look fixedly at the tips of my shoes."[23]

At the same time, Mitterrand did not discard his strong belief in increasing European unity, although the European idea was embodied in a European Economic Community that was an expression of the successes of late-twentieth-century capitalism. In 1972, before signing the Common Program, Mitterrand had to fight leftists at the PS Suresnes congress, who demanded a policy of neutralism with complete departure from the Atlantic alliance. In 1973 at the party's Bagnolet congress still another formal debate was needed to determine PS policy on Europe and France's membership in the European Community (EC). Mitterrand needed simultaneously to speak to the more leftist militants and those sickened by years of compromise, to call out to Communist voters over the heads of their leaders, and to hold on to old SFIO members who wanted a pro-European policy.

Did Mitterrand ever believe in his own highfalutin leftist language? Certainly he did not take it at the letter. But by adopting a language that was not his native speech, Mitterrand encouraged emulation. The young followers of the CERES naturally welcomed the marxophonic mode. It excited many other new PS members and those reawakened to politics by 1968 and formerly discouraged by the bureaucratic politics and seedy compromises of the old SFIO. The SFIO standard-bearers who had rallied to Mitterrand, such as Gaston Defferre in Marseilles and Pierre Mauroy in the north, had a horror of being identified as the right wing of their party and also fell in with the fashion.

The spread of leftist language only confirmed the apprehensions of those on the Right and Center (and some on the Left), who saw with dramatic clarity all the dangers of a Communist alliance, while discounting Mitterrand's ability to keep control of it.

The evidence of the succeeding decade is that Mitterrand knew well what he was doing in the area he best understood—the political and institutional one—but made grave mistakes in the economic area, where he was not only ignorant but also insouciant.

The Common Program reflected Mitterrand's views on yielding power when the Left lost an election, on adherence to the European Community, and on remaining (provisorily, at least) in the Atlantic alliance. But France's nuclear deterrent was to be abandoned (the pacifist and even neutralist current in the PS was still strong). In the economic negotiations, however, Mitterrand settled for a vaguely worded call for nationalizations, set in a framework of anticapitalist language that could only discourage or frighten medium and small entrepreneurs, whose cooperation was necessary for the Common Program's economic success.

The rise of the Socialist party from 1972 until the victories of 1981 stemmed from its growing acceptance by both believers and skeptics: Some voters desired to believe in it; some who wanted to vote against the Right hoped that most Socialist promises would not be kept. Communist voters became more reconciled to voting for Socialists (and especially for Mitterrand); leftist Socialists supported a leader they had regarded with deep suspicion a few years earlier; less leftist Socialists comforted themselves with the idea that strong leadership more than made up for deficiencies in economic perception; uncertain voters tested out the idea that Mitterrand's PS could control the Communists and without overly radical measures could improve a system exclusively directed since 1958 by the Gaullists and their allies.

Mitterrand's prestige grew when in the legislative elections of 1973, nine months after the signature of the Common Program, the PS won 19.3 percent of the vote, the PCF 21.4 percent. Both parties could draw comfort from results better than those of the disastrous elections after the events of May 1968. But the Socialist vote was higher than it had ever been since erosion began in 1946. Mitterrand's objective, however, was the presidency. President Pompidou's term would run out in 1976. In 1973 it was already clear that the president's health was failing.

Pompidou died in April 1974, just as the economic crisis had begun. In 1972, he had dropped Prime Minister Chaban-Delmas, whose "new society" had failed to avert the sharp left turn of a newly united opposition, and the president moved toward a more openly proclaimed conservative capitalism. Chaban was the Gaullist party's candidate to succeed Pompidou and suspect to many in his party as too social democratic. The other conservative candidate was Valéry Giscard d'Estaing, perennial economics minister under de Gaulle and Pompidou and leader of his own party, the Independent Republicans. A faction of Pompidou loyalists in the Gaullist party led by the late president's protégé Jacques Chirac refused to support Chaban, who was easily eliminated in the first round. In the second, Mitterrand faced in Giscard a younger opponent whose immense self-assurance, especially on economic topics, left the Socialist leader at frequent disadvantage. Giscard campaigned on the slogan "change without risk."

In the second round of voting Mitterrand was outpointed by an able adversary. The French electorate was uneasy at the potential weight of the Communists in a future government, but Mitterrand nevertheless won 49.3 percent of the vote to Giscard's 50.7. The loser was momentarily discouraged, but the Left in general took this narrow defeat as a presage of victory on the next occasion. Later in 1974 the ranks of the PS were swelled by the adherence of the former PSU leader Michel Rocard and some of his associates, as well as leaders from the formerly Catholic and democratic-leftist Confédération Française Démocratique du Travail (CFDT). These new recruits from the former leftists of 1968 were soon to show themselves the modernists of the PS (or as the CERES said, meaning it of course as an insult, the "American Left").

PS victories in by-elections triggered a sudden and ferocious PCF attack on the PS. The Communists had suddenly realized during summer 1974 that the enormous prestige accruing to Mitterrand was benefiting the Socialists, not themselves. Their calculation of 1972 was proving false. They sought to energize their ranks with a torrent of abuse against the PS, accusing it of having taken a sudden turn to the right. Mitterrand's reaction to this storm was essentially to stand on the defensive. He was still aiming at the Communist voter over the heads of the party chiefs, and he saw that the Politburo's tactic was to provoke him into angry reply and then invoke party loyalty against an accuser.

By late 1975 the PCF leaders had decided to call a halt to their criticism of the PS. Almost simultaneously, the party underwent what seemed almost a camp meeting conversion to the milder Italian style of communism. "Eurocommunism" was supposed to be the conversion of major Communist parties to a prodemocratic stance and a critical view of the Soviet Union. For the PCF Eurocommunism turned out to be a false face, assumed in part to imitate the electoral successes of the Italian party. Eurocommunism fit well, however, with the needs of 1977, when nationwide municipal elections meant that renewed good relations with the PS were essential. The PCF expected and received large gains in those elections.

The parliamentary elections of 1978 were more important; they could open the door to power on a national level, with Communists obtaining important ministries. But the French Communists were not gloating over a victory that advance polls depicted as almost certain. They were asking themselves whether it would indeed be a Communist victory in any meaningful sense or instead make them the electoral prop for a more powerful Socialist party over which they would have only limited control. By early 1977 the PCF leaders had decided that they must try to extract maximum concessions from the PS, renegotiate the Common Program to permit more nationalizations, and fashion machinery that would give the PCF and the CGT control of powerful administrative councils in nationalized industry.

The Socialists had supposed that the PCF was interested in fighting loyally at their side in the elections—though they expected a power struggle once victory was won. Too many concessions before the elections risked strengthening the PCF hand by frightening hesitant voters and would endanger the Socialists' own future hegemony in government. Therefore they held firm—and the Communists broke off negotiations. In March 1978, despite polls that showed a strong possibility of victory for the no-longer-united Left, second-round results returned a conservative majority to the National Assembly. The PS, which had hoped to be the largest party in an assembly numbering 477 seats, had only 104. France had looked at the possibility of a government of the Left (or a government shared by two quarreling parties of the Left) and flinched. Mitterrand's strategy seemed to have failed.

Against All Hope

The Communists had sabotaged what had once seemed certain victory. They hoped that in its disappointment the Socialist party would fall to quarreling, that Mitterrand would leave the scene, and that they could rebuild a powerful and hegemonic Communist party on the ruins of the PS. Socialist infighting began promptly on schedule. Mitterrand's response to the quarrel sought by the Communists had always been to turn the other cheek and remain "unitary for two." Michel Rocard and his friends had always been skeptical of a "unity" that enforced the pursuit of an economic policy increasingly out of line with the economic realities of the late 1970s. The Rocardians (and others) doubted that Mitterrand could or would lead the PS in 1981 in what would be his third try for the presidency.

Rocard was convinced that a new strategy and a new economic line were needed. Immediately after the election he criticized the PS campaign—and implicitly its strategy—he was in fact declaring his bid to take over the party and become its 1981 presidential candidate. But Mitterrand, despite moments of discouragement, did not mean to cede the leadership.

No one in the Mitterrand clan that had followed him from the CIR to the PS or among his younger disciples had much love for Rocard. Among the younger leaders were men like Lionel Jospin, whom Mitterrand chose to succeed him as first secretary of the PS in 1981, and Laurent Fabius, who became in 1984 his second prime minister. For them, Mitterrand *was* the PS, and any attack on him or the line he had followed since the Epinay congress of 1971 was lèse-majesté—and a threat to their own positions in the party.

Members of the Mitterrand clan had no intention of letting Rocard and his friends evict them. In mid-June 1978 thirty friends of the first secretary signed a text rejecting "any search for a professedly technical and modernist solution that would place our party in mortal peril." An unintended effect was to push Pierre Mauroy into Rocard's arms. Mauroy, the number-two man in the PS, had not been informed of this démarche, which was signed by several national secretaries of the party. He was both furious at the slight to his authority and suspicious of a total takeover by Mitterrand henchmen.

Amid great press and television publicity Rocard moved toward inevitable confrontation at the PS congress held in Metz in April 1979. Mauroy had wanted only to move Mitterrand toward a new line but ended as Rocard's ally. Skillful as always at inner-party maneuver, Mitterrand again allied himself with the leftist CERES to outflank Mauroy and gained a majority at the congress. A defeated, but still determined, Rocard announced his continuing candidacy unless Mitterrand were to run. Mitterrand delayed declaring himself until early November 1980. Maneuvered into believing that the first secretary would not run, Rocard declared formally in October and was then forced into a humiliating withdrawal.

These maneuvers were not merely incidents in the biography of Michel Rocard; they had an effect on the PS as a whole. From spring 1978 to late 1980 the PS was caught up in an internal power struggle that left little time for more important affairs. Because Rocard carried the banner of economic modernism against the first secretary's "archaism," the Mitterrandists took up the chant "we are all archaic." As the economic crisis worsened and unemployment rose, the PS shut its collective mind against any rethinking of its economic program, much of which had been questionable in 1972 and was now eight more years out of date. In the faction-ridden party that Mitterrand had fostered, new ideas could not simply bubble up from below—they had to be carried by a faction. If this faction was not in the majority, its ideas would be rejected. Because the Mitterrandists were uncertain whether they could hold the party in 1979–1980, the party apparatus simply sat on its dossiers and refused to consider new economic problems. It was easier instead to follow its leftist bent: When Mitterrand brought the CERES back into the party majority, he gave its leader Jean-Pierre Chevènement the job of drawing up the 1980 "Socialist project." The result was a pompous, dogmatic, and thoroughly unrealistic manifesto.

Giscard in replacing Pompidou had hoped to create a less polarized society and to seduce a part of the Left to work with the Center. The revived Left could, however, see no good in Giscard, even when his government adopted an abortion law and lowered the voting age to eighteen. Meanwhile, the narrow margin of Giscard's election victory frightened those in power; it presaged more trouble in municipal elections and the National Assembly elections of 1978. The heads of big business became more willing to negotiate with labor, the minimum wage was increased, and despite the economic crisis, employers allowed salaries to go up—by 20 percent between 1974 and 1981. The conservative reaction to 1968 and to the rise of the Left thus gave ground on social affairs and increased France's future economic problems—though the Left could not see that.

In a further complication, the crisis brought on by the 1974 oil shock was first judged to be temporary. In 1975 Giscard's first prime minister, Jacques Chirac, tried to jump-start the economy by pumping in more liquidity—and merely succeeded in creating a situation in which France had ingloriously to retire from the newly established "snake," the predecessor of the European Monetary System (EMS). After Chirac resigned for his own political reasons in 1976, Giscard picked a professor and civil servant he introduced as "the best economist in France," Raymond Barre. Barre concluded that France was living above its income. Periodic devaluations had resulted only in higher inflation and more devaluations, an endless cycle. He favored a strong franc based on a deflated economy.

Socialist economists looked at the deepening crisis and a rapidly rising unemployment rate (which in the 1960s had been well below 3 percent). They diagnosed the acuteness of the crisis as a result of the austerity "imposed on the workers" by Barre and the unwillingness of French capitalists to invest in new industry. For them, the twin ills of the French economy were a slowdown in domestic demand and the weakness and inapt orientation of productive investment. "Relaunching consumption and nationalization thus constituted the two aspects of a policy acting on both supply and demand."[24]

By 1981, when Mitterrand became president, PS economic ideas were willfully retrograde. Journalist Roger Priouret wrote presciently in June 1980 that any Socialist president would find himself burdened with demands legitimated by the PS as well as the PCF, facing an electorate informed by both parties that the economic crisis had been "manufactured" by the government and the bosses.[25]

Mitterrand, the brilliant political tactician, had won out over Rocard, a mediocre one. By not changing his program and by refusing to quarrel with the PCF (though he criticized its leaders), Mitterrand had won over the million Communist voters in 1981 who voted for him on the first round. In 1981 the French Left was still intensely ideological. Too few Socialist militants and voters (and very few Communists) were ready to believe in Rocard's economic realism. If Mitterrand had been less vague on economics and less opportunist, the Socialists might have thought more deeply about the economic problems of 1981. But if Mitterrand had behaved differently, would the Socialists have won in 1981?

Questions like those are of course impossible to answer. One can analyze the opportunistic and demagogic tactics Mitterrand employed in refounding the Socialist party and winning the confidence of a large majority of the generic Left, but no one can say what might have happened if . . . The only alternative presenting itself was the Rocardian model. Fifteen years later, Rocard told an interviewer that the Left electorate would indeed have understood the program he advocated in 1978–1979, and a Socialist victory in 1981 would have ensued.[26] But even he doubted that the PS would have accepted the later compromises of 1982–1984, had he, not Mitterrand, made them.[27] The Communist-controlled CGT would certainly not have accepted them.

Mitterrand's success in 1981 was purchased at the expense of professing the ideas of 1972. Without doubt, many mistakes in detail made in 1981–1982 could have been avoided by a more economically alert president and party. But the larger frame of reference was an ideologized Socialist party still wet from the backwash of May 1968, and a *peuple de gauche* with long memories.

The burden of the Socialist past hung upon Mitterrand. So did the whole mythology of the Left. The latecomer to socialism assumed the mythology, tradition, and nonsense together. It was a heavy burden, but it is hard to see how he could have escaped it.

2

Socialism in One Common Market Country

The Third Round

The American constitutional system stipulates a ten-week interim between an election and the inauguration of a new president. France knows little delay. On May 21, 1981, ten days after the election, Giscard departed the presidential palace, the Elysée, and François Mitterrand became the fourth president of the Fifth Republic. He faced the hostile National Assembly elected in 1978. His first political choice was whether to compromise with it in some way, temporizing, or to use his presidential powers to dissolve it immediately and hope that new elections would bring in a Left majority.

Mitterrand wasted no time. He appointed the veteran Socialist politician Pierre Mauroy as prime minister and immediately dissolved the National Assembly. Mauroy formed a ministry composed almost entirely of Socialists. It was designed to handle the immediate concerns of government until the new assembly could be elected. Again, there was little delay; the parliamentary elections—often referred to as the "third round" (after the two-round presidential elections)—were scheduled for June 14 and 21.

Even before Mitterrand announced dissolution, the third round had begun—in the ranks of the old majority. Giscard's own Independent Republicans (renamed the Parti Républicain [PR]) were part of the umbrella coalition called the UDF (Union pour la Démocratie Française), of which the other members were the Centre des Démocrates Sociaux (CDS), heirs to the briefly powerful Christian Democratic MRP of the Fourth Republic, a remnant of the once-powerful Radical Socialists, and a right-wing Socialist splinter group.

Giscard's first prime minister, Jacques Chirac, now his rival, led the larger and better-organized Rassemblement pour la République (RPR), the neo-Gaullist party.

With 150 seats in the assembly elected in 1978, the RPR had frequently frustrated Giscard and his prime minister Raymond Barre; the UDF had had only 138 seats. The Socialists, for their part, had had only 104 seats in that assembly.

The UDF was Giscard's movement, and when he fell, there was confusion in its ranks. Giscard attacked Chirac for undermining his presidential campaign (true enough—Chirac's candidacy was to a considerable degree responsible for Mitterrand's victory). The worried UDF deputies, however, needed not recrimination but unity and hastened to approve a plan advanced by Chirac for a united conservative ticket.

Chirac talked confidently of victory but may not have expected it. Polls already showed that Mitterrand's victory was not unwelcome even to many who had voted against him. The question remained whether the Socialists and their smaller allies could win the 240 seats needed for a majority, or whether the Communists would hold the balance in the new legislature. The Communists hoped to win. Rapidly rallying to the standard of Union of the Left they had earlier abandoned, they hastened to declare that they were ready to assume responsibility "at all levels of national life." The Socialists gave them a cautious welcome, reminding the PCF that the Socialists had not altered the positions criticized by the Communists for the past three years. Nevertheless, the PS was ready to deal with a humbled PCF and, knowing that their party would still need electoral help, renegotiated the traditional agreement to support the best-placed candidate of the Left in the second round.

In the first round of the elections the Communist vote rose less than 1 percent above Marchais's poor score in May. The second round confirmed and exaggerated the results of the first. The Socialists alone had a clear majority—269 seats plus another 20 held by smaller allies. The Communists had lost half their seats; the conservative forces were also reduced by half. Jubilant, still incredulous, the Socialists saw themselves the masters of France, carried along by a wave of support they had long hoped for, but had never before received. After twenty-three years in the political desert, the Socialists had finally won their victory.

The New Men

During the next fourteen years the French became familiar with a new set of Socialist leaders previously little known to the public at large. With a few exceptions, the ministers of the first and second Mauroy governments would remain in most of the Socialist governments formed during Mitterrand's two terms. Leading figures not in the first two governments were Lionel Jospin, Mitterrand's replacement as first secretary of the PS, an important minister and factional figure in the second Mitterrand term, Socialist presidential candidate against Jacques Chirac in 1995, and prime minister after the upset election in 1997; Pierre Joxe, a Mitterrand associate from CIR days, who served first as chairman of the PS faction in the National Assembly and thereafter headed important ministries; and Pierre Bérégovoy, secretary-general of the Elysée (presidential chief of staff) and afterwards minister of social affairs, minister of economics and finance, and finally prime minister. Close Mitterrand associate Roland Dumas became foreign minister in 1984 and was reappointed in all other Socialist governments.

Pierre Mauroy as prime minister was by constitutional definition "chief of the government" and number-two man in the new governmental system. He proudly traced his proletarian descent from a long line of woodcutters in the old forests near the northern city of Cambrai. Mauroy *père* became a teacher, rising to be an inspector of schools. His son, born in 1928, became a professor of technical education and a militant of the SFIO, traditionally strong in the north country. A protégé of Guy Mollet, Mauroy thought himself the SFIO leader's heir until he was passed over in 1969. He then moved closer to Mitterrand. Deputy first secretary under Mitterrand, Mauroy in 1973 was also elected mayor of Lille and a deputy to the National Assembly.

Mauroy had led the old SFIO forces that combined with Mitterrand's CIR and the CERES to make Mitterrand leader of the PS. He had sided with Michel Rocard in 1979 and found himself in the minority at the PS congress of Metz. His SFIO past and alliance with Rocard inclined the more inquisitorial members of Mitterrand's entourage to treat Mauroy as a moderate (a dirty word in French leftist usage). The label was neither accurate nor easily suffered; both as prime minister and thereafter Mauroy was at pains to stress that he was very much on the Left. Tall, broad-shouldered, outgoing, an orator overly given to length and flowery Socialist clichés, the new prime minister was to prove a hard worker and courageous leader in facing the bitter choices that would soon present themselves.

Economy and Finance Minister Jacques Delors was still an outsider in the first year of Socialist power. Later his prestige rose as his predictions came true. Born in 1925, early active in progressive Catholic youth organizations, Delors had been a key adviser to liberal Gaullist prime minister Chaban-Delmas in 1969–1972. He joined the PS in the early 1970s and became a Mitterrand partisan, even though his economic views were close to Rocard's. Able, ambitious, and cautious, he annoyed Mitterrand by frequent complaints and threats to resign, but the president came close to making him prime minister in 1983. After Mauroy resigned, Delors did not care to serve under Laurent Fabius, who had been his insubordinate junior minister for the budget. Mitterrand then helped Delors become president of the European Community Commission, where he rapidly distinguished himself by firm management and planning for a more united Europe. Repeatedly reelected, he served for ten years. Delors was much solicited to run as Socialist candidate to succeed Mitterrand in 1995, but he declined for mixed personal and political reasons.

The new interior minister and minister for decentralization, Gaston Defferre, was at seventy-one the oldest man in the government. Socialist mayor of Marseilles for nearly forty years, Defferre was a respected elder statesman. Foreign Minister Claude Cheysson, born in 1920, was an ex-diplomat and ambassador, and former European Community commissioner. A strong believer in aid to the Third World, a good linguist with excellent English and German, Cheysson would carry plain speaking to the lengths of foot-in-mouth disease, as in the uproar immediately after General Jaruzelski's coup against Solidarity in late 1981, when he said, "Of course, we shall do nothing." (No one did do anything, of course, but Cheysson won no admirers for truth telling.) He was replaced in 1984 by Mitterrand's friend and associate Roland Dumas.

Charles Hernu, born in 1923, the new defense minister, had been a journalist, politician, and a Mitterrand admirer since the early 1960s. In the early 1970s Hernu was one of the few leading Socialists convinced that the new PS had to support a strong nuclear defense. He won the party over in 1977 (with Mitterrand cheering him on but leading from behind), when the PS finally abandoned its traditional pacifism. Hernu was to be popular with the military, but he torpedoed himself in 1985 with the *Rainbow Warrior* affair, when intelligence agents acting on his authorization blew up a ship in a New Zealand harbor belonging to the ecologist organization Greenpeace. In the scandal that followed, Hernu denied knowledge of the matter but was forced to resign.

Justice Minister Robert Badinter, born in 1928, was a close friend of Mitterrand but not a member of the PS. The appointment of this wealthy and successful trial lawyer at first scandalized doctrinaire Socialists, who protested the nomination of a noncomrade and *grand bourgeois* to the cabinet. He became a Socialist hero as the minister who brought about the abolition of the death penalty and as a champion of judicial reform. Badinter also became the target of bitter attacks, sometimes covertly anti-Semitic, by an opposition that accused him of being soft on crime. In 1986 Mitterrand named him president of the Constitutional Council (the closest French equivalent to the U.S. Supreme Court) for a nine-year term.

The new education minister (who in France controls the teaching personnel and much of the curriculum at all levels) was Alain Savary, born in 1918. As a deputy and minister in the Fourth Republic, he was deeply involved in decolonization in North Africa; he resigned in disgust from Guy Mollet's cabinet when the prime minister did not disavow the hijacking of a plane containing Algerian leaders flying over international waters. Savary and Mitterrand were on distant terms; as a leader in the small Autonomous Socialist Party, Savary had blackballed Mitterrand when he tried to join its ranks in the early 1960s, and Mitterrand had displaced him as first secretary of the PS in 1971. As education minister, Savary tried to steer into safe harbor a bill reconciling state-financed church education with the secular state system, only to fail when intransigent Socialists provoked intransigent Catholics and a monster demonstration opposed the government in the streets of Paris.

Law professor Jack Lang, born in 1939, minister of culture, made himself a name in the early years as a noisy leftist nationalist who attacked the United States for its "cultural imperialism" (the television series *Dallas* was a major offender). He ended as one of the most popular Socialist ministers and delighted his constituency by doubling the cultural budget. Lang served in every Socialist government.

Jean-Pierre Chevènement, born in 1939, was a graduate of the Ecole Nationale d'Administration (ENA) and an ex–civil servant in the Finance Ministry. A deputy at thirty-four, he led the CERES, the most leftist faction in the PS. He was minister for scientific research and technology in 1981, taking on the industry portfolio as well a year later. His interference in the management of nationalized industry infuriated managers, and in the cabinet reshuffle in 1983 Mauroy offered him a different portfolio. Chevènement chose instead to resign, letting it be known that he opposed the new austerity policies. He returned to office in July 1984 as education minister, and in 1988–1991 was defense minister, resigning over disagreements on the Gulf war.

Michel Rocard had made at least pro forma peace with Mitterrand. He was still the head of a faction that questioned the wisdom of many current Socialist ideas, and his continuing, though frustrated, ambitions to take over the party caused most of its leaders to regard him with deep distrust. Rocard became minister for economic planning and development, a seemingly important post with little staff and no independent funding; it turned out to be a gilded cage. In 1983 Rocard took over the agriculture portfolio, but he would resign in 1985 to pursue his presidential ambitions, renounce them again, and become prime minister in 1988.

There were six women in the new government. (Under Giscard, two women had been appointed ministers, a first in France.) Edith Cresson, born in 1934, was agriculture minister. She quarreled with the farmers' lobby and was moved in 1983 to the post of minister for foreign trade, where she was more successful. In 1991 Mitterrand was to name her France's first female prime minister. One other woman had the title of minister; two others were junior ministers and another a state secretary.

Communist leader Charles Fiterman was the most senior of the four Communist ministers in the government and the only one who was a member of the PCF Politburo. As minister for transport, he proved an effective executive. His PCF colleagues were Civil Service Minister Anicet Le Pors, Health Minister Jack Ralite, and Minister for Professional Training Marcel Rigout. Former foreign minister Michel Jobert, who was not a Socialist but had quarreled with Giscard, became minister for foreign trade. He left the government in March 1983. One minister and one state secretary represented the Left Radicals, the PS's small satellite. In all there were forty-three cabinet members. Seventeen ministers were under fifty. Six were graduates of the prestigious Ecole Nationale d'Administration. Only one minister had engaged in private business, but fifteen were or had been teachers, and ten others members of the civil service. Only three had been ministers before. Twenty-three of them, however, had administrative experience as mayors (and as is permitted by the French system, remained in the job while serving as ministers).[1]

The Socialist party organization was stripped of many of its experienced leaders, as its chiefs became ministers and took their aides with them. With the exception of the four Communists, Michel Jobert, and two Left Radicals, the entire government and an overwhelming number of its staff came from the Socialist party. Its power and consequent responsibility were now enormous.

Governing in a Hurry

Before the June election victory the Socialists had worried whether Communist participation in the government would be needed to secure a parliamentary majority. Thereafter, they saw inclusion of Communist ministers as a minor risk, largely compensated by tying the Communist-controlled CGT to government policy. Although Communist voters might think their party's entry into the government the logical result of the resurrected Union of the Left, the Communist leaders knew better. They had sabotaged what seemed like certain victory in 1978 to escape Socialist hegemony and in 1981 were obliged to enter the government in a far less favorable position. By entering it they meant to satisfy their rank and file, draw whatever benefits they could from participation in government, and try to heal the electoral wounds of the presidential and parliamentary elections.

The first months of the new administration saw a long honeymoon with public opinion, or, in the more theological French phrase, a "state of grace." But the president and his team were in a hurry. They knew their majority guaranteed them a minimum of five years in full power and spoke frequently of the importance of this "long duration" afforded them by the institutions of the Fifth Republic. Subconsciously, however, they could not quite believe it. The periods when the Left had been in power had always been brief. Because so many of their promises meant upsetting an economic status quo placed in limbo by the elections, delay was impossible for reasons both economic and political.[2]

Communist polemics had consistently maintained that the reformist Socialist leaders were not workers, were only verbally leftist, and in practice were "trained bears" anxious to serve the interests of their secret allies in big capital. The president, the prime minister, and the vast majority of the Socialist party were determined to show "the people of the Left" that those charges were lies. Given the big majority of 1981, what economic arguments could have sufficed to block measures thought politically necessary? In retrospect, even the cautious Jacques Delors agreed: "The Left [read PS] would not have been credible if it had not taken the measures due its electorate. The sin of treason is more mortal than that of error."[3]

Nationalization

Prominent in Mitterrand's electoral platform, the "110 proposals," was number 21, which read: "The public sector will be enlarged by the nationalization of the nine industrial groups foreseen by the Common Program and the Socialist program and of the steel industry and the armaments and space activities financed by public funds. The nationalization of credit and insurance will be completed." At the opening session of the new assembly on July 8 Mauroy made this proposal the centerpiece of his general policy declaration.

Nationalization had figured large in the Common Program of 1972, although oddly enough it was not part of the ancestral heritage of the French Left. But the idea was taken up by social planners in the 1920s and early 1930s and gained popularity at the end of World War II. The Left coalition presided over by Charles de Gaulle then nationalized the three biggest savings banks, the railroads and the airlines, electricity and natural gas production and distribution.

The Socialists had espoused the idea of nationalization for a variety of reasons, not necessarily consistent with one another. For the CERES and some others, Communist advocacy might almost have sufficed: If the biggest party of the Left, the party of the workers, demanded it, then the PS could not take the side of capital. The Socialists agreed to nationalization in 1972 for one set of reasons and then found others. The original purpose was "to seize the commanding heights of the economy." The major conglomerates built up under Pompidolian capitalism had to be removed from the control of big money. Under public ownership, key industrial sectors would become show windows of economic democracy and social innovation. As time went on, Socialists also argued that French capitalists were not investing enough. They were building or buying plants outside of France and therefore, in their selfishness, causing unemployment. French industry had to be restructured, made more efficient, more competitive—and capable of employing more workers. Mitterrand stressed a nationalist argument in a September 1981 press conference:

> The nationalizations will give us the tools for the next century. If that were not done, instead of being nationalized, these enterprises would speedily be internationalized. I refuse an international division of labor and production decided on far away and obeying interests other than our own. Nationalizations are an arm of the defense of French production.[4]

The French public was not opposed to nationalization in 1981; a SOFRES poll of early October 1981 showed 50 percent of the population favoring it. De Gaulle had set a precedent for such action, which could not be branded as intrinsically leftist. The French state had bulked large in the economy ever since the time of Louis XIV's finance minister Colbert, and state action since 1944 had rebuilt the French economy from the abyss of defeat and wartime destruction.

Opponents of nationalization had arguments both doctrinaire and practical. They feared its indefinite extension, although Mitterrand insisted that those firms not on the list would be let alone "at least until a national decision by popular consultation (parliamentary or presidential elections) should decide otherwise."[5] Almost all bosses feared the encroachment of the CGT in their businesses (some of them having previously excluded it by using company unions). They expected constant government interference, pressure to hire without permission to fire. And above all, they thought state control hopelessly inefficient, even if the new masters did not eject them from their positions of power.

Although everyone in the new government agreed on the principle of nationalization, there was disagreement on the manner of implementing it. Should all the industrial groups on the list be nationalized 100 percent, or would a 51 percent control suffice? Should all companies owned in whole or part by nationalized conglomerates be taken over also, as the Communists and some CERES members wanted? How were shareholders to be compensated? How quickly should the government proceed?

Ideology and practical reasons both argued for speed: The Left wanted a display of firmness, but business executives also needed to know where they stood: The economy could not be left in limbo. Mauroy proposed nationalizations to the National Assembly in early July, but discussions concerning ways and means continued until September. Delors, Rocard, and Badinter advocated control without full takeover, Mauroy wanted nationalization at 100 percent, and some of the exchanges were heated.[6]

In the end Mitterrand opted for full nationalization. The five conglomerates nationalized in 1982 were the Compagnie Générale d'Electricité (electronics, naval construction, cables, computers, telecommunications), the Compagnie Générale de Constructions Téléphoniques (formerly ITT-France), Péchiney-Ugine-Kuhlman (aluminum, ferrous metals and copper, chemical products), Rhône-Poulenc (chemicals), Saint-Gobain-Pont à Mousson (glass and plastics), and Thomson-Brandt (electronics and telecommunications). Two big steel companies, Usinor and Sacilor, which had been extensively bailed out under Giscard, were taken over by conversion of their debt into stock held by the state. The Dassault airplane construction firm, whose principal customer was the state, was also on the list. The nearly nonagenarian Marcel Bloch-Dassault had seen his company nationalized before. He compromised with the government, asking only that he be left in technical control of his firm. The state also acquired control over the computer firm CII Honeywell Bull and Roussel UCLAF (pharmaceuticals), both partly owned by foreign capital (U.S. and German).

Matters were more difficult with Matra, a conglomerate prominent in the manufacture of sophisticated armaments, but with substantial holdings in publishing and radio stations. Since only the arms sector was profitable, the final compromise stipulated a 51 percent share for the government, thus guaranteeing the survival of the entire company. Thirty-six banks were also nationalized—most notably the major investment banks Banque de Paris et des Pays Bas (Paribas) and Banque de Suez; the major savings banks had been nationalized in 1945.

Debate on the nationalization law opened in the National Assembly on October 13. At once the minority conservatives introduced a large number of amendments and objections designed to provoke and frustrate the Socialists. After the Socialist majority had approved the bill in late October, it was rejected by the Senate, delayed when the Constitutional Council decided that the terms of payment were insufficient, and became law finally in February 1982.

Economic Problems

The strongest element in François Mitterrand's socialism was a passion for social justice. The Fifth Republic had enlarged the welfare state, but the Left believed that much remained to be done. A famous report of the Organization for European Cooperation and Development (OECD) of July 1976 on income distribution in major countries cited France as having the highest percentage of annual income going to the richest 10 percent of its citizens. The raging double-digit inflation of the late 1970s had increased the inequalities felt by elderly and lower-paid citizens, who were already hard hit by an indirect taxation that burdened food and other necessities with a 7 percent value-added tax (VAT).

Economic prognostications, particularly OECD estimates, suggested that in 1982 the twenty OECD countries would have an average growth of 2 percent in gross national product (GNP), but demand for French exports would rise by 6.25 percent.[7] Mitterrand's economists told him that since the new Reagan administration in Washington intended to reflate the U.S. economy, France could launch itself on the cresting wave of a world economy. Comforted by such prophecies, the new government proceeded to follow an economic policy shaped by its political needs and social aspirations. Aside from extensive nationalization, Mitterrand had promised to raise the minimum wage and old age pensions, set retirement age at sixty, cut the work week, introduce a fifth week of paid vacations, and, above all, reduce unemployment. Rapid economic growth was a necessity if all these measures were to be paid for.

The heads of the major nations met for the annual economic summit in Ottawa in July 1981. Making his first appearance on a world stage, Mitterrand added his voice to a general European demand for the United States to cut interest rates. Ronald Reagan was not interested. "The new administration didn't really have a policy on interest rates," remembers Henry Nau, senior National Security Council staffer for economic policy. "High interest rates were [Federal Reserve Bank chairman] Paul Volker's policy; we went along with it."[8]

Undeterred by this setback, the new French government went ahead with an ambitious program. It had already raised the minimum wage (*salaire minimum de croissance,* or SMIC) by 10 percent in early June, with immediate effect on 1.5 million workers. (Eight more increases would raise its nominal value by a total of 38 percent by March 1983.) Manual laborers making roughly a third more than the *smicards* felt a more gradual effect, and more highly salaried workers, very little.[9] The government undertook to compensate business directly for half the increased social burden imposed by this rise.

Family allocations were raised as well. The Barre government (worried by a birthrate that had begun to sink after a thirty-year rise, an increase unknown in France since the early nineteenth century) had raised payments to families for the birth of a third child by 5,000 francs. The Socialists not only raised this allocation by 25 percent but also increased payments to families with two children. Minimum old age pensions, languishing in 1980 at 57.6 percent of the minimum wage, were raised 62 percent in the first two years of the Socialist administration. To those should be added increased rent subsidies, aid to poor farmers, and a rise in compensation for part-time unemployment. Altogether, the cost for all social measures was 200 million francs in the second half of 1981 and 800 million in 1982.

Mitterrand had promised in 1981 that the workweek would be reduced from forty hours to thirty-five, a measure expected to create new jobs. The CGT wanted that done at once, with compensation for a forty-hour week. Mauroy favored a gradual reduction of the workweek but worried about any wage reduction. Acting without fully consulting his prime minister, Mitterrand opted in January 1982 for the thirty-nine-hour week paid as forty. Only a few thousand jobs were created instead of the hundred thousand jobs optimistically estimated. The extra costs did not affect industry as much as might have been expected; they were compensated by a gain in productivity. The precedent of a drop in hours worked without a drop in pay did, however, block any further motion toward a thirty-five-hour week. In retrospect, this drop was recognized as the kind of action the government should have left to labor-industry bargaining rather than enacting it by decree.[10]

All of the government's actions had stressed greater social justice, but PS economists also expected that the liquidity injected into the economy would greatly expand consumer spending and bring about new growth in the French economy. Here they seriously miscalculated two factors. In late 1980 and early 1981 Giscard's prime minister Barre (for reasons not unconnected with the forthcoming elections) had raised old age pensions, granted new aid to investment, and altered the practice of previous years by excluding increases in the cost of oil from energy bills paid directly or indirectly by the public. These measures alone had stimulated growth by around 0.4 percent in 1981 and were only imperfectly integrated into the Keynesian measures of the Socialist economists.

The second and more important miscalculation was the estimate made in mid-1981 that the French economy had sufficient capacity to fill the consumer demand that would result from reflation. The money injected into the economy found French consumer production unprepared to handle it. The consequent rise in imports, particularly from West Germany, swiftly placed heavy pressure on the balance of payments.

For several months the government's economists believed that their reflationary measures were successful. But December 1981 saw a steep decline in the balance of trade, which continued into 1982. In October 1981, 92.3 percent of imports were covered by exports; by the following June this index had dropped to 79 percent.

In the ten days between the election and Mitterrand's entry into office an already declining franc had plunged rapidly, as nervous capitalists took their money out of the country. Some technicians asserted that a rapid devaluation of the franc was essential. CERES leader Chevènement was already arguing that France should shake off the constraints of the European Monetary System.

Mitterrand wanted none of it. Devaluation had a political symbolism that he understood well; the economic implications were less clear to him. Defense of the franc was a strong nationalist affirmation—had not de Gaulle defended it in the turmoil after 1968? Mitterrand intended to include the Communists in the government after the elections (and he did not at first know or perhaps even expect that the Socialists would have an absolute majority). All that would certainly frighten the world financial community. Devaluation smacked of unreliability. Furthermore, devaluation was incompatible with the government's policy of reflation—a policy that all candidates in the 1981 race had backed in one way or another. Whatever technical advantages devaluation might present, it seemed politically risky.

Some economists have argued in retrospect that a speedy and prophylactic devaluation would have cleared the air, since the government found itself obliged to devalue the franc in October—and then twice again. The October devaluation was by 8.5 percent (3 percent devaluation of the franc, 5.5 percent revaluation of the deutsche mark). In agreeing to do that, West Germany insisted that France deflate somewhat, reducing its 1982 budget by 15 billion francs.[11]

The devaluation did not do much to change the economic picture, as Delors himself had foreseen when he argued vigorously in the Council of Ministers in early October for a tighter budget and slower expansion of buying power. An angry François Mitterrand, whose eye was still fixed firmly on his political problems, told Delors: "The people who voted against Barre's austerity policy won't quickly accept a return to constraints. . . . In any case, the Right will do everything to capsize the policy of change, which is backed by public opinion."[12]

The economic news grew worse in January and February, as both Delors's and Mauroy's economists had warned them. Some of the president's advisers preferred to believe that the tardy world economic recovery would begin within six months. (In December 1981 the OECD was still predicting an average 2 percent growth in 1982 for its member nations; the real figure was minus 0.3 percent.)

Meanwhile the process of reflation set in motion in summer 1981 continued inexorably into 1982. Only one-quarter of the new expenses had been pumped into the economy in 1981, and the economic effects of Barre's reflation were slightly more important to the economy in 1981 than those undertaken by the new government.[13] Barre's injections of liquidity into the economy had, however, been a temporary measure, like a reflation attempted by Chirac in 1975. The Socialist government's deflationary measures could not be easily abrogated; they were designed as permanent social ameliorations. Unable to stop a process it had set in motion for political and social reasons, the government would find itself condemned for the next three years to continue releasing buying power on the one side while sopping it up on the other.

Mauroy was not convinced of the need for drastic action until the spring of 1982.[14] Meanwhile, his economic advisers, together with two of the top economists on the presidential staff (now alerted to the crisis), met constantly with Delors's people to plan a counterattack on the economic front. The president's attention was riveted on the economic summit to be held at the palace of Versailles. Hoping to convince the G-7 leaders to approve an ambitious program of worldwide economic expansion, Mitterrand resolved to impress them—and especially Ronald Reagan—with the splendors of France. He insisted that nothing be done to diminish the Versailles summit, at which he appeared so regal, so solitary in his splendor, that an irreverent minister, remembering Giscard's predilection for Louis XV, whispered to his neighbor, "I never knew that Louis XIV had succeeded Louis XV."[15]

A Slight Case of Hubris

The Versailles summit marked the end of phase one of the Mitterrand presidency, when the Socialists basked in unwarranted self-assurance, displaying an arrogance based on misreading the election results. Their victory had been too big. Returned on the flood tide of Mitterrand's victory and an unprecedented parliamentary majority, many Socialists thought in 1981 that their new power might last for twenty years. Simultaneously, they overreacted to the bitter language of the conservative opposition. Its world turned upside down, the Right gave full expression to its indignation and its fears. In the early months it had still another reason for strong language: The spokesmen of the Right were not yet preaching entirely to the converted but were also intent on winning back those moderates who had voted for Mitterrand and had to be brought back into the fold.

A Socialist government was bad enough, but a Socialist-Communist government! Unused to opposition, the Right freely employed wild language, charging the new government with collectivizing or sovietizing France, and declared that a government taking such measures was not legitimate.

Ever since they had signed the Common Program with the Communists, the Socialists had proclaimed their attachment to the principle of alternation in power. Leninist tactics were not for them; power won through the ballot box would be yielded if the ballot box went against them. To be told that they were dangerous to French democracy, society, and institutions was an insult, an idea to be entertained only by unspeakable reactionaries. The Socialists naturally reacted with resentment and a self-satisfied assertion of good conscience.

Thus feeling themselves provoked, and armed with a happy sense of destiny, the Socialists let power intoxicate them, and foolish words issued from their lips: "Its [the Right's] supreme value is money" (Pierre Mauroy); "The French people know quite well that freedom is on the Left" (PS deputy leader Jean Poperen). Most damaging of all was a phrase uttered by a young Socialist deputy, the diminutive and dogmatic André Laignel. Replying to the objections of former justice minister Jean Foyer during the nationalization debate, Laignel said, "You are legally wrong, because you are politically in the minority."[16] His words would go echoing down the years of Socialist power.

On top of that, the Socialist party congress held in Valence in late October 1981 displayed an ugly triumphalism that shocked the country. A speech by PS leader Paul Quilès drew the most attention. He demanded a purge of those who were resisting or obstructing the new regime. It would not be a systematic purge of high civil servants and chiefs of industry, but: "It would be naïve to leave in place people who are determined to sabotage the policy desired by the French: rectors, prefects, the heads of national industry, senior civil servants. We should not say 'heads will roll,' like Robespierre in the Convention, but we must say which ones, and quickly."[17]

Not that many heads did roll, although conspicuous ones had already fallen. The Socialists had constantly complained over the years about tight government control over radio and television, and Mitterrand had promised a pluralist media. But the new government also thought that many television officials and editors who had risen in the Pompidou and Giscard era were its enemies. The result was a rapid purge of the directors of the three national networks, of news editors and anchormen.

Communists had always been excluded from television. The PCF now pressed for the hiring of Communist journalists. Some were taken on, although not always the ones at the top of the PCF preference list.

No government action could be more conspicuous than one that caused the disappearance of familiar faces from the tube. By purging TV personalities, by permitting themselves to use arrogant and imprecise language, by playing the Jacobin, 1793 style, the Socialists accredited the accusations of the opposition. The hubris of Valence was not easily forgotten; even *Le Monde,* long friendly to the government, would write in 1984 that the term *Valence* still symbolized a sectarian image that had stuck to the Socialists.

The government continued to alienate powerful special interests. Agriculture Minister Edith Cresson tried to buck the farmers' association, the Fédération Nationale des Syndicats d'Exploitants Agricole (FNSEA), by giving preference to an insignificant alternative organization, and a similar attempt to bypass the Conseil National du Patronat Français (CNPF), the employers' association, was a useless provocation. The meaning of such gestures for many people suspicious of, but not yet hostile to, the new government was that the Socialists were both incompetent and sectarian. Mitterrand declared on the day he took office that "the political majority has rejoined the sociological majority." He meant that an electorate that should have voted for the Left in 1978 had now taken a fundamental decision to shift left and stay there. In other words, the Socialists had been swept into power not merely by a few percentage points in the presidential race and given full control of the assembly by 38 percent of the vote; their victory had been brought about by the ineluctable forces of history and sociology. Socialists could not believe that once the country went for them, it would ever again wish to vote against them. With this blithe assumption that History had taken out a PS party card, and a serene confidence that they were the party of freedom (though unsure of this virtue in their Communist partner), the Socialists made the grave error of believing that a temporary plurality of votes conferred nearly unlimited legitimacy for change.

From Laignel's concept of "politically in the minority, thus legally wrong" it followed that a Socialist legitimacy emerging from a relatively small majority at the polls made conservative objections illegitimate. Small wonder that conservatives already inclined to shout "sovietization" found their fears confirmed.

In fact, the Socialists had mistaken a delirious honeymoon for a stable marriage. The honeymoon soon ended. Confidence in Mitterrand's ability to resolve France's problems was measured by polls at 74 percent in June 1981, but began to decline in September, and had dropped below 60 percent by December. The January 1982 by-elections for deputies whose elections had been invalidated for irregularities returned the one opposition member previously elected and unseated three other deputies elected on the PS ticket. All four had won earlier by a margin of a few dozen votes; the by-elections gave the opposition candidates much larger majorities. The March 1982 cantonal elections for *conseillers généraux* (delegates to departmental assemblies) confirmed this pattern. The honeymoon was over.[18]

Had the PS ever had a chance to create a new majority on the basis of the results of May and June 1981? Probably not, for as electoral analysis has shown, Mitterrand won in 1981 by rallying almost all the Left vote and gaining nearly a million votes from disgruntled neo-Gaullists who refused to vote on the second round for Giscard d'Estaing. The subsequent legislative elections were marked both by heavy abstention on the Right and a desire on the part of moderate voters to give the new president a workable majority. When this majority did not show itself moderate, the momentary fellow travelers of June 1981 promptly redefected to the Right.[19]

Yet any serious attempt to hold them would have collided with the political necessities that ruled out cautious economic policies in the first months: The new government felt obliged to meet the expectations cherished by the Left electorate. Even if the Socialist tribunes had held their tongues, their acts would not have pleased the fringe voters of 1981. If the government had done what sober hindsight identifies as the rational thing, it would have been untrue not only to its promises but also to itself; rather than gaining another electorate, it would have lost its own. Mitterrand retained the trust of his core electors in the increasingly difficult times of 1982–1985 by keeping his early promises.

Parenthesis Without an End

Socialist self-confidence did not last long after the Versailles summit; the economic realities the Socialists had rejected were about to demand recognition. Still unpersuaded of the need for drastic economic measures, Mitterrand reluctantly agreed to a devaluation—after Versailles. Immediately after the summit, Mitterrand gave a press conference still suffused with optimism. Four days later France devalued by 10 percent (with the mark reevaluated by 4.25 percent, the franc by 5.75 percent). Mauroy was applauded when he told the congress of the CGT that prices would be frozen, hooted at when he announced a four-month wage freeze. The Communist party and the CGT chiefs went along with the plan—reserving their criticism for later.

The full plan for *"rigueur"* (as austerity was prudishly baptized) was composed of three measures: a wage and price freeze until the end of October and a 1 percent rise in value-added taxes (the VAT on food, which Mitterrand had promised to abolish altogether, was reduced from 7 percent to 5.5 percent). In addition, social spending was cut, in part by the price freeze on pharmaceuticals and doctor bills, in part by a minimum payment for hospitalization expenses.

Mauroy's polls showed that the French people understood the need for a more realistic policy and might welcome it, but the new policy was clumsily presented and extensively misunderstood. Mitterrand himself had not been convinced that a change of course was necessary or if it was necessary, that the one chosen would do the job. The new measures were set forth as short-range ones and presented to the country as "a parenthesis in the process of change." The PS deputies did not understand the new necessities, resented the new language, and, by showing their resentment, braked change. Both Mitterrand and Mauroy felt the need to go easy on their own troops and on the PCF—or rather on the CGT. Meanwhile French businesspeople were still doubtful of the social measures of 1981, deeply suspicious of the price freeze, and resentful of Socialist charges that their reluctance to invest was willful sabotage of the economy.

If Mitterrand had fully engaged himself in the program of attenuated austerity begun in June 1982, he might have explained it more clearly to the country. Instead, the government went on emphasizing that the policy of reforms would continue. Mauroy had worked easily with Delors in convincing the president that a change was necessary in June. Now he disagreed with the minister of economy. He wanted to downplay *rigueur* and emphasize that the government had not really changed or abandoned its program.[20]

Mitterrand looked for a way out. The outline of a new policy had been suggested to him by some of his advisers in the crisis of June 1982. They argued for boldness, a severe but salutary jolt to the economy. The rules of the European Monetary System (EMS) made dramatic and competitive devaluations almost impossible; France would have to leave the EMS to regain full economic independence. Had not Giscard twice left its predecessor arrangement, the "snake," and returned? Mitterrand, they argued, could do the same. This advice came both from members of the government and from old friends of the president who had his confidence. The Delors-Mauroy course was wrong, they said; France had to follow another policy.

The Legislative Record

Socialist success depended on economic policy, and Socialist failures were ultimately rated by the voters as preeminently economic. But the new government also hoped to be judged on its ambitious reform program. In attempting a great deal, it undoubtedly dissipated its energies. Convinced that things left undone in the first two years risked not being done at all, the government introduced bills on judicial reform, new labor laws, and important new laws on decentralization, plus much lesser legislation—meanwhile fighting the time-consuming nationalization bill through the National Assembly.

Not all new laws were controversial; some were passed with little or no opposition. The abrogation of the death penalty was approved in September 1981 by threefourths of the deputies, notably including Jacques Chirac. Other legal measures that received high priority were the abolition of the special court set up at the end of the Giscard administration to hear security cases and the repeal of a severe 1970 law directed against rioters. Legal reform had long been high on the Socialist list, but once achieved, the reform met with a mixed reception. As the incidence of crime increased, abolition of the death penalty became unpopular; in 1984, polls showed that 61 percent of the French wished to reintroduce the guillotine.[21] The opposition found much approval for its charge that the Socialists were soft on crime and terrorism, although this topic was more successfully exploited in 1983 and thereafter by the emergent National Front (Front National, FN) of Jean-Marie Le Pen.

Another top priority was decentralization. A series of laws first limited the power of the prefects, who would no longer be chief executives of the departments, and then transferred central powers, responsibilities, and resources to the towns, departments, and regions. (See Chapter 7.)

Extensive changes in industrial relations, dubbed the Auroux laws, were introduced by Labor Minister Jean Auroux and enacted by parliament. A new authority for television and radio was created to loosen the government's grip on the electronic media; abortion became reimbursable by social security; a series of grandiose public works was announced; and a new savings system indexed the interest rates of modest bank accounts.

The public's awareness of all these laws was not great and its enthusiasm hard to detect. Worries about taxes, unemployment, and harder times ahead remained as always the bread-and-butter issues. As 1982 wore on, discontent and pessimism were everywhere evident. In July, the monthly SOFRES poll on satisfaction with the prime minister registered a dip for Mauroy to 39 percent. Except for a slight rise in September–October, the curve would continue to decline. The president's public relations adviser, Jacques Séguéla, had been telling him since spring that Mauroy had been the man for a time of dreams but was out of place in a time of austerity. Other advisers agreed. Mitterrand hesitated, believing that he could afford only one change of prime minister during the life of the legislature, a change that must signal a new period. In August he summoned Mauroy to Latché, his country hideaway in the pine downs south of Bordeaux. The two men talked at length, as the president sought to reassure himself that the new economic policies would work rapidly. In the end he told Mauroy that he would give him four more months to succeed.[22]

The polls told Mitterrand that although his prime minister was rapidly losing popularity, he himself still retained the confidence of more than half the electorate. But the government had much to worry about. By-elections for *conseillers généraux* and the occasional mayor continued to register a tilt toward the Right. The Socialists had vowed to solve unemployment, but instead it increased by 14.9 percent in the first year after they gained office. The government was obliged to raise energy prices as world prices rose and to make employees pay more to balance a threatening social security deficit. Popular confidence in the government as a whole was eroding. (A SOFRES poll in early August 1982 registered 57 percent who thought that the government reacted from day to day, without knowing where it was going; worse, 33 percent who called themselves PS voters agreed.)[23]

The government's day-to-day conduct did frequently produce an impression of confusion and dissension. The Mitterrandists did not easily accept the authority of Mauroy, "the loser at Metz," and an eager press gave full play to rumors of arguments within the government assiduously leaked by bickering ministerial staffs. Declarations by ministers were frequently contradicted by the prime minister or the president. Mauroy's style, orotund and eagerly optimistic, met frequently with skepticism and sometimes with scorn.

The opposition was powerless to defeat bills in the National Assembly. The Senate possessed delaying powers only. For parties accustomed for twenty-three years to believe that their ranks constituted the natural leaders of the country, the frustration was immense. They could only vent it in bitter speeches and in the columns of the conservative press. Press lord Robert Hersant's newspapers, particularly the Paris *Le Figaro* and *France Soir,* plus the independent Paris tabloid *Le Quotidien de Paris,* the weekly newsmagazine *L'Express,* and to a lesser extent its rival *Le Point* abounded in criticism that descended frequently into invective.

In opposition the Socialists had not been too restrained in their own vocabulary of criticism; had not the president himself written a book twenty years earlier in which the whole Fifth Republic was derided as a "permanent coup d'état"? But Socialist thin skins betrayed inexperience in office. When the crowd at the Fourteenth of July parade jeered at Mitterrand, no fewer than three top PS leaders issued communiqués (uncoordinated) denouncing plots by factious elements and evoking the memory of the Fascist leagues of 1934.[24]

As polls and by-elections alike indicated ebbing confidence in the Left government, an opposition that had been stunned by defeat plucked up its spirits. In 1982 a wave of rumors traversed Paris-in-the-Know: Mitterrand was dying of cancer; a new presidential election would come soon, and the Right would return to power. After Mitterrand's death in 1996 a controversial book by the president's doctor revealed that he had indeed been suffering from prostate cancer diagnosed in the fall of 1981. The president, who when elected had promised full and faithful bulletins on his health, enjoined strict secrecy on his doctor. The disease did not handicap Mitterrand until 1992; the secret was kept, and the rumors died away.

Chirac meanwhile allowed his lieutenants to fire away at the new government. He himself was at first concerned to build up his stature as the unquestioned leader of the opposition, a bit above the daily fight in the trenches. All that ended in summer 1982, when the government produced a new law designed to diminish Chirac's position as mayor of Paris. In the name of decentralization, the twenty arrondissements of the capital would each become a town in itself, with the mayor of Paris (master of a multibillion-franc budget and boss of 40,000 employees) reduced to the role of a senior coordinator. (Although gentrification had pushed most of the old Parisian working class and much of the lower-middle class into the suburbs, the Socialists still hoped to take over a number of town halls within the city.) Chirac accused the government of balkanizing the city. Why Paris only, and not Socialist-ruled Marseilles, demanded the opposition? The Socialists retreated—Paris, Marseilles, and Lyons would have multiple mayors but would each remain one city. The government ended by showing itself both heavy-handedly partial and politically clumsy. It had succeeded only in uniting the RPR with a UDF still resentful of Chirac's takeover of Paris in 1977. In the 1983 municipal elections the Socialist maneuver proved a spectacular failure, as Chirac's partisans took all twenty Paris arrondissements.

The autumn of 1982 saw no economic improvement. The American economy was barely beginning to take off, too late to help the French, and the other European economies were nearly stagnant. French exports to West Germany sank steadily throughout 1982.[25] Unemployment leveled off as a result of reflations and other actions, but did not diminish. Inflation decreased slightly, but remained close to double digits.

The government was slowly losing the confidence of its own inner constituency and not gaining that of French business. Enjoined by a Socialist-Communist government to invest at a time of high inflation and falling profit margins, company directors, not unreasonably, chose to wait. Rapid rises in the minimum wage, the fifth week of paid vacation, the thirty-nine-hour week paid as forty did not endear a Socialist-Communist government to businesspeople, whose attitude already ranged from suspicious to hostile. A darkening economic picture in 1982 did nothing to lessen their doubts about a government they neither liked nor trusted. When the government declared that the measures it had taken toward *rigueur* were temporary, a "necessary parenthesis" that once closed would permit further steps on the march toward socialism, the business class (for once) believed them, though many workers did not. Business nourished only the gloomiest views of the future.

Given this climate, it was hardly surprising that the twice-devalued franc came under increased attack in autumn and winter 1982, as the need for a long-range austerity policy became plainer and the government continued to issue confusing statements. Through the cloud of language the French people perceived that the situation was growing no better and feared it might grow much worse. Meanwhile, there was no consensus within the Socialist party on what to do, and none in the government. Mauroy, more and more under the influence of his economists and in general agreement with Delors, understood clearly that a new and greater austerity was necessary. But his intellectual acceptance of this necessity warred with his visceral dislike of it. Furthermore, he had every reason to believe the president far from ready to approve more austerity and quite ready to entrust whatever new actions might be taken to a new prime minister.

As always, Mitterrand was thinking in political, not economic, terms. Although he had told Mauroy in August that he gave him four months to succeed, he had not meant to replace him in December—because the president's eyes were fixed on the municipal elections set for early March. France holds all municipal elections simultaneously every six years, with two rounds, as in legislative and presidential elections. In the 1977 municipal elections the Union of the Left at its most united had won city council majorities in 159 of the 221 cities that had more than 30,000 inhabitants. Seventy-two big-city mayors were Communists. All signs suggested that in 1983 the Left would not do well. Thirty-four members of the Mauroy cabinet were also running for election or reelection as mayors; severe losses for them would be a disavowal of the government. Mitterrand reasoned that if that should happen, he would need a new prime minister. But a new chief of government would also need to embody new policies, if the old ones seemed rejected. The ideas of those who favored a break with Delors's version of conventional austerity appealed ever more strongly to him. Those plans were bold, different, dramatic; if successful, they would permit a dramatic breakout from the trench warfare in which Mitterrand felt entrapped. Their advocates were old friends, ministers, personal advisers. Mauroy often met them in the presidential antechamber as he left Mitterrand's office at the end of the day. He gave them the name of the spectral presences in a famous Marcel Carné film of the 1940s, *Les Visiteurs du soir,* the "night visitors."

The "Other Policy"

Pierre Mauroy's intellect had conquered his instinctive aversion to austerity but was still at war with his sentiments, and his oratorical style served sentiment rather than intellect. The collection of his speeches as prime minister, significantly titled *À Gauche,* demonstrates that although he did not hide the problems presented by the policy of *rigueur,* his desire to be optimistic got him into trouble. One celebrated example came in a television interview in February 1983: "I will try to show tonight that finally the big problems are behind us. In June, we had to make choices. In November, we had to fix governmental policy. But now governmental policy is fixed, and I will show you that all the traffic lights for governmental policy, or practically all, are finally showing green."[26]

If Mauroy was referring to a hard battle won, he was disingenuous at the least, for he knew that the battle as he conceived it was far from won. Municipal elections in three weeks might remove him from office and open the way to a change of policy if a much feared swing against the Left was too great. Nine months after the first decisions on austerity, François Mitterrand was still hopeful that other roads might be found. When the 1982 decisions for *rigueur* and devaluation were being made, Mitterrand had warned Mauroy and Delors at the end of a stormy Council of Ministers meeting, in the hearing of the other ministers, "If we do not succeed in this second phase, a third one could lead us to exit from the EMS."[27] Here was an invitation to dissenters to present an "other policy." The "night visitors" were pressing him to switch to one.

They were Jean Riboud, president of the giant multinational Schlumberger, publicist and sempiternal idea man Jean-Jacques Servan-Schreiber, Industry Minister Jean-Pierre Chevènement, plus two ministers personally very close to Mitterrand, Pierre Bérégovoy and Laurent Fabius. Their advice—that France need not remain in the European Monetary System and accept its constraints, its frequent and humiliating negotiations with the Germans—was appealing to a man who detested feeling trapped. The way to regain growth and pursue a Socialist course was to go it alone, pursue a partially protectionist course, cut interest rates, and do everything to build up French industry and its internal market. Later, France might return to the EMS, or like Great Britain, remain outside. Mauroy regarded all that as both anti-European and terribly risky; he did not think that French industry had the élan to fill the role assigned.

The polls had gloomy news for the Socialists in the election month of March: Only 39 percent of respondents gave their confidence to Mauroy, 48 percent to

Mitterrand. The first round of the municipal elections on March 6 seemed to confirm PS fears, but in the second round the Socialists rallied. Worse hit were the Communists. The Socialists lost Nantes, Grenoble, Brest, and Chalons-sur-Saône but were happily surprised to hold embattled Marseilles. Indeed, those cities where ministers were also mayors (or candidates, like Bérégovoy and Edith Cresson) almost all ended in the Socialist column. Except for Marseilles, the biggest cities had gone against the Left, with a crushing defeat in Paris. The balance of the country had shifted to the right. But since they had expected worse results and more humiliating ones, the Socialists could think that a glass they had feared more than half empty was really almost half full.

Mitterrand's reaction to the second round was relief; the vote had not obliged him to jettison Mauroy. The "night visitors" had, however, convinced him to change economic policies. "At the rate the external deficit is going, plus the difference between our inflation rate and that of our partners," they whispered, "France will be a colony of the deutsche mark in two months. By January 1984 the IMF (International Monetary Fund) will call the tune in Paris."[28]

The adventurer in Mitterrand was excited by ideas suggested by Riboud, an old friend and a big capitalist who was also a man of the Left. Riboud believed he could reestablish the dynamics of growth within three years. France would then be independent and freed from the fetters of its capitalist partners. Severe but temporary austerity would permit imaginative and successful policies.

The morning after the municipal elections, the Paris daily *Libération* published what seemed an authoritative story by its chief editor Serge July, based on diligent leaks from Mitterrand's staff. It asserted that Mauroy would soon depart to make way for "the other policy," which would begin by floating the franc and proceed to stronger action against imports. Arriving at the Elysée, Mauroy was not surprised to find that those were indeed the president's ideas—but Mitterrand wanted him to remain as prime minister to carry them out.

The prime minister asked for a few hours to think it over, consulted with his disapproving entourage, and returned a negative answer. "I do not know how to drive on an icy road," was his comment. But the media expected the president to comment on the election results—and, of course, confirm the rumors. Having nothing to announce, Mitterrand was obliged to deny that any broadcast had been planned or that any change of prime minister was in the offing. He announced that he would speak to the nation ten days later. Together with the *Libération* story, these actions implicitly told the country that the government was without a prime minister and hesitating between two policies.[29]

The crisis of March 1983 was the hinge event of 1981–1986, perhaps of the entire Mitterrand presidency. In May 1981 and June 1982 policies had been suggested that might have taken France out of the European Monetary System and turned it toward a go-it-alone policy. June 1982 had seen the decision for *rigueur*, which was to persist; in this sense the turn away from the original socialist policies dates from then. But Mitterrand had taken no final decision. In 1983 the president decided to go it alone—and then reversed himself. He hesitated, as he consulted with his closest advisers, with the most famous French economists, and with a variety of other pundits, political and economic. Leaks from these consultations suggested to the media that the president was irresolute. In fact, he seems to have decided fairly rapidly against the "other policy," but for several days more was still seeking a political and economic solution to the now-evident crisis.[30]

Mauroy had declared his opposition to the president's plan and was packing his bags. Delors, along with most of the government's economists and key advisers at the Elysée, produced a continual series of memoranda on the precarious state of French finances. Budget Minister Laurent Fabius, a proponent of the "other policy," was now briefed by Treasury chief Michel Camdessus that French monetary reserves were only 30 billion francs, not enough to survive the hammering of speculators once the franc was allowed to float. (Even in a free float, the franc would still have had to worry about its relation to the dollar, and the dollar continued to rise.) A devaluation of 20 percent would automatically send the foreign debt from 330 billion francs to 400 billion. Many of the president's technicians warned him that if the franc were set free to float, it would immediately sink by 20 and perhaps 30 percent. No one would lend to France. The effect of higher prices on imports (dollar-denominated energy in particular) would be immediate, whereas any positive effect on exports would be much slower in coming. Once out of the European Monetary System, France could expect no support from its European ex-partners. The only defense of the franc would then be to hike interest rates from the prevailing 14 percent to 20 percent or higher. No one would invest at such rates.

The advocates of the "other policy" had told Mitterrand that the arguments of the orthodox faction seemed plausible only because they had the computers to extrapolate results. If we had the same resources, they argued, we could show why our ideas are better. But "their ideas were so vague," charged former Mauroy top aide Henri Guillaume contemptuously, "that they had no details to back them up";[31] indeed they were unable to furnish Mitterrand with a list of proposed immediate measures. Nor did all advocates of the new policy agree among themselves. Some advocates of the "other policy," including Chevènement and Riboud, favored a protectionism that meant closing French borders to other European goods, which some others contemptuously termed "Albanian" tactics. The "other policy" was clearly a leap in the dark.

Once Mitterrand had recognized the political danger, he agreed that conventional austerity must continue. But still another scenario had been suggested to him by his advisers, that the Germans could be persuaded to revalue the mark enough to permit France to avoid devaluation.[32] Furthermore, he was still looking for a prime minister. For a week, Jacques Delors thought the nod would go to him. He knew that Mitterrand detested the idea of going to the West German government cap in hand to ask for a favor. Negotiating feverishly with the West Germans, Delors arranged for Bonn's finance minister Gerhard Stoltenberg to come secretly to Paris to prepare the next meeting of the EC countries. To reassure Mitterrand, Delors reported that he had pushed frankness with the Germans to the point of insult, accusing them of causing monetary disorder in Europe.[33] In Brussels, Delors let it be understood that if he failed to get the devaluation agreement, Mitterrand might revert to the "other policy."

Whereas Delors had demanded a major German revaluation, he had finally to content himself with a 2.5 percent devaluation for the franc, the mark rising by 5.5 percent. To accompany devaluation, the French government would be obliged to extend the policy of austerity, not for a few months, but for years. To carry out this policy, Delors believed not only that he had to be prime minister but also that he had to have the economics and finance portfolios, like Raymond Barre under Giscard.

This gesture of distrust toward Bérégovoy and Fabius was a tactical error. Delors, they charged, was "too greedy." Besides, he had no following in the Socialist party. He was a latecomer, the brains behind the policies of Gaullist prime minister Chaban-Delmas. Mitterrand listened. He did not feel comfortable with Delors and disliked his frequent offers to resign when decisions went against him. For a day, Bérégovoy hoped to be prime minister. Mauroy prepared his formal letter of resignation, which he delivered to the president on March 22. Half an hour after leaving the Matignon he was back. At the last minute, Mitterrand had decided to name him prime minister again.

By March 1983, Mitterrand should probably have taken the advice given him by his image artists to get rid of a prime minister unsuited to the new dispensation. The president's difficulty was that he did not have a candidate available who could assume the symbolism of the new policy—and Mitterrand was perhaps not certain exactly what the new policy was to be. He had thought of Delors and rejected him. Pierre Bérégovoy was loyal, if not exciting, but he had been an advocate of "the other policy" until the end. So had Laurent Fabius, who according to most accounts changed his mind only in the decisive last week of the crisis. Besides, he was young and needed more experience; he had never headed a major ministry. Michel Rocard was not to be trusted, a choice of last resort. Mauroy was faithful, diligent, honest— and when his usefulness ran out, he could be trusted to go quietly.

The new austerity plan, still called *rigueur,* was designed to sponge up the excess demand that the government's earlier measures had continued to spill into the economy. It aimed at equilibrium in the balance of payments in two years and in so doing accepted what the Socialists had violently rejected two years earlier—low growth or none. Buying power was siphoned off by a 10 percent obligatory loan figured as a surcharge on income tax (for households paying more than 5,000 francs in tax), a surtax of 1 percent on income, taxes on alcohol and tobacco destined to refloat social security (Bérégovoy had already set a 20-franc-per-day cost-sharing fee for hospital stays in November 1982), and higher electricity and gas prices. Railroad tickets and telephone rates were raised by 8 percent in April instead of later in the year, which was customary. The state also scaled back or delayed its outlays by 24 billion francs and took some measures to encourage savings.

The most visible and instantly irritating new measure was a ban on the purchase of foreign currency, limiting tourist expenses to 2,000 francs per adult per year, with the use of credit cards abroad restricted to business trips. In a country where vacations are sacred and every year millions plan to travel abroad, this irruption of state power into private family planning brought into question the government's foresight, planning, and honesty. An already skeptical public had watched Mauroy saying, "All the stoplights are green" and "There is no secret plan for more austerity in the files." After a year of semi-rigor explained as a parenthesis, there had come another crisis, a third devaluation of the franc, new taxes, and austerity without a visible end.

If the economic policy adopted in June 1982 involved long-term austerity, why had the government not explained that to the country? If the policy of March 1983 was new, people wanted to know how it was to be distinguished from the old one, and how long it would continue. Those already hostile to the government found the confusion of March 1983 just one more example of incompetence and said so loudly. Mauroy's satisfaction rating in the SOFRES poll fell from 45 percent to 33 percent between March and May.

Before the crisis of March 1983 it had been possible for some Socialists to think that the economic constraints weighing on France were temporary and contingent, to be conquered by bold measures and a firm will to prevail against all difficulties. The great lesson of March was that a middle-sized capitalist country with a network of economic and political ties to its neighbors in the European Community could ignore or shake off these ties only at extreme peril, both economic and political—in fact, could not shake them off at all. Once the lesson sank in, only the Communists could be found to dispute it.

Mitterrand himself may not have understood that completely at first; there is some evidence that he continued to hope that an improvement in the Bank of France's reserves would permit him to go back to the "other policy" later in 1983.[34] But in early June Mitterrand began to adopt the new dispensation as his own.

When in September 1982 he had mysteriously declared, "I do not make socialism my Bible," he had not specified what new scriptures he had adopted. On June 8, 1983, he declared, "There is no other possible policy," and admitted that mistakes had been made. "It's true, perhaps we were dreaming in 1981."[35]

Slowly, the country began to believe that the new economic severity was a real change and not a patch. That did not make it more palatable to Socialists. Jean Poperen, number-two man in the PS, attacked the government: "Jacques Delors has hit the wrong target again. He has undertaken a program of classic deflation, while making it easy for entrepreneurs, bosses, and farmers. . . . He demands the most from salaried workers, specialized workers, white-collar workers, [who were] the support and the electorate of François Mitterrand in May 1981."[36]

This was a single-mindedly political discourse. Other Socialists began openly to admit their failure to understand the workings of the economy. Looking about them for a familiar conceptual framework to explain the setback and to discern the outlines of the future, they found little guidance. Was socialism *à la française* to be nothing more than any policy conducted by a government composed of Socialists?

Individuals, party, prime minister, president—everyone began to search for some larger meaning and came up with diverse answers.

Ideological Drought

The confusion and dejection in Socialist ranks after 1983 arose from the shattering of hopes that had nourished and conditioned the Socialist revival, hopes profoundly affected by the intellectual climate that had set in after World War II. From the Liberation until the early 1970s the winds of political and intellectual fashion in France had blown steadily from the left. The ideological climate turned in the mid-1970s, although as often happens with climatic change, it was not immediately recognized. In 1981 the Socialists could think their triumph was the natural culmination of a long struggle by the Left. In reality, Socialist victory was the belated result of causes that were ceasing to operate, a fact the Socialists were slow and exceedingly reluctant to apprehend.

The PS that Mitterrand took over in 1971 had no unitary ideology, but all its members drew on the traditions of the Left. Building a new party on the ruins of an SFIO largely discredited by its opportunism and competing actively with the PCF within the framework of their alliance, Mitterrand's PS had needed to refurbish its leftist rhetoric. The standard-bearer for leftist ideas in Mitterrand's new PS was Jean-Pierre Chevènement's CERES, boasting until 1977 one-quarter of PS membership, opposed to the Communists on organizational principles, but not in policy. Advocacy of nationalizations, denunciation of capitalism at home and abroad were obligatory.

The leftist rhetoric of the PS necessarily drew on the common fund of leftist ideas in France. Leftists of all stripes had agreed from the early postwar years that a gradual and reformist course was impossible for France. "A serious effort at economic renewal would have such broad social and political consequences that only the partisans of revolutionary change could accept them," wrote a reproving critic of Raymond Aron's *Opium of the Intellectuals* in 1954.[37] For many Leftists, therefore, the Communist party remained the only agent of change.

In the 1970s Mitterrand espoused a Marxoid language, saying at the Epinay congress when he had just won leadership of the PS in alliance with CERES: "He who does not accept the *rupture* [break] . . . with capitalist society . . . cannot be a member of the Socialist party."[38] Mitterrand nevertheless remained wary of the potential power of CERES, evicting it from the PS's governing majority at the Pau congress in 1975, only to bring it in again as a weapon against Rocard at the Metz congress in 1979, where the majority motion stated, "Our objective is not to modernize capitalism or to temper it, but to replace it by socialism."[39] In 1980 Chevènement was given the task of drawing up the *Projet Socialiste*—which Mitterrand did not use as his platform when he ran for the presidency in 1981.

"Breaking with capitalism" sounded brave and resolute, but it hid a multitude of ambiguities. Capitalism had a negative ring in the ears of the French Left, rather similar to the American "robber baron capitalism." Connotations aside, however, capitalism necessarily involves the market, and the French Socialists did not propose to abolish markets. "The common-denominator philosophy of the PS at the beginning of the 1980s was social redistribution to curb the crisis, [plus] structural reforms to diminish the influence of big capital and reorient investment."[40]

Nationalizing a number of key conglomerates and banks while leaving large chunks of the economy in private hands was thus supposed to enable the creation of a new society by seizure of the "commanding heights of the economy." But this French economy was still part of the world capitalist economy, and the reflation of the economy by a sudden injection of new buying power made sense only on the assumption that France was launching itself onto a cresting wave of growth, to be stimulated notably by the United States. The attempt to create socialism was thus dependent on a new spurt of capitalism, which failed to arrive according to the timetable widely predicted. The inability to create economic growth using the policies of 1981–1983, plus the conditions accompanying negotiated devaluations, forced the cutback on the social program. Here was the logical consequence of France's failure to launch itself out of the orbit of European and world capitalism. Banal economic difficulties brought about by the imprudent but essentially Keynesian policies of 1981 (not by the more socialist nationalization policy, which merely failed to serve its stimulative purpose) suggested to both the country at large and many of the Socialists themselves that their program had failed.

Socialist beliefs of the 1970s had asserted the possibility of a profound change that was never called revolution but that owed a good deal to pre-Marxist and Marxist ideas of revolution. Once the Socialists discovered that the measures of 1981–1982 could not reverse unemployment or restore prosperity, disillusionment set in, encountering and fitting well with the new and ideologically disabused ideas already abroad in the country. A nonideological party might have been less affected by failure. By 1984 the French Socialists had gained a certain sense that their ideology had run dry. The Communist party ceased after mid-1984 to guarantee a Left majority, and an influential intellectual community that was now anti-Left found the PCF increasingly offensive on ideological grounds. With the resurgent Gaullists and UDF baying at their heels, abandoned by the opinion makers, and beaten down by an economy unresponsive and ailing, the Socialist government faced a seeming infinity of problems.

Legislation and Its Discontents

By late 1983 many French Socialists had begun to find the institutions of the Fifth Republic an unexpected burden. Before Mitterrand's election they had distrusted a presidentialized system designed permanently to exclude them. In June 1981, the guarantee of five years in control of the state seemed a marvelous dream realized. At that time, they were still guided by the aims expressed in their 1977 language for the revision of the Common Program: "To break the domination of big capital and set in motion a new economic and social policy, rejecting the policy of the present government, the government will progressively carry out the transfer to the collectivity of the most important means of production and financial instruments now in the hands of dominant capitalist groups."[41]

Two years after they had attempted to put these brave words into action some Socialists yearned for the irresponsibility of the Fourth Republic, which would have dismissed them from office after the setbacks of 1983, leaving behind the monument of their legislation. In two years the Socialists had introduced laws concerning almost all of the promises Mitterrand had made in 1981. As *Le Monde*'s chief political writer noted: "Concentrating so great a number of reforms in the first months of the *septennat*—nationalization, decentralization, workers' rights—so-called structural reforms, the Left rapidly exhausted itself: Suddenly it found itself without a project."[42] In one sense the Socialists had done their work. In any event, they were weary and without further ideas they could call their own, just at the point when they had to adopt unwelcome economic policies.

The existence of the temptation to lay down the burden exemplified a widely shared and formalistic conception of government as the power of prescriptive law. The Socialists' yearning for the freedom of the Fourth Republic bore the impress of the long years of opposition, the notion that the Left was the force of innovation, the Right that of administration. Not all Socialists shared this view, of course, and least among them the tenant of the Elysée palace, who was intensely conscious of the fact that his lease ran for seven years.

The myth of the Revolution and experience in short-lived Left governments of the Third and Fourth Republics suggested that the power of the Left to alter France lay in massive doses of legislation, rapidly injected. It followed also from the myth of 1789 that those favorably affected by such legislation would support the party or forces that had introduced it (although the evil forces of money always intervened to deprive them of power).

The Socialists were therefore surprised and disappointed, as they watched their popularity steadily diminish, to find that their laws and measures weighed so lightly in the balance of popular approval. Here was naïveté. Apart from actions that put money immediately into people's pockets (but raised the danger of inflation), many of their measures were too technical, complicated, or far-reaching to affect or even influence the general public in the short run. Decentralization had no daily effect on the average citizen, nor did legal reform. Some legislation on civil liberties actually became unpopular—notably abolition of the death penalty and restriction of police freedom to stop and search. As crime mounted, it did no good for professors to demonstrate in the pages of *Le Monde* that its cause was not abolition of the death penalty but rather deep-seated sociological problems. It was far easier for the opposition to charge that the Socialist government was soft on crime.

The mass of substantive legislation that had occupied the attention of government and parliament in 1981–1982 was also slow to excite enthusiasm. Announcement of new legislation was usually followed by a long parliamentary debate, and many months later by a brief notice that the law was actually in effect. Whereas the nationalizations announced in 1981 and carried out in 1982 occupied the complete attention of the managements affected, they made much less difference to the workers involved and no obvious difference at all to the rest of the population.

Here was the dilemma: Immediate measures improving the lot of the socially disadvantaged affected a relatively small part of the population, which voted for the Left in any case. Once implemented, many new statutes aggravated the economic crisis, provoking an austerity that restricted further social legislation and increasingly collided with the pocketbook interests of the lower-middle and middle classes. Ideas on social, judicial, and governmental reform that conscientious citizens on the Left (and not the Left alone) had cherished over the years produced limited electoral resonance once they had been enacted into law. Could the Socialist government have managed things otherwise, and would a more participatory variation of leftist government have evoked greater enthusiasm and support? Certainly workers' enthusiasm even in 1981 was less than that displayed for the Popular Front. But enthusiasm in 1936 had taken the form of factory occupations, which scarcely aided the Blum government. It is easier to note that the Mitterrand government consulted too little and decreed too much than to know whether a more determined and skillful effort at participatory government would have made a major difference. Indeed, commenting on French socialism's lack of integral ties with labor, a PS leader remarked wryly in a private conversation in 1987, "If we had had ties to the unions like those of the Labour party or the SPD, we would never have been able to do the things we had to do in 1983 and 1984."

The Socialists had held unrealistic expectations that their electorate would give the same value as they did to the measures they promised and delivered. Despite the successful passage of much legislation, they disappointed their voters. Nevertheless, if Left voters did not get all they expected, it was not the shortfall in genuine socialism that hurt the government the most. Mitterrand and the Socialist deputies owed their elections to the accident of an electorate more determined to reject Giscard and company than to choose socialism. Mitterrand's "sociological majority," the wage earners who were the vast majority of French men and women, was not in its majority composed of workers. The Socialists had briefly constructed a majority that included a significant fraction of the middle class and rapidly lost much of it again.

As noted, the Socialists had excellent reasons to give priority to their core constituency. In the hubris of the first year they also quite unnecessarily provoked business and farmer organizations by favoring splinter groups thought to be pro-Socialist. Yet arrogance and a bias toward the underprivileged were not the principal reasons why they lost much of their temporary middle-class constituency. Much of it would have remained loyal to the choice made in 1981 only if the Socialists had been able to do everything right, making a rapid dent in unemployment, meanwhile cutting inflation and improving the economy. The mistakes and bad luck of 1981–1982 ended this possibility.

The conservative opposition rallied as early as 1982—after an initial stunned incredulity. A small majority of the French had not wanted conservatives to govern France forever, but the opposition still benefited from a cultural prejudice that held the politicians of the Right to be the natural forces of government. Naturally, the outs also benefited from the very French pleasure of savagely criticizing the ins. Adopting a new free enterprise philosophy gilded by the 1983 upturn in the American economy and made relevant by the failures of the magic wand of Socialist *dirigisme,* the Right found a newly pleasing language to use with the French electorate. Jacques Chirac triumphed in every arrondissement in Paris in the 1983 municipal elections. A seemingly discredited Raymond Barre, his policies revalidated by reluctant Socialist imitation, moved up in the polls as Mauroy's ratings sank, and Barre began to prepare himself for the challenge of the 1988 presidential race. Polls showed that an electorate grown doubtful of the Socialists was skeptical of the opposition's ability to do much better—but was nevertheless inclined to test its claims. By mid-1983, as the government grew visibly weary, the opposition in France—unlike that in Britain or Spain—increasingly appeared a viable alternative.

The Problems of Pierre Mauroy

Weary and short of ideas the government might be, but under the Fifth Republic it had to persevere. It had squeaked past the test of the municipal elections; everything else, however, seemed to be going badly. An opposition press now in full cry, charging universal incompetence, cheered on the numerous demonstrations of late spring and summer 1983: by farmers in Brittany and elsewhere, by hospital interns and clinic chiefs, medical students, and small entrepreneurs. The streets of Paris and numerous other cities were frequently blocked by protesters. The progovernment papers spoke of "right-wing gangs," and some leading Socialists wondered if force might not be needed to break up demonstrations, while the rightist *Figaro* gleefully accused the government of seeing plots everywhere.

The period from spring 1983 to the change of prime ministers in July 1984 marked a transition within Socialist government. The Socialists were attempting to understand the changes in policy that events had forced on them and to cope with an economy still in decline, an opposition on the rise, and an ideology in tatters. President and prime minister reacted differently to these problems. François Mitterrand had begun as early as September 1982, though hesitantly and with many contradictions, to take his distance from socialism.[43] His interest in "the other policy" in early 1983 was not necessarily proof of a diehard attachment to socialist ideas; one of the chief influences on him at that time was Jean Riboud of Schlumberger, who believed that French business needed an electric shock to awaken it to competition. And as always, Mitterrand's nationalist views caused him to look for solutions in which international constraints could be lessened, if not removed. Meanwhile, the very socialist Pierre Mauroy opposed the "other policy" in part because he did not believe French business capable of responding to the challenge.

By mid-1983, Mitterrand was in search of a new theme. He wanted to give the lie to opposition charges of incompetence, to reassure the French that austerity would not last forever, and to talk up growth as the way out of the nation's troubles. But he also knew that the high taxes needed to support the social costs of more than 2 million unemployed and of all the other expenses he had inherited or incurred had exasperated a middle class that felt itself pinched.

The sophisticated politician's eye roved over political successes achieved in other countries; U.S. tax cuts were popular. In June 1983 Mitterrand told a radio audience that the total burden of taxation and social security had gone from 42 to 44 percent, which he termed the outer limit. (The Treasury wanted to raise social security contributions by another percentage point.) To offset the rise, the president opted for a surtax hitting high incomes, which brought in little revenue. The 1984 budget contained new surtaxes, continuation of the extra 1 percent tax for social security, and a rise in some value-added taxes.

An IFOP poll in autumn showed that 63 percent of those surveyed thought the government's economic record was negative. In mid-September 1983 Mitterrand went on television and showed himself the last of the Laffers. Announcing that too many taxes asphyxiated the economy and cut back tax income, he declared that the 1985 budget would have to come down by 1 percent at least. (In preparing the 1984 budget, Mauroy and Delors had assumed that fiscal pressure would unfortunately have to increase again in 1985.) Mitterrand had not adopted Reaganism—far from it—but he had shown that in searching for new ways to appeal to the nation, he was not to be hemmed in by the boundaries of any doctrine.[44]

Mauroy had courageously taken the lead in difficult economic decisions in both June 1982 and early 1983. Now he was suffering from the stings of all the nettles he had grasped. The logic of long-term austerity meant a revision of optimistic plans to reopen declining coal mines in his native north, as well as major cuts in the workforce of the deficit-ridden steel industry of the north and Lorraine. Mauroy wanted to soften the blow by extending the process over time. At the end of 1983 the emphasis in the Elysée was again on shock tactics. A rapid operation, cutting where surgery would be necessary sooner or later, might at least help the government gain credit for courage. The positive action accompanying these cuts was to seek growth by aiding new industry and investing in high technology, described as the road to future job creation. Those were the ideas of the president and his advisers—particularly his chief idea man, Jacques Attali, and his protégé Laurent Fabius, since March 1983 minister of industry.

Mauroy, in contrast, saw the working class of his own industrial north as the core constituency of the Left. Anything but pro-Communist, Mauroy believed that the social forces shoring up the Communist party represented a part of the electorate that the Socialists would never be able to reach. The support of voters from this irreducible Communist minimum would in his view always be necessary for a genuinely social democratic policy. Believing that the intransigent leaders of the PCF would ultimately have to accept the fact that their party could no longer grow and might well continue to shrink, the prime minister opposed an industrial policy that would burn PS bridges to the PCF and its electorate.[45]

Both arguments were as much political as economic and were affected by considerations of timing. Mitterrand and his advisers had their eyes fixed on the legislative elections of March 1986. If the economy continued to lose speed, the elections would bring disaster to the PS and perhaps force the president to resign, ending the whole Socialist era with a whimper. But in almost three years much could be done to retrieve the situation, conceivably even to win those elections. Consciously or unconsciously, Mauroy had a different perspective. He knew that his stewardship as prime minister would terminate by the end of 1984 at the latest, and although he certainly did not desire defeat in 1986, his thinking was not centered on this date.

Mauroy was furthermore whipsawed by the contradiction between his need to defend austerity policies to the Left constituency and his natural tendency to sound as optimistic as possible. Mitterrand watched his prime minister's credit diminish and waited. The next electoral contest was the election for the European Parliament in June 1984. Sometime thereafter a change in prime minister might be necessary.

As 1983 dragged on, bringing new crises in the important automobile industry, where both nationalized Renault and privately held Peugeot-Citroen were fast losing their market share in France and Europe, the political logic of rapid and dramatic action appealed increasingly to Mitterrand. Not only Fabius and Attali but also Delors now argued that the government must not appear to be bogged down and defeatist. Mauroy's go-slow ideas inevitably fell into this category.

In pursuing the logic of dramatic action Mitterrand was implicitly breaking with the policy of alliance with the Communists that he had followed since 1965. In mid-1983 he seems to have persuaded himself that since the PCF had not left the government after the municipal elections (their most logical departure point), they would swallow almost anything and remain in the government until 1986.[46]

Pushing the Communists this hard was a gamble; the PS might still need a coalition partner, and in 1983 it was unclear that in 1984 PCF fortunes were destined to sink lower. In July 1984, when Mitterrand chose Laurent Fabius to succeed Mauroy and the PCF left the government, its share of the vote had already fallen to 11.28 percent. But in 1983 the PCF had not yet gathered the nerve to leave the government; the leadership feared that the party base would not have understood the break.[47] In 1984, Mitterrand may have hoped that the Communists would remain in the Fabius government, but he could not logically have expected them to do so, since both their political and their social reasons to remain in government had disappeared.

The political decisions made in 1983 well before Fabius's appointment led toward a new policy. The government could no longer describe itself as the engine of social change. In the future it would need to appear as the agency of strong and sensible orthodox administration, dedicated to the modernization of the French economy, socialist only because more sensitive than the Right to the pain caused by inevitable surgical operations. The new economic policies meant that the Socialists were unable to do much more for the core Left electorate. To have a presentable record in the March 1986 elections, they were obliged to go in chase of the mildly left-center voters whom they had disenchanted in 1981–1983. That was in any case the electorate most likely to be pleased by their new economic policies.

The period between March 1983 and Mauroy's resignation in 1984 is both confusing and confused; neither Mitterrand nor Mauroy was ready to face the logic of the president's choices. Mitterrand should have named a new prime minister in March 1983, one who could pursue austerity while giving the government the new goal of modernization. Instead he temporized, choosing Mauroy again rather than Delors (Fabius seemed too inexperienced) because he thought Mauroy safer. He wanted to keep his options open for a later change of prime ministers, in 1984. He thought, rightly or wrongly, that retaining Mauroy also helped him to manage the Communists.

Mauroy, however, was seen by the country and by himself as a champion of orthodox socialist ideas. Unwilling to appear merely as an administrator, and unable to find a conspicuously socialist agenda in economic measures, Mauroy began to emphasize other promises made in Mitterrand's "110 proposals." His policy was to please and remotivate a dispirited Left. Meanwhile, the new economic policies directed by Delors might win back left-center voters. Mitterrand assented to this double-tracked scheme. In retrospect, it is clear that Mauroy's tactics would have worked only if each constituency involved had listened to the right tune and remained deaf to the appeal not meant for it. Master politicians (and Mitterrand was one) can sometimes bring off such a stratagem. But evidently neither Mitterrand nor Mauroy had yet understood in autumn 1983 that they (and particularly Mauroy) had lost the strength essential to this maneuver, the ability to define a policy convincingly to the country on one's own terms. The next months would show that this capacity had passed instead to the opposition.

Mauroy's first target was the press empire of Robert Hersant, the French Rupert Murdoch. De Gaulle's government in 1944 had decreed a limit on the number of newspapers that could be owned by one person, a principle largely infringed by Hersant's growing press acquisitions. Like Murdoch, Hersant was something more than a rich man with an appetite for gobbling up papers—French newspapers (such as the old *Figaro,* which he acquired in the late 1970s) were slackly and wastefully run. Hersant had understood how to modernize both administrative and printing operations. But the Socialists hated him as an ambitious press lord of the Right with aspirations to acquire still more papers and radio stations—and eventually television channels when that became possible.

Hersant was tainted with charges of collaboration in his extreme youth—although they had not excluded him from membership in Mitterrand's own small party, the UDSR, when he was a deputy during the Fourth Republic. In the Fifth Republic, he and most of his papers moved to the right, and after May 1981 his flagship, the Paris daily *Le Figaro,* became the most vociferous and frequently violent media opponent of the government.

Nevertheless, Mitterrand's old friend and aide André Rousselot had negotiated with Hersant in 1981–1982, hoping to purchase the popular Paris daily *France Soir*, which he believed the press magnate wished to sell. Without a daily press outlet of its own, the Socialist government and party found itself frequently frustrated by the way in which the independent press on both left and right explained and criticized its actions. The Socialists believed in a free press. They also wanted to be understood, lovingly.

Many Socialist leaders, including Mauroy and his entourage, noted that no French party had been able to sustain a profitable Paris daily (the Communist *L'Humanité* was no exception, being heavily subsidized). They would have preferred to acquire provincial newspapers to support the party. In any case, Hersant was not negotiating seriously with Rousselot. He had his eye instead on a prestigious Grenoble daily, *Le Dauphiné Libéré*, with wide circulation in the Isère department and much of the important Rhône-Alpes region. Mitterrand lieutenant Louis Mermaz, Socialist boss of the Isère, would have liked to acquire the paper or at least dissuade Hersant by denying him credit from the nationalized banks. For whatever reason, nothing was done to block Hersant's acquisition of the paper in 1983. Thereafter, Hersant lost interest in negotiating the sale of *France Soir*. Thus mocked, the Socialists found the Hersant empire an ever more tempting target.[48]

When Mauroy told the Socialist congress of Bourg-en-Bresse in October 1983 that "the exercise of democracy demands pluralism and clarity . . . a halt to the creation of ever more powerful and monolithic press monopolies," he was wildly applauded. A month later the government adopted a bill "to guarantee freedom of the press and readers' free choice by limiting concentration." Immediately baptized "the Hersant law" and violently criticized by the right-wing press (not Hersant's alone), the bill was passed by the National Assembly after lengthy and stormy sessions, during which the opposition introduced no fewer than 2,600 amendments. An appeal to the Constitutional Council produced the Solomonic verdict that the law was constitutional—but could not apply retrospectively, a judgment glossed by the satiric *Canard Enchaîné* as declaring that no one but Robert Hersant might possess a press empire.

The Socialists therefore failed to force Hersant to cede a part of his empire either to them or to neutral forces. Worse, they played directly into the hands of an opposition now trumpeting the superiority of economic liberalism (Adam Smith– or Reagan-style) over stumbling socialism. Blindly confident that civil liberty was their own exclusive property, the Socialists did not see that in backing a bill designed to curb the powers of a press lord, they were giving their opponents a means to link the cry of freedom for the economy to freedom of the press, and thus accredit the blanket charge of "collectivism."

The Second-Biggest Demonstration Ever

In 1981 Mitterrand had included in his "110 proposals" the rash promise to erect a "unified and secular public education system." The pursuit of a highly modified version of this pledge ended in June 1984 in a fiasco that brought down the Mauroy government.

In the 1980s approximately 16 percent of French children attended private schools. Perhaps half of their parents were practicing Catholics. Church schools (especially on the secondary level) had grown increasingly popular as French public education battled unhappily with the same intractable problem that confronts American secondary education in the late-twentieth century: the lack of any philosophical consensus on the minimum content of general education in a mass society where the old classical curriculum seems of uncertain relevance. Doubts abounded on the value and content of experiment and innovation, while disciplinary problems were spreading in often overcrowded classes taught by underpaid teachers.

A poll commissioned by the Education Ministry in 1982 showed clearly that all these factors influenced the parents who sent their children to private schools. Although two-thirds of them wished their children to receive religious instruction, only 10 to 15 percent considered that the principal reason for their choice of institution. They named instead discipline, quality of instruction, ease of contact with the teachers, and the assurance that their children would receive an education respecting traditional values.[49]

The church schools were regarded by the adepts of secular education as a throwback to a period before universal, public, and secular education had been guaranteed in France. The village schoolmasters had in the late-nineteenth and early-twentieth century been the shock troops of republican socialization in a premodern France where the ordinary people, who teachers thought had been easily manipulated by proclerical government under Napoleon III, were to be educated in sound republican values by men immune to reactionary clericalism. The quarrel with the church had simmered down by the mid–twentieth century, but secular education as the supreme value of the republic remained a dogma for many on the Left.

In 1959 Prime Minister Michel Debré had brought in a law providing government funding for teachers' salaries in Catholic schools, even though a petition against it gathered 11 million signatures. The Guermeur law of 1977 gave church schools rights that state schools did not possess and sometimes accorded them funds for subject matter they were unable to teach. However, in 1978 only 33 percent of respondents in a poll desired integration of private schools into the public system. With Alain Savary, Mitterrand and Mauroy had chosen an education minister with a long record as a principled and patient Socialist able to negotiate with all parties. The PS leader most identified with the claims of lay education, Louis Mexandeau, was significantly passed over for the education job and given another ministry. In 1981 the Catholic hierarchy could believe that if the extravagant language of Mitterrand's promise was not meant literally, then the fact that church schools enjoyed strong support might enable Catholic educators to sign a peace treaty with the paladins of secularism and resolve the church-state education question once and for all.

In retrospect, it was clearly a major error to promise an educational system that was both unified and secular. Formulated in the heat of the campaign, the promise had been drafted to please a powerful PS constituency, the Fédération de l'Education Nationale (FEN). Oddly enough, in view of the enormous fuss aroused in 1984, the education plank played no great role in the 1981 election campaign. To counter rumors that the Socialists intended to cut off payments to private schools or rapidly absorb all Catholic-school teachers into the state system, Mitterrand promised in an open letter of May 1, 1981, that the new dispensation would result from "negotiation and not from a unilateral decision," and that nothing would be done abruptly.[50]

The negotiation proper began in 1982 and lasted for two years, during which Savary and his staff worked hard to frame a compromise law that could accommodate the demands of moderates on both sides of the question. On the left, the leaders of one group advocating secular education, the Centre National d'Action Laïque (CNAL), allied to but not identical with the FEN, refused to believe that public opinion supported public aid to church schools. "Public funds for public schools, private funds for private schools" was their war cry. On the right, deep suspicion of the real intentions of the government was fed by the declarations of the CNAL and excited by politically inspired denunciations of the government's whole educational policy.

Savary's attempts to reform state education centered on the idea of increased decentralization to promote initiative in individual schools. He ran into a wall of mistrust constructed over fifteen years by ever increasing criticism of French education in the mass age. The years 1983–1984 saw publication of a number of "why Jeannot can't read" books, with titles like *Your Children Don't Interest Me Any More, Do You Really Want Idiot Children? The Massacre of the Innocents.* Denouncing lowered teaching standards and laxity in discipline, such books sold well and were publicized in television discussions.[51]

Savary's pedagogic reforms were thus easily confused by the general public with an increase in laxity, while the opposition's politicians denounced the introduction of a tutorial system suspected of being ideological. Against all this, the private Catholic school (known in France as the "free school") offered an alternative that parents might or might not choose, but that was at least reassuringly present.

To these factors must be added the immigrant question, which by 1983 had emerged in the political consciousness as the most acute social problem of contemporary France (see Chapter 4). Products of a birthrate still governed by the customs of a peasant society, the numerous children of North African immigrants were moving into the schools of the large inner cities. Often speaking limited French, they filled already crowded classes and slowed the process of instruction. Mitterrand had promised in 1981 that maximum class sizes would be reduced to twenty-five, but that was possible only in private schools.

Mauroy emphasized the Hersant law and the Savary school bill to placate a Socialist party badly in need of some nourishment other than the distasteful fodder of *rigueur.* The opposition, no less political, rapidly saw that both bills fit neatly with its tactic of denouncing the Socialist-Communist assault on liberty. By early April 1984, when the Council of Ministers adopted the Savary law, *Le Figaro* was attacking the "murder of the church schools," and the talented polemicist Jean-François Revel was heaping wood on the fire by announcing that "all education in the proper sense is from now on positively forbidden."[52]

The temperature rose as the Savary bill approached its National Assembly reading. In the course of negotiations, the idea of the unified secular school system had melted away. The bill made concessions to the church schools that the CNAL found intolerable, guaranteeing state payment of the teachers in church schools and basic school expenses, leaving only upkeep to the diocesan authorities.[53]

The church hierarchy in turn was troubled by an article stating that teachers in private schools who had passed their state certification examinations could, if they so wished, apply for civil service rank (become *titulaires*) in the state teaching establishment. This provision was objectionable because Catholics feared it might open the way for complete state control of private teaching, allowing the state to assign private-school teachers (like their public school colleagues) anywhere in the country. That could break up the free schools. However, the hierarchy quietly let the Elysée know that it would not oppose this point if guarantees were given that the state would not push hard to implement the provision.

On March 5, a rally against the Savary bill sponsored by the well-organized private parent-teachers associations (PTAs) drew nearly a million people to Versailles. Leading opposition politicians were conspicuous among them. On April 25, the CNAL organized a counterdemonstration in Paris—also against the Savary bill—which drew 75,000 people. In the front ranks marched not only the CNAL leaders but also PS first secretary Lionel Jospin, PCF secretary-general Marchais and part of his Politburo, and Pierre Joxe, Socialist leader in the National Assembly. In mid-May, Joxe and other Socialist leaders in the assembly told Mauroy that they would not vote for the bill as it stood; amendments were needed. Carefully steering between two opposing extremisms, Savary had produced a bill supported by the government, the church hierarchy, and the Catholic PTA leadership. Challenges came not only from the lay side but also from Catholics and from politicians of the Right uninterested in successful compromise. Warned by Mauroy that Socialist deputies would insist on amendments, the church negotiators repeated their opposition to absorption of private-school teachers into the state system. The prime minister attempted to appease them. Both sides threatened new mass demonstrations. European elections, which would be fought on almost exclusively domestic questions, were scheduled for June 17; the government seemed trapped between two forces.

Mitterrand had become increasingly pessimistic that any compromise was possible on the school question. However, the affair had already gone so far that a prudent retreat was not possible; a frustrated and unhappy Socialist party lusted for the red meat of laicism. Mitterrand continued to drop hints to the clerical camp that he wanted a compromise, but with his intimate advisers he had already begun to consider other ways out of his dilemma.[54]

On the night of May 22 the National Assembly passed the Savary bill with amendments reluctantly accepted by Mauroy. One amendment stipulated that towns were not obliged to finance private nursery schools and tied creation of new ones to the prior existence of public nursery schools in a town. A second stated that towns need not pay their share of school expenses until a majority of teachers in private schools had—after a six-year discretionary period—accepted the status of state employee. Although the state would guarantee to meet such payments for eleven years, it would not guarantee them forever (as Mauroy had allegedly promised the church negotiators).

The amendments did not seriously alter the thrust of the Savary bill, affected only a small proportion of state payments for church education, and left a great deal of room for future adjudication. But they tilted a precarious balance in the Catholic camp. The cardinal archbishop of Paris told *Le Monde* in an interview on June 5 that Mauroy had broken his word. The prime minister consulted the president, then hotly denied this on television.

The European elections of June 17 further weakened a stumbling government. In balloting marked by a 43.3 percent abstention, the PS vote fell to 20.76 percent, and the PCF to 11.28 percent. The combined list of the Right had done less well than it hoped, but with 42.88 percent, it still outweighed the combined Socialist and Communist vote. The unwelcome surprise of the elections was the sudden rise of Jean-Marie Le Pen's racist National Front, with 11 percent.

One week later came a great Parisian demonstration against the Savary bill organized by the Catholic PTA associations. (The bill still had to go before an obstructionist Senate.) Both the government and the Catholic forces had worried about the dangers of a mass demonstration in Paris degenerating into clashes, but the impressive organization of the march and the quiet determination of the marchers thwarted any such dangers. Its good temper, discipline, and sheer size astonished a government and a nation well accustomed to mass demonstrations. Wave after carefully timed wave of demonstrators, between 1 and 1.4 million people, emerged from metro stations, buses, and trains, marched to the place de la Bastille, and dispersed. They kept coming for twelve hours, Bretons in costume shepherded by their priests, Alsatians, southerners, each group with its own flag and a common slogan, "The free school will live!"

Paris had seen immense street demonstrations before, the great crowds of May 1968 (the biggest being some 200,000) or the pro–de Gaulle response to May 1968 on the Champs Elysées (500,000). But with the exception of the passionate manifestation of joy that brought nearly 2 million Parisians and suburbanites spontaneously together to welcome de Gaulle on the morrow of liberation in August 1944, the Catholic forces had mobilized the biggest demonstration the French had ever known.[55]

The Savary law had sown discontent both on the secular left and the Catholic right. It was also judged severely by the general public. Polls in June 1984 showed that 55 percent of the French thought the bill infringed on liberties. Almost certainly many people thought the Left mistaken in reopening the church-state question, which was widely perceived as anachronistic. Furthermore, as Serge July pointed out, the government made a serious error in allowing the debate to be framed in terms of uniformity, by emphasizing the idea that teachers should all be government officials, and in speaking of a state monopoly over the schools. Those were the values of the old Jacobinism, which the opposition had abandoned and condemned in the Left. By incurring once again the charge that the Left wanted to collectivize everything, the government revived all the old doubts and fears.[56]

After so stunning a show of disapproval immediately after the disavowal of the European elections, the government would have great difficulty in continuing as if nothing had happened. But how could it extricate itself from the situation into which it had blundered?

In the meantime, the opposition announced its intention to fight the Savary law in the Senate all summer long and suggested that Mitterrand should consult the people in a referendum on the matter. Mauroy opposed any such idea, keeping to an interpretation of the constitution that permits referenda only on questions of the "public powers." He toyed with the notion of a giant secularist counterdemonstration. The Senate was impotent to kill the education bill and would have to release it by September. And while the ultras of the RPR were talking of "a prerevolutionary situation," the president, however embarrassed he might be by the drop in Socialist fortunes, reaffirmed his support for the Savary bill in televised remarks on July 5.

On July 8, however, he summoned his counselor on constitutional matters, Michel Charasse, and PS first secretary Lionel Jospin to Latché, his country home, and laid out his plan to escape from the corner into which the government had painted itself. Both men were sworn to secrecy.[57]

Mitterrand then departed on an official visit to Jordan. He was spending more and more time traveling outside France as his popularity dwindled; his trip to Moscow on June 22–23 and the successful resolution of contentions with Britain at the June 25–26 EC summit at Fontainebleau were largely eclipsed in the public mind by domestic furor.[58] (The Fontainebleau summit can now be seen as a milestone in rebuilding the EC from the quarrels and failures of previous years.)

On July 11, when Mauroy went out to Charles de Gaulle Airport to greet the president on his return (a procedure the prime minister had grown to detest), he was dumbfounded to learn Mitterrand's new plan: a referendum—with a difference. Mitterrand announced his intention of going on television the next day to propose a double referendum, one to permit votes on general questions, followed by another affording a popular vote on the school question.

Mitterrand sought, however, to appease Mauroy's fears for the future of the Savary law. Not until a television interview three days later, on Bastille Day, did the president admit that the process of a referendum was incompatible with urging passage of the law by the Senate. After praising the honest effort made by Savary, Mitterrand concluded: "But it is evident that my opinion is not shared by a very large number of French people. Thus, as I have just said . . . I worry about what the people who don't agree with me are thinking, and I take it into account."[59]

Mitterrand had not thought it necessary to warn either his prime minister or his education minister that he was withdrawing the Savary bill. Savary immediately told the prime minister that he had been disavowed and would resign. His decision made

Mauroy choose not to serve Mitterrand for a final few months, as the president desired, but to resign immediately on a political issue, to "fall on the Left." His resignation and the appointment of thirty-seven-year-old Laurent Fabius as his successor were made public on July 17.

These details of a ministry's fall are a striking illustration of François Mitterrand's idiosyncratic mixture of indecision and sudden resolution, his unwillingness to share his thoughts even with close collaborators, and finally his resourcefulness, very lightly ballasted by ideology. He had overtly backed Savary until the end in a course that required delicate maneuvering, hoping that he might succeed. At the same time, he was far from confident of success and was never emotionally involved. He apparently concluded that he could not stop Pierre Joxe from pushing amendments in the assembly, or use Jospin to hold off the wave of anachronistic secularist sentiment that had broken out in the PS. In retrospect, he maintained that it had been necessary to let the drama play itself out, to let the extreme secularists see that the country was not with them. It is likely enough that he saw this outcome as one of the incidental advantages if the Savary bill failed.

Mauroy had pushed harder for the Savary bill than had Mitterrand. Though he had acceded somewhat reluctantly to the assembly's amendments, the bill was part of his campaign to provide the Socialists with compensation for the retreat elsewhere. The emotional charge the bill carried for the Socialists, paralleled on the other side for the defenders of church schools, greatly hindered presidential mediation, and Mitterrand was obliged to stand helplessly by as the situation worsened; he could hardly have expected the massive demonstration of June 24.[60]

Seizing the opposition's idea of a referendum to turn it against them carried some risk, but the president foresaw correctly that the opposition would refuse to give him the powers implied by the first referendum, since the right-wing Senate by law had to concur on the text of a referendum. "The president began the process leading to a referendum that he did not desire. The Senate was obliged to think up quibbles and arguments to refuse organization of a referendum on the school question that it had noisily supported."[61]

In September the Senate predictably blocked the referendum. Mitterrand's game of mirrors had dazzled everyone; the president was quit of the Savary law and could still tell himself and the country that he had first tried to save it and then bowed honorably to the weight of public opinion. The imbroglio forced Mitterrand to change prime ministers slightly ahead of his planned schedule and humiliated him, despite the skill he showed as an escape artist. In the end, however, he came out better than one might have expected at the time. The leaders of the opposition had marched in the ranks of the protesters, but they did not command them. The wave of protest against a perceived Left threat to liberties swelled up, broke, and did not rise again. June 1984, with the European elections and the school demonstration, was the low point in Mitterrand's first term.

Mauroy had soldiered through a difficult three years at the Hôtel Matignon. His authority as prime minister had been limited by extensive interference, by jealous surveillance in his first year on the part of Pierre Bérégovoy as secretary-general of the Elysée, by ministers and party figures who appealed over his head directly to Mitterrand, by interministerial committees in which presidential aides appealed over his head, often pretending to an authority not expressly given them. Mauroy had, however, shown great courage in retreating from policies he had initially advocated and desired, working effectively with Delors and a small team of like-minded presidential advisers and ministerial staffs.

Mauroy was a far more genuine socialist than many Johnny-come-latelies who had sneered at him as a right-winger. Once the turn away from original socialist policies had been made, he wanted to brake the headlong restructuring that was abolishing jobs. Failing in this, he invested his energies in noneconomic issues, which played straight into the hand of the opposition. He left behind him a blurred impression of his record in office. His misleadingly optimistic television performances had provided much ammunition to his critics. Fabius the modernizer would manage to symbolize better than Mauroy many of his predecessor's accomplishments. With a better sense of public relations, Fabius was also able to present himself as a new man with new policies.

3

Thirty-Six Months
at the Center

Fabius Socialism

During the curious interim between the June 24 demonstration against the Savary law and Mitterrand's withdrawal of the law on July 14—another interregnum like that of March 1983—*Le Monde*'s chief political writer Jean-Marie Colombani asked in a front page analysis-editorial: "What does one do when one is in power and has just been disavowed, and when less than two years remain before the real rendezvous with the public's verdict?" Since votes lost by the PCF were no longer moving to the PS column, it was clear, he wrote, that to remain viable, the PS had to conform its rhetoric to its policies and seek to build a social democratic bloc—a party sure of at least 30 percent of the vote.[1]

Always resistant to exterior constraint, Mitterrand had been putting off the moment for making economic policy conform with political rhetoric. When as a result of Mauroy's resignation he was faced with an immediate need to choose a new prime minister, he picked the person most in tune with his new ideas, Laurent Fabius.

The "young prime minister whom I have given to France," as Mitterrand referred to Fabius in his paternalistic way, had been very much on the Left when that was Mitterrand's stance. In 1979, when Mauroy and Rocard challenged Mitterrand at the PS congress in Metz, Fabius had lectured Rocard on the meaning of socialism. Until March 1983 he had been an advocate of high taxes for the rich and of the "other policy"—leaving the EMS—changing his mind late in the day after an alarming briefing on the state of French reserves.

Fabius had been a member of the PS for ten years when he was named prime minister, the youngest man to hold the job since the reign of Louis XVIII. Son of a rich Parisian antique dealer, the precocious young man graduated from both the Ecole Normale Supérieure and ENA, taking high honors and opting for the *grand corps* of the Conseil d'Etat. An accomplished horseman and man about town, he seemed destined to join the gifted and gilded *énarques* clustering around one of their own, Valéry Giscard d'Estaing. Instead he joined the PS, where he rapidly impressed its first secretary.[2] Mitterrand liked to surround himself with bright young men, pushing forward their careers more rapidly than those of their elders. Among the most prominent were Jean-Pierre Chevènement, Pierre Joxe, Jacques Attali, Lionel Jospin—men who in their different ways aided and complemented Mitterrand without posing any threat to his position. Fabius was first in this class. Beginning as a member of the PS Economic Commission, he rapidly became director of Mitterrand's cabinet, then a national secretary of the PS. In 1977 he was "parachuted" into the Socialist constituency of Le Grand–Quevilly, an industrial suburb of Rouen, to become deputy to its aged and popular mayor. Working hard at his new job, passing out leaflets at factory gates, Fabius, who "had learned to speak Socialist language quite correctly," then succeeded the mayor as a deputy in 1978.

Named budget minister in 1981, Fabius was promoted in March 1983 to minister of research and industry. He headed a superministry to which telecommunications had been added, a move that brought more independent access to funding than this ministry has usually possessed. Industrialists who had disliked his interventionist and dogmatic predecessor Chevènement were pleased. Others were not. *Le Monde,* more critical of the Socialists than in 1981, entitled one article on Fabius's nomination, "A Mysterious Young Man" and another on his record as industry minister, "The Art of Dodging."[3]

In July 1984 the unanimous opinion was that Fabius was his master's voice. "Mitterrand appoints himself prime minister," said the conservative *Quotidien de Paris,* echoed on the Left by *Libération:* "Mitterrand prime minister." Having taken as his first prime minister a man who symbolized the ideas of traditional socialism, the president was now choosing a close collaborator who had no following of his own but who symbolized the change in Socialist policy. Fabius stood for only one thing—modernization, the new leitmotif of the Mitterrand administration.

The Fabius ministry itself was only partly new. Jacques Delors departed for Brussels to become president of the European Community Commission. He was replaced as minister for economy and finance by Pierre Bérégovoy. Michel Rocard, agriculture minister since 1983, remained in his post. Claude Cheysson remained at the Quai d'Orsay (which the Socialists had renamed external relations) for some months yet before departing to become once again an EC commissioner. He would be replaced by Mitterrand's friend Roland Dumas. Pierre Joxe moved from leadership of the Socialist fraction in the National Assembly to become interior minister and take a new hold on the government's troubled dealings with the police. And Jean-Pierre Chevènement returned to occupy the siege perilous of the Education Ministry.

The new prime minister declared his program in late July: heavy emphasis on modernization amid continued austerity. Growth presupposed a solid production apparatus, but modernization might cost jobs before it produced new ones.

Investment, reduction of the burden of social costs falling on industry, a move toward freeing industrial prices, lower taxes—these were the main points made by the new Socialist chief of government.[4]

The country reacted well to the change: Fabius's initial poll ratings were far higher than Mauroy's had been toward the end. The government's core constituency was still sulking, and the Communists had begun to hammer away at government policies, but at least policy and rhetoric were in line again. Chevènement and Fabius sought a quick compromise on the church education question. Negotiating quietly, they worked out a compromise by which the government would finance private education (the principle of which had never been at issue, except in the superheated rhetoric of some secularist fanatics).

The concessions of the 1977 Guermeur law, which even many church officials thought indefensible, were largely rescinded, and the Debré law of 1959 was reaffirmed in December 1984. (In June 1992 Jack Lang, who had become minister of education, signed an agreement with the secretary-general of the Catholic teachers, settling their financial claims on the government. Old-fashioned Socialist anticlericalism was dead.)

Chevènement made himself improbably popular in circles where he had been a *bête rouge* by promoting a return to the three R's in education. The singing of the "Marseillaise," dropped for many years, was reintroduced into schools. Discipline and classroom authority were emphasized. Many teachers were displeased, but the public loved it. At a minimum, Chevènement had hit on a brilliant stroke of symbolic politics. Part of Savary's problem had been that too many people believed that experimentation (begun long before 1981) had wrecked public education. Savary's innovations were therefore suspect and government interference in private education automatically bad. Chevènement's back-to-basics was understood as "no experiments" and met approval.

Pierre Mauroy's thirty-seven months as prime minister had begun with boundless optimism. They were filled with the actions of a government in a hurry first to make its mark, then to correct a slide, and finally trying frenetically to please the Socialist deputies by veering to the left. Laurent Fabius's twenty months began at the low point of July 1984, with a near-certainty that the PS would lose control of the National Assembly in March 1986. A dejected PS was still only beginning to come to terms with the idea that too many of its old ideas had been illusions. Fabius's mission was to present the new face of the Mitterrand administration. In the 1970s, the Left had rejected the idea that it should "manage the crisis." Now the task was to show that the Socialists *could* manage the crisis—better than the Right had done, more humanely, and with more vision for the future.

Accordingly, the achievements of the Fabius government have a largely non-Socialist flavor. His economics and finance minister, Pierre Bérégovoy, was proud of having created a financial futures market—a good idea, but not one he would have propounded at the Metz congress in 1979. The government also discovered a means of bringing much-needed private capital into nationalized industry, by selling up to

15 percent of the stock of certain companies owned by nationalized conglomerates. With a renewal of business confidence, the Paris stock market took off.

Bitter Medicine

The principal task of the new government was to show that the Socialists, now governing alone, were, above all, modern administrators of the enterprise called France. Fabius hastened to set the tone of a new beginning. At his first meeting with the Council of Ministers as prime minister, after a brief and chilly homage to his predecessor, he concluded, "But that is the past, and we are here to prepare the future."[5]

Modernization was not, however, a complete break with previous Socialist ideas. The nationalizations had been justified on social grounds, but still more on nationalist ones, as the defense of French independence. Modernization would serve the same purpose—with one significant shift: Much of modernization was supposed to arrive as a result of European cooperation; Mitterrand had brought back from a visit to Silicon Valley in March 1984 a new fascination with the electronic revolution. This idea of France's new horizon appealed greatly to him as a way out of the crisis—this "third industrial revolution," where Europe lagged behind the United States and Japan, was to be accomplished by Europe-wide R and D.

Jacques Attali, Mitterrand's close adviser, had written in 1978, "When the twenty-first century begins, France will have become either a branch office of the United States of America, or else the matrix of a new form of progress."[6] By 1984, a journalist could write: "opening to the outside was no longer considered as the great danger that threatened our independence, restricted our autonomy of decision. It became the stimulant that spurred on our inventive genius, developed our trade, compressed our prices for the greater good of consumers and their purchasing power."[7]

After the turnaround of March 1983, Mitterrand began to turn his attention to European integration, although the theme did not emerge clearly for another year at least. The prime minister would handle the domestic part, in which modernization would take on a socialist aspect, to be seen as an essential policy neglected in the past by the old conservatives—the current conservatives, sneered the Socialists, could only borrow from the United States. "Today the Right can no longer modernize. It can only go abroad to hunt for a model that is not transposable to France," stated the text of a Socialist national convention in December 1984.[8] (Nationalist discourse still had a useful target, the United States.)

Before modernization could make much progress, the government had to continue reconstruction, which meant further job cuts and continued austerity. Austerity meant holding down consumption, which in turn guaranteed low growth. Nationalized industry had been discovered to be in far worse shape than the Socialists had originally suspected (in 1984 only one of the major conglomerates that had been taken over in 1982 was in the black). Having precluded any private investment in these industries, the government had in effect bought the privilege of investing large amounts of money in nationalized industries just to make them profitable again. At the same time, it was trying to encourage investment in private industry by business-people who were reluctant to invest, for both economic and political reasons. Since the policies of 1981–1982 had already raised taxes and social costs, and the social security system required a larger budget to cope with unprecedented unemployment and early retirement, the government found that its total control of credit gave no new freedom to invest and expand. Expensive bailouts of dying industries like coal mining had to be reconsidered in terms of cost, not just jobs saved.

By 1983 the Socialists had discovered that the French economy was weak and could hardly bear the additional social burdens they had placed on it. If it was to grow, they must spend government money selectively and encourage private investment more successfully than they—or Raymond Barre—had done. Profit, which had been a dirty word to Socialists, suddenly became a favorable reference. Once the Socialists had understood that the goose of capitalism did not automatically lay golden eggs, they began to revise their ideas of the importance of enterprise, entrepreneurs (formerly known as capitalists), and profit.

The government realized that intravenous feeding of dying industry was not really good politics and very bad economics. Laurent Fabius wrote in May 1983, shortly after he had become minister for industry, that the stake in modernization (henceforth his favorite word) was "the fate of our youth, the rank, the weight" (then the nationalist note) "and the independence of France in the next twenty years."[9]

But the human cost was terrible. In Lorraine alone, 20,000–25,000 jobs in steel production were suppressed. (The industry had already lost 38 percent of its jobs between 1974 and 1981; this blow cut another half of the region's jobs. The total cut in steel employment was around 30,000 jobs nationally.[10] Lorraine workers marched through the streets of Paris, backed by the CGT. Three PS deputies from Lorraine demonstratively resigned from the party (and quietly rejoined it).

An overmanned automobile industry hard hit by Japanese competition in its export markets found it necessary to cut 20,000 jobs, and the ailing tire industry, despite the entry of Japanese capital, lost another 10,000 jobs.[11] The government was obliged to authorize more firings at Renault, where 4,500 workers lost their jobs in 1984 and another 12,500 in 1985. Although Peugeot-Citroen-Talbot was not allowed to fire all the personnel it desired, the Fabius government authorized 2,000 firings in August 1984 and 10,700 in 1985. Peugeot recovered before Renault, making a profit in 1985, whereas Renault, in the process of profound reorganization, did not expect to see black ink before the end of 1987.

Another crippled industry was shipbuilding, hard hit by Asian competition in a shrinking market. Public money flowing into the shipyards, which employed around 25,000 workers, cost the state an average 100,000 francs per worker per year in the 1980s. The plan for cuts in shipbuilding (part of the private sector) called for the gradual loss of 6,000 jobs.

These cuts were only part of the jobs that French industry was losing. But they were concentrated regionally, in Lorraine, the Nord, in Auvergne, and the industrial upper Loire, areas where the Left in general and the CGT in particular had traditionally been strong. To provide jobs and hope in these regions, the government announced the creation of special zones where special financial incitements would draw new investment. A plan worked out together with the unions was proposed to lighten the blow for workers thrown out of their jobs.

With the announcement of all these measures, the Left government had undertaken a series of actions that it would have severely condemned had a conservative government dared to put them forward. The Socialists had been elected on the promise of reversing the advance of unemployment. Instead they were now deciding the cessation of tens of thousands of jobs. The decision to act quickly rather than to drag out a painful process over a period of years may have been affected by Mitterrand's political desire to present a fresh, new balance by 1986, but by any reckoning, it was a difficult and courageous step. It struck directly at the Left constituency and was followed by fiscal measures that, encouraging new investment, inevitably favored a constituency belonging to the Right. Unemployment soared in 1984, from 2,181,000 to 2,456,700, leveling off in 1985 before rising again by an additional 103,000 at the end of 1986.

Gradual Improvement

In September 1984 the Council of Ministers kept Mitterrand's promise to reduce taxes by proposing a budget designed to lower individual taxes by 5 percent, abandon the 1 percent surtax for the social security funds, and cut business taxes. The political effect of those actions was, however, dampened by the concurrent rise in consumption taxes, especially on gasoline and telephone service. In October, the government also financed special measures aimed at relieving poverty by raising income tax on the very rich by half a percent.

At the same time, the stringent measures undertaken in 1982–1983 began to produce beneficent effects. The inflation rate in France had been consistently high throughout the 1970s. Prophets of gloom had announced that Socialist policies would kick it from the 13.6 percent rate in Giscard's last full year of office toward 20 percent. The wage and salary freeze of 1982, followed by the deindexation of wage increases, broke the vicious circle of inflation linking wage and cost increases.[12]

What conservative governments had feared to do, a Socialist government accomplished. As a consequence, inflation rates began to fall. In 1984, the year of discontent, they ended at 6.7 percent, down from 9.3 percent the preceding year. In 1985 they receded to 4.7 percent, and in 1986, to 3.1 percent. The falling price of oil aided this last drop, but a perception that inflation was finally sinking helped to redress the credit of the Socialists as capable administrators.

An annual poll asking whether the past year seemed good, bad, or average for the French as a whole showed a steady rise in 1983 and 1984 over the 50 percent who thought it bad in 1982. The 1985 figures dropped to 42 percent. Asked about inflation, 76 percent of respondents said in 1982 that they expected more than 8 percent for 1983; 49 percent adhered to this opinion for 1984, and only 34 percent for 1985. At the end of 1985 only 6 percent remained that pessimistic. Writing at the end of 1986, two leading pollsters and political scientists fixed the change in the reigning climate of pessimism in the first half of 1985, noting, however, that the French remained uncertain and apprehensive about the economic future.[13] The change in prime ministers thus provided a caesura for a period that was perceived as a failure. The economic decisions taken in 1982–1984 were slowly taking effect and gradually becoming evident to the public.

The PS in 1984

The Socialist party by mid-1984 was groggy, like a spirited but inexperienced fighter who has led too often with his chin. Had the institutions of the Fifth Republic permitted it to retreat and nurse its bruises, it might have been happy to subside into resentful opposition. Since it could not, individual Socialists began to examine what had gone wrong, often with amazing candor. It was relatively easy to explain that Giscard and Barre had left them with an economy in far worse shape than they had expected. However, they had persistently argued before 1981 that the crisis was largely the result of selfish and incompetent behavior by French capitalists and their friends in government. They had genuinely believed that they could turn the situation around, creating social justice and fuller employment at the same time.

The Rocardian faction of the PS had always argued that the crisis was real, but Rocard had been beaten at the 1979 Metz congress. As woes mounted, he and his friends continued to say, "we told you so," which was humanly understandable but did not endear them to their fellow Socialists. The Mitterrandists lamented that they had waved the magic wand of socialism, and nothing had happened. What was to be done? What did they need to jettison, what had they already jettisoned, what did they really believe in?

The PS was still divided into its constituent factions, although the necessities of government muted their clash. The Mitterrandists led by First Secretary Jospin followed the president's lead (not always without misgivings). The Rocard faction was badly represented in government and hampered by its leader's position as a minister—until he seized the chance to break out of his cage in opposing Mitterrand's 1985 decision to adopt proportional representation. The CERES too was restrained by the intermittent presence in the government of its leader, Chevènement. The same problem held back the Mauroy faction until July 1984. The weight of the factions could not be ascertained by the vote on their propositions at party congresses, since this procedure was left in abeyance in 1981 and 1983. So the factional movements stirred restlessly, their contours visible, but their exact sizes only vaguely discernible, like bodies under a blanket. They only knew that some day—soon, if the president were forced out of office in 1986, or perhaps somewhat later—they would struggle again to determine the course of the Socialist party.

As the young prime minister incessantly celebrated the virtues of modernization, a certain number of leaders who had always been on the Left of the party, like Jean Poperen, suggested that the question had to be viewed "from a class viewpoint," which presumably meant that the spirit of enterprise and the new cult of the entrepreneur were not their highest values. Other Socialists, both Rocardians and those who saw Laurent Fabius as the new leader, were determined to marry the spirit of enterprise to socialism.

A Rocardian deputy commented: "Taking enterprise into account is not a temporary concession. It is one of the axes around which our socialism will be built." But others were not so sure. A deputy from the Nord declared: "No one is calling into question the values of socialism, liberty, justice, solidarity, responsibility. Our values remain true, but we are now in a situation where we cannot translate them into action in a period of change." She found that Fabius "lacked utopia, lacked breadth."[14]

The PS, not just Fabius, had lost the utopian spirit. As long as the party had seemed condemned interminably to the snowy wastes of the opposition, regular draughts of utopian brandy had kept socialist ideas alive. But utopian intoxication collided with the sobering tasks of administration, with its daily compromises and inevitable discouragements. Its replacement (nonintoxicating) was to be the sober pleasure of good management. An idea that had migrated from Catholic doctrine into French socialism, that money and profit are intrinsically dirty, had to be abandoned.

The Fabius government would also witness the reconciliation of most of the Socialist party to the notion that it was really social democratic. French Socialists had objected violently to the idea of accepting social democracy until the early 1980s. Some also argued that social democracy involved close cooperation with a unitary trade union, which would be impossible in France. But that was a taxonomic argument, not a political one. The real objection was that social democracy, even in Sweden, implied a compromise with capitalism that they had proclaimed unacceptable.

Here was the central Socialist myth. When Mitterrand told the editor of *Libération* in May 1984[15] that the idea of a mixed economy played a central role in his economic thinking, many commentators interpreted it as a key change. Some Socialists scoffed, pointing out that the PS had never intended to wipe out the private sector. Nor had they, but they had overemphasized the importance of the public sector, believing that control over it would place a Left government "on the commanding heights of the economy." Instead, they had to bail out failing industry and cut thousands of jobs. The new cult of enterprise—among the Socialists, but also on the Right—came from an increasing recognition of the fact that *dirigisme* either of the Left or of the Right was not capable of creating productive employment for the 1980s or beyond.

Celebration of the entrepreneurial spirit might be necessary, but it did not make a Socialist. Could the PS strip away its myths, lose its illusions, and still be Socialist? The Rocardians thought so. The Mitterrandists were uncertain, including many who had been vociferously on the Left in 1981–1982. Here was the implicit course of their president, the explicit course of their young prime minister. Was there a political majority in the country for this new Left—where the Communist party could play no real role? What would the new spirit mean in the legislative elections of 1986? And if the president were so badly disavowed in 1986 that he had to resign, what would be left for them?

New Worries for Fabius

Although in early 1985 the economic picture was slowly brightening and Fabius's image, as reflected in the polls, soared above Mauroy's in his last year, the government had new worries at home and abroad. The headlines were full of stories about kidnappings of French diplomats and journalists in Beirut and bombs exploding in Paris. Added to that, the long-simmering ethnic problems of the French overseas territory of New Caledonia not only troubled that island but also entered into French domestic politics in late 1984 and early 1985.

Annexed by France in 1853, New Caledonia had been first a penal colony, then a major source of nickel ore. The high price of nickel in the 1970s attracted new immigrants, who became a sixth of the total population of 150,000. Approximately half the population were autochthonous Melanesians, not granted the right to vote in this French overseas territory until 1952. A radicalized independence movement, the Front de Libération Nationale Kanak Socialiste (FLNKS), pitted the natives (Kanaks) against the Europeans (Caldoches). Until 1981, government policy had been to increase autonomy under the aegis of the "national" parties, particularly the Rassemblement Calédonien pour la République (RPCR), which was close to the RPR and included some Melanesians.

In 1981, the Socialist government had attempted a new policy of balancing the claims of independence-minded Kanaks and loyalist Caldoches. The plan was to increase self-determination (on a regional basis) and explore an autonomy that might lead to independence inside the French Community. The ambiguity of this scheme led the more militant FLNKS to call for independence immediately, while the Caldoches feared that the Socialist government planned to abandon them. In January 1985 several armed FLNKS militants were killed by French gendarmes. One was a top leader of the movement. The government sent out Edgard Pisani, a former Gaullist minister who had joined the PS in the 1970s, to represent it in New Caledonia and propose rapid measures for self-determination. His stay was troubled by much disorder, including murders of both Europeans and Melanesians. Pisani presented a plan calling for independence in association with France, with a special status for the Europeans. More violence caused Pisani to declare a state of emergency after Caldoche demonstrations in the capital city, Nouméa.

A violent debate in France accompanied the events in New Caledonia. The opposition attempted to take maximum advantage of the government for actions described as dilatory, lax, and equivocal. The RPR leader in the Senate, Charles Pasqua, even threatened the president with an accusation of treason for illegal acts.[16] All ex–prime ministers and former president Giscard joined in a declaration against the government's policy, and the New Caledonian imbroglio seemed for a moment to open a new abyss of unpopularity for the Socialists.

In late April 1985 Fabius decided to defuse the situation by delaying the referendum until after the 1986 legislative elections. He calmed the situation by proposing the division of the island into four regions, each with an elected council, plus a territorial congress made up of all council members. Three of the regions would give the FLNKS a majority. Pisani, who had lost the confidence of the European population, was recalled and given the consolation post of minister for New Caledonia. In the September 1985 regional elections, anti-independence forces won 60 percent of the vote, with 80 percent of the voters participating.[17]

A Scandal in Auckland

More trouble arrived in July 1985, when an explosion in distant New Zealand sank the *Rainbow Warrior*, a ship belonging to the ecology movement Greenpeace. The *Rainbow Warrior* had been anchored in Auckland harbor, preparing to lead a demonstration against French nuclear testing in the South Pacific. Two bombs timed to explode at intervals sank—but did not destroy—the ship. The second bomb killed a crew member, a Portuguese photographer who was a Dutch citizen. Two days later the New Zealand police arrested a couple posing as Swiss tourists named Turenge, who were rapidly uncovered as Dominique Prieur and Alain Mafart, officers of the French external intelligence service, the Direction Générale de Sécurité Extérieure (DGSE). Implicated in the sabotage action, they were charged with murder.

High officials of French intelligence had convinced themselves that the Greenpeace expedition was a major menace to their nuclear testing and heavily penetrated by agents of Soviet espionage.[18] The French naval authorities in charge of security at the Mururoa atoll test site had warred with Greenpeace before—in 1972, when there was a near battle, and in numerous subsequent acts of sabotage to Greenpeace boats, including apparent arson against one in a Chilean port. In 1985, Greenpeace proposed to sail into Mururoa waters with the *Rainbow Warrior* and three smaller craft, making it more difficult for the French navy to board and intercept them all. The mother ship carried television gear equipped for satellite broadcast, ready to demonstrate provocative French action.

The ambiguous word chosen by the authors of the 1985 operation was *"anticiper"*—to forestall. The *Rainbow Warrior* would never be allowed to sail into Polynesian waters. The first explosion was supposed to frighten the crew from the boat, the second would then sink it; no one was supposed to be killed. French intelligence had, however, thought very little about the dangers of an action unavoidably stamped with French fingerprints, conducted in a harbor of a foreign country whose government was already on record as anxious to gain domestic credit by protesting nuclear weapons in the Pacific.

The *Rainbow Warrior* was sunk on July 10; the president and prime minister learned of it the same day and immediately understood that French services were involved; Mitterrand had assented to the idea of "forestalling" the arrival of the *Rainbow Warrior*. According to the reconstruction of the affair in *La Décennie Mitterrand*, however, neither the chief of Mitterrand's general staff, General Jean Saulnier, who had to sign the credits for an operation costing at least $500,000, nor the president himself had been briefed on the details of the plan.

The Auckland police rapidly determined that the "false Turenges" had made numerous telephone calls to Paris. Interior Minister Pierre Joxe, asked for help by the New Zealand police, stalled; when he learned that the phone number called was one belonging to the Defense Ministry, he immediately ordered all such numbers changed and immediately informed Mitterrand.

For more than two months the president stalled for time. Defense Minister Charles Hernu was responsible for the actions of the DGSE, and Mitterrand was reluctant to fire Hernu, an old comrade in arms from the 1960s, and a Socialist who was genuinely popular in the army and officer corps. Hernu, believing that it was his duty to cover up for the DGSE, claimed at first that if "the false Turenges" were DGSE officers, they had not placed the bomb. DGSE chief Admiral Lacoste refused to disavow his officers. Prime Minister Fabius insisted that Hernu come clean and succeeded only in stiffening his resistance.

In the first week of August the French press began to publish articles implicating the DGSE in the Auckland sinking. Mitterrand immediately reacted by ordering the government to conduct a "rigorous" investigation. Fabius commissioned a report of inquiry from a distinguished Gaullist, Bernard Tricot, a former secretary-general of the Elysée. Tricot's report, published in late August, was based on information provided by the DGSE and Hernu. It admitted the presence of French agents in New Zealand but asserted that their action had been limited to reconnaissance. Since this amounted to saying, "Yes, we had intelligence agents in the area, but the sabotage of the Greenpeace ship was an inexplicable coincidence that has nothing to do with France," it is hardly surprising that only 17 percent of the public claimed to believe the report. Tricot himself admitted that his sources might have sought to deceive him.

In the meantime, Mitterrand had demonstratively reiterated an order to the armed forces to halt any incursion into the waters of the testing site at Mururoa island, by force if necessary. He followed this up with a lightning trip to Mururoa on September 12, taking Hernu with him, and declaring on his return that France would continue nuclear testing as long as it thought tests necessary to its defense. He had already, on August 1, promoted General Saulnier to chief of the Army General Staff.

The French press showed more initiative in investigative journalism than had been customary in such affairs, pointing out that an expensive operation of this type had to be approved at high levels. Finally, on September 17, *Le Monde* disclosed that the actual sabotage had been conducted by a team of French frogmen that had swiftly been removed from the scene. These revelations ended the determination of the president and his men not to know anything about the affair. Mitterrand had been reluctant to part with Hernu. But on September 20 he finally had to let him resign and on the same day dismissed the head of the DGSE.

Fabius instantly named Transport Minister Paul Quilès to replace him, with instructions to conduct a real investigation. Two days later Fabius announced on television that the DGSE, acting on orders, had sunk the *Rainbow Warrior,* and a few days later he told the country that after Quilès's investigation he had questioned Hernu and Lacoste, and "my conviction is that the responsibility was at their level." This formulation barely hid the fact that neither Hernu nor the admiral would admit giving the order.[19]

The protracted scandal had cost Mitterrand prestige and a minister. Both he and Fabius had known in sufficient if not full detail of the operation since mid-July. After the scandal broke, Mitterrand was conspicuously uninterested in clarifying the matter and very much interested in displaying his concern for national security, whereas Fabius pretended until mid-September that he knew nothing of the matter. (*Le Figaro*'s wicked cartoonist Jacques Faisant thereafter always portrayed him carrying a protective umbrella.)

Hernu was not a scapegoat—the responsibility for approving an operation foolish in conception and bungled in execution was clearly his. The opposition, now in full cry after Mitterrand, studiously refrained from attacking the government on a security matter, even when the senior Gaullist Tricot was brought in to cover the government. The French in general remained unexcited about the affair, and the damage to the government's reputation arose mainly from its clumsiness at cover-up and denial. Hernu remained popular, and Mitterrand's and Fabius's poll ratings did not sink. The overall view of the uninformed public was summed up in a quote from a taxi driver: "Terrific, that Hernu! He was damn well right to sink that Russian boat!"[20]

The Politics of the 1986 Election

Fabius's relative popularity did not rub off on the Socialist party. In the March 1985 cantonal elections it lost seven more presidencies of departmental *conseils généraux*. The Left now controlled only twenty-eight of the one hundred councils in mainland and overseas France. The cantonal elections again demonstrated that there was no hope of recreating a workable Left majority in the 1986 parliamentary elections. The president was obliged to face instead the prospect of a heavy right-wing majority in 1986, one so large and intransigent that he might be forced to resign.

In those circumstances, Mitterrand looked again at his 1981 campaign promise to introduce electoral reform using proportional representation. (The election laws in France have been changed ten times since 1871; this would be the fourth change since 1945.) In April 1985 the government announced that it would bring in a proportional representation bill, and it was duly passed by the National Assembly in June. The new law was drawn up to protect a PS standing alone and reduced in strength against a landslide that would throw its leaders out of national office. Voters had to choose from inflexible party lists, and the department, instead of the smaller electoral districts, became the basic voting unit. There was to be only one round instead of two, and departmental lists winning less than 5 percent of the vote would be disqualified. The new law did include much-needed redistricting, in which the Parisian representation dropped from 31 deputies to 21, Paris suburban departments became more fairly represented, and glaring inequalities disappeared. Several departments gained new seats; only Paris actually lost any. The new total of deputies in the National Assembly was 577 instead of 485, counting departments and territories outside metropolitan France. This increase was maintained in 1986 when the new conservative majority dropped Mitterrand's proportional representation, restoring single-seat constituencies and the winner-take-all system.

The first result of the proposal to change the election laws was the resignation of Agriculture Minister Rocard. He based his resignation on opposition to proportional representation, but he had clearly chosen the opportunity to take his distance from a government that was doing little for his image and too much for that of Laurent Fabius. He planned to try another run for the presidency in 1988 and announced his candidacy in June 1985.

The summer of 1985 had seen a quarrel between Fabius and PS first secretary Jospin about which of them should have the principal responsibility for the conduct of the 1986 National Assembly election campaign. Fabius was attempting to deemphasize socialism, talking of a Front Républicain designed to bring in sympathizers who did not wish to call themselves Socialists. Jospin was wary of slogans that were not explicitly Socialist. He also saw Fabius as a rival to his own position and future ambitions. The Rocard faction might become his ally. There was also a real danger that factional maneuvers too clearly aimed at boosting Fabius might even push the Rocardians out of the party. Mitterrand, taken by surprise, decided in favor of Jospin. Five years later, after the bad blood between Fabius and Jospin had split the Mitterrandists and caused the disaster of the party congress in Rennes, Mitterrand told an interviewer: "I must say that I had not realized how great their differences were."[21]

By the fall of 1985 the Socialists were concerned with the preparation of a legislative election they knew they could not win, in order to secure Mitterrand's position for the final two years of his term. If the years 1986–1988 did not go too badly, the Socialists might hope to win another presidential election. But with the president's record considered negative by 55 to 60 percent of the electorate, another Mitterrand candidacy then seemed unlikely. The most plausible Socialist replacement for him appeared in summer 1985 to be not Fabius, but Rocard.[22]

Rocard spent most of 1985 after his resignation from the government in reorganizing his own faction in the party. Elections for departmental delegates to the Socialist party congress scheduled for October in Toulouse showed that Rocard's followers represented 28 percent of the party, with special strength in the west and fairly good overall representation. Rocard had never been a team player, but the Mitterrandists had never wanted him on the team either. Now it looked as if they must prepare for that possibility. Rocard's main programmatic point was to insist that the PS fully accept the identity created by its party's record in office and not backslide into the left-wing ideologizing of the 1970s.

Rocard spoke on the first day of the PS congress to an audience prepared to hear and perhaps be impressed by him. But he made a poor speech and once again raised doubts about his talent as a political tactician. The next day, Laurent Fabius filled the congress's emotional needs by attacking the opposition leadership as a "mediocre wax museum" and succeeded in making the assembled Socialists forget that many of them did not love him very much. His listing of economic achievements won only polite applause, but the congress loved the red meat.

On the ideological front, the congress demonstrated that the PS accepted Rocard's positions, less because they were his than because there could be no turning back from the president's and party's record of 1983–1985. The final resolution of the congress stated, "There are constraints that no power can shake off in a democratic and open society." It continued: "The crisis has put this brutal truth in sharp light: The only revenue that can be distributed is the counterpart of that which can be produced and sold. The Socialists have taken better account of the necessity to remain competitive, to make profits in order to invest, to contain the costs of production."[23]

Fabius seemed to emerge from the Toulouse congress as the charismatic leader of a party newly united around the idea of modernization. Three weeks later, he appeared on television in a debate with Chirac meant to build him up as the new leader of the Left. Attempting with short sharp questions to provoke the conservative leader, he fell victim to his own tactics when Chirac told him, "Please let me speak and stop interrupting constantly, a bit like a yapping little dog." To this insult the younger man replied to the former prime minister with hauteur and a scornful gesture: "Listen, you are talking to the prime minister of France."

Fabius had blundered; his arrogant rejoinder seemed to sum up a chilly and dismissive aspect of his personality that was already troubling the public. In early December he made another error. When Mitterrand unexpectedly received the visiting Polish leader Jaruzelski, author of the 1982 coup against Solidarity, Fabius, without giving any explanation, told the National Assembly that he was "troubled" by the president's action. Although the Socialists were also disturbed, they were more upset at Fabius's attempt to take his distance from his chief.

Fabius's poll ratings went into a steep decline. Jospin could direct the campaign, but who was able to carry the banner for the PS? The result was the president's return to the political arena. In October 1985 it had seemed to many Socialists that even if he were not swept away by the tides of 1986, he would depart two years later. By early 1986 it was clear that only François Mitterrand could save the fortunes of the PS—and his own.

4

From Confrontation to Cohabitation

The Waning of the PCF

For many years after World War II, the Communist party dominated the French Left. The wellspring of faith in Communism was a belief in the purgative and creative powers of revolution, the elemental force born in France in 1789, reborn in Petrograd in 1917. As the representative and ally of the Soviet Union in France, the Communist party could inspire and lead a far wider constituency than its actual membership. The Paris mandarinate of the upper intelligentsia (heavily pro-Communist in the postwar years) also influenced hundreds of thousands of lesser opinion makers throughout the country, not least in the lower intelligentsia typified by secondary-school teachers. Two of the three independent teachers' unions—those of secondary-school teachers and of university professors—were dominated organizationally by Communists. Not all or even a majority of teachers were Communists, but the vast majority of them were and remain on the Left. Like haute couture from the Paris salons descending to the mass garment trade, opinion fashioned in Paris spread to the provinces.

In the post–World War II years, as reports of Soviet brutality in bringing the Eastern European countries under their domination multiplied, and as defectors brought out more and more details on the horrors of the 1930s being repeated, French Communists and fellow travelers refused to credit their testimony. The root cause was a passionate desire to believe in the thaumaturgic October Revolution. That revolution, incarnate in the Soviet Union, could perhaps make mistakes, thought these French Leftists, but it could not commit crimes—or else the world made no sense. This deformation of reason into rationalization forged an almost impenetrable armor against unpleasant reality. The Soviet Union and the French Communist party might err—but one should not dwell on it. In the polarized world of the Cold War they were the only sources of hope. "We must not destroy hope in

Billancourt," said Jean-Paul Sartre in 1952 (referring to the Renault autoworkers, hence the proletariat in general).

The shocks of Hungary, Khrushchev's secret speech, the Prague spring, had moved much of the intelligentsia from its earlier faith, but many still believed, as did hundreds of thousands of workers and employees. Many who became doubtful about Soviet communism found surrogates in other revolutions: China, Cuba, Vietnam, Cambodia.

In the mid-1970s, however, change finally came to the fellow-traveling intelligentsia and the much larger mass of PCF members who listened to the leaders of their party. Two interlinked ideas central to the French Left—the cult of revolution and admiration for the Soviet Union—underwent a number of attacks within a relatively brief period. The desire to believe had resisted the assaults of Khrushchev's secret speech and the Hungarian revolt, rationalized and trivialized the suppression of the Prague reformers. The edifice of belief could not hold against the fresh battering of the 1970s, against an accumulation of attacks striking it from all directions. The myth of the Soviet Union was shaken by attacks from Maoist China and by the *gauchisme* of 1968; the justification of revolution was called into question by Solzhenitsyn's *Gulag Archipelago* and the horrors of Cambodia; and the surrogates for Soviet revolution were devalued by the Khmer Rouge horrors and the collapse of the Cultural Revolution with the fall of the Gang of Four. All these conjoined within a few years: it was too much.

Pro-Soviet French Communists had been outraged by the party's brief period of Eurocommunism, but party members harboring some doubts about the Soviet Union were probably more numerous. Once the party admitted that the Soviet Union was highly imperfect, a taboo had been broken, and taboos, like Humpty-Dumpty, are hard to mend. The anger of many in the party ranks at the PCF's sabotage of the Union of the Left in 1978 did not abate, although the PCF score in the European elections of June 1979 remained at 20 percent.

Two years later a quarter of the Communist electorate abandoned Marchais to vote for Mitterrand in the first round of the presidential elections. Once the hemorrhaging had begun, it continued in 1984 and thereafter. With its electoral losses, the PCF also increasingly lost the capacity to bully the Left into silence.

PCF criticism of government policies in 1982–1984 would have had much greater impact on the government and the Socialist party if the PCF had not been both electorally weakened and intellectually discredited. (In fact, PS independence from the PCF might not have been possible at all.) Sociological change—the weakening of the industrial working class by a switch to tertiary activities—obviously played a major role. But the ideological change involved in a waning of faith clearly helped to precipitate the electoral collapse of the PCF in 1981–1986.

Exit the Communist Party

After the defection of a quarter of its electorate in the first round of the 1981 presidential elections, the PCF had little choice but to support Mitterrand in the second round. (There were, however, some limited sabotage actions consonant with the original intent to destroy Mitterrand, in which trusted militants were urged to vote for Giscard in the second round.) In 1981, with new legislative elections imminent, the PCF also needed PS support for its leading candidates in the first round. Its plausible hope that the Left would not have a majority without Communist deputies was frustrated when the PS won a majority on its own, whereas the Communists elected only half their previous deputies. Nevertheless, the party believed, thanks in part to the power of the CGT, that it could still exercise great influence on the government. That was also the fear of the conservatives, and of a not inconsiderable number of Socialists as well. In fact, the PCF entered the government in 1981 more as a hostage than as an associate. The Socialists also took care to limit the amount of patronage the Communist ministers could exercise.

Fears that Communist ministers could fill the civil service with their appointees were based on their success in so doing in 1944–1947. The circumstances were in fact quite different: In the immediate postwar period the civil service had been purged of the most egregious Vichyites, leaving many openings for deserving Resistance fighters, many of whom were, of course, Communists. The window was not nearly so wide open in the 1980s.[1]

The PCF might desire and receive some concessions in personnel matters, but government policy was decided by the Socialists alone. Mauroy's rule was never to create a situation where the chief of a major administration was a Communist if the CGT controlled the base. Thus when Health Minister Jack Ralite wanted to appoint a comrade as director of hospitals, Mauroy broke this office off from the Health Ministry and gave it to one of the prime minister's collaborators, with instructions to keep an eye on personnel changes. Similar dispositions were taken with Fiterman's Transport Ministry. The suburban transport system, the RATP, where autonomous syndicates were in the majority, was given a Communist president, but Matignon's man went to the national railroads, where the Communist unions were strong.[2] The very anti-Communist union Force Ouvrière (FO), however, found itself dealing with Communist ministers in the areas where it was most concerned, and considered itself very badly dealt by.

Except for sensitive posts, the presence of party members in the government apparatus had never been taboo in the Fourth or Fifth Republics. Civil Service Minister Anicet Le Pors, well known as a Communist, had risen during the Giscard administration to the position of chief of the Finance Ministry division for economic forecasting. Personnel policy was always merely to restrict their presence and their influence. In the 1980s the Communists could have left their mark on French bureaucracy only if they had been given time and opportunity to install a large number of party members permanently in important jobs. Neither was granted to them.

Communists in high positions had no influence on defense or foreign affairs—and neither did most Socialists. The Communists' effect on governmental policy could be seen only in sectoral questions, as when Health Minister Ralite ended the custom of having beds in public hospitals available to the patients of doctors with partially private practice. Doctors were incensed.

The PCF pushed hard to have Communist journalists hired by state-controlled radio and television channels. In one such case, the government chose none of the men recommended but hired instead a Communist journalist in partial disagreement with his party. Many of the French objected on principle to the presence in the government of a party that made itself an apologist for Soviet actions in Afghanistan and for Jaruzelski's coup in Poland, and that called for French nuclear weapons to be counted with American ones in negotiations with the Soviets. When the investigation of Communist fraud in a number of city campaigns in 1983 caused the election of a several Communist mayors to be invalidated, the opposition was (unsurprisingly) much more vociferously indignant than the Socialists. But some Socialists, mostly admirers of Michel Rocard, also felt it shameful that their party, with its proclaimed democratic principles, maintained its alliance with a party that had so clearly relapsed into its old ways after the ambiguous and abortive attempt at change known as Eurocommunism.

After the renewed signs of decline in the European elections, "reformers" of a Eurocommunist persuasion in the Communist ranks made bold to challenge Secretary-General Marchais, whose twelve-year tenure had been a long string of disasters for the party. One of the dissidents was the minister Marcel Rigout. Marchais was firmly in command of the party apparatus and beat them off, using the standard Communist "any criticism approved by outside forces only proves how right I am" tactic.

When Mauroy resigned and was replaced by Fabius, the hard-line members of the Politburo decided that this was an excellent opportunity to detach the party from complicity in a government that, with Fabius at its head, would clearly continue the policies of industrial restructuring that the Communists found difficult to swallow. Three of the Communist ministers favored remaining in the government; Marchais was undecided, having recently spoken in favor of remaining in government. The hard-liners pointed out to Marchais that by taking the lead again in a party of opposition, he could better rally his troops against dissidents, depicted as pro-Socialist and opportunistic.[3]

Polls had shown that a majority of the Communist electorate favored continuing participation in the government. After the damaging zigzag tactics of 1978–1981, the party had to worry about the manner of disengaging from the government. It could afford to look as if it had been pushed (though the Socialists did not want to push it), but not as if it had jumped. Fabius's nomination gave the Communists a chance to represent their departure as the result of an unacceptable Socialist démarche—a push. Thus, Marchais could and did jump.

The twenty-fifth PCF congress in the following February set its new policy as the establishment of a "new people's majority rally," an empty formula that could not hide the fact that no one was rallying to the PCF and that it represented a smaller minority than at any time since the 1920s. The reformers were allowed to express themselves at the congress but were strongly criticized by the leadership. Some reformers, such as Pierre Juquin, were not reelected to top posts and began to move toward an open break with the party. The following months saw the resignations from the Central Committee of other reform-minded leaders. The party was turning inward on its hard core.

Communist departure from the government did the PCF no more good than its previous presence. The National Assembly elections of March 1986 saw its share of the vote sink to 9.7 percent, a regression to its position of 1924. In Paris, where the PCF had seven deputies in 1973 and three in 1978, its score fell below 5 percent of the vote and it won no seats at all.

The bitter criticism the PCF lavished on the Fabius government won it no credit with its former voters. In those departments where the massive job cuts of early 1984 had been most grievous, the PS suffered slightly in the 1986 elections (still improving its record over that of June 1984), but the PCF continued to sink, finishing well behind its 1981 vote.

After the 1984 elections, and still more after March 1986, observers began to speak of a historic decline of the PCF. Three elections in five years had seen the party vote cut in half from the 20-plus percent of the vote it had held throughout the 1970s. The pattern of decline was nationwide and would continue. The lackluster André Lajoinie polled only 6.8 percent of the vote in the presidential elections of 1988, although his party made a partial recovery in the subsequent parliamentary elections, at 11.4 percent.

Municipal elections in 1989 saw Communist losses of a number of cities, and in the European elections that same year the PCF tally was only 7.7 percent. It had 9.1 percent in the 1993 elections (in which the Socialists received only 17.4 percent). In 1995 Robert Hue, who had replaced Marchais as secretary-general, won 8.7 percent. However, Hue's gains over Lajoinie, seven years earlier, were largely due to slightly increased votes for the more sympathetic Hue in areas where Communist strength was negligible, "passing from extreme marginality to marginality, and in any case incapable of profiting from it on the municipal, cantonal, or departmental level."[4]

François Mitterrand had told the Socialist International in 1972 that his ambition was to reduce the Communist vote to 15 percent. In 1981 he hit his mark, in 1984 overshot it, and by 1986 there was little left to shoot at. The Communists had not been wrong in 1977 when they charged that the PS wished to use them only as an electoral prop. But after 1984 the prop was too short to do the Socialists any good, nor was it offered to them. The vote subtracted from the Communist column did not go to swell the Socialist vote after 1981. It is of course impossible to determine just which voters have moved from one party to another over the past few years. But the aggregate Left, which had had 50.2 percent in the first round of the 1978 legislative elections and 55.64 percent in the 1981 legislative elections (marked, however, by high abstention), had actually dropped to 43.96 percent in the 1986 elections, and in 1993 to 35.02 percent (although two-thirds of the 7.64 percent garnered by the two ecologist formations can also be reckoned as a Left vote).

In the departments of the Mediterranean littoral and in some big cities, a part of the formerly Communist vote had gone to the National Front (FN). Some of the

Communist voters had retreated into persistent abstention. Worse, the National Front was now consistently outpointing the PCF in every election, taking from it what Georges Lavau described as its function as a tribune, the party of protest. In the 1993 elections the Communist share of votes among those eighteen to thirty-four years of age was less than half of what it had been in 1978. In the 1995 presidential elections, the perennial Trotskyite candidate, Arlette Laguiller, who in 1981 gained only 2.3 percent of the vote, won 5.3 percent, more than half of Hue's score, while Le Pen took 15 percent. Worse still for a party that had always proclaimed itself the party of the workers, the PCF candidate in 1995 received only 15 percent of workers' votes, whereas they gave Lionel Jospin 21 percent and Le Pen 27 percent!

The working class itself had changed greatly in a few decades. In 1975, the number of industrial workers reached a peak: 40 percent of the working population—dropping to 33 percent in 1987. Tertiary occupations increased, and even industrial jobs were often skilled oversight rather than heavy labor. Finally, the real proletariat in France was increasingly foreign, especially Maghrébin—and even where the younger generation had French citizenship, the party neither sought their adherence nor did they look to it.

Within two decades the Communist party had thus declined from a position of great political and electoral force to near irrelevance. Given the two-stage run-off system, the Socialists have remained interested in electoral alliances—but since the Communists are now entirely dependent on them to elect officials at almost any level, their bargaining power with the PS has decreased. Control of the CGT (itself much diminished but still powerful among public workers) remains the chief power in the hands of the Communist party. But the PCF appears to have lost the power to regenerate itself.[5]

Enter the National Front

From 1945 to 1953 the extreme Right had won only a minute portion of the vote in France. It rallied with the Poujadiste movement in 1956 (12 percent of the vote) but collapsed again after de Gaulle returned to power. In the presidential election of 1965 Jean-Louis Tixier-Vignancour (a lawyer who had defended both Marshal Pétain and the generals who rebelled in Algeria) won only 5.28 percent of the vote.

In the following years the extreme Right was divided by its internal quarrels. Jean-Marie Le Pen, one of its most talented politicians, who had been elected to parliament as a Poujadiste at twenty-eight, got 0.74 percent of the vote when he ran for president in 1974. In 1981 Le Pen was unable even to get the 500 signatures of *notables* needed to enter the presidential race. In his warm-up speeches for a campaign he could not undertake, he placed relatively little emphasis on immigration, preferring to emphasize the thermonuclear threat, Communism, France's energy deficit, and the disproportion between the demography of the "white races" and those inhabiting the Third World.[6]

When Le Pen ran for the National Assembly in June 1981 he won only 4.38 percent of the vote in a Paris constituency. With the triumphant rise of the Left, the forces of the extreme Right seemed to have become a minority inside a minority. The rise of the National Front therefore came as a surprise to French politicians.

Two years later Le Pen's National Front had been reorganized, had found its dominant theme, and made its first breakthrough: Le Pen won 11.26 percent running for a seat on the Paris city council in 1983. Proof that this was no fluke came when a supplementary municipal election in the small industrial city of Dreux, fifty miles west of Paris, gave Le Pen's lieutenant Jean-Pierre Stirbois 16.72 percent of the votes. Stirbois was then brought onto the opposition list headed by the RPR and UDF, which was consequently able to oust the Socialist mayor and city council on the second round. In October 1983 another such municipal election in the Paris Red Belt town of Aulnay-sous-Bois ousted a Communist mayor, with the help of FN votes.

These signs warned of the storm that broke in the European elections of June 1984. In France (as elsewhere in Europe) they were conducted on purely national issues. Deputies to the European Parliament had little or no power, and voters felt that no great responsibility attached to their choices. The FN received 10.95 percent of the vote, the PCF 11.2. One party was rising, however, the other sinking. Because the French were used to a much bigger and more threatening Communist party and to a negligible vote on the extreme Right, Le Pen's party appeared as the victor and Marchais's formation the loser.

The National Front now ran as the champion of the native-born French against North African immigrants, against crime and unemployment (with the Arab presence seen as a cause of both evils), and for law and order in a France allegedly governed by a lax and incompetent Left. Those were not new problems, but the election of a left-wing government allowed them to be seized upon by an extreme and demagogic movement.

Few thought that the FN would disappear in the 1986 assembly elections (and after Mitterrand had decided that they would be held under proportional representation, no one at all). The question remained how an extreme Rightist who had been around a long time had suddenly found a hearing in 1983–1984. Le Pen is a talented demagogue, but his talents do not date from yesterday.

North Africans, or Maghrébins, are heavily concentrated in the working-class areas of big cities. Thus in 1981 immigrants of all nationalities made up 20 percent of the population of Paris, 16 percent in Lyons, 15 percent in the Paris suburban departments of Seine-Saint-Denis and Val-de-Marne, and 12 percent in Marseilles. North Africans accounted for approximately half of this number, but as they were geographically concentrated and physically distinguishable from Europeans, their presence was the more obvious.[7]

The problem in France is not precisely racial, at least not in the most obvious sense of the term. Rather, it is cultural. There had long been large numbers of non-Europeans in French cities, but by the early 1980s the French had become uneasy about the apparently unassimilable Moslem North Africans. An undoubted contribution to this new fear of Islam came from the rise of fundamentalism in Iran and from the inextricable tangle of Lebanon (where French diplomats and soldiers had been constant targets, and where 58 French soldiers were killed in a terrorist attack on the same day in October 1983 that 239 American marines lost their lives).

The Islam known to France since Napoleon's expedition to Egypt, the conquest of Algeria in the 1830s, and French hegemony in Syria and Lebanon had been a culture on the defensive against aggressive Western values. Even the war in Algeria had been lost to a National Liberation Front led by a Westernized elite fighting in the name of national independence. In the 1980s, however, although many of the French believed that pluralist education would assimilate Moslems in France to French values, many pessimists (only a minority being intellectuals) agreed with Louis Pauwels, the rightist editor of *Figaro Magazine,* that "this ignores the fact that our values are disappearing and that Islam more than ever honors its own, seeing our societies becoming sillier and decomposing ever more each day."[8]

Polls on French attitudes toward North African immigrants in October 1985 indicated a 31 percent approval rating for Le Pen's views that the massive presence of immigrants posed a danger to France. The same polls showed nearly as many approving his defense of traditional values. (Ten years later, 28 percent thought immigrants a danger—but those approving Le Pen's defense of traditional values had increased to 41 percent.)[9]

What respondents mean by traditional values is unclear; they are apparently referring to vague Le Pen slogans like "France, first of all," (and in 1995, undoubtedly also reacting favorably to Le Pen's opposition to the Maastricht treaty and European integration).

Crime and the National Front

The incidence of crime had climbed steeply in France with the rise of urbanization and prosperity. Between 1963 and 1983 the incidence of burglary, the most common crime, was multiplied by a factor of fourteen. Violent crimes against both persons and property nearly doubled between 1972 and 1983, but only a small part of them involved physical violence. The big cities were naturally hardest hit by the rise in crime. Nearly one Parisian in five was touched by crime of some sort in 1983, and the cities of the Mediterranean littoral and Lyons were also heavily affected.[10]

The alarming rise in crime had begun well before Mitterrand's election. However, a large part of the public came to believe that the Socialists were encouraging crime by their naïveté and laxity. Discontent began early and increased in intensity. In May 1984 only 28 percent of SOFRES respondents believed that the government's record on public safety had proved satisfactory; the statistic dipped to 25 percent in May 1985 and 22 percent in May 1986.[11] Much of the aversion to Socialist policies on public safety was directed against Justice Minister Robert Badinter. A former criminal lawyer, author of the law abolishing the death penalty, advocate of reform in

French criminal justice, and a Jew, he was a magnet for criticism. His predecessor as justice minister, Alain Peyrefitte, went as far as to write in June 1983: "M. Badinter has continued to be the defender of criminals while being the minister of justice. . . . For the sake of France and of justice, I only hope that the immense talent of M. Badinter, the most brilliant of criminal lawyers, will again be used judiciously, that is, in the service of famous criminals."[12] When an ex-minister and member of the Académie Française could venture to describe an honorable political opponent in such scabrous terms, there was ample room for less eminent demagogues to follow.

The opposition's efforts to exploit fears created by the rise in crime ended by playing into the hands of the demagogue Le Pen. Peyrefitte and his friends in the RPR and UDF had not been able to reduce crime; Le Pen had the advantage of being a political outsider. He excited support by linking the rise in crime to the presence in France of 3 million North Africans.

The incidence of crimes committed by foreigners was in fact higher than their proportion to the total population. Analysts explained the disparity by referring to high rates of unemployment, particularly among the large numbers of young North Africans, plus inferior and crowded housing conditions. Those not disposed to be analytical found it easier to listen to Le Pen's demagogy.

Mitterrand had opened himself to accusations of being "soft on crime" in 1981 when he granted amnesty to 6,200 prisoners (about 14 percent of the prison population). Such amnesties are traditional after the election of a new president. Among those amnestied were unrepentant terrorists of the Action Directe group, who were not yet guilty of major crimes but were later to murder General René Audran and Renault chief Georges Besse.

In any case, abolition of the death penalty was badly received by a police force largely suspicious of the Left. In May 1983 three policemen were killed in one day while checking the identity of a suspicious person. The murderer turned out to have been released from prison two weeks earlier.

Unassimilable Moslems?

Le Pen has made the French more uneasy than they otherwise might have been about the immigration question, but the problem is nonetheless a real one. According to the 1990 census, there were 4.2 million individuals living in France who were considered immigrants, of whom 1.3 million had acquired French citizenship. Of these, 56.6 percent came from the countries of the European Union (40 percent being Portuguese). Another 12.5 percent had been born in the countries of the former Soviet bloc. But when the French speak of the immigrant question, they are not talking of any of those immigrants or usually of the 9.2 percent of other immigrants born in Asia. They mean the Moslems—most of them from the Maghreb, 147,000 from Turkey.[13] But they also mean Moslems not counted as immigrants by the French census: Beurs (the name of young Maghrébins for themselves, "backslang" for *arabe*) and Harkis (Algerians who fought for France in the Algerian war). On the other hand, they do not generally include the immigrants from sub-Saharan Africa in this category, although 40 percent of them are also Moslems.[14] In 1990 Pierre Joxe, the interior minister, gave a figure of 3 million Moslems in France. The FN has always insisted that the real figures are much higher because of extensive illegal immigration.

Le Pen and the National Front have exploited a confused sentiment of estrangement in one's own country, which is felt by many French men and women walking the streets of the North African quarter in big French cities. Many who detest Le Pen worry about the problem of assimilating the younger generation of Maghrébins. Some in this younger generation are apparently unsure whether they want to be French, and whether becoming French means renouncing their cultural heritage. Even the National Front did not originally propose expelling the Maghrébins en masse (although Le Pen has increasingly made noises to this effect). For the FN's purposes the controversy is more useful when agitated than solved. It campaigned against the automatic accession to citizenship of young Maghrébins born in France, advocating making naturalization a favor, not a right. Knowledge of French would not suffice; respect for French law, culture, and history would figure in. And the possibility of losing French nationality or having it stripped away would be written into law. (The Pasqua laws on naturalization of 1993 essentially met this demand—but Le Pen's vote in 1995 rose again.)

In the 1960s, when hundreds of thousands of young Maghrébins were imported to help a rapidly expanding French economy in need of cheap labor, no one had worried about them. In 1974, with the first oil shock, the government stopped all importation of labor and attempted to convince foreign workers to go home, using financial incentives. However, there was no work to be found in their North African homelands and few acceded. Instead, family immigration increased. Young men who had perhaps thought they would work for a few years abroad and return home to start a family either sent for their wives or brought in brides. The high birthrates natural to Third World countries produced a new crop of North African children (automatically entitled to French citizenship). By the early 1980s, the presence of North African families had become increasingly evident in the poorer quarters of French cities.

First to complain were the Communists, who then controlled many of the suburban towns with high worker populations, especially in the "Red Belt" around Paris. In late 1980 the Communist mayor of the suburb of Vitry led a group of men who bulldozed the power supplies and staircases of a hostel used by immigrant workers. Responding to the immediate hostile press reaction, Secretary-General Marchais insisted that no racism was involved, but that Communist-run municipalities had been allocated too many immigrants, who were a drain on public housing resources, social services, and schools.[15]

The children born in the 1970s were flooding into schools, where they inevitably caused problems. The North African (and other) immigrant populations were largely drawn from the peasantry of their home countries, and North African peasants often were illiterate, although many of the men, at least, could speak some French (post-1974 immigrants were usually better educated).[16] Their children, carrying little cultural baggage, were inevitably both handicapped in their schooling and a drag on their classmates.[17]

To the problem of large numbers of North Africans already in the country was added the question of illegal immigration: The number of illegals was difficult to estimate and therefore subject to demagogic exaggeration. In 1981 the new government had "exceptionally" regularized the status of 130,000 illegal immigrants, a majority of them Maghrébins. The total number of illegal immigrants was estimated (confidentially) at 300,000. With a Maghrébin population increasing both in size and public evidence, the talented demagogue Le Pen thus had little difficulty into making them the focus for dissatisfaction and increasing the power of his National Front.

François Mitterrand privately saw the FN as a force that split the Right, but no real threat. In spring 1982, after the FN won less than 1 percent of the vote in the cantonal elections (which saw an increase for the Right as a whole), Mitterrand acceded easily to a request by Le Pen for radio and television coverage of the National Front's congress. The taboo once broken, Le Pen was interviewed more frequently on the news hour as the 1983 municipal elections approached, with probable advantage to his party. (The Trotskyite parties, which drew votes from the Socialists and Communists, were not so favored.)

In an interview in the week after Le Pen had made his first major breakthrough in the 1984 European elections, Pierre Bérégovoy told a journalist: "We have every interest in pushing the National Front. It keeps the Right from being elected. The stronger it is, the harder we'll be to beat. It's a historic chance for the Socialists."[18] That was a confidential reaction; the Socialists in general and in public spoke of the FN as detestable and fascist. The PS gave its support to SOS-Racisme, a pro-integration movement that sprang up in 1984; its motto was "touche pas à mon pote" (hands off my buddy). Intended to counter the FN with a discourse of tolerance wrapped in the rhetoric of the younger generation, the movement received much publicity for a while. It was supported by the Elysée, which also hoped to gain some political advantage by appealing to the young Beurs.

Nevertheless, some PS deputies who did not much like the FN would still say things privately like, "I wish I had an National Front candidate who'd get 10 percent in my district—that'd help me."[19] In 1986, the leaders of the RPR and UDF detected no Socialist displeasure in results that held the conservatives to a tiny majority. In the two following years, controversy raged whether electoral alliances with Le Pen were permissible. After the regional elections of March 1986 the RPR and UDF accepted FN alliances in several regions in order to have a majority in the local councils. These actions brought loud cries from the Socialists. Some conservatives asked whether alliances with Le Pen were any worse than the Socialist alliance with the Communists; the Socialists found it easiest to shout down this question.

The question of whether to accept local alliances with the National Front has been crucial. It applies differently in legislative, regional, and municipal elections.

Where there are second-round runoffs, as in legislative elections, 12.5 percent of the votes are necessary for a candidate to remain in the race. The Socialists and Communists have long practiced a system known as *désistement,* in which the candidate with fewer votes—usually well above the minimum—stands down in favor of the better-placed one. A number of UDF and RPR figures, particularly in the south, where the FN is strong, have argued that local alliances do no harm, and that *désistements* in favor of the National Front were far less sinister than those of the Socialists aiding Communists.

But in the legislative elections of 1988 there was only one case in which a successful National Front candidate was given a leg up by the respectable Right (despite a *désistement* agreement in the populous Bouches-du-Rhône department). Majorities in regional councils had earlier been formed with the aid of FN counselors, however.

After 1988, the principled opponents of the FN on the Right were joined by those who had concluded that little advantage could be found in alliances. In March 1990 Jacques Chirac told an audience of RPR officials in Toulon (an area where the FN was strong) that 40 percent of the FN's voters came from the Left and would always vote against the mainstream Right; 15 percent were *"pétainistes-nazillons-OAS,"* implacably opposed to Gaullism, and the remaining 45 percent were *"braves gens de droite,"* who would end by voting for the mainstream Right with or without electoral agreements.[20]

As time went on, it became evident that the National Front was capable of taking away Socialist votes as well as those of the Right. By the time the FN had eaten so deeply into the working-class vote that it outperformed all other parties in the elections of the 1990s, Socialists had learned that any earlier complacency was misplaced, and conservatives, that FN voters were not easily seduced by anti-Maghrébin legislation.

If the National Front had never existed, or if (like the Republikaner party in Germany) its threat had rapidly diminished, there would still have remained an extensive malaise in France about the presence of a large number of immigrants coming from areas outside the occidental tradition and likely to assimilate slowly if at all. The word "identity" has become a cliché, used in academic meetings as a sort of aspirin of the intellect that handles all problems, but there is still no doubt that the challenge of a large number of Moslems in this ancient (now largely nonpracticing) Christian country has awakened fundamental doubts and questions on the meaning of the French identity today. A group of distinguished intellectuals asked to consider the future of French identity reported: "French identity is in disarray. It does not appear as robust as it once was, capable of absorbing and assimilating without difficulty influences and inflows from abroad."[21]

To a considerable degree the problem is one of perceptions, since the second generation of the Maghrébin immigration is rapidly becoming more French, though perhaps neither integrated nor assimilated. Ninety-two percent of Algerian and 94 percent of Moroccan immigrants from North Africa who arrived in France before the age of sixteen can speak and read French, whereas only 8 and 18 percent respectively can both speak and read Arabic. According to a survey cited by Dominique Schnapper, about 5 percent of young Moslems in Marseilles actively declared a belief in God, 87 percent of the boys and 72 percent of the girls said they did not pray, and 94 percent of the boys and 45 percent of the girls did not observe Ramadan. Islam for them has a value of giving identity. Schnapper spoke of the development of a French Islam—a personal religion.[22]

French Jews have of course long practiced Judaism as that sort of personal religion (though this "assimilationist" idea is now much contested by Sephardic Jews of North African origin). Anti-Semitism nevertheless persisted—and it is difficult to believe that a fear of Islam will vanish because the children of Islam have modified their practice of it.

The ability of Islam to cause consternation in a France still fixated on monoculturalism was demonstrated in 1989 when a school principal in a Paris suburb refused entry to the school to three teenage girls who insisted on coming to their classes wearing the traditional Moslem scarf covering the head and neck. Numerous Socialists sided with the principal, defending the importance of forbidding religious symbols in a public school—the scarf was frequently described in the press as a veil. The whole controversy went on hot and heavy for two months, until Education Minister Jospin, who had kept his head in all this, appealed to the Council of State, which sensibly decided that it was up to the principal to decide—the fate of the republic was not at stake. In the wake of this controversy, the widow of a National Front leader won a by-election to parliament in the city of Dreux, where National Front strength had first been shown. The government responded by declaring that France was "no longer a land of immigration" and announced a campaign to ensure against the entry of more foreign workers.

The Socialists were thus yielding ground—just what they had accused the parliamentary Right of doing. To compensate, they introduced or reemphasized programs to help integrate resident immigrants, which had a marginal effect at best. The high unemployment rates of young Maghrébins and their heavy presence in the joyless concrete housing of industrial suburbs ensured tension—which did not fail to explode. Riots occurred in the years after 1981 in the Lyons suburbs of Villeurbanne, Vénissieux, and Vaux-en-Vélin, in housing projects where the residents ranged from 37 to 80 percent Maghrébin. In 1991 there was a wave of violence at Mantes-la-Jolie, near Paris, where largely North African youth looted, burned cars, and attacked firemen.

In 1993 the returning Right swiftly amended the naturalization laws (see Chapter 6) and broadened police powers. As noted, these measures were designed to appease current or potential FN voters—and in 1995 failed to do so.

After the end of the Cold War diffuse but widespread French fears of future trouble focused on the countries of the North African littoral, fears ignited by the spread of fundamentalism and subsequent terrorism in Algeria (see Chapter 9). A fundamentalist victory in Algeria, which could spread to Tunisia and Morocco, would undoubtedly trigger a wave of refugees from the most Westernized classes. It is uncertain how welcome they would be in France.

If there should be no massive increase in immigration, can French society integrate the Moslem minority, coming to terms with both the inequalities facing that minority and its own fears for the homogeneity of French society and its traditional identity? To a polling question of early 1995 on the attitudes causing them the greatest worry for the future, 56 percent of respondents replied "racism" (59.5 if one excludes respondents over sixty-five).[23] Nevertheless, the continued electoral growth of the National Front argues that a large minority (greater than the FN's electoral strength) is actively racist or tends to racism.

What of the Maghrébins themselves? According to a 1994 survey, 60 percent of young Beurs consider themselves well or fairly well integrated into French society. The criteria here are varied: fluent French spoken as their maternal language, the possibility of marriage with a non-Maghrébin, and an expressed willingness to fight for France should need arise. Interestingly, young women feel they have more future than young men—despite the restrictions Moslem custom places on them. For example, only one-quarter of them feel they are worse situated than the rest of young French women in gaining an education—although 55 percent doubt they are as well placed as other women in the job market.

Some data, like the preceding, are relatively hopeful. There are also warning signs, such as the fact that 14 percent of respondents told pollsters they approve of Moslem fundamentalism.[24] Some of these young people are presumably potential recruits for terrorism. An extended terrorist campaign could easily turn those "native" French somewhat disposed toward greater integration toward hostility and cause a permanent setback in ethnic relations. There is thus an implicit alliance between the racists of the National Front and the fanatics of the Groupe Islamique Armée who operate in France. As the twentieth century draws to a close, no confident predictions for the improvement or deterioration of ethnic relations in France can be made.

The Return of the Right

After their double defeat in 1981 French conservatives could not believe what had happened to them. At first they thought it quite possible that the Left might remain in power for decades, as they had. Hopelessly in the minority, with a total of only 155 seats—a third of the National Assembly—the younger neo-Gaullists and Giscardians fought a rearguard action against the nationalization laws, while their leaders stood aside.

During the Socialist "state of grace," the old leaders of the former majority were in discredit. Giscard and Barre were generally unpopular; Chirac was blamed by the Giscardians for bringing down Giscard and for mistakenly believing that the Socialists could be defeated in the "third round," the National Assembly elections. But Chirac was the strongly entrenched leader of a disciplined party, and recovered rapidly.

The first sign that the Socialist victory was fragile came in January 1982 when conservatives won all four by-elections for seats where the June elections had been invalidated, unseating three Socialists. The March cantonal elections showed a further falling away from the Socialists. The June 1982 economic crisis, triggering a second devaluation and the beginnings of austerity, gave the conservatives new hope. Election after election—the municipals of 1983, the European elections of 1984, and the cantonal elections of 1985—furnished solid proof of what polls had already shown: a strong and unprecedented swing in popular opinion away from the Left.

The defeat of 1981 evoked a need to restate the reasons for and nature of conservative opposition to the Left majority. In the Fifth Republic until 1981 an ideological Left had faced a much less ideological Right, which did not even have a name for itself. The term *Right,* discredited by Vichy, had by 1945 become taboo, and the conservatives in the Fourth Republic shunned it. In the Fifth Republic, from de Gaulle through Giscard, they referred to themselves, like barbarian tribes whose name for themselves means simply "the men," as the Majority. This led to limp and tautological election slogans like "the Majority will win a majority!"

Conservatives in the Fifth Republic had felt no need to reverse the nationalizations carried out by General de Gaulle's government in 1945. They believed in capitalism, but with an economy directed by the state. In the mid-1970s, when Raymond Barre began to speak of liberalizing the economy, he was bitterly attacked by Chirac:

> To abandon oneself to the play of economic freedom and international competition alone is to renounce control over the future, to abandon oneself to the unforeseeable. Raymond Barre likes to quote Frédéric Bastiat . . . [who] said some very good things. But he wrote in the first half of the nineteenth century, and he accorded a religious confidence to the providential harmonies of nature. Since then, one has become much more suspicious about the consequences of *laisser-faire* and *laisser-passer,* which are not all necessarily favorable.[25]

But the Raymond Barre decried by Chirac as too much of a Manchester liberal told the editor of *L'Expansion,* the French *Fortune,* in that same year, 1978, that his liberalism was not much different from that of social democratic governments, adding that he did not exclude recourse to nationalization or to massive state aid for declining industry.[26]

This discourse was tailored for the 1970s. Both men were addressing a current of opinion influenced by the ideas of the Left, and neither thought it profitable flatly to contradict those ideas; both were also defending the record of the interventionist state capitalism of the Fifth Republic. When the victorious Socialists carried *dirigisme* further than the Gaullists had done, it became politically necessary for conservatives not just to dissent mildly, but instead to find ideas that would decry the validity of government intervention. Purely French production of new ideas was momentarily insufficient to meet this need, and recourse to imports was inevitable.

On the offensive against Giscard and Barre in 1981 and preparing to run for president, Chirac found such new ideas in the New World. Visitors to the United States reported the popularity of a newly elected Ronald Reagan and the usefulness of a combative free enterprise ideology. Even before Mitterrand's victory Chirac had ceased to attack Giscard and Barre for espousing the ideas of nineteenth-century free enterprise and began to denounce their creeping socialism, "the cunning collectivism that has developed in the last seven years."[27] And Chirac's campaign slogan in 1981 "Chirac, Maintenant!" was an echo of the American "Reagan, Now!"

After the election the virtues of free enterprise *libéralisme* were praised by Chirac's younger advisers, like the brilliant *énarque* Alain Juppé. The RPR, which needed to counteract a Left that spoke of liberty while allocating more power to the state, would in future call for less state in the name of liberty. Here it departed from the tradition of Gaullism and the philosophy of Charles de Gaulle. The historian René Rémond wrote: "There was no body of thought more unitary and less disposed to share power with other authorities than that of Charles de Gaulle, nor more convinced that only the state is capable of perceiving the general interest and making it prevail over the egoisms of interest groups."[28]

The Gaullist synthesis in both domestic and in foreign affairs had, however, exhausted itself by 1980. Its political heirs still wished to exploit the general's name, but they increasingly found his ideas outdated. French social scientists who analyzed responses to a questionnaire given delegates to the November 1984 RPR congress concluded that de Gaulle's name had for them an emotional and symbolic value, but that the label "Gaullist" did not commit them to a policy or an ideology.[29]

When conservatives had controlled the government in an expanding economy, they had found a powerful argument against the Left by pointing to the welfare measures that they had introduced. In a contracting economy, the cry of "We could do it better" in social policy was clearly no way to return to power. Something new was needed.

As Suzanne Berger pointed out in a highly perceptive analysis, new investigation into the values of free enterprise had begun even before the Socialist victory, prompted by the crisis of directed capitalism and resentment against the *dirigisme* of late Giscardianism.[30] Henri Lepage's *Demain le capitalisme* sold 40,000 copies in 1979 and was followed in 1980 by *Demain le libéralisme*. When Socialists defeated conservatives in France, and Reaganite Republicans beat Democrats in the United States, the transatlantic example seemed to light the way, even before the U.S. economy improved. Publicists described Ronald Reagan's America in glowing terms—Guy Sorman's *La Revolution conservatrice américaine*, published in 1983, rapidly became a best-seller. Another best-seller, François de Closets's *Toujours plus*, criticized trade union privilege, power, and selfishness, and raised the question of whether unions were necessary or even legitimate. Other books about the virtues of deregulation, supply-side economics, and less-intrusive government rapidly followed. Publishers remarked that the flood of leftist literature before 1981 had nearly dried up, to be replaced by dozens of books criticizing the Left and advocating new ideas for the Right.

The new French liberals differed from the Reaganites by not attacking the welfare state. They concentrated instead on the pernicious effects of too much state power and the pervasive influence of the unions. These two themes had clear antecedents in French political thought. A newer development was their cult of the entrepreneur, no great hero in earlier French conservative thinking. (The entrepreneur would soon be adopted by the Socialists as well.)

As the Socialists faltered and the European elections showed that the Left would almost certainly be defeated in 1986, the conservative parties became more and more confident that they had done well to choose a new ideology—now glorified by the flourishing condition of the U.S. economy in 1984. One sign of their new confidence was a change of label: They began unabashedly to refer to themselves collectively as "the Right," with no apologies to anybody and no adverse reaction from the country.

Though far more closely united in parliament than in the quarrelsome Giscard years, the Right was still divided on party lines. The RPR leader remained Jacques Chirac, strong despite his errors in 1981. No one in the UDF had equal prestige or power. Giscard's immediate postelection error of denouncing Chirac for treason had been a mistake. Although the younger parliamentarians had not intended from the outset to take over the Parti Républicain (Giscard's own party, the largest element in the UDF) from Giscard, alienation grew among many of them. As a conservative journalist remarked: "Giscard has an amazing power of inspiring hatred—because he is both chilly and cutting, so they grew to hate him." Worse, as time went on, his popularity did not rise as that of the Socialists sank. But Giscard's disgrace did not cling to his second prime minister. After sharing unpopularity with his president, Raymond Barre in 1983 became the most popular figure on the Right.

Why Barre, not Giscard? The former president had dwindled in defeat. His Olympian certitudes had offended too many people, especially since they had often revealed themselves to be wrong. People still remembered the early efforts at folksiness (inviting the garbage collectors to breakfast) and later the reports that Giscard had the presidential family served at table before distinguished guests. They found the folksiness phony and the snobbism all too plausible. Barre had been kept out of the 1981 election campaign (too unpopular), an exclusion for which he could later be thankful. But his real credit lay in Socialist discredit—and the fact that the new government had been obliged to adopt policies barely different from his.

Condemned by Chirac for liberalism in the 1970s, Barre in the 1980s declined to be swept away by the neoliberal enthusiasm. As a young professor he had anticipated the 1980s vogue for Friedrich Hayek by translating his *Scientism and Social Science*.[31] Having long before assimilated liberal ideas, Barre refused to show the enthusiasm of the newly converted. Very likely this contributed to his renewed popularity. The French looked at the choirboys of neoliberalism and found that an astonishing number of them had been trained in the Ecole Nationale d'Administration, the main nursery for the acolytes of the overpowerful state. People questioned the sincerity of their conversion.

The newly confident Right knew by 1984 that it would win the 1986 legislative elections. The real prize in the Fifth Republic is the presidency, and the 1988 presidential campaign began in early 1983. Chirac would obviously run again. Giscard wanted to avenge his defeat, but even in 1983 it was clear he might not find enough backers. Barre too had presidential ambitions; his problem was that he had no party behind him. Born in 1924 on the French island of Réunion in the Indian Ocean, he had been a professor of economics and one of the commissioners of the European Economic Community before Giscard brought him into the government in 1974. In 1976 he became prime minister when Chirac resigned. Although he was elected to the National Assembly for the first time in 1978 as a UDF member, he had always taken a stance above the parties. But if he were to run for president he would need UDF support.

The UDF was not a tightly organized party like the RPR but a coalition of parties (see Chapter 2). In 1982, the Parti Républicain, the strongest element in the UDF, elected a new young secretary-general, François Léotard. An *énarque*, deputy, mayor, and son of a mayor of the Mediterranean port of Fréjus, Léotard soon showed that he had ambitions of his own and only limited loyalty to Giscard. He and his political friends were all deputies or were elected deputies in 1986 and were all in their forties in the 1980s. They became the leading advocates of *libéralisme* in the PR. Léotard's influence in the PR and the UDF was challenged by informal organizations loyal to Barre, which the former prime minister began to set up in 1983. His strongest support lay in the CDS, but a strong minority of influential members of the PR inclined to him also.

The power of neoliberalism drew the RPR and UDF together. In the 1970s the Gaullist movement had moved away from the general's vague but strongly held ideas about "participation," toward Pompidou's more orthodox capitalism, while remaining interventionist. RPR adherents tended to think of the UDF as generally to the right of them (as evidenced by Chirac's 1978 disquisitions on Barre's outmoded nineteenth-century liberalism). By the mid-1980s, the RPR had itself moved to the right. Although RPR cadres looked down disdainfully on the UDF as incoherent and badly organized, they saw little ideological difference between the two parties.[32] There was more distance on the matter of *libéralisme* between Barre and the enthusiastically liberal *"bande à Léo"* than there was between the Léotardians and the RPR.

The approach of the 1986 National Assembly elections encouraged the Right to run joint candidates in a large number of constituencies. Agreement came more easily because it was worked out by the party leaders, with Barre standing aside and proclaiming that any "cohabitation" with Mitterrand after the election would be a mistake. Both Barre and Chirac saw the 1986 election as a proving ground for the presidential elections of 1988. Polls showed the electorate opposed to the Socialists—but skeptical that the Right would manage the country better. Barre staked out high constitutional ground when he argued that the presidency would be diminished by cohabitation, although observers speculated that he really wanted to put his new popularity to the test rapidly, after a Mitterrand resignation, rather than wait two more years. Chirac needed to forge a new popularity by serving as a successful prime minister. Advised by Edouard Balladur, then a little-known figure (though briefly secretary-general of the Elysée under Pompidou), Chirac had decided that Mitterrand would not resign if he lost his Socialist majority, and that it was inadvisable to attempt to force him to do so. *Cohabitation,* a term launched by Balladur in a much remarked *Le Monde* article in September 1983, was thus a necessity.[33]

From the watershed of the European elections of June 1984 to the March 1986 elections, therefore, the parties and personalities of the Right advanced toward a battle that would decide much, but would not be decisive. The Socialists too looked beyond 1986 to 1988. The calculations of both, however, were affected by Le Pen's National Front, the new force that had suddenly arisen on the extreme right wing of French politics.

5

Cohabitation

The Election of 1986

By early 1986 the stringent economic policies launched in 1982 and 1983 had begun to bear fruit. Inflation was down and expected to sink further, the wave of mass layoffs in industry seemed to have ended, and the nationalized industries were beginning to show a profit. Citizens, if not optimistic, were at least less pessimistic about the future. A poll taken in December 1985 showed that only 38 percent of respondents characterized 1985 as a bad year for themselves and their families. In earlier year-end polls 44 percent of respondents had thought 1983 a bad year, and 54 percent had viewed 1984 in the same way.[1]

Nevertheless, the polls of early 1986 clearly indicated that after swinging toward the right in 1982, the country had not again altered course. The themes dear to the Right—the importance of industry, profit, admiration for business success—had gained an approving audience among a majority of the French. The Socialists (without the Right's evangelistic enthusiasm) had emulated the conservatives in praise of the entrepreneurial spirit. Although the country had taken note of this change, it was not sure what to make of it. A confident opposition found it advisable to campaign against the errors of 1981–1982, suggesting that they would be repeated should the PS continue in power.

The RPR program for the 1986 elections, entitled "The Renewal," proclaimed that the Socialists had failed in everything they had attempted. It nevertheless took care to emphasize that the thirty-nine-hour workweek, the fifth week of paid vacations, and retirement at sixty were not threatened. Neoliberalism was heavily stressed. "Renewal," proclaimed the program, "turns its back uncompromisingly on socialism, but turns its back also on the interventionism sprung from our Jacobin tradition." And under the rubric "Give the economy back the means of development" appeared the message: "What has characterized French society for nearly twenty years is the result of French people's labor, confiscated by the state. This spoliation went on quietly in the past, and became triumphant in 1981."

Chirac's RPR, the largest party on the Right, was thus asserting its agreement with a Parti Républicain that under François Léotard had gone over completely to free enterprise and Reaganite principles. And the RPR was openly admitting that it had turned its back on methods of controlling the economy held valid by Chirac's great patron Georges Pompidou.

The Socialists were well aware that they had no chance of winning the elections. (The president's proportional representation law was a purely defensive measure designed to hold on to a maximum number of seats in the assembly. The Socialists could not have won a majority under its provisions even in the flood tide of 1981.) At the very most they might hope for a legislature with no clear majority, which would give Mitterrand a freer hand. But that assumed that National Front deputies would not be accepted into a coalition and was a recipe for dissension, muddle, and drift. The Socialists' best hope was to rally as much of their 1981 electorate as they could. To do that they had to admit some of the errors of 1981, while trumpeting the virtues of a courageous and effective administration since 1983.

Both the PS and the RPR thus confessed past errors and presented themselves in a new light for the future. Each attacked the other, however, as basically unchanged. The RPR and UDF claimed the Socialists would resume their old ways if they could; the Socialists sought to present the Right as partisan, selfish, and interested in the welfare only of the rich. The first PS election poster showed a frightened woman calling out, "Help!!! The Right is coming back!" This was deemed too defeatist and was replaced by a Disneyesque Big Bad Wolf addressed by Red Riding Hood *La France*: "Tell me, pretty Right, why do you have such big teeth?"

Under the new proportional representation law, 50 of the 97 departments had only 2 to 4 seats, a total of 149. In almost all departments the first choice candidates of the three large parties were assured of victory. To guarantee that a system favoring larger parties would help them, the RPR and UDF concluded a pact for joint candidacies in two-thirds of the departments. The smaller parties—the PCF and National Front—could win only where they had strong local support, or in very large departments where even 5 or 6 percent of the vote might suffice to gain a seat. The system was so predictable that the *Nouvel Observateur* could come out on February 14 with a (largely accurate) feature article entitled, "The 448 deputies already elected." That presumed a mere 129 seats left in doubt.

The only question left to the voters was whether they wanted a greater or lesser disavowal of Mitterrand. In either case his proportional representation law would hold off a landslide favoring the Right. Mitterrand presumably would not have to resign, but if the vote went heavily against the PS, his position would be seriously weakened. Voters were unsure how a conservative majority and a conservative prime minister would contrive to coexist (or, as the new expression had it, cohabit) with a Socialist president whose seven-year term did not end until May 1988.

Tradition holds that the French have little or no ability to allow their institutions to evolve gradually, that they remain rigidly the same until abrupt change brings new institutions and the republic acquires a new name—or number. It would be more correct to say that the frequency of abrupt change in French history has led to a general apprehension that French institutions can stand few shocks. The prospect of cohabitation engendered considerable anxiety, enhanced by constant discussion in the press, radio, and television.

Although the framers of the 1958 constitution had not expected perpetual parliamentary majorities, all elections from 1958 to 1981 had returned National Assemblies in which conservative forces dominated. In 1973, Georges Pompidou had declared in the face of the new Union de la Gauche that if his government lost its majority, he would resign. Taken as a warning to the electorate, even a threat, the statement played its intended part in a comfortable conservative victory. In 1978, when a Left victory seemed overwhelmingly probable, Giscard had told the nation that he would not resign—but warned that he would then have no powers to block the programs of the Left. In 1986, Mitterrand had no temptation to resign or power to warn. His aim was to hold 30 percent of the electorate, hang on, and fight another day.

In 1984 the noisier members of the opposition had declared that there could be no question of living together with François Mitterrand, who would be disavowed by the electorate and must be driven from the Elysée if he persisted in holding on to his office. Someone even suggested that Mitterrand could be evicted by cutting off the electricity in the presidential palace. Gambetta's famous demand that President MacMahon submit to legislative will or resign, *"se soumettre ou se démettre,"* was extensively quoted by the journals and orators of the Right. Presidential hopeful Raymond Barre announced that no good could come out of cohabitation, which would bring in two years of confusion and drift, meanwhile eroding the strong presidential institutions of the Fifth Republic. As polls showed Barre far more popular than Chirac at this time, he appeared to be hoping that a rapid showdown between a conservative majority and an intransigent president would force Mitterrand's resignation and a new presidential election.

In taking this stand Barre made what proved to be a serious strategic error. He had no party behind him that could enforce such a decision. His announcement that he personally would vote no confidence in any government intending cohabitation might influence his friends but could not bind them. In April 1985 only 41 percent of UDF voters and 39 percent of RPR voters approved Barre's position.[2]

Jacques Chirac saw in cohabitation a means to refashion an image still overshadowed by a reputation for impetuosity and inconstancy. Edouard Balladur, now one of Chirac's closest advisers, had been advocating cohabitation as a necessity since September 1983. Balladur argued that the constitution was sufficiently flexible to fit a situation in which the president's party no longer had a majority. The equilibrium between the two offices and the two personalities would be delicate, conflicts would be possible, and the government might lose some of its efficiency. But that would be the result of a popular decision that must be taken into account.[3]

Chirac was long uncertain whether he should head a government of cohabitation. In May 1985 he told a radio interviewer that he had no intention of taking the job and no vocation for it.[4] Apparently Chirac feared that he might be bogged down in an association with the Machiavellian Mitterrand, with Barre sniping from the sidelines and dividing the governing majority. However, since Barre was well ahead of him in the polls, Chirac, as a future presidential candidate, needed the prime minister's office to renew his reputation. After the October 1985 television debate between Chirac and Fabius, when the young Socialist leader torpedoed his own prestige and advanced the cause of Jacques Chirac, little doubt remained that Chirac would demand the prime ministry. With Fabius among the walking wounded, it became more necessary than ever for Mitterrand to take an active role in the campaign. Mitterrand began with a television interview in mid-December 1985, followed by mass rallies in the home constituencies of his two prime ministers. Polls showed that by the end of the campaign two-thirds of the electorate felt that the president had not exceeded his constitutional role in campaigning for his party.[5]

Mitterrand's main theme was "do not turn back." He picked up on an idea suggested by one of the better Socialist campaign posters, showing a pretty girl with a sheaf of wheat and the slogan, "I want to harvest what I sowed on the Left." The Socialist campaign also dwelt on the divisions of the Right—its disagreements on cohabitation and its temptation to compromise with the National Front. Some leaders of the UDF and RPR seemed open to a deal with Le Pen. Others, particularly Chirac, were not. The issue was complicated by the simultaneity of legislative and regional council elections; a politician might oppose opening the ranks of the parliamentary majority to Le Pen and company and still admit the possibility of forming regional alliances with them.

In a very real sense the 1986 election was the first round of the 1988 presidential race. No one knew whether the period of cohabitation would last for the twenty-five months officially separating the two contests, but it was clear to all that to remain united and combat ready, the Socialists needed to win at least 30 percent of the vote. For Chirac the 1986 election was a rung on the ladder he must climb to reach the presidency. For Barre, the election would test his prophecy that cohabitation was a mischievous policy and bound to fail—its success or failure affecting his own presidential candidacy.

Those whose fortunes were not immediately involved in the next presidential election saw the legislative elections as more important. The new young leaders of the Parti Républicain knew that victory meant their emergence into full public life as ministers, promotion of their several careers and of their free enterprise ideology. Jean-Marie Le Pen sought to confirm and enlarge the successes of 1984, thus forcing the other parties to recognize him as a legitimate and major player. The Communists desired to win back their losses of 1981 and hoped that a Socialist defeat would bring disunity to the PS and allow the PCF to emerge again as the dominant force on the Left.

Opinion was uncertain whether cohabitation would or would not weaken the presidential office. Many argued that with the president in the Elysée warring with the prime minister in the Hôtel Matignon across the Seine, France would become ungovernable and return to the piteous state of the Fourth Republic.[6]

Although it had been clear since 1984 that the Right would win the 1986 elections, it was not until August 1985 that the new leaders of the Parti Républicain met together with Chirac to agree that they would not side with Barre against cohabitation, nor back any other RPR figure (such as Mitterrand's friend Jacques Chaban-Delmas, mayor of Bordeaux) against Chirac. For the first time it became clear to Chirac that Léotard and his friends had no intention of helping Giscard in any ambitions he might have to become prime minister. Their quid pro quo was major ministerial positions.[7]

In mid-January 1986 the RPR and UDF produced a joint campaign platform that backed away slightly from some of the extreme neoliberalism of the earlier years. (In 1984 a neoliberal economist had even proposed to sell off the national forests.) The nationalized sector would be privatized—but the process would be spread out over the five-year term of the legislature. The allies promised a return to the old election procedure with single-member constituencies, the removal of price controls, changes in state control of broadcasting, firm measures on law and order, tax cuts, and much more. The five-week vacation and the thirty-nine-hour week would not be touched.[8]

There was much overlap here with the real program of the Socialists. The Fabius government had moved toward removal of price controls, had improved relations with the police, and had taken a tougher line on crime and terrorism. It had even moved one step toward denationalization by selling shares in the subsidiaries of nationalized firms. The electorate, however, still mistrusted the Socialists. No one in the campaign was talking much about reducing unemployment. (The Socialists were acutely conscious that their 1981 promises to reduce it now looked ridiculous, and the Right knew itself powerless to bring rapid improvement.) The voters, however, consistently listed that as their highest national priority, and the Socialists' record weighed heavily against them. Other issues hurting the Socialists were crime and the immigration question. Though the voters of the National Front placed those higher on their lists than did others, they ranked high in all lists of concerns.[9]

The campaign itself was slickly Madison Avenue, evidence of an Americanization of French manners that marked an immense change since the days when the French feared that if they drank a dubious brew called Coca-Cola they would cease to be the heirs of Descartes, Racine, and Corneille. The principal PS slogan, "A France that's winning," was balanced by the RPR slogan "On to tomorrow!" A campaign that took place during an exceedingly cold winter was illustrated by RPR campaign billboards and posters showing politicians in shirtsleeves, the head of the party list in each department photographed with Chirac, all grinning inanely in the best American manner, their neckties blowing in a studio wind.

The trend of polls appeared to show that although the electorate had focused in early January on the disappointments brought them by five years of Socialist rule, many (though not a majority) had concluded by election day, March 16, that the total Socialist record was not so bad—that Mitterrand and his prime ministers had shown courage and the ability to learn from their mistakes. This change was reflected in the final election results, when the PS exceeded the crucial barrier of 30 percent.

The conservatives had won, but had not triumphed. The "breakwater" of proportional representation had deprived the RPR/UDF alliance of the big majority it would have won under the old election law: The National Front had 35 seats for its 9.82 percent of the vote, whereas it would have had none before. The total vote of the Right was 54.6 percent, but the respectable Right, with its 44.68 percent, had only 291 seats, for a majority of 2.[10] On the left, the Socialists had shored up their position, but the Communists were no longer even arithmetically a possible coalition partner, and the combined votes on the Left represented one of the worst scores of the Fifth Republic—44 percent.

There could, however, be no talk of a triumphant Right hounding a disavowed Socialist president out of the Elysée. The Socialists and their small allies had won 32.6 percent of the vote and with 216 deputies were the strongest single party in the new National Assembly. Cohabitation was a political necessity. And the man who had decried it, Raymond Barre, had disappointed his supporters by demonstrating short coattails in his home department of the Rhône, distanced by a Socialist ticket led by Charles Hernu.

Barre had proclaimed that he would not vote confidence in a cohabitation government. But the Right's exiguous majority gave him and his friends no choice on voting confidence, even as it removed any possible doubt in the conservative ranks that Chirac was their necessary choice for prime minister. Mitterrand, in his best mysterious manner, encouraged rumors that he might choose Jacques Chaban-Delmas, the popular former health minister Simone Veil, or even Giscard. His game was to keep his choices open, but still more to nail down an agreement with Chirac that his privileges as president would be respected, and that the new government would not seek to humiliate him. Chirac had long since decided that he wanted the job, and Mitterrand had decided that "Chirac is the most hard-line [of possible choices], and I have to take the hard-liner. To beat him up, and chew him up in the government."[11] For Mitterrand, the 1988 presidential election campaign had already begun.

On the Tuesday after the election Elysée secretary-general Jean-Louis Bianco announced that the president had asked Chirac to see whether he could form a government. On the following day, Chirac's nomination was formally announced. The five years of Socialist power had ended, and a coexistence of uncertain duration had begun.

Chirac Returns

Energy and ambition were the most striking characteristics of the new prime minister, whose rapid career had been marked both by ability and unpredictability. Born in Paris in 1932, Jacques Chirac descended from two grandfathers who were Radical Socialist schoolmasters in their native south-central department of the Corrèze. His father had abandoned teaching for banking, rising to be a bank director and financial adviser to the airplane builder Marcel Bloch-Dassault.[12]

Chirac studied at the Institut d'Etudes Politiques (Sciences Po), did his military service in Algeria, commanding a platoon on the Algerian-Moroccan border, and then continued his studies at ENA. He spent a few months in the United States, where he went to a summer session at Harvard Business School and rose from dishwasher to counterman at a Howard Johnson's. The experience of combat and command in Algeria were formative experiences in his life; he discovered the pleasures of action.

The Chirac who returned to Paris from Algeria in 1957 to enter ENA was not yet a Gaullist, although the inability of the Fourth Republic to master the Algerian problem was now plain to him. In 1959 he graduated sixteenth in his ENA class—good enough to be assigned to the prestigious Cour des Comptes. In 1956 he married Bernadette Chodron de Courcel, daughter of a distinguished aristocratic family, whom he had met at Sciences Po. The keys to success—slow or rapid—were in his hands.

Success was rapid. In 1962 he became a junior member of the staff of the new prime minister, Georges Pompidou. The young *chargé de mission* for questions of transport and civil aviation rapidly discovered that in his position he could deal as an equal with government ministers. His energy and authority were noted by his elders, including Pierre Juillet, the mysterious, irascible political brains of the Pompidou period. Pompidou was not long in taking notice of this rarity among young bureaucrats, one who never explained why something could not be done but instead went out and did it. Pompidou called him affectionately "my bulldozer." In 1967, Chirac was encouraged to run for the National Assembly in the Corrèze. After a narrow victory over a Communist in this left-wing territory, he remained tireless in the service of his increasingly devoted constituents, even after he was elected mayor of Paris.

In the next seven years the young civil servant turned deputy became successively state secretary for employment, budget minister under Economy Minister Valéry Giscard d'Estaing (one of the few people who ever intimidated Chirac), minister for parliamentary relations, agriculture minister (a very popular one), and briefly, just before Pompidou's death, interior minister. Under Pompidou, Chirac was powerfully influenced by Pierre Juillet and his coadjutor Marie-France Garaud. Secretive, power hungry, right-wing, they hated Pompidou's first prime minister Jacques Chaban-Delmas. On Pompidou's death, Chaban declared his candidacy for the Elysée. Chirac had neither love for nor faith in Chaban and could expect nothing from him. Chirac first tried to block Chaban by inciting Prime Minister Pierre Messmer to declare his own candidacy. When that failed, he prevailed on a number of Gaullist deputies to sign a letter that cast doubt on Chaban's chances. Without openly opting for Giscard, the other conservative candidate, Chirac torpedoed a Chaban candidacy already listing to port. In the first round, Giscard had more than twice Chaban's percentage of the vote and went on to win narrowly over Mitterrand.

Giscard rewarded Chirac by making him prime minister. Chirac was apparently not certain he wanted the job—not because he lacked ambition, but because his real design was to take over a Gaullist party in disarray. Giscard mistakenly thought that his young prime minister would tame the Gaullist party for him; instead, Chirac began to reorganize it in his own image. Within two years, the two men had fallen out, and in August 1976 Chirac resigned. In 1977 he ran for mayor of Paris against Giscard's candidate and made the city his fief. Strengthened by this victory, he thought that the RPR plurality won in the 1978 parliamentary elections should give the party a major voice in the cabinet and the government's decisions. Giscard did not see it that way.

In late 1978, preparing for the first European elections to be held by popular vote, Chirac once more let himself be influenced by his familiar demons Pierre Juillet and Marie-France Garaud. Their hold on him was the despair of the rest of his entourage. In Juillet and Garaud a Gaullist nationalism bordering on caricature, mixed with deep contempt for modern society and reformist temptations, blended together with a tactical sense capable of both amazing coups and incredible blunders. Scornfully domineering, they had maneuvered Chirac since his days as a young state secretary. Once when he expressed his gratitude for their aid, Juillet remarked, "This is the first time a horse has praised its jockey."

The RPR appeal for the European elections, drafted by Juillet but signed by Chirac and issued in his name, said yes to Europe, but no to "a vassal France in an empire of merchants. . . . As always when France is about to abase herself, the party supporting foreigners is at work with its calm and reassuring voice. Frenchmen, do not heed it." This mixture of Napoleonic war propaganda and bombastic Gaullism of the worst period struck an entirely false note. The RPR was criticizing the economic policy and European vision of a government it claimed to support and alienating public opinion where it thought to attract it. The proof was its score in the June 1979 European elections: 16.25 percent, at bottom—behind the PCF (in its last hurrah at 20.57 percent), the PS (23.57 percent), and the UDF ticket (27.55 percent).

Breaking with Juillet-Garaud after the disaster of 1979, Chirac began to explore non-Gaullist free enterprise ideas. But the shadow of the "infernal couple" still hung over him. Who was this man, wondered an uneasy public, this leader so energetically decisive and so undecided, so prompt to charge in an uncertain direction, so charismatic (for his own flock) and so easily manipulated by his counselors? Did he have any fixed ideas, or only fixed ambitions?

Chirac's problem in March 1986 was thus the double dilemma of time and program. He had a maximum of twenty-five months before him to establish a record that would banish abiding doubts on his constancy and character. His government faced not only the unknowns of cohabitation with a Socialist president determined to maintain his prerogatives but also the problems of a coalition in which his RPR had 145 deputies and the UDF 129. The coalition, which included some other conservative deputies, was soldered together by the slim majority of 2. The rivalries between the leaders of the RPR and the young Turks of the UDF, most vociferous champions of the new *libéralisme,* were, however, barely hidden.

The Dynamics of Cohabitation

Cohabitation had always been understood as a transition, an interval before the next presidential election. Still, there was much debate about the length of the interval and fear that the strong presidential institutions of the Fifth Republic might be permanently affected by a period in which the president would take a backseat to the prime minister. The drafters of the constitution of 1958 had provided for a strong president, able to reinforce the powers of the prime minister, his nominee, on the assumption that the National Assembly would continue to be dominated by the multiple and shifting party alliances of the Third and Fourth Republics. In fact, de Gaulle had enjoyed a de facto majority in 1958–1962; thereafter all presidents had controlled an assembly majority and had increased their powers. Now the question was whether practice could elucidate a potential problem left unmentioned in the constitution: Would the president be able to block the new majority, and if so, would he have to be forced from office, incurring a dangerous precedent like that with MacMahon in 1877–1879? Or would the prime minister so whittle down a presidential power more customary than statutory that the office would be permanently altered?[13]

Although these were serious and important questions, events conspired to make them less relevant than they seemed to observers in 1986. Cohabitation did go to term, presidential powers suffered no lasting damage, and Mitterrand's reelection in 1988 revived the familiar pattern of a strong president who can dissolve an inconvenient assembly to seek a better one. Yet the institutions of the Fifth Republic might have suffered some of the damage needlessly feared if Mitterrand, the master of maneuver, had not protected both his political fortunes and his office so well. The second cohabitation in 1993–1995, with a president who was very ill and in any case a lame duck, was very different, yet in many ways determined by the precedents of the first cohabitation. In retrospect, the struggles of this first cohabitation appear as a shadow play, where no blood is sought or drawn, but where the most skillful actor wins the prize.

One major uncertainty soon disappeared, as it became evident that neither the president nor the prime minister had any interest in hastening the presidential election. The country liked the idea of cohabitation—at least for a while—and might punish the author of a sudden and partisan rupture. As Balladur put it: "It's the opposite of a Western—the one who draws first is dead." Chirac needed to establish a record. Mitterrand was intent on reworking his image to become a father figure who would smile on what was done well, meanwhile reproving mistakes. Cohabitation was defined by their several needs, reciprocal yet antagonistic. It was less a struggle for power—the constitution clearly gave that to the prime minister—than for the semblance of power. Mitterrand could not permit himself to be humiliated and had to continue to be conspicuous in the determination of foreign policy, even though its diplomatic and economic machinery was controlled by Chirac. Above all, Mitterrand needed to embody the supreme political-moral authority in France. If he lost that, he would be seen only as an aging man, feebly remonstrating from his gilded palace against the actions of his vigorous and decisive juniors.

Mitterrand's interest was thus to let the country believe that it was governed by a dyarchy, sometimes concordant, sometimes discordant, where one power could check the other. Chirac stood to lose at this game, but lacking sufficient popularity to win an immediate presidential election, he was obliged to go on playing it to the end.

In this curious period Chirac's UDF allies, the Socialist party, and indeed the National Assembly itself were pushed to the sidelines. Chirac's small majority, need for discipline, and lack of time obliged him to enact his program as rapidly as possible—by decree where he could or, often, by legislative choke-off. (The notorious Article 49:3 of the constitution permits a government to force the assembly to choose between a negative confidence vote and automatic passage of a bill.) In 1981–1986 the deputies had found themselves merely the foot soldiers of their commander in the Elysée, as so often before in the Fifth Republic. In 1986–1988 the National Assembly did not regain stature, as some had thought it might. Instead it was commanded by a different executive, the prime minister. Meanwhile, Mitterrand's Socialist party was upstaged by the president. It had to support him, and it could not get far ahead of him on pain of damaging its leader. In this waiting role its first priority was to maintain its unity and hope that as the new majority committed inevitable mistakes, the Socialists would look better.

The tone for mutual forbearance between president and prime minister was set in the first meeting after Mitterrand asked Chirac to try to form a government. The two men knew each other only slightly and disliked each other; each was convinced the other was an unprincipled opportunist. Mitterrand had already made clear in a television interview in early March that he would resign rather than yield his essential functions. But Mitterrand knew that whatever was still Gaullist about Chirac forbade him to strip the president of his powers in defense and foreign affairs, and he could surmise that Chirac had no interest in a speedy election. In their first conversation, Mitterrand posed three conditions: that the new government not seek to humiliate the president, that it not seek to reestablish the death penalty, and that the president's right to participate in decisions on defense and foreign affairs be respected. In return he agreed to sign the laws passed by the new majority in the National Assembly (which he had no authority to veto).

Balladur and Chirac had drawn up a sort of contract of cohabitation, which stated that the new government intended to promulgate laws by decree (which would be ratified later by the assembly). Mitterrand refused to sign this contract and thus tie his hands. Chirac, however, made a somewhat amended version public that evening; he may not have expected any great problems with the president on signing decrees—on which the constitution was ambiguous—not specifying whether the president was or was not obliged to sign them. Three years later, Balladur regretted that Chirac had not insisted that Mitterrand sign this contract and had not threatened a crisis if he refused.[14]

Mitterrand also made it clear that he wanted a veto power on the designation of the foreign and defense ministers, so that those chosen would be persons he could work with in confidence. This led to a comedy act in which Mitterrand vetoed his old rival Jean Lecanuet, president of the UDF, as a potential foreign minister and the ambitious young PR chief François Léotard, who aspired to be defense minister. It is unlikely that Chirac much wanted either—both were UDF leaders who might cross him. The government that was announced four days after the election was a nearly even balance of RPR and UDF personalities. As foreign minister Chirac chose Jean-Bernard Raimond, previously Mitterrand's ambassador to Moscow. Defense Minister André Giraud, a senior technician who had been industry minister under Giscard, was also uncontroversial. The most important minister (the only one with the honorific title *ministre d'Etat*) was Balladur, Chirac's gray eminence since 1980, after the RPR leader broke with the Mephistophelean Pierre Juillet.

Another important figure in the new government was Interior Minister Charles Pasqua. Born in 1927, the son of a Corsican policeman, Pasqua was a teen-aged member of the Resistance in his native Alpes-Maritimes. From this experience he drew a taste for action and clandestinity and an unshakable loyalty to Gaullism. He had an important role in the Services d'Action Civique (SAC), the Gaullist security squads of dubious memory, dissolved in 1981 after one group murdered a renegade and his whole family. Pasqua was a prime organizer of the June 1968 march up the Champs-Elysées opposing the May disorders, which drew half a million people into the streets in support of de Gaulle; he proudly displays a painting of it on his office wall. Twice in the cohabitation period Pasqua would urge a repetition of this populist rallying technique. Together with his junior minister for public security, Robert Pandraud, a civil servant with years of experience directing the police, Pasqua intended to reassure a nervous France (and the voters of the National Front) by playing the tough cop.

The justice minister was Albin Chalandon, civil servant, banker, ex-minister, ex-head of the oil firm Elf-Aquitaine. René Monory, another ex-minister, received the education portfolio. The young Turks of *"la Chiraquie"* entered the government: Philippe Séguin, an able, ambitious young left-Gaullist, had the difficult Ministry for Social Affairs and Employment. As junior ministers, Alain Juppé, with the budget, Michel Noir, foreign trade, and Camille Cabanna, privatization, were supervised and sometimes smothered by their chief, Edouard Balladur.

The UDF leaders, with François Léotard's friends *(la bande à Léo),* had lesser jobs. Léotard had to content himself with the Ministry for Culture and Communication, his friend Alain Madelin was industry minister, and their associates Jacques Douffiagues and Gérard Longuet junior ministers for public works and transport, and the post office and telecommunications. These men, mostly in their early forties, were the most enthusiastic and noisy advocates of free enterprise *libéralisme* in the government, as opposed to Balladur or even Chirac, graduates of the school of Pompidolian *dirigisme.* The most prominent Barre supporter in the cabinet was Pierre Méhaignerie, president of the Centre des Démocrates Sociaux, who consented to take the technical Ministry of Public Works, Housing, and Regional Development. There were no women among the senior ministers, but one was a junior minister and three were state secretaries. Valéry Giscard d'Estaing would have been willing to return to his old post as minister of the economy but was not offered the job, and Chirac looked past him to patch up a quarrel with another old enemy, Jacques Chaban-Delmas, by backing him as president of the new National Assembly. Raymond Barre remained ostentatiously out of the government of cohabitation that he had denounced as a mistake.

The government's program was to free the economy by privatizing nationalized industry—both that taken over in 1982 and also those industries nationalized in 1945 by General de Gaulle's government. The government would bring back the old system of majority voting, free up prices, and lower taxes, attempt to cut unemployment, and balance the social security system. Tougher measures against crime and terrorism were promised, as well as a law to make it harder for young foreigners born in France (mostly North Africans) to become citizens automatically. Before the new government was a week old, Mitterrand declared that he would not sign a decree abolishing restrictions on firing workers. He followed that with a message to the new assembly on April 8 declaring that he would not automatically sign decrees *(ordonnances)* set before him; they must be few in number and their purpose so clearly explained by enabling legislation that the parliament and Constitutional Council could judge them.

A government in a hurry needed decrees to save both time and potential stress within its small majority. Chirac needed to impress the country with the verve and rhythm of his new government. The president, however, intended to stand as the champion of measured procedure against rashness, haste, and retrograde legislation. To emphasize that he was a guardian of, not a participant in, the new government, he forbade his own staff to sit in on interministerial meetings (where Chirac did not want them anyway) with the exception of defense and foreign affairs.

The question of just how much authority the president would retain in foreign affairs arose immediately. When in early April 1986 the U.S. government requested permission to overfly France to bomb Tripoli, by common consultation and agreement both Chirac and Mitterrand refused. Afterwards, when Chirac claimed that the president had concurred with his decision to refuse, presenting himself as the principal personage in this joint decision, Mitterrand was furious.[15]

Chirac wanted to represent France alone at the Tokyo G-7 summit in early May 1986, arguing that the economic and monetary decisions to be discussed there were in the prime minister's domain, not the president's. Naturally, Mitterrand refused, but Chirac's decision to accompany Mitterrand to the Tokyo economic summit completely upset the protocol-sensitive Japanese. Unused to roosters with two heads, Gallic or otherwise, they could find no way to seat Chirac at the opening banquet for chiefs of delegations. The efforts of Chirac's staff to exert influence on a meeting already almost completely prepared merely confused diplomatic contacts, while Chirac's explanation to Prime Minister Nakasone that the French president henceforth had a merely ceremonial role in foreign affairs was promptly leaked to the press and had to be denied.[16]

This preliminary skirmishing on the domestic and diplomatic fronts set the tone for the months to follow. Mitterrand declared on May 18 that his duty was "to permit the majority elected by the people to govern," but also "to intervene each time that a decision might harm the unity of Frenchmen, appear unjust or exclude . . . part of the French people." Following this logic, the president refused to sign *ordonnances* on the privatization of sixty-five industries, banks, and insurance companies, on a new electoral law, and on new regulations on working hours, forcing Chirac to push bills for these measures through the National Assembly. The government thus did not save time on these and other matters that Mitterrand refused to approve, and risked seeming to move more rapidly than carefully. The president also did not hesitate to make plain his disapproval of some ordinary bills presented to the National Assembly, such as the law on dismissals and a new statute for New Caledonia.

In other legislation, the government repealed the surtax on large fortunes and enacted an amnesty to repatriate funds that had illegally left the country in the days when the Socialo-Communist menace had panicked some of the rich. Both of these measures were unpopular; they also gave the new Socialist opposition an opportunity to cry that the Right was repaying its paymasters. The result of the government's haste and the president's skillful maneuvering was that by October 1986 Mitterrand's popularity had soared to 61 percent.[17]

The government's privatization law of August 6, 1986, provided for changes over a five-year period in the status of eleven industrial groups, three giant insurance companies, and fifty-one banks. After the partial conversion of the oil company Elf-Aquitaine to the private sector, a campaign designed to create a popular mass capitalism on the Thatcher model opened in late November 1986 with the privatization of the glass and plastics giant Saint-Gobain. This operation was heavily oversubscribed. Economy and Finance Minister Balladur was encouraged to move rapidly toward twelve other privatizations in 1987, involving 6 million stockholders—until the stock market crash of October 1987 brought a temporary halt. In this process the government privatized two giant investment banks taken over in 1982, Paribas and Suez, and a major deposit bank, the Société Générale, which had been in the public sector since 1945. After the first tremors of the crash had passed, the government also privatized the munitions firm Matra in January 1988, but then paused to await the elections. Six of the major industrial groups taken over in 1982 remained in the public sector at the time of Mitterrand's reelection.

As a means of defending major industries or banks against raiders, Balladur built a regulation into the privatization scheme stipulating that selected purchasers would in exchange for a fixed price for stocks obligate themselves to keep the stock purchased for two years and sell in the three following years only with the approval of the board of directors. These so-called stable blocs of holdings, or *noyaux durs,* made up 25 to 30 percent of the total capital. Balladur selected the core shareholders, companies and individuals who were in many cases close to the RPR. This operation was severely criticized, not only by the Socialists, but also by Raymond Barre. The *noyaux durs* controversy and the relative loss of confidence in popular capitalism consequent to the 1987 market crash considerably dampened the political usefulness of Balladur's privatizations.[18]

The president had refused to sign a privatization decree, but the Socialists were unwilling to defend their nationalizations to the last trench. In April 1988 Mitterrand declared on television that he would proceed to no new privatizations before 1992 and suggested that he would do nothing to renationalize companies. Bérégovoy's preference lay with a state sector able to raise capital by issuing blocks of nonvoting stock, the tactic he had used with some small companies in 1985. He thought the state should be able to create new companies, if its intervention is needed, but also be free to sell off companies.[19]

The first privatizations went off well and were very popular, bringing in millions of new, small stockholders. But unemployment continued to rise, and in August 1986 Social Affairs Minister Séguin frankly admitted that France would have to accustom itself to at least 2.5 million unemployed for a long time.[20] The need to alleviate an unemployment characterized by long duration and less and less softened by insurance became plain to all. But as all parties realized that no measures would shrink unemployment quickly, politicians became more and more wary of talking about it; the 1988 presidential campaign heard none of the promises to cure joblessness that had resounded in 1981 and even (to a much lesser extent) in 1986.

Chirac and his interior minister Charles Pasqua intended to show they could do much better than the Socialists (and win over voters from the National Front) by showing themselves the determined enemies of illegal immigration, crime, and terrorism. Bombs had continued to go off in Paris and elsewhere—beginning in March just as Chirac was named prime minister. In the first two weeks of September 1986, after terrorist bombs bloodied Paris, the government imposed visas for all foreigners except nationals of the European Community and Switzerland and ordered soldiers to patrol the frontier. The police were again authorized to check identity documents at will and multiplied their efforts. One hundred and one illegal Malian immigrants were demonstratively flown home on a government chartered aircraft. Despite the terrorist carnage, the government continued to benefit from greater approval on the topic of internal security than on any other question.[21]

The Chirac government's first serious setback came from an unexpected but familiar quarter: lycée and university students. Junior Minister for University Affairs Alain Devaquet had worked out what seemed a moderate reform for a pressing problem. The French university system is obliged to accept all students who pass the baccalaureate examination, a number enormously swollen in the past forty years. The establishment of new universities in the past generation has not sufficed to control this problem; classes are overcrowded and the prestige of a university education has fallen. Devaquet's law would have permitted each university to set its own admission quotas for the different faculties. In addition, each university would have handed out its own diploma and not a uniform document issued by the state. Registration fees (French universities are free) would have been set at 450 to 900 francs.

The government thought that opposition to the bill might come from its own right wing in parliament, but not from the students. It was therefore taken by surprise in late November when, after the Fédération d'Education Nationale and the PS called for a demonstration against the project, more than 100,000 students gathered at the place de la Bastille to denounce the law. Four days later, after coordination committees had sprung up at most universities and many provincial lycées, another sea of students took to the streets—200,000 in Paris, 300,000 in the provincial cities—far more than the mostly amateur organizers had expected.

The students were neither violent nor particularly angry. They were, however, frightened by a badly explained education bill that they feared would limit their access to universities, force them into undesired career choices, and devalue diplomas issued by the less prestigious universities. Some also feared that the registration fees, minor in themselves, were the thin edge of the wedge for tuition charges.

Unrest continued, with another monster rally on December 4 that saw more than 500,000 students in the streets. The government wavered, and the younger UDF and RPR ministers, horrified at the idea of losing a generation hitherto rather favorable to *libéralisme,* demanded that Chirac withdraw the bill. Chirac did not want to disclaim Education Minister Monory (Devaquet's chief) and the only major CDS politician who backed him rather than Barre for president), and Monory stubbornly refused to retreat. Chirac, remembering May 1968, feared that if he withdrew the bill, he would seem to be taking orders from the street. Interior Minister Pasqua was at first flexible, then shifted to toughness and advocated a countermarch of RPR partisans, à la 1968. On the night of December 5, after disorders of unclear origin, Pasqua's police took their truncheons to a young Algerian-French student with weak kidneys who died of the beating. The government had to back down in disarray, while Mitterrand hastened to visit the dead boy's family.

The student troubles at the end of 1986 broke the momentum of the Chirac government. The prime minister had shown himself imperceptive and irresolute while the dissension within his government was widely reported, then brutally resolute, and finally compelled to give in. Mitterrand, meanwhile, had appeared as the high guarantor of calm and measure.[22]

Troubles did not come singly. In December there were wildcat strikes by railroad workers and by personnel of the Paris metro and suburban railroad. France was briefly paralyzed, in a winter of extreme cold. Chirac felt obliged to cancel a special January session of the National Assembly and postpone controversial measures. A bill on restriction of automatic naturalization (principally aimed at young North Africans) was deferred until a blue-ribbon commission could mull it over; it was finally postponed until after the next election. Unemployment continued to increase, and the government's handling of social affairs was judged ineffective.

Generally approved by a bare majority of the people when it took office, the Chirac government's popularity had risen, with momentary dips, until the disaster of the November education crisis and the strikes. Thereafter it skidded, diminishing throughout 1987.[23] However, the departure of the Socialists was still not much regretted, and in February 1987, after the student troubles, only 31 percent of SOFRES respondents wanted the Socialists to return to power as rapidly as possible.[24] The voters thus seemed to be in the process of withdrawing the credit they had tentatively advanced to the Right, yet unready to give it again to the Left. In this state of indecision and disillusion, a majority of the people and even half the Socialist supporters thought there were few basic differences between the PS and the parties of the Right.[25] Ideologies were at a discount, and the weight of the personalities of rival candidates for the presidency became increasingly decisive.

Toward the Presidential Election

Jacques Chirac had hoped that his record as prime minister would efface the doubts about his character and judgment disturbing many of his compatriots. He had known from the beginning that Mitterrand would be spared the unpopularity that accompanies responsibility and would seek to rebuild his own prestige at his prime minister's expense. But the president had turned seventy in 1986. He might or might not seek reelection, and if he did not, the Socialist party had no popular choice to succeed him. In the meantime, Chirac had to worry about Raymond Barre, the rival in his own camp.

Barre's standing in the polls suffered during most of 1986 from his opposition to cohabitation. But by early 1987 both supporters of the RPR-UDF and voters at large consistently began telling pollsters that they thought Barre the best candidate of the Right in 1988.[26] Barre's strength lay in his air of assurance and the popular confidence in him as the best man to assure economic growth. Against the energetic but erratic Chirac, he was Mr. "Slow and steady wins the race," and he dubbed himself "the tortoise."

Barre had always disdained organizational politics and the little world of politicians, which he scornfully termed "the microcosm." His friends had, however, built up a network of Barrist committees all over France. He enjoyed the particular support of the CDS leaders, whereas the young leaders of the Parti Républicain eyed him with mistrust but admitted that they would have to back him. His relations with his original patron, ex-president Giscard, were correct but distinctly cool. But Giscard remained unpopular and had lost his grip on the levers of party machinery in his old Parti Républicain.

Would Mitterrand be a candidate again in 1988? His popularity had plunged to its nadir in late 1984–1985; in January 1985 only a third of poll respondents considered the balance sheet of his administration to be positive, and his unpopularity diminished very slowly in the course of 1985.[27] At the PS congress in Toulouse in October 1985 the general tone was defensive—few thought the president could do more than hold out through the hard times of cohabitation to come. If the PS could eke out a respectable score in 1986, Mitterrand would not be forced from office and the PS could avoid the round of recriminations and the bitter power struggle that would almost certainly accompany total defeat. The most plausible PS candidate in 1988 was thought to be Rocard or perhaps Fabius.[28]

Mitterrand's performance in rallying his party in the 1986 elections and his consistently skillful conduct of cohabitation changed all that. As early as June 1986 a poll showed that 47 percent of voters and 74 percent of Socialist voters wanted him to run again in 1988.[29] When a Socialist party congress met in Lille in April 1987 to prepare the 1988 elections, there was no discussion of Mitterrand's candidacy, precisely because almost all the Socialist leaders were convinced that he would run again. Michel Rocard continued to insist that he too would run for president, but he was now felt to be more an alternative than a real rival to Mitterrand.[30]

The president's popularity as the great cohabiter held steady throughout 1987, reaching the heights attained in early 1982 before disappointment had set in. His opponents took comfort, however, from polls reflecting doubts about his earlier record and on the wisdom of choosing him for another seven years. Nevertheless, polls after June 1986 consistently showed that Mitterrand would defeat either Chirac or Barre in the second round in 1988. Chirac and Barre partisans could only hope that the popularity of the president-arbiter would not transfer itself to the president-candidate once he finally declared himself. Mitterrand was in no hurry to declare. Lesser candidates, like the soporific André Lajoinie of the PCF or the able demagogue Jean-Marie Le Pen, needed a head start, announcing their candidacies in 1987. (A battered Georges Marchais grimly held on to power in the PCF but had no wish to head a ticket almost certain to see the worst score the party had ever had.) There were the usual minor candidacies, including an ecologist, Antoine Waechter, and a dissident Communist slate headed by former Politburo member Pierre Juquin—now backed by one of the Trotskyite groups. Chirac formally declared his candidacy in January, Barre in early February. Mitterrand delayed until March 22.

By this time all doubt about his decision had disappeared, but instead of anticlimax, he had achieved an effect of welcome confirmation. Mitterrand had no laundry list of new proposals to submit to the French this time. He ran as a candidate in whom the people could have confidence, and a poll in late March suggested that the frequent reproach of inconstancy had for a large majority yielded to admiration for his ability to adapt to changing situations.[31] Although he did not renounce his past as a Socialist, Mitterrand laid his major emphasis on reunifying the French and imbuing them with a sober determination to face the economic challenges of the 1990s and beyond, building a strong France in a more unified Europe.

Confidence was also Barre's stock in trade, and in some mysterious way as confidence in Mitterrand was confirmed, confidence in Barre ebbed away. The networks of *notables* he had set up throughout the country corresponded to an electoral technique that might have worked twenty or thirty years earlier but that was no longer effective in the television age, which revealed him as a wooden and uninspiring performer. A steady decline in his ratings set in after the new year began, unchecked by his formal declaration of candidacy. By March he was clearly far behind Chirac, whose ratings were rising. Without the formidable party machinery Chirac possessed in the RPR, and given only perfunctory support by the young leaders of the Parti Républicain who were already calculating the terms of an alliance with Chirac, Barre had no hope of emerging successfully from the first round.

The first round on April 24 confirmed Barre's collapse—a poor showing of only 16.53 percent. But Chirac had done badly as well. Generally credited in the polls until the end with around 23 percent, he ended with 19.95. The major surprise of the first round was Jean-Marie Le Pen's unexpected 14.38 percent—polls had credited him with 12 percent at the most. Mitterrand, with 34.11 percent, had run slightly behind polling predictions. The Communist party had its worst score in history: 6.76 percent.

Le Pen had clearly taken votes from all sides—many from the RPR, certainly, but also from voters reckoned in the Mitterrand column, and National Front strength was impressive in towns and industrial suburbs that the PCF had formerly dominated. Le Pen's strength increased in the cities of the Mediterranean littoral, where he had already shown himself strong. He had 28.34 percent in Marseilles, 25.92 percent in Nice, 27.04 percent in Toulon. His average vote in the ten biggest cities in France was 17.52 percent. He had made inroads into small towns, where there were few or no immigrants, and in the countryside. For once, Le Pen was taken at his self-estimate when he called his results "an earthquake."

Chirac knew that he could not expect to win in the second round unless all the Le Pen voters backed him, and he could not realistically hope to garner them all, or even all of Barre's. His campaign in the next two weeks was directed to narrowing the gap with Mitterrand—hoping perhaps for a miracle, but really attempting to maintain his position as leader of the Right after the election.

He evidently hoped that headline-grabbing actions overseas would help him. Pasqua's emissaries had been negotiating with Iran to free the remaining French hostages held in Lebanon well before the elections, and after several hitches they were released early in the week before the second round. Immediately thereafter, French gendarmes in New Caledonia stormed a cave on an outlying island where a commando of Kanak guerrillas were holding French hostages—the hostages were rescued, but two gendarmes and nineteen guerrillas were killed. (Mitterrand had signed off on this operation, however.) The next day, Paris announced that Captain Dominique Prieur—one of the two French intelligence officers caught by New Zealand in the *Rainbow Warrior* affair and sentenced to ten years imprisonment—would be flown back to Paris. Chirac had negotiated an agreement with New Zealand to commute the sentences of the two officers to three years on a remote French Pacific island. Prieur's partner, Major Mafart, had already been brought back to France because of illness (not severe enough to keep him from taking a course at the Ecole de Guerre); and Captain Prieur was expecting a baby (her husband had joined her on the island—reportedly with a strong hint from Chirac that he would do well to get his wife pregnant).[32]

The release of the hostages was popular, but Chirac (or Pasqua) had probably overdone the sensational action. Desire among swing voters to vote against an RPR apparently ready to make deals with Le Pen played a large role in second-round reactions (especially after Pasqua was quoted as saying that the values of the National Front did not differ from those of the RPR). In any event, Chirac's score in the second round on May 8 was only 45.98 percent, against a triumphant 54.02 percent for Mitterrand. Exit polls showed that the president had won almost all of the Communist and other extreme leftist vote, four-fifths of the ecologists, 22 percent of Le Pen voters, and 13 percent of Barre's.[33]

6

Mitterrand II

The Rocard Ministry

Mitterrand's victory had been expected. What Mitterrand might do with that victory remained unclear. He had been elected as a unifier, favored over Chirac because the traditional Left electorate retained confidence in him and a significant portion of the center-right voters preferred him to Chirac, a man of many contradictory policies and no clear core identity. But Mitterrand had run on the slogan "France Unified" and a deliberately vague policy of *ouverture*—"opening." At a minimum, it meant there would be no return to the policies of 1981–1983. In 1988 Mitterrand intended to continue the role he had assumed during cohabitation, the guarantor of social justice.

In the "Lettre à tous les Français," which he sent out in millions of copies in early April 1988, Mitterrand offered a very modest proposal, nothing like the platform he had run on in 1981, the "110 proposals." There were no major social reforms. Instead he aimed at maintaining and preserving social security and adjusting the minimum wage. He also proposed a new minimum revenue payment for the "new poor," those not covered by any other social measures.[1]

In theory, this position left much room for agreement with the Centrists in the CDS and with some other Barre supporters. The Chirac government had changed the election law back to the "first past the post" system obtaining before 1985. Thus a Socialist party that might not have a majority in the country presumably needed a coalition partner. The question was the terms on which these partners might be available. Months before the election, Mitterrand had been dropping hints to the Centrists that a coalition might be possible.[2]

The Right still had a majority in the National Assembly, but Chirac had declared that he would resign if defeated. Mitterrand's choice of prime ministers was limited: He needed someone who shared his general outlook and who could symbolize the idea of *ouverture*. Renaming Fabius would look like the mixture as before; Delors was needed in Brussels. Pierre Bérégovoy was now well seen by the business community, and the Socialist party's economic ideas now largely coincided with Rocard's, although many doubters remained. These men were the obvious candidates. Rocard was more popular and a better politician, whereas Bérégovoy would be seen as too close to the president to provide the shielding effect traditionally attached to the prime ministerial office.

The president's relations with the man he would choose as his third Socialist prime minister had long been strained. Rocard had his own following, some of it people who had followed him from the PSU, some from the CFDT, the formerly Catholic trade union, some new adherents who from the first had found Rocard's views on economics more realistic than the Common Program. Mitterrand had been suspicious of Rocard and his people since they were brought into the PS in 1974. He remembered too well how he and his own small group had taken over the PS from outside, and he feared a reprise. Gilles Martinet, one of Rocard's friends, recalled Mitterrand's sharp remark to him in the mid-1970s, "Remember, Martinet, this party is not for the taking—it has been taken."[3]

In 1981, Rocard was given the Ministry for the Plan and the prestigious title of minister of state, but no real responsibilities or funding, then in March 1983 the Agriculture Ministry, where he did well. By 1984, he and Delors—the naysayers of 1981—were the only popular Socialist politicians. In April 1985 Rocard surprised Mitterrand by resigning from the government, allegedly because he disapproved of the new election law on proportional representation, but no doubt also to give himself more freedom for another try at the presidency.

By early 1987, it seemed probable that Mitterrand would run again. In February, he invited his old rival to the Elysée and, telling him that he had not yet decided, suggested that as the only alternate Socialist who could win, Rocard begin campaigning. Mitterrand may or may not have already decided whether to run again; he appears in any case to have been intent on making peace with Rocard. In December 1987 he summoned Rocard again to tell him he had decided to run, and dangled the prime minister's office before him—warning, however, that he had not made a final choice.[4]

The day after his election, Mitterrand still had not revealed his intentions to Rocard. He reportedly told Bérégovoy, who still nourished a tiny scrap of hope that the nod would go to him: "We have to get over the Rocard problem. People would not understand it if he doesn't get his chance. It's his turn."[5] Late on the next afternoon, after Chirac had formally submitted his resignation, Rocard's appointment was finally announced.[6]

The nomination was well received (with some grumbling from the left wing of the PS), but cabinet appointments led to a controversy that immediately laid bare the ambiguities attached to *ouverture*. The Rocard government would be seventy-five votes short of a majority in the National Assembly. If Rocard's new government was to be a coalition, it would depend on the acquiescence of the UDF—or more precisely, the Centrists of the CDS, the UDF component most disposed to cooperate.

Mitterrand was convinced that if he did not dissolve the assembly quickly, the momentum of the presidential election would be lost.

Rocard immediately met with three top leaders of the CDS, Pierre Méhaignerie, Jacques Barrot, and Bernard Stasi. They knew already that Mitterrand intended to dissolve the assembly but hoped for a new decision from Rocard. Méhaignerie proposed a possible contract for governing, envisioning a Centrist group of forty to sixty deputies—which implied reintroduction of proportional representation. But the Centrists feared to lose their seats in a rapid election and insisted on nondissolution. Rocard had already agreed with Mitterrand that dissolution was entirely necessary, and he himself opposed proportional representation. He had hoped to work out an arrangement whereby the Centrists would run on their own account, with programs more or less parallel to his, not criticize the government too much, and afterwards rally in a formal coalition. Mitterrand vetoed this idea, saying that the only acceptable coalition basis was the rally by individual Centrists. He no doubt knew by then that a number of individuals would indeed rally.[7]

It is clear in retrospect that there was no chance for a real coalition. Had Mitterrand then launched the idea of *ouverture* purely as an electoral gimmick to garner votes, as the Rocard group later concluded? Not necessarily. For the Centrist Bernard Stasi, the decisive factor in Mitterrand's behavior was his 54 percent majority in the presidential election (and, probably, the polls that then suggested a large Socialist majority in case of new legislative elections).[8] Had Mitterrand won with a slight majority and feared to dissolve, he might well have pursued the idea of a coalition.

Valéry Giscard d'Estaing, visibly pleased by the defeat of his two former prime ministers and rivals, smoothly argued for "constructive opposition." Mitterrand instead signed up leading non-Socialist politicians to enter the government on an individual basis. Three former ministers under Giscard, who were not personalities of the first rank, accepted portfolios in the new government. So did a leading nonparty industrialist and a senior magistrate, who became ministers of industry and justice. But the nomination of thirteen ministers from the Fabius government (seven in their old ministries, including Bérégovoy, Dumas, Joxe, Lang, Michel Delebarre, with Chevènement at Defense), delineated a government dominated by Socialists. Lionel Jospin became minister for education, with the rank of minister of state.

Although 40 percent of the new ministers were not PS members, the opposition immediately charged that Mitterrand (who had handpicked them) had produced a false opening and a real Socialist hegemony, using the same old people. This accusation was hardly disinterested. Giscard desired to retake the leadership of the Center, and he needed to hold on to the largely Catholic CDS. The CDS in turn was restless under the UDF tent in close proximity to a domineering and insistently free enterprise Parti Républicain, and tempted by the notion of a real Center party that might exercise the pivot role played by the Free Democratic party in West Germany. Raymond Barre, little damaged by defeat because Chirac had also done poorly, looked on benevolently and did not discourage Centrists who consulted him about entering the Rocard government. Meanwhile Giscard discouraged his party friends (notably Simone Veil) from entering the new government.

On May 14 the president announced that he was dissolving the assembly and called for elections to take place on June 5 and 12. Believing that it would have a large majority, the Socialist party offered (on presidential instructions) to support the candidacies of non-Socialist ministers as well as other prominent non-Socialists. The maneuver did not sit well among PS militants, as always unhappy at the idea of leaving cherished positions to outsiders who had been political opponents.

On the evening before Mitterrand dissolved the assembly, the now merged Mitterrand-Mauroy factions of the Socialist party (the other factions having withdrawn) met to choose a new first secretary. Lionel Jospin had announced several months earlier that he wished to leave the post. The declared candidate was former prime minister Laurent Fabius, who had the president's all but explicit support.

Many Socialists disliked this gifted but overly smooth young man who had skated too easily and too fast from the left to the right wing of the party. Having lost a fight with Jospin in 1985 over preeminence in the 1986 parliamentary election campaign, Fabius had decided that to position himself as a future presidential candidate he needed first to strengthen his position inside the party, then head it. He devoted the fallow years from 1986 to 1988 to making the rounds of the local party federations and cultivating their leaders. With the president's backing for the vacant first secretary's job, Fabius apparently thought he was a shoo-in.

Mitterrand saw a PS with Fabius controlling the party apparatus as a check on Rocard, telling the younger man just before the election, "If I name Rocard to Matignon, the condition sine qua non is that you direct the party."[9] But Fabius as first secretary prefigured Fabius the ambitious presidential candidate, and many PS leaders were unwilling to see this issue strongly influenced seven years before the next election. The powerful, usually ultra-loyal Mitterrandist Henri Emmanuelli encouraged Mauroy to contest the candidacy. (Mitterrand wanted Mauroy to become president of the National Assembly; Mauroy was lukewarm.)

Jospin had made it clear that he disliked the idea of Fabius as his successor but had initially refused to organize the opposition to him. In the caucus Jospin now told the PS leaders that the president took no position on candidacies, having determined "to cut the umbilical cord" with the party. That was immediately denied by Bérégovoy, who had spoken with Mitterrand that morning. Jospin cut him off, saying no one there was authorized to be the president's spokesman. Mauroy spoke of the need for a first secretary who would not make the party the machine for his own (presidential) ambitions. Mauroy was elected by a respectable majority including Mitterrand intimates Claude Estier, Louis Mermaz, and Roland Dumas.

By advancing his young protégé, Mitterrand had inadvertently opened a succession crisis within the week of his reelection. The PS had been Mitterrand's electoral machine in 1981, and the party had been obliged to follow him through the bad years after he and it lost popularity and through the trials of cohabitation. At the beginning of a new term, the Socialists wished to show independence, especially those who were upset by the president's encouragement of an opening to the Right.

On May 22 (when the most recent poll suggested a "pink wave"—a large PS majority) Mitterrand told reporters that too large a Socialist majority would not be healthy. Some commentators have supposed that he was deliberately trying to hurt the fortunes of a party that had slipped out of his control. It is more likely that he wished to keep open aspects of *ouverture* in the face of a PS that was showing itself restive—and Mitterrand probably expected at least a comfortable majority.[10]

The Socialists fought the campaign on the theme of "support the president," and used the threat of possible alliances between the Right and the National Front as a bugaboo. The Right campaigned largely on local themes. The result was to emphasize the strength of local notables both of the Left and Right. Abstention was at record highs in both rounds—34.26 percent in the first round and 30.05 in the second. After the first round it was clear that the pink wave predicted by pollsters had failed to materialize, but fresh polls predicted a small but comfortable Socialist majority.

A number of non-Socialist ministers and even PS figures (including two close collaborators of the president) were defeated in the first round. "Parachuted" into unfamiliar constituencies, none of them had much opportunity to court their new voters. Some were outpolled in the first round by Communists. A PCF taken for dead after the disaster of Lajoinie's 6.76 percent showed that it still had drawing power in selected constituencies, polling 11.32 percent. In contrast, the National Front ticket had not done nearly so well as Le Pen's presidential candidacy—9.65 percent against 14.43 on April 24.

A week later an extraordinarily close second round produced more surprises. The PS needed 289 seats for a bare majority; it won only 276. The Right had fewer seats than in 1986, the National Front had won only 1, and the Communists (backed by the PS in the second round where they had come in ahead in the first) had an unexpected 27 seats.

Exit polls did not explain the unprecedentedly high level of abstentions, but one poll did indicate the mixed motivation of an electorate that had produced this result. It found 56 percent of respondents saying that they did not wish to see a PS majority, and 59 percent who did not want an RPR/UDF majority. (Nevertheless, 63 percent had wanted to see a majority of some kind emerge from the vote.)[11]

In the ultimate irony of a presidential-legislative campaign billed as a move toward the center, the voters had produced a Socialist-Communist majority like the one feared in 1981. But nothing in the political landscape resembled 1981— Georges Marchais instantly announced that his party would not cooperate with the Socialists, and for Rocard and Mitterrand what was left of *ouverture* forbade all but small tactical deals with the PCF.

Mitterrand confirmed that Rocard would continue as prime minister and told the country that the constitution provided for just such contingencies as the present one, noting that a number of stable Western European democracies operated with coalition majorities. The second Rocard ministry, formed in late June, had twenty-six PS ministers, and three from the MRG. Fourteen others were "technicians" and six UDF. Twelve ministers were new. The PS executive bureau expressed "le trouble" of the Socialists on the entry of Barrist mayors of Metz and Auxerre, Jean-Marie Rausch and Jean-Pierre Soisson, into the government, and inclusion of other Centrist personalities formerly close to Giscard, now closer to Barre. Composite as it was, the Rocard government was not a real coalition; it was rather a Socialist government with non-Socialist participation.

The National Front had bitten deeply into the strength of the conventional Right, which was in disarray, suffering from the disappointed ambitions of too many leaders. The immediate effect of Mitterrand's precipitate dissolution of the National Assembly was to weld together a Right that was coming apart. Chirac intended to rise from his ashes to lead the Right; Giscard hoped to reform a more powerful UDF and outmaneuver Chirac. Neither had lost the ambition to be a presidential candidate again, and although public opinion polls showed neither one overwhelmingly popular, Chirac retained control over his party; Giscard was trying to control his, as Léotard yielded the presidency of the UDF in June 1988 to him.

Raymond Barre, still popular and respected, intended to remain in politics, or slightly above them, and become the godfather for Centrist forces. His relations with Mitterrand warmed once the elections were over. After the legislative elections CDS leader Pierre Méhaignerie, proud of his party's fifty seats, announced the formation of a parliamentary group independent from the UDF called the Union Démocratique du Centre (UDC). The UDC, nevertheless, remained affiliated with the UDF and gradually moved back toward it as Socialist fortunes fell. No one in 1988 would have dared to predict that five years later the Right would have more than 450 deputies in the National Assembly.

Victory for What?

The kind of government Mitterrand proposed and the policies the Rocard government expected to follow had been presented only in general terms. The ideologically tinted programs of 1981 were ancient history, and the declaration of general policy made by Rocard at the end of June 1988 was deliberately down to earth and modest.[12]

What remained of PS ideology? The party's own statement was contained in a program agreed on in January 1988, designed to be concordant with but separate from the personal platform that Mitterrand would publish. It attempted to retain a distinctively Socialist identity while taking account of what the Socialists had learned in 1981–1986. Thus the utility of public ownership was affirmed and *libéralisme* decried, but the program did not call for renationalization of privatized industries. (Mitterrand came out for a policy of no new nationalizations, no privatizations, soon baptized "ni-ni," or neither-nor.)

"The state neither can do everything nor should it," said the program. "Transformations can work only at the rhythm by which citizens become aware of their necessity and legitimacy. . . . A parliamentary majority can translate options into law, but for them to become deeds, in a complex society, minorities must accept them."[13] The PS had come a long way from the *rupture* of 1981.

Despite that, the Socialists still felt uncomfortable if they defined a strategy that excluded the Communists—and included the Center.[14] Mitterrand had to take account of this. Two years later, a poll conducted at the Socialist party congress indicated that 81 percent of the party cadres questioned wanted the party to try to reassemble the Left rather than opening to the center (supported by only 14 percent). Only 33 percent of those cadres favoring Rocard wanted the center opening. Furthermore, whereas 51 percent of Rocardians favored further individual entries into the government by people coming from the Right, only 17 percent of Mitterrandists liked the idea.[15]

When Mitterrand named Rocard as prime minister, gossip in Paris immediately supposed that the job was a poisoned gift, which would speedily destroy Rocard and make way for a more favored Mitterrand follower. A good deal of subsequent evidence suggests that Mitterrand did not expect Rocard to be a great success, and that he would have been quite content to dismiss him in two years or less.[16] The economic prognostications of early 1988 were gloomy, and Mitterrand may well have expected that a slow economy would rapidly sap Rocard's popularity, leaving opportunities for a more desirable successor as the recession waned.

Rocard was instead aided by an economic uptick that lasted two years and complicated any such presidential intent. The Gulf crisis, which began in August 1990, precluded a change of prime ministers until after the threatening war had come and ended. But what overall domestic design, if any, did Mitterrand have for his new term, particularly for the five years in which his party had near control of the legislature? His priorities on European integration are clear, but one is obliged to conclude that the vague language of the "Lettre à tous les Français" reflected the president's vague thinking on domestic policies.

Rocard had a program, but not a very exciting one. In a famous phrase he spoke of his "duty to be boring" *(devoir de grisaille)* and, in another uninspiring image, of the need to "repair the elevators." He believed in government by consensus, without overly grand ambitions for reform. His critics, both in the Socialist party and on the Right, were to accuse him of immobilism, a disinclination to do anything bold or unpopular, in order to preserve his image for the presidential race in 1995. Very much the technocrat, Rocard has been a genuine believer in the cumulative effect of nonresounding reforms. In a 1996 interview he recalled that he had compared politics to tree farming—a long and patient labor. He admitted, however, in a 1993 TV interview, that he probably should have pushed reform faster and harder than he did.[17]

Rocard had had little leeway in naming his first government—Mitterrand, naturally, chose the ministers for foreign affairs, the economy, and the interior, and he wanted his old guard: Joxe, Poperen, Dumas, Mermaz—and Edith Cresson. Most of them had slight regard for Rocard, considering him a lightweight. Rocard had wanted some nonpolitical figures in his ministry. Here too he drew criticism. In the best Jacobin tradition Henri Emmanuelli said suspiciously: "There is here the beginning of an ideological drift, which, taken too far, could threaten the foundations of democracy. Where does civil society get its legitimacy? If it does not come from the voting booth, that could look like an attempt by the establishment to get its hands on the government."[18]

Rocard had more influence on the composition of his second government than on the first; after much criticism of the earlier list Mitterrand had decided there should be parity between Socialists and non-Socialists. After interfering a great deal with Mauroy's government, less with Fabius, and per force far less with Chirac's, Mitterrand did allow Rocard to govern.[19] But he also organized little whispering campaigns against Rocard—protecting and encouraging what the Rocard staff considered troublemakers, meanwhile smiling benevolently.

At the outset, Rocard had to face the near hostility of many of the PS leaders (whom the press had now baptized "the elephants"), many of whom were installed as ministers in his own government. His first crisis, successfully surmounted, came in an overseas French territory.

In January 1988 Chirac's minister for Overseas Territories Bernard Pons had introduced a statute according considerable autonomy to the territory of New Caledonia but renouncing the plan introduced by Fabius that gave the Melanesian majority representation in three of the island's four regions. A crisis ensued in April when the FLNKS, the independence movement, called for a boycott of the presidential and territorial elections; there followed the assassination of four gendarmes, with twenty-seven others taken hostage.

The elections were marked by disorders, and most of the Melanesian population abstained from voting. Pons demanded that the FLNKS be banned; Mitterrand refused. On May 5, three days before the second round of the presidential election, the military liberated twenty-three hostages, but two soldiers and nineteen Melanesians were killed—some, according to a subsequent military investigation, after they had surrendered.

Given this unsettled situation, Rocard acted within a week of his nomination, dispatching prefect Christian Blanc to mediate and settle the problems between the French Caldoche settlers and the native Kanaks. On June 26 Rocard announced the "Matignon agreement" with the Caldoche leader Jacques Lafleur and Jean-Marie Tjibaou, the FLNKS leader, specifying that the Pons statute would be suspended and a new federal statute would be worked out, to be the subject of a national referendum before the end of the year. On November 6 the referendum was approved by 80 percent of those voting, although with a disappointingly low participation in a population wearied by presidential, legislative, and cantonal elections in one year. With this success, Rocard had shown that he was capable of decisive and intelligent action, and his credit rose in the country and in his party.

Autumn in France is traditionally marked by strikes, and 1988 was no exception. A major strike of hospital nurses occupied the headlines in October. A Socialist government was embarrassed by wage claims that might lead to general inflationary demands. Postal strikes in mail-sorting centers in October, then a strike in the Paris subway lines gave the government more headaches. The nurses went back to work, and the subways were running again by the week before Christmas, although army trucks had been needed in November to help suburbanites get to work. No French government ever looks good in these periodic crises, but Rocard had managed fairly well. When in early December the RPR proposed a motion of censure against the government, condemning "the degradation of the social situation," the UDF did not sign it (though most of its deputies voted for it). Barre and three other Centrists refused to vote for the motion, which failed. The statistics at year's end showed it had been a good year: The gross domestic product (GDP) growth rate was 4.5 percent over the previous year, and inflation dropped to 3.1 percent.

In March 1989 at the municipal elections the Socialists won back thirty-five cities that they had lost in the 1983 downturn, although Chirac and his party continued to control all twenty arrondissements of Paris. The prime minister had perhaps not won these elections—but would have been attacked by his own party if they had gone badly. These elections also saw a breakthrough by the ecologists, who had previously hovered around the 3 percent mark in various elections, but now won more local counselors than did the National Front, in some cases getting more than 15 percent in second-round contests. In the May 1989 elections for the European Parliament, ecologist leader Antoine Waechter's list took 10.7 percent of the vote—whereas a PS ticket led by Laurent Fabius got only 23.6 percent.

Rocard's Reforms

In 1986 the Right had hastened to abolish the tax on large fortunes introduced by the Socialists in 1982. This political error ended by costing Chirac votes. The new government now introduced a more tactfully worded variant on the old tax, a "solidarity tax on fortunes," intended to finance a minimum revenue for the extreme poor. The tax exempted those with a total fortune below 4 million francs, as well as art holdings and enterprise capital, and rose to a maximum of 1.1 percent on fortunes of 20 million francs or more.

At the end of November 1988 the assembly approved a guaranteed minimum income, the *revenue minimum d'insertion* (RMI) to aid the increasing category of the very poor, those "excluded" from the wage-earning society. People over twenty-five with no other income could apply for a small sum, less than the minimum wage, which would be given them through councils in the departments for a period of three months to a year while they prepared themselves for work. Originally intended to go to 800,000 people, and to cost 6 billion francs a year, the RMI ended by going to far more recipients, as unemployment increased. Not precisely a welfare entitlement, in the American sense, or a contract with the individual, the RMI was intended both to aid those entirely devoid of income and to give them a hand toward finding work. Since there frequently was no work to be found, the RMI became a sort of lowest security net. The RMI was, however, well accepted—and continued by conservative governments after the 1993 and 1995 elections.[20]

Rocard thought his policy of small and quiet reforms the only one possible; he did not seek to steal the limelight from Mitterrand. In 1996 he told an interviewer: "I wanted to emphasize 'the boring small duties,' and so, neither necessarily desiring, or certainly being able to do things that made a big splash, we did important things—but without much media attention, except when there were quarrels and dissension."[21]

Rocard cited a number of important but not resounding measures he took: Social Affairs Minister Claude Evin, one of the few Rocardians in his government, made a start on control of health expenses, using not state constraint but contracts between the state and the various corporate bodies, involving in all sixty-three contracts. He began with the private clinics—a large chunk—with an agreement to level out expenses, then the analysis laboratories—another expensive sector. The first contract for general practitioners was negotiated only in April 1991, having met strong opposition, and Rocard's successors did not push the idea. Reduction of health expenses was one major way of cutting the budget deficit, seen as far too high. However, when Rocard left office, only a part of this program had been completed, and not the largest.

One of the most important—and controversial—measures of the Rocard government was the introduction in late 1990 of a new tax entitled the *contribution sociale généralisée,* or CSG, which undertook to shift part of the burden of social security deductions—in France taken directly from salaries—to a generalized tax. The deduction from salaries for old age insurance, for example, hit only incomes at or below 11,000 francs per month in 1990. Thus a poorly paid worker had to contribute a sum levied on his whole salary, whereas an executive making 33,000 francs a month had to pay only on a third of it.

The CSG was intended to relieve burdens on people making less than 18,000 francs a month. However, as it was levied on all revenues, including pensions and money going to those unemployed who still paid income tax, older people were hit more heavily and were not pleased. The CSG was a redistribution among generations, not just of class.

In proposing the CSG Rocard had first to fight his economics minister Pierre Bérégovoy, who worried about a measure that would be seen as a tax. The CGT and the FO were both opposed, as was the PCF, and the Right. The Fabius faction argued that the tax should be deductible from income tax, which would have reduced budget receipts.[22] Rocard was forced to use the Fifth Republic's choke-off device, constitutional Article 49:3, winning his vote of confidence by only four votes, as the Communists abstained and Barre with three others voted with the government.

Despite the lack of a majority in the assembly, the Rocard government was usually able to find a de facto majority by looking to cooperative Centrists on many issues, and the Communists on issues with a left-wing flavor. In Rocard's three years in office, the Centrist deputies either abstained or voted for the government's bills, whereas the Communists abstained half the time and voted against the rest. The Rocard government used Article 49:3 on more than twelve texts—although the total of uses was higher—twenty-nine times, because in some cases it was used on the first, second, and third readings of a bill.

Rocard's "stereo-majority" was made possible by remarkably skillful parliamentary tactics, described by their engineer, Rocard's parliamentary aide Guy Carcassonne in the terms of an old joke: "To sell something you have to someone who wants to buy it isn't business; to sell something you don't have to someone who doesn't want to buy it, that's business. But to sell something you don't have to two parties, neither of whom have the least desire to buy it, but who also don't want the other fellow to buy it, that's an art."[23]

Other Rocard reforms included modernizing changes in the status of the Post Office, Telephones, and Telecommunications, creating two autonomous agencies, one for the post office, the other called France-Télécom. Another was a reform in management of government workers, getting rid of all sorts of rigidities and allowing more negotiation by personnel, who were encouraged to contribute ideas, not just to accept orders. The hope was that the new spirit would also save money.

The Rocard government also began a reform of the penal code. Former Justice Minister Robert Badinter, now president of the Constitutional Council, wanted a special session of parliament devoted to it. But since Rocard's staff concluded that the very extensive texts required much time to work their way through the parliament, the work was done gradually, some of the legislation continuing until 1993.

A final reform, prepared before Rocard's dismissal in May 1991 but voted afterward, was a bill to control government telephone tapping, denounced by the opposition as hypocritical. Although the question of who was a security risk remained open, the law probably did curb the previously extensive use of taps.

Many of Rocard's reform measures were important, but few if any were dramatic. Rocard's popularity remained high during all three years he was prime minister, descending from the two-thirds of respondents who approved of him when he began to an average above 50 percent in his last year in office.[24] This high opinion was not, however, shared by his critics in the Socialist party, notably Laurent Fabius, who spoke of a "social deficit" in Rocard's policies as early as 1989. Fabius, now comfortably installed as president of the National Assembly, with an office in a splendid palace next to the assembly building, was busily building up his own clientele.

The continued sniping from his own Socialist ranks at the prime minister and his determination to carry out quiet reform contributed to Rocard's reputation for "immobilism," which was largely unjustified. The word "prudent"—not meant as praise—occurred often in press descriptions of his actions and propositions. Having discovered that lobbies and corporate interests were far stronger than he had thought, blocking reforms once the details came out, Rocard decided to create the preliminary steps for reforms. But by the time he left Matignon too little had been really accomplished, hence his appearance as a competent administrator but not a reformer.

Even in the estimation of one of his friends—Gilles Martinet—Rocard's constant weakness was a fixation on the goal of the presidency. If he had undertaken big reforms, without Mitterrand's agreement, remarked Martinet, Mitterrand might have dismissed him sooner, but he might have emerged with a better record as a future candidate. Certainly Rocard avoided clashing with the president, believing that if they did not quarrel Mitterrand would have to back him in 1995 for the presidency, or at least not block him.[25]

Only a caricature of Michel Rocard, however, would picture him as someone who designedly avoided bold measures and sedulously cultivated a president ill disposed to him. Rocard genuinely believed that consultation and the necessarily slow winning of consensus were the keys to real reform. If Rocard hoped to have five years as prime minister and return to power as president in 1995, ambition certainly played a large role. But a not inconsiderable factor was his deep conviction that problems are solved, not by government fiat, but by long, patient, and difficult negotiation with all involved.

In 1989 Rocard had told the PS steering committee:

> You do not change society without the means, you do not change society without time, you do not change society without having power. . . . Without means: [where] administration and transformation come together, for only a prosperous economy offers room for movement. . . . Without time: for none of the ills our society suffers from will disappear from one day to the next. . . . Without power: that is without the confidence or complicity of a majority of the French, even if relative. One must not confuse shocks and changes.[26]

The counterpart of Rocard's many positive qualities was a strong technocratic tendency and an underdeveloped sense of how to manage the political aspect of problems by working on public opinion. Mitterrand, a master of maneuver, found little in common with his prime minister. There was "a cultural divergence" between the two; Mitterrand believed in political confrontation to mobilize the electorate, using the forces of positive law and the power of the state, whereas Rocard sought the widest possible consensus in civil society.[27]

Rocard and Mitterrand

The tension between Mitterrand and Rocard was described in the title of a journalist's book as "quiet hatred," although the hatred seems to have been mostly on Mitterrand's side, whereas Rocard strove to gain his difficult chief's approval. Mitterrand did not try to micromanage Rocard—but since the ministers in Rocard's government were mostly the president's favorites, he never lacked for reporting on his prime minister, and it is not implausible that some Mitterrand intimates systematically poisoned the president's mind against Rocard.

Mitterrand had given Rocard no credit for the good results of the municipal elections in 1989, allegedly concluding because of the high abstentions that the results were due to confusion on the Right. He also apparently believed that Rocard's good ratings in the polls would not be transferable to the PS in 1993, because Rocard was more popular with Centrists than with sure Socialist voters.

Mitterrand approved Rocard's holding the line against wage demands, but thought his technique too cold, that he was too much the frigid administrator. He was quoted as saying, "Let him reform with moderation, since it's his style—but let him reform." He also reproached Rocard for taking the Centrists too much into account. (The prime minister could not, after all, pass laws without some of their votes in the assembly.) The Elysée also encouraged one of its "court Leftists" (former Trotskyites who maintained a cozy relation with the president) to publish a pamphlet against the prime minister, attacking him for timidity and complaisance in reassuring the forces the PS had just beaten.[28]

Perhaps because Mitterrand had moved so far from the policies he had espoused in 1981, he needed to believe that his government could correct the abuses of the market economy by using the power of the state. Rocard did not disagree with the end but considered that Mitterrand's means, notably increased taxes, were no longer appropriate, and that only growth could cut down unemployment. Rocard's policies accordingly placed less emphasis on social policies to counteract unemployment, and more on lowering taxes to reduce labor costs for firms.[29] The president found it easy to misunderstand this, telling his entourage that Rocard was too timid, too pragmatic. "Luckily I myself am still on the Left."[30]

A Disaster in Brittany

Seven years after the turnaround of 1983, the Socialist party still had not redefined its ideology to fit its policies. In 1989 First Secretary Mauroy demanded an "ideological" party congress to reformulate Socialist ideas. The last congress, held in Lille in the cohabitation year of 1987, had not been able to do much on this account. No one could know, when the next congress was set for March 1990 in the Breton capital, Rennes, how little ideology would be discussed there and how disastrous the congress would be.

At a PS congress, delegates vote on programmatic statements called *contributions* rather than for tickets, with the results assigning proportional strengths to the *courants* (factions). A new first secretary was to be elected (or reelected) and a new steering committee. Factional rivalry was thus inevitably connected with programmatic (even ideological) competition. The Rennes congress, however, saw factional rivalry raised to the highest power.

Laurent Fabius had been organizing a subfaction in the Mitterrandist camp since his failure to be elected PS first secretary in May 1988. Fabius's reproach (already over a year old) that Rocard lacked a grand design and that his policies suffered from a "social deficit" echoed the grumbling heard emerging from the Elysée palace. According to Fabius and his friends (who included ministers Pierre Bérégovoy, Michel Charasse, Jack Lang, and Paul Quilès, all close to Mitterrand), the PS no longer appealed to "that which is moving in French society." Fabius also argued that the PS must become a modern mass party and begin by drawing "sympathizers" closer to the party.

The other leader of the Mitterrandist-Mauroy faction, Lionel Jospin, remained hostile to Fabius's design to use the PS as a trampoline for his presidential ambitions.

The struggle between them threatened to split the PS majority. The texts each sponsored had a more leftist thrust than that offered by Rocard's friends. The logic of confrontation with Fabius, however, pushed Jospin closer to Rocard.

As the Rennes congress approached, Mitterrand worried that the Fabius-Jospin feud would allow Rocard to take over the Socialist party; he warned Rocard not to attempt that. Rocard had been working to improve his relations with Jospin, if only to ensure himself against a possible Fabius-Jospin alliance, which would threaten his position. Each subfaction admonished the other that a split would be the best way to give the Rocardians the strongest role in the party.

A mid-January meeting of the PS steering committee failed to produce agreement. Neither Jospin nor Fabius was willing to cede key offices in the party to the other. Encouraged by Mitterrand, Fabius was confident of winning. When in late January Mitterrand took Fabius with him on a trip as a clear sign of his favor an angry Jospin decided to work more closely with Rocard.[31]

At Rennes, the two ex-Mitterrandist factions faced each other, each with slightly more than 29 percent of the delegates. Chevènement's ex-CERES, now Socialisme et République, had 8.5 percent, Jean Poperen's faction a bit more than 7 percent, and two small groups 2 percent together. The Rocardians, with 24 percent, clearly held the balance.

Fabius apparently hoped to exploit the president's much-advertised preference for him and to benefit from a generalized feeling that First Secretary Mauroy was not the strongest possible leader to take the party toward the crucial 1993 elections. In the maneuvering Fabius played up the Rocardian menace, warning of "the reverse of the Metz congress"—the Mitterrandist win over Rocard and Mauroy in 1979. And Fabius's spokesmen claimed that he was being excluded. "Nobody is excluding anyone," thundered Jospin, "unless he wants to exclude himself."

The haggling went on behind the scenes until dawn on the last morning of the congress, Mauroy willing to make compromises on personnel, Jospin less willing, and the Rocardians, finally showing their hand, backing Jospin. As neither side would give way on ceding key offices, no result could be announced to the waiting congress, which broke up in total confusion and without decisions.

The Rennes congress showed the Socialist party to the country as a group of politicians using the language of ideology to squabble over power, and worse, unable to agree. The obvious outcome should have been a Rocard-Jospin alliance. But that was exactly what Mitterrand would not hear of, and Jospin, though he had defied Mitterrand to block Fabius, was not willing to defy him again. Back in Paris, the warring factions put a temporary patch on party quarrels. Pierre Mauroy was reelected without triumph, and a Fabius ally was made number-two man. But a congress that all factions had advertised as meant to strengthen the party ended by discouraging militantism and disgusting militants. Rennes began the decline of the Socialist party that culminated in 1993 with a shattering defeat.

The spectacle of a botched congress was sufficiently serious for President Mitterrand to feel himself obliged to devote forty minutes to the subject in a television interview a week later—far too much. He seemed to be admitting the new status Rocard had apparently gained at Rennes. "If the present prime minister succeeds sufficiently in bringing the current majority to electoral victory in 1993, he will be in a position to be everyone's candidate for the presidential encounter. . . . My wish is that . . . Michel Rocard remain in office as long as possible. There is nothing to gain from a kind of continual instability."

Nothing in this language meant what it seemed to say. Mitterrand, having told Rocard before Rennes that he was not to mix into party affairs, and giving him to understand that he himself was backing Fabius, felt that Rocard had disobeyed his injunction: Don't exploit a family quarrel to improve your own fortunes. Rocard and his staff remain convinced that Mitterrand never pardoned Rocard for Rennes. After March 1990 he began planning to get rid of this prime minister who had disobeyed him and nearly taken over his party.[32]

Jean-Paul Huchon, Rocard's chief aide, noted that things began to go badly from June 1990 on. In a speech in Auxerre on May 29, 1990, Mitterrand demanded that the government pursue "more social policy." He was reacting in part to a report that showed that as of the end of 1988 the gap between rich and poor, which had been diminishing until 1985, had widened again. It was in this context that Rocard announced his intention to proceed toward introduction of the CSG.[33]

Pierre Bérégovoy, Rocard's minister for economy and finance, had sided with Fabius at Rennes and before. He was, however, even more opposed than was Rocard to raising taxes. The devoted Mitterrandists thus did not invariably agree with the president on policy. Rocard, regardless of his policies, however, found himself consistently on Mitterrand's wrong side.

In October 1990 lycée students began a series of demonstrations all over the country to protest insecure conditions, overcrowded classes, and dilapidated buildings. (Jospin as education minister had already increased his budget, but given the swollen classes and ill-paid teachers, much remained to be done. See Chapter 7.) Mitterrand now reverted to the tactics he had used to harass the Chirac government during cohabitation, taking sides with the students against his own government. On November 12, during a monster student demonstration that was accompanied by some pillaging and car burning, Mitterrand received a delegation of young people at the Elysée and declared to them that eight-tenths of their demands were reasonable. When one student asked him where all the billions for education had gone, he replied, "I wonder myself." Jospin was acting prime minister, in the absence of Rocard, who was visiting Japan. He watched on television as the students' spokesman delivered a message from the steps of the Elysée: "The president agrees with our demands. Now it's time for the government to assume its responsibilities." A furious Jospin understood that the blow was aimed at him and Rocard, a species of revenge for the Rennes congress. Rocard, returning, saw himself obliged to allocate an extra 4.5 billion francs to the education budget—adding them to the budget deficit.[34] *Le Monde* cartoonist Plantu depicted Mitterrand as a lycée student with a boom box, doing the hip-hop while spray-painting a wall with "Jospin, du pognon!" (Jospin, some bread!)

Cresson, Briefly

By summer 1990 Mitterrand was considering a change in prime ministers, a project made more difficult by the Iraqi invasion of Kuwait and the subsequent Gulf war. Rocard's staff believe the crisis prolonged their time in office. Mitterrand meanwhile continued to mull over choices for prime minister. One of his criteria was that the new one should not have ambitions for the presidency; his choice should also ideally produce a sense of surprise and pleased shock. One obvious (and hopeful) candidate, Pierre Bérégovoy, did not answer this last criterion. Another did: Edith Cresson, minister for European affairs—a Mitterrand follower since the days of the Convention des Institutions Républicaines, and agriculture and foreign trade minister in the 1980s. Cresson was unhappy in the Rocard ministry and by April 1990 had negotiated a position in private industry. Asked to delay her resignation, she finally left in early October, with a letter to Mitterrand denouncing the absence of a "grand industrial project." Several months earlier she had denounced the "Japanese invasion" of French markets—at a time when Rocard was preparing a trip to Japan that he hoped would be fruitful.

In December 1990 the president told Cresson that he saw only three possible candidates for the Matignon: herself, Bérégovoy, and Roland Dumas, remarking that Dumas might be the best; he told her a few weeks later that he might choose Bérégovoy. In early February 1991, Mitterrand hinted strongly that she would get the job, requesting her ideas on a list of ministers, and so on. In order not to attract press attention, he told her to enter the Elysée by the garden door, which gives on the quiet Avenue Gabriel, rather than the Faubourg Saint-Honoré street entrance, where the press corps lies in wait.[35]

Rocard's prime ministry came to an abrupt end on May 10, 1991, when Mitterrand told him he wanted his resignation in a week. After rumors of the change escaped, Mitterrand moved the date up to May 15. Rocard later said, "I was fired." Mitterrand did not tell him he meant to replace him with Edith Cresson.

Only two of the Fifth Republic's fourteen prime ministers in 1958–1995 served longer than three years, four for approximately three, the rest for two or less. Rocard was not much surprised to end his service in three, though he may have hoped to serve longer. He was, however, offended when he learned the name of his successor, of whom he had a low opinion.

Despite rumors of a change (Paris always buzzes with rumors), the dismissal of Rocard on May 15 and the nomination of Cresson created a sensation. Later, as her star was sinking, it was easy to remark, "Wearing a skirt does not make one a Margaret Thatcher," but the immediate reaction to the nomination of the first female prime minister in France was strongly positive, and not just among women.

Cresson had excellent contacts in the business community, which welcomed her, but the rhetoric as she began had the resonance of a move to the left—what Mitterrand described as a "new élan"—if only to demarcate her from the "conservative" Rocard—whom she proceeded to criticize until he wrote her in protest.

Cresson had seen herself as a prime minister with a Superministry of the Economy. But Mitterrand chose her ministers, and the most important of them was Pierre Bérégovoy. With oversight over the ministers of industry, foreign and domestic trade, and posts, the minister of the economy and finance had created a species of Japanese MITI. Cresson could name only a few of her own ministers, of whom the happiest choice was Martine Aubry as minister of labor. Aubry, daughter of Jacques Delors, was an *énarque* who had earlier made her mark as the principal drafter of the Auroux laws on labor; she was to become one of the new hopes of the Socialist party.

The major reason for a more leftist rhetoric was Mitterrand's desire to give new hope to the Socialist electorate, which he felt Rocard had neglected. A more tactical aim was to secure the cooperation of the Communists in the National Assembly, who had again voted against the government in a final vote in December on the CSG. But if Mitterrand had thought through the idea of a turn to the left, he would not have made Bérégovoy a sort of vice prime minister. The deflationary policies pursued by the powerful minister under Rocard were continued under Cresson; she was to struggle against them without avail. If Mitterrand had genuinely wished to change course, he would have dropped Bérégovoy and the *franc fort* (strong franc). Instead, he merely dropped Rocard and encouraged Cresson to talk a more leftist line.

Cresson's maiden programmatic speech to the assembly was disappointing, judged as vague and poorly drafted. She spoke of giving more muscle to the productive apparatus and struggling against inequalities and poverty, with unemployment as the prime target. But the unchanged priorities entrusted to Bérégovoy meant that there would be little but a change in rhetoric. Cresson's popularity lasted a month. Her poll ratings then plummeted and kept going down.

By most accounts, Cresson had a bad eye for choosing staffers. Her chief aide and gray eminence was Abel Farnoux, a middle-aged businessman who had her ear on everything and who, sitting at the end of the table in ministerial meetings, annoyed the ministers by addressing them all with the familiar "tu" and interrupting in a loud voice. Farnoux organized a paragovernmental liaison with business, called *groupes d'études et de mobilisation* (GEM), with twenty-one regional groups. Not very much came of them, but coming after Cresson's initial leftist language, they met with deep suspicion from Socialists, who saw they were filled with business people from the Right.

Cresson undoubtedly had bad luck. Her first month in office saw violent incidents in the industrial city of Mantes, near Paris, in which a policewoman and a young Algerian were killed. Pressed by Bérégovoy and Mitterrand to do something about the deficit in social security funding, she agreed to a 0.9 percent rise in pay deductions for sickness insurance, which was predictably unpopular and brought professionals into the street in protest.

Some of her troubles came from a serious case of foot-in-mouth disease. When the stock market went down after she had announced a new tax, she said, "I don't give a hoot about the stock market" ("Je n'ai rien à cirer avec la Bourse"). She described the Japanese as "ants." When a journalist dug up an interview she had given four years earlier in which she had said that the English were not interested in women and a quarter of them were homosexuals, she was foolish enough to confirm the story. When she announced that illegal immigrants would be expelled, using special charters, the immediate reaction was favorable. But then she told a TV interviewer: "Charters are for people who go on vacation at low prices. Here it's free, and not for vacation." The Left remembered that it had been shocked when in 1986 Interior Minister Charles Pasqua expelled 101 Malians by charter—and asked itself about its new prime minister.

The snipers in the PS who had harassed Rocard reloaded to fire again at Mitterrand's new prime minister. She complained that they objected to having a female prime minister, but although there was some of this, the jealousy was unisex, especially on the part of Bérégovoy and Dumas, who had hoped to have her job and saw their chances disappearing.

A prominent Socialist militant, a veteran of Mauroy's staff, commented: "One of the functions of a prime minister is to be shot at from all sides, and if you can't take it. . . . Cresson took it badly, and complained. Also, a prime minister has to work very hard, and she didn't work hard enough." Another remarked, "Certainly there was sniping against her, and Béré thought he should have been at Matignon instead of her, but . . . "

Cresson talked tough in public, with a deliberate touch of vulgarity, which went over badly. But inside her government she lacked authority, partly because she was seen to be poorly organized. The Matignon, remarked one inside observer, is like the place de la Concorde at rush hour. Cresson's Matignon was in a perpetual administrative traffic jam, and things did not get done.

Mitterrand, who continued to defend Cresson against her critics, obviously had not realized that her very real qualities did not extend to the ability to run the government. But even a well-organized and abler prime minister would have run into severe problems in the summer of 1991 and thereafter. The economy had flourished in 1988–1990. Now it began to turn down. The last poll taken under Rocard, published after he had left office, showed a drop in confidence. Cresson's first polling figures equaled Rocard's final ones, but then began a rapid drop.

Unemployment had reached a level in the mid-1980s at above 2.5 million. It diminished somewhat between September 1988 and the early spring of 1991. But by June 1991 it had reached 2.7 million and thereafter renewed its ominous ascension, quarter by quarter, reaching nearly 2.9 million by December. A new access of gloom already perceptible in late 1990 increased rapidly. To the question, "Do you expect that the situation of the French economy will deteriorate in the coming year?" in December 1988, 32 percent had said yes; in October 1989 only 21 percent, but in December 1990, 45 percent and in December 1991, 55 percent.

To a similar set of questions, whether the situation of the French economy had in the past year improved, deteriorated, or remained the same, 36 percent said "worse" in December 1988; 24 percent in October 1989; 53 percent in December 1990, and 76 percent in December 1991.[36] Thus the relative optimism that had set in during the late 1980s, especially in 1988–1989, fell off in late 1990 and collapsed in 1991.

Although two political scientists could write, "The French would rapidly perceive that the president of the republic had changed prime ministers without a major political reason . . . essentially because he was tired of cohabiting with Michel Rocard," only 30 percent of those queried in a poll taken soon after the change in prime ministers much regretted losing Rocard.[37] And Cresson's increasing unpopularity did not change opinions—Rocard's popularity dropped below that of Jacques Delors after May 1991—though still remaining higher than that of other Socialist leaders. One of the traditional uses of prime ministers in France is to serve as a shield for the president, allowing his public standing to remain high, and to take the brunt of unhappy public opinion. Mitterrand's popularity diminished along with Cresson's.

The Scandals

Economic troubles and increasing pessimism were not the only factors that pulled down Cresson, Mitterrand, and the Socialists in general. The year 1991 saw a quickening in the flood of scandals that ultimately discredited the Socialist party and tarnished its president's reputation. Before March 1986 two scandals had created a sensation: that of the "Vincennes Irish," the arrest by the Elysée's special antiterrorist cell of an alleged IRA terrorist group in August 1982, which turned out to be based on bad information and was followed by fabricated proofs, and the *Rainbow Warrior* affair. Neither of these cases had been politically exploited by the opposition, however.

During the 1986–1988 cohabitation period, both sides began digging for mud to throw. Interior Minister Charles Pasqua opened the assault with the scandal of the Carrefour du Développement, a semigovernmental organization supposed to provide aid to the Third World. He accused former minister for cooperation (African affairs) Christian Nucci of skimming off money earmarked for African affairs, directing it into party use and perhaps his own pocket. Mitterrand protected Nucci as best he could. Nucci aide Yves Chalier, who apparently siphoned off about 10 million francs for himself, was allowed to escape from France using a passport in a false name issued him by Pasqua in return for information against his boss. Pasqua then refused to explain his actions, alleging "defense secrets."

In November 1987 the Socialists were accused of granting licenses to the Luchaire company to sell arms to Iran, despite the embargo, in return for kickbacks to the party. The Socialists in turn cried out against Justice Minister Albin Chalandon, who had had a profitable account in an illegal bank run by the Chaumet brothers, well-known jewelers who had gone bankrupt earlier in the year. None of these affairs, however, had the political effect of the series of scandals that began in 1989.

François Mitterrand had always advertised his contempt for money. The Socialists had always felt themselves morally superior to the Right, suspected of all manner of deals and corruption. Accusations and indictments for corruption thus affected Socialist morale and the public view of the party even more than did scandals past and present attributed to the Right.

The first serious scandal that cropped up in 1989 involved Roger-Patrice Pelat, a rich businessman and perhaps Mitterrand's closest friend. In 1988, the nationalized French aluminum company Péchiney purchased Triangle-American Can. The U.S. Securities and Exchange Commission noted that large blocks of American Can stock had been bought just before the announcement of the company's sale at more than five times its previous stock quotation. SEC investigations rapidly discovered that Pelat and some associates had made profits of several million francs from insider trading.

The precise informant has not been identified, but Alain Boublil, then director of the cabinet of Finance and Economy Minister Pierre Bérégovoy, was implicated, along with Max Théret, a prominent businessman who had been one of the financial backers of the Socialist party. Pelat was indicted for insider trading in February 1989. Asked about the case in an interview a few days before the indictment, Mitterrand defended his friend, who had been a butcher's apprentice before the war, evoking their hardship together as POWs, his courage and energy in the Resistance. Mitterrand asked, "Must I quarrel with him because he was poor, very, very poor, and then became rich, not as a financier but in industry?" He ended, however, by saying that if it should be shown that Pelat had committed a crime, he would have to reconsider their relationship.[38] Pelat died of a heart attack a few weeks later.

In June 1990, a former director of Bérégovoy's cabinet, Jean-Charles Naouri, was accused of insider trading, along with four others, in the purchase of the Société Générale bank. In October Jean-Michel Boucheron, former PS deputy and ex-mayor of Angoulême, briefly a junior minister in the first Rocard government, was suspended from the PS because of an inquiry into Angoulême finances. Boucheron had organized a series of shadow firms in Angoulême destined principally to enrich himself. In February 1992 he fled to Argentina after being indicted for corruption, abusive use of public funds, and interference with justice.

The expenses of the French political parties had continued to grow throughout the 1980s. Parties on the Right had traditionally been financed with contributions, most of them from big business. Lacking a similar source of major funding, the Left established a system using a series of dummy consulting firms that performed little or no work for contractors working for municipalities but that collected substantial commissions. This system had been brought to a fine art by the Communist party in earlier years, and in 1972 Pierre Mauroy, then Mitterrand's number two in the PS, had copied it first in the two big northern departments of the Nord and Pas-de-Calais, then systematized it nationally, in order to prevent individual cities or federations from skimming off receipts or appropriating money. A whole series of consultancies, or *bureaux d'études,* had been set up, of which perhaps the biggest was called Urba. Urba had originally been so open that it had a stand at Socialist party congresses, at which it proposed its services to local militants for their towns.

The whole subject of political finance in France had been hidden behind a veil of scrupulous hypocrisy, shared by all participants. If these practices had continued for years, more or less openly, why was the climate changing by the end of the 1980s?

One major reason was the tremendous increase in election expenses, coupled with a drop in the zeal and number of party activists who had formerly furnished cheap or unremunerated labor in putting up posters, sending out mailings, and so on. Television, responsible for astronomic expenses in U.S. politics, is furnished free to French candidates, but other expenses are high—campaign newspapers, direct mailings, chartering airplanes, and constant polling, perhaps the most expensive single item. The 1988 presidential campaign (where no other positions were to be filled) was declared, in what was certainly a low estimate, to have cost Mitterrand and Chirac each not quite 100 million francs—but may have cost three times as much.[39]

The rise of expenses in the 1980s was accompanied by a rise in investment in public works, which under the new decentralization laws were increasingly administered by cities and towns. The number of opportunities for skimming off funds by demanding a percentage from contractors (or being handed money by contending contractors) increased greatly. All political parties were involved in similar operations and, in the absence of public funding, considered them necessary, hence not immoral. The judicial authorities customarily did not follow up on such cases when the police stumbled upon them.[40] Politicians had been so accustomed to the general complicit silence that they discounted the idea of any of their sins being brought home to them, and hence took few precautions. A system that before the 1980s had been passed over discreetly became more corrupt, and more evident, even as some individuals took advantage of it to fill their own pockets.

In March 1988, just prior to the presidential elections, the National Assembly passed the first law on public financing of French elections, with some measures intended to control expenses and sources, as well as the obligation for candidates at most levels to declare their financial holdings. But in effect the law "encouraged a situation in which public finances were added to secret financing, instead of replacing them."[41]

The increased freedom exercised by print and electronic media is a prominent factor in the public emergence of scandal on matters already widely known to the political class. In 1973 the French domestic intelligence service had been caught red-handed planting an extensive network of microphones in the offices of *Le Canard Enchaîné,* the satiric weekly, which has always prided itself on being critical of power. Despite the fact that the paper revealed the names of the intelligence officers involved, no indictments were brought, the rest of the press made no great fuss, and the case was simply passed over. By the late 1980s, the climate had changed.

Another new and still more important factor was a new access of independent spirit on the part of investigating magistrates, a novelty in France. Former justice minister Robert Badinter remarked on the new status of magistrates: "They never lacked the capacity to be independent—they lacked the daring to exercise independence. Now that they have found it, there is no way back. Before, they exercised timid self-restraint, avoiding areas that were not, in fact, forbidden, but that they regarded merely as dangerous."[42] Guy Carcassonne remarked that in France, justice had always been servile, and for a long time the magistrates had wanted more independence, without knowing how to get it. Then a few of them led off and showed the others that it was up to them to assert themselves.[43]

The new dispensation began in 1991, with the zealous activities of a young magistrate named Thierry Jean-Pierre. He picked up information that went back to April 1989, when an investigation by the police into an affair of false receipts in Marseilles found notes taken by an employee of Urba-Gracco on most of the meetings of the committee coordinating the whole network of consultancies maintained by the PS.

These notes, including names, dates, and sums, were quite sufficient to force the opening of a case, and the two policemen who had seized the documents asked the public prosecutor to do so. The Marseilles prosecutor's office asked advice from its hierarchical superior, the Ministry of Justice in Paris, which delayed a reply.

News of the search at the Urba office in Marseilles was immediately relayed to Paris, where its import was instantly evident. Within two days, it was the subject of a high-level meeting of horrified officials: Justice Minister Pierre Arpaillange, Interior Minister Pierre Joxe, Economics Minister Pierre Bérégovoy, and from the PS, Henri Emmanuelli and Louis Mermaz, as well as Rocard's top aide Guy Carcassonne and Elysée deputy secretary-general Christian Sautter.

Arpaillange was a former high magistrate, one of the nonparty ministers selected by Mitterrand in 1988. His reaction was that the discovery of the Urba documents had to be legally authorized so that the documents could be seized. Faced by the extreme reluctance of the others, Arpaillange threatened to authorize Marseilles to open an investigation. The alternative was to convince the chief of the Urba office in Marseilles (lodged temporarily in jail) to agree to surrender the documents. Arpaillange added that if he was unable to keep the Marseilles magistrates (some of them nominated by his RPR predecessor) from opening an investigation, rapid passage of an amnesty law could avoid a wave of indictments among Urba officials and Socialist officeholders. Arpaillange's solution was adopted. In the meantime. however, the policemen who had made the discovery, Antoine Gaudino and Alain Mayot, had drawn up a detailed listing of the documents they had seized, describing in detail the system of false receipts that brought in 100 million francs a year, two-thirds of which went to the Socialist party.[44]

Paris blocked the Marseilles investigation, and the persistent policeman Antoine Gaudino was transferred to the drug squad. He had, however, already furnished the inventory of Urba documents to his Marseilles superiors, who had sent it to the Paris public prosecutor's office—which demanded permission from the Justice Ministry to search the Urba offices in Paris.

Mitterrand decided to take the offensive by generalizing the problem. In an informal press conference on May 14 he declared himself worried by evidence of the damaged functioning of democracy and called for a law that would impose democratic rules for election and party financing, going down to the town and city level.

Rocard, who favored a new law on party financing with real teeth in it, was confronted by party leaders Mauroy and Emmanuelli, who demanded that the text include an amnesty for offenses connected with party financing. Rocard's first reaction was that the party should collectively admit its guilt and demand judgment. Unsurprisingly, this idea only awoke the suspicion among Socialists that Rocard was taking his distance—the Rocardians had benefited very little from Urba. Finally, all hands agreed there must be an amnesty law or, better, an amnesty clause in the over-all law on party financing.

Before a law could be introduced, leaks to the press produced most of the text of the Gaudino inventory, making it clear to anyone why the Socialists urgently desired an amnesty. The climate had become too hot for rapid passage of a law before the end of the spring-summer assembly session. A magistrate in Nancy created a stir when he denounced the idea of deputies' voting amnesty and whitewashing them-selves. The RPR denounced amnesty as a scandal. And a Paris magistrate indicted both the Marseilles Urba figures and Gérard Monate, head of the entire operation.

In this impasse, Mitterrand decided to wait out the summer, and above all to seek support from the other political parties, all more or less involved in questionable op-erations. Guy Carcassonne, Rocard's parliamentary wizard, tested the idea of an amnesty that would exclude cases of personal enrichment—and all parliamentarians. The businessmen who had paid up and the Urba staff (considered as honest victims by the PS) would escape prosecution. Carcassonne warned the PS leaders, however, that inclusion of an amnesty clause in the text of the bill on public financing would frighten skittish opposition members. It was decided to submit an amendment at the second reading, after the Senate had passed the main law. Originally, a Centrist deputy had agreed to submit the amendment, but the Centrists then backed out and a Socialist deputy who had made a specialty of amnesty laws proposed the amend-ment. The RPR deputies, with a few exceptions, voted against it, as did the Communists (generally agreed to have carried off the prize for hypocrisy in a stiff competition). Two-thirds of the UDF deputies abstained, as did most of the Centrists.

The new law provided that infractions of the law committed before June 15, 1989, were amnestied where the matter concerned direct or indirect financing of electoral campaigns or parties and political groups. Although parliamentarians were excluded, the press was quick to charge hypocrisy, noting that since intermediaries were amnestied, the judicial dossiers lost most of their force. Challenged by the Constitutional Council, the retouched law was voted again in April 1990. The gen-eral public had by this time heard enough to conclude that the politicians, notably the PS, had amnestied themselves.

When proceedings against Christian Nucci were dropped in April 1990 because of the amnesty, there were protests from the five magistrates from the commission on the rarely used High Court of Justice, which had been working on his case. One of them declared, "We are made responsible for the non-pursuit of M. Nucci before the High Court, whereas in fact the deputies have whitewashed themselves with this amnesty law, tailor-made for Nucci." Nucci appears to have benefited from large sums for his electoral purposes but not to have enriched himself—unlike his aide Yves Chalier. The Socialists had desperately wanted the amnesty for the overall reasons already discussed, but the language in it had indeed been fashioned to spare Nucci.[45] (Chalier was condemned in April 1992 to five years in prison for stealing public money and was released in 1994.)

There is general agreement that the amnesty law did lasting political damage to the PS. A poll immediately after the declaration by the five judges saw 76 percent of respondents thinking that the amnesty of Nucci was shocking. The damage extended to the political class in general, seen as "all rotten"—80 percent of respondents thought there were as many dishonest politicians on the Left as on the Right.[46] If no further scandals had followed, the public might have forgotten the matter. But many scandals did follow.

In January 1991 Le Mans magistrate Thierry Jean-Pierre entered on the scene and started to unravel another part of the Urba web. He gained access to the notes seized by Gaudino in Marseilles and, following up on this, in April 1991 conducted a search of the Paris office of Urbatechnic, another PS consultancy. The deputy justice minister termed this a "judicial burglary" and pulled Jean-Pierre off the case. He was replaced by Renaud Van Ruymbeke, who continued the investigation with equal zeal.

The Urba cases kept expanding, involving municipalities all over France and resulting in the indictment of Urba officials. In January 1992 Van Ruymbeke conducted a judicial search of PS headquarters in Paris, producing evidence that in July provoked the indictment of former party treasurer Henri Emmanuelli. Justice Minister Michel Vauzelle indignantly denounced a "government by judges," and Emmanuelli, receiving the letter of indictment, said that it was the Socialist party that was being indicted.

Jean-Pierre and Van Ruymbeke became nationally known figures, and their celebrity emboldened other magistrates. Although the French corruption scene was not comparable to the wave of investigations and arrests in Italy that ended by destroying both the Christian Democratic and Socialist parties, the accusations and indictments convinced the French public that the self-righteous Socialist party was thoroughly corrupt. A list published in 1995 of 100 elected officials who had been accused or indicted of various forms of corruption showed that exactly half were members of the PS.[47] During the years 1990–1993, however, most of the public attention was directed to a seemingly endless list of solely PS derelictions—and the moral standing of the party continued to sink.[48]

Contaminated Blood

Another harmful and long-lasting scandal broke in October 1991, with the indictment of four senior physicians connected with the Health Ministry and the National Center for Blood Transfusion, together with a public controversy on the responsibility of three ministers. The AIDS epidemic had become evident in the early 1980s, spreading rapidly to France. Researchers soon concluded that it was spread by a retrovirus, usually by sexual contact, but also by contact with infected blood. The Center for Blood Transfusion was slow to recognize the risks incurred by hemophiliacs, who needed regular transfusions. By early 1985 an American process to heat the blood supplies and kill the AIDS virus was proposed to the French authorities, who instead decided to wait several months until a French product was ready. They continued to sell blood that they knew was probably contaminated by the AIDS virus. Worse still, the blood supplied was collected from a multitude of unscreened donors, including prison inmates—and thus even more dangerous than it might otherwise have been.

One of the doctors indicted, former director of the Health Ministry Jacques Roux, was also a member of the Central Committee of the Communist party. He (and his party's press) noisily contested his guilt and insisted on the responsibility of the three Socialist ministers involved: Edmond Hervé, who had been state secretary for health, his supervising minister Georgina Dufoix, ex-minister of social affairs, and the prime minister of the period, Laurent Fabius.

Brought to trial in 1992, former chief of the transfusion center Michel Garretta, Roux, and a third doctor were found guilty; a fourth doctor was acquitted. The opposition attempted to bring the ministers involved before the rarely used High Court of Justice, the only jurisdiction competent to handle such a case. This attempt failed, but the case itself has remained on or near the front pages and regular TV coverage. The chief actors here have been the families of the hemophiliacs, outraged because no one had received a sentence longer than four years—the maximum for the crimes in the indictment: "failure to aid persons in danger, and sale of substances that are falsified and corrupted, harmful to health." An indictment for poisoning sought by many would obviously have incurred graver penalties.

The technical complications of the "contaminated blood" scandal are such that it remains extremely difficult to determine the exact degree of fault, both of the doctors and their political superiors. At the very least, the doctors were guilty of almost incredible bureaucratic stupidity, and their superiors of failure to grasp the dangers involved. The general public, hearing and reading constantly about the scandal, could only conclude that the Socialist administration was culpably incompetent.[49]

In all these affairs, financial and otherwise, the attitude of the Socialist government was defensive, with a general reluctance to admit any charge, and as in the Urba case, the government denounced investigative magistrates or blocked criminal proceedings.[50] Ex-minister Georgina Dufoix, criticized in the contaminated blood case, caused a stir by declaring herself "responsible but not guilty." In Mitterrand's second term, she was a presidential counselor and head of the French Red Cross. It was her inattention to dangerous consequences that permitted another scandal: permission for the Palestinian terrorist Georges Habache to be hospitalized in France in January 1992—whereupon she was finally dismissed.

Enter Bérégovoy

Pummeled by bad news domestic and foreign (see Chapter 9 on Mitterrand's foreign policy), the prestige of the government and president dropped steadily into 1992. By December 1991 it had become clear that the PS would do badly in the regional and

cantonal elections the following year; in March 1992 Edith Cresson's approval ratings stood at only 22 percent. In the one-round regional elections on March 22 the
PS got only 18.3 percent of the vote (in 1986 it had received 29.88 percent). Two rival ecologist movements together took 14.37 percent, the National Front 13.9 percent, the RPR and UDF together only 33 percent, and the PCF 8 percent. In the
two-round cantonal elections on March 22 and the following week, the PS did frac-
tionally better, with 18.94 percent. The expected result was Cresson's resignation on
April 2; she had served only ten and one-half months. To no one's surprise
Mitterrand replaced her with Pierre Bérégovoy. Finally the ambitious minister had
his long-awaited chance, but he knew it had come very late.

Two months earlier, shortly after a PS congress that had finally officialized the
identity of the PS as a social democratic party (to a general lack of interest), Pierre
Mauroy arranged to step down as first secretary. He negotiated an agreement between Rocard and Fabius for the latter to succeed him in the party, with the understanding that Rocard would be recognized as "virtual candidate" for the presidency
in 1995.

The day Fabius took over at the PS rue de Solférino headquarters, Renaud van
Ruymbeke searched the PS offices; it was a bad start. The opposition later attempted
to bring Fabius, Dufoix, and Hervé before the High Court of Justice as responsible
in the contaminated blood affair. That was a political operation, but in December
1992 it finally began, dragging on endlessly and blocking any ambitions Fabius
might have still had to run for president in 1995. Emmanuelli, succeeding Fabius as
president of the National Assembly, the third-ranking official in the state, would be
indicted in July 1992.

Bérégovoy's new ministry lacked Lionel Jospin, replaced as minister of education
by Jack Lang, who also remained culture minister. The ministry included prominent
businessman Bernard Tapie, a self-made businessman who had become a celebrity
and a favorite of Mitterrand's, and who then entered politics. He was made minister
for urban affairs (although there were already doubts about his probity), was indicted two months later for misuse of company funds and—reluctantly—resigned.
Bérégovoy had defended him in early May, and days after the indictment Mitterrand
paid tribute to his "energy and imagination." Tapie rejoined the government in
December 1992 after the charge was dropped. He was to occupy the chronicles extensively in the next few years, as he pursued his political career even while being indicted on several other charges, including fixing a football match and perjury. After a
long series of appeals, he was sentenced to jail in 1996.

Beset by these scandals (his own was yet to come), Bérégovoy knew he had barely
a year before his party had to face new legislative elections in March 1993. An opposition that had taken three and one-half years to recover from the defeats of 1988
was pulling itself together and gaining strength from the discredit of the Cresson
government, scandals, and the decline of the economy. Nevertheless, in April 1992 it
still seemed possible for the new prime minister to produce a credible result in the
next elections. Although the Socialist party had done badly in the 1992 elections,

the combined vote of the RPR-UDF was also down, 8 percent less than in the 1986 regionals; new strength had been shown only by the ecologists, whose advance was difficult for the Socialists to accept, but whose electorate came for the most part from the Left. As Cresson's and his own unpopularity deepened, Mitterrand had begun to think of a return to proportional representation for the next elections, but the Socialists wanted none of it. Even Fabius resisted his argument that without alliances the PS would do badly, explaining that the party was less controllable than in 1986, and that many of the 282 deputies, inevitably evicted from favorable positions on a proportional list, would form their own lists and cause more trouble.[51] In June 1992 a sudden shift in opinion produced new momentum for the opposition, as voters came to believe it might have solutions where the Socialists had failed.[52]

Bérégovoy began bravely, with a declaration to the National Assembly that if "eleven months are a short time, they suffice to decide, to explain, to convince." He gave himself two priorities: the struggle against unemployment and the eradication of corruption. Unemployment in March 1992 stood at 10.3 percent of the workforce, and despite Bérégovoy's good intentions, it had climbed another percentage point to 11.3 by a year later—past the fatal figure of 3 million unemployed.

In his two periods as minister of the economy and finance, from 1984–1986 and 1988–1992, Bérégovoy had accomplished much: He had renewed and modernized the Paris stock market, now more important than ever before, created a futures market, overseen freeing of exchange and prices, and above all had been a tenacious advocate of a strong money vis-à-vis the deutsche mark, the *franc fort* (see Chapter 8 for an extended discussion). Initially an advocate of the "other policy" in 1983, he had accepted Mitterrand's policy of working toward an increasingly strong European union, which meant that instead of reverting to the earlier tactic of competitive devaluation, France had to pursue the idea of competitive disinflation, which in practice meant tying the French franc to the mark.

As prime minister, "Béré" continued his former economic policies. He was convinced that an improved trade balance would lead to creation of more jobs. In the years of renewed prosperity between 1987 and 1990 the French economy had created more than 800,000 jobs—but only dented unemployment, which never dropped below the 1983 level of more than 2 million unemployed. In 1992–1993, very few jobs could be created. Entering office, Bérégovoy rashly promised to wipe out long-term unemployment within six months. In December the results were out: The figures on the 900,000 unemployed for over one year had decreased by 6 percent—but at the end of December 1992 their ranks had filled again, and there were still 880,000 long-term unemployed.[53] The GDP had grown by only 1.6 percent in 1992. The 1993 budget, however, had been based on estimations of higher growth in 1992 and especially in 1993, and the deficit shot up.

Bérégovoy had worked for low inflation, stable prices, and the increased competivity of French industry. He won the praise of the international financial press and of French business. But as the number of scandals mounted, along with the unemployment statistics, this champion of fiscal orthodoxy began to lose popularity.

Despite his worker credentials (unusual in the PS) and long adherence to socialism, Bérégovoy was widely and correctly seen as the prime minister of a period of acquiescence (other than verbal) in a decline in popular incomes and a rise in social problems.

Bérégovoy bore another burden—one that was initially supposed to be an advantage but turned out not to be. In December 1991 France and the other European Community countries had signed the Treaty of Maastricht, to create a European Union including a future common currency and common foreign and security policy. In June 1992, after a referendum in Denmark had rejected the treaty, Mitterrand decided to submit the treaty to a referendum in France (see Chapter 9). The treaty turned out to be more divisive than integrating; its ratification in the referendum of September 20, 1992, showed the electorate almost evenly split, divided on lines of class and education. Much of the Socialist electorate did not heed its leaders, especially in the traditional Left areas of the south and the industrial north. This setback, so close to disaster, was not the last.

In early February 1993 *Le Canard Enchaîné* published a story that in 1986 Mitterrand's great friend Roger-Patrice Pelat had given Bérégovoy an interest-free million-franc loan to help him buy an apartment in the fashionable sixteenth arrondissement. Pelat had died in March 1989, but his name was by now well known as the businessman who had profited from inside trading in the purchase of Triangle-American Can by Péchiney. The investigation of the affair had pointed a finger at an anniversary party given by Bérégovoy in November 1988, at which his then chief aide Alain Boublil, Lebanese businessman Samir Traboulsi, and Pelat were present. All three had been indicted.

Other stories about Pelat's earlier activities were coming out—that he had had 5 million francs of free work done on his country property by a construction company, covered by false receipts. Pelat had allegedly used his influence with Mitterrand to get the company contracts to build a hotel in North Korea. Furthermore, Pelat's fortune had allegedly been built on the sale in 1982 of his company, Vibrachoc, to the recently nationalized Compagnie Générale d'Electricité. Pressure was allegedly exerted from on high to force the sale of a company that in any case was worth far less than the 110 million francs paid for it.[54]

Pelat had made the loan to Bérégovoy in 1986, when the Socialists were out of power; there was nothing illegal about it, and Bérégovoy had recognized the debt. But Thierry Jean-Pierre, who had dug up the dossier, raised the question whether the loan had not been a gift, with expectation of future favors. (The magistrate was preparing to launch himself into a political career on the Right.) Pelat's sons told the press that Bérégovoy had repaid half the money in 1992, after fiscal authorities had discovered the debt, and had already paid the other half in antique furniture and books. According to one of Bérégovoy's friends, the Pelat sons were trying to help him by launching this implausible story—but as Bérégovoy did not collect rare objects, it only got him into worse trouble.[55] The prime minister, pestered by journalists and heckled at meetings, became more and more depressed. Bérégovoy, who had prided himself on his probity and called for greater public honesty, now saw his reputation destroyed.

Bérégovoy had hoped to bring PS fortunes through the coming storm of the 1993 elections on March 21 and March 28. When the second-round votes were counted, the PS had suffered its worst defeat since 1967. The outgoing assembly had numbered 282 Socialists and associated Left; the new one had only 61. The Right had won an enormous majority: 484 seats out of 577. Bérégovoy believed that his own scandal had dragged the party down. On May 1 he killed himself.[56]

Cohabitation II

The suicide of Mitterrand's last Socialist prime minister marked the end of "the Epinay cycle,"[57] which began with the Socialist party takeover by Mitterrand in 1971. Under Mitterrand's leadership the PS had increased membership, found more voters and near success at the polls, conquered the presidency in 1981, and, after the cohabitation of 1986–1988, found victory again. In May 1993 *Le Point* could write: "With the death of Pierre Bérégovoy, a period is ending . . . the Mitterrand era is closing in an atmosphere of tragedy. The funeral of the former prime minister was also that of a certain kind of socialism."[58]

Never a friend to Mitterrand or his men, the Paris weekly nevertheless signaled the inevitable symbolism of this death—of the defeat of a socialism seen as too little social, too lost in the delights and temptations of power. And the odor of financial scandal, which apparently obsessed a proud and sensitive man and drove him to suicide, was a part of the moral laxity that characterized altogether too many Socialist officials. Even the charges of complicity in the terrible scandal of contaminated blood leveled against former ministers Georgina Dufoix and Edmond Hervé, as well as against ex–prime minister Laurent Fabius, blended, not entirely logically, into this pattern of a lapsed ethic and a party gone wrong.

François Mitterrand still had two years of his term to serve, but on September 16, 1992, it was announced that the nearly seventy-six-year-old president had undergone an operation for prostate cancer. Mitterrand's doctor unhappily signed a mendacious communiqué stating that the cancer was in an initial stage; in fact he had been secretly and successfully treating him for the condition since it was diagnosed in late 1981. But the president rapidly resumed an intense schedule, flying off on a visit to Israel and Jordan on September 25.[59]

In March 1993 Mitterrand appeared physically able to serve out his term, but politically he was entering a cohabitation very different from that with Jacques Chirac seven years earlier. Given his age, his health, and the health of the Socialist party, there was no question of a resurrection in 1995.

A second cohabitation was not automatic. In September 1992, shortly after the president's operation, Jacques Chirac had called for Mitterrand's resignation after the elections if the opposition won a large majority. His idea was supported by a number of leaders in the RPR and UDF. Some supposed that Mitterrand might try to escape from the dilemma of a second cohabitation by calling for a constitutional amendment to change the presidential term to five years—and then resigning to give the example. According to one of his counselors, he decided against any such idea because he might not have been able to get the amendment through the parliament. (The Senate, controlled by the opposition, might not have consented.) Also, since the PS was heading for a severe defeat, Mitterrand thought it better for the PS to have two years in the opposition before facing the next presidential election—which he doubted it could win—rather than face it in the conditions of early 1993.[60]

Mitterrand gave an interview to *Le Monde* in early February 1993 to say that he had no intention of resigning, that he and no other would name the prime minister, and that he would take no one who did not favor building Europe. Between the two rounds of the election, when it was already clear that the Socialists would do poorly, Chirac returned to the attack, arguing that since Mitterrand would be disavowed by universal suffrage, he should serve the national interest by resigning. Knowing that the opposition was not united, Mitterrand sent word that he was prepared to fight. Giscard immediately criticized Chirac's statement. Edouard Balladur, who expected to become the next prime minister, explained that the opposition had to assume the responsibilities of power.

Still master of the RPR, Jacques Chirac had decided that in 1993 he would not again become prime minister, but would let his chief counselor Balladur assume the job; meanwhile, he would concentrate on becoming president in 1995. What he did not yet know was that Balladur, always so loyal in the past, had come to the conclusion sometime after 1988 that Chirac was unelectable. When in February 1993 Chirac reverted to the line that Mitterrand had to leave immediately if the elections went overwhelmingly against him, Balladur began to think Chirac wanted to make a quick bid for the presidency. He solicited the support of Senate President René Monory as an intermediary with Mitterrand for Balladur's becoming prime minister and hinted broadly, "It's necessary for me to go to the Matignon for what comes afterward" (i.e., to run for president). In January 1993, when Balladur dined with a small circle close to Monory, the talk turned to Chirac's presidential hopes and Balladur expressed the view that he was finished. Chirac did not realize at first that this old friend had deserted him, but very quickly caught on. Oddly enough, he did not show particular emotion. His analysis was that Balladur could never be elected. Balladur also learned what Chirac was saying about him—and all that caused bad blood between them.[61]

Mitterrand was as always unwilling to let his hand be forced and did not wish to let it seem that he was appointing a prime minister by the grace of Jacques Chirac. He waited a day, did not send for Balladur to confer with him, and then went on television to announce Balladur's nomination. In his speech Mitterrand emphasized that he intended to watch over "the continuity of our foreign and defense policy," ensure that the Maastricht treaty would be implemented, and work to preserve national unity, "which rests upon the social cohesion of our country." Later that evening Balladur went to the Elysée, where he and the president agreed that both would "respect the institutions." Balladur emerged to declare that he had "accepted the president's decision" to nominate him.[62]

Born in Smyrna (Izmir) in 1927, Edouard Balladur descended from an originally Persian family converted to Roman Catholicism in the fourteenth century by Dominican missionaries, which had prospered under the Ottomans and been given French protection because they were Catholics. In 1926, Balladur's father acquired French citizenship, and he took the family to France when Edouard was a small boy.[63] Balladur had graduated from ENA like so many of his contemporaries who later acceded to high political office. There followed the prestigious Conseil d'Etat and a post in Georges Pompidou's prime ministerial cabinet. He rose to become secretary-general of the Elysée in Pompidou's last year as president. Suave, unctuous, polite, he appeared the model of the upper bourgeoisie, to which he had not belonged as a child. A vaguely clerical appearance attracted nicknames such as "the cardinal" and later "Your Sufficiency." In 1986–1988 *Le Monde*'s cartoonist Plantu invariably caricatured him borne in a sedan chair.

Balladur was a model of caution. He remembered the turbulent year 1968 and the experience of a triumphant Right that had charged back into power in 1986, only to be evicted again in 1988. In 1983 Balladur had developed the theory of cohabitation, which had not worked for Chirac. His new analysis was that a cohabitation that avoided the confrontations of 1986–1988 would succeed where Chirac, the hard charger, had failed. Balladur had neither the design nor the temperament to challenge the presidential prerogatives Mitterrand most cherished. In addition, Balladur had supported the Maastricht treaty and believed in the *franc fort*.

Balladur had not been especially popular before he was named prime minister, but within a month of his assuming office his poll ratings shot up, and after five months at the Matignon he was more popular than any prime minister before him. These figures were the more surprising, since unemployment remained high, pessimism had not diminished, and growth had not picked up. Balladur's popularity, in fact, derived in large measure from the fact that he was not a Socialist. His policies were not remarkably different from those of Bérégovoy—except for a commitment to explicit rather than gradual privatization. But whereas the Socialists—even Bérégovoy at the end—seemed to stand for shoddy morality, Balladur appeared sincere, honest, and efficient. With a strong majority behind him and a no-nonsense air, he exuded a pleasing sense of authority. These appearances were to fade somewhat in the next two years, as a number of prominent politicians of the Right were involved in their own scandals, finally including several members of Balladur's own government. But the initial impression of the new prime minister was almost entirely positive.[64]

His new government was composed of twenty-nine ministers, of whom the most important were Charles Pasqua, returning as interior minister, Alain Juppé, minister for foreign affairs, and Edmond Alphandéry, economics minister. In most French governments this last post is extremely important. However, the minister was not given the Finance Ministry, as was usual. It went to Balladur's close associate Nicolas

Sarkozy, an energetic young politician with ambitions to become Balladur's prime minister after 1995. The post of president of the National Assembly was given to another rising Gaullist politician, Philippe Séguin, no friend of Balladur's, who had strongly opposed the Maastricht treaty.

Mitterrand's popularity did not benefit from the popularity of his prime minister and the success of a cohabitation that the voters of the Right had not much wanted. His poll ratings improved only a few points over the depths to which they had sunk between December 1991 and the end of 1993. The prime minister did not seek to confront him, and the president acquiesced in most of the new government's actions, although he did not renounce occasionally objecting, as when he raised doubts in July 1993 on the government's plan to privatize twenty-one corporations, banks, and insurance companies. He also objected to a change in the Falloux law of 1850, which limited the amount of financial support the government could provide for private schooling. The diminished Left opposition offered more than 3,000 amendments, exhausting the fixed period of the regular session, and Mitterrand refused to call a special session of the parliament to continue discussion. The changes were nevertheless passed in December 1993, against the opposition of the president and the teachers' unions—but withdrawn in January after demonstrations.

Balladur's technique of governing resembled in many ways that of Rocard: Advance slowly after discussions and negotiations and break off when the going becomes too rough. François Mitterrand had complained that his prime minister suffered from immobilism when the prime minister was called Michel Rocard. He may very well have come to dislike a prime minister named Balladur for the same reason.[65]

The work of privatization went forward with the sale of the giant Banque Nationale de Paris and the chemical conglomerate Rhône-Poulenc in October-November 1993, followed in 1994 by Elf Aquitaine (33 billion francs), Renault (in part), and the major insurance company Union des Assurances de Paris. The profits from these privatizations helped the government to pledge to limit the deficit left behind by Bérégovoy and cut income taxes. In addition, a 40-billion-franc loan launched by Balladur in June was oversubscribed, bringing in 110 billion francs.

In his first policy declaration to the National Assembly Balladur had emphasized his intention of conducting privatizations and reforming the nationality laws. This latter task was dear to Interior Minister Pasqua, who remained convinced that the best way to cut down the voting power of the National Front was to meet Le Pen at least halfway. In June the Council of Ministers adopted the "Pasqua laws," which entered into force in November after a number of objections by the Constitutional Council and necessitated an amendment to the constitution. The principal change affected the application of the law of the soil *(ius soli)* traditional in France: Children of immigrants born on French soil were no longer automatically entitled to French citizenship but had to request it between the ages of sixteen and twenty-one. That not only left these young immigrants in limbo but also meant that foreign parents legally resident in France could no longer request French nationality for their minor children, formerly a means of consolidating permanent residence, since the parents of a French child could not be expelled.

Other provisions regulated the conditions for the entry and stay of foreigners in France, posing obstacles to obtaining permits for permanent residence, family re-grouping, refugee status, and, in some cases, marriage. The law facilitated the expul-sion of foreigners, some of whom had lived in France for years but could no longer renew their residence permits, thus becoming "illegal aliens." (This provision gave rise to a major incident in summer 1996, involving a group of Africans who sought refuge in a church in Paris from which they were expelled by the police.) Mayors re-ceived authorization to suspend for a week the celebration of the marriage of a French citizen with a foreigner and raise the question with a magistrate, if they sus-pected a *mariage blanc* (i.e., only for the purpose of regularizing status). The laws also gave the police increased powers to stop and search on mere suspicion.[66]

The target of these laws was of course not Portuguese or Spanish nationals resi-dent in France, but Moslems, in the first instance, North Africans. The efficacy of the Pasqua laws as a firebreak against the National Front may be measured by Le Pen's increased percentage in the 1995 presidential elections and FN successes in the 1995 municipal elections. A February 1995 poll found 54 percent of respondents agreeing with the proposition that "today, in our country, more is done for foreigners than for the French." In September 1996, after Le Pen had launched one of his sea-sonal provocations by speaking approvingly of the inequality of races, 40 percent of poll respondents said that although not close to the FN, they approved of some of its ideas.[67]

The month of August 1993 saw intense speculation against the franc that threat-ened the existence of the European Monetary System and continuation of the Maastricht treaty (see Chapter 8 for a more detailed discussion). The crisis was reme-died only by a Brussels agreement enlarging the EMS bands from 2.25 to 15 per-cent. Balladur did not take advantage of this theoretical space, however; although the franc-mark ratio deteriorated, France did not devalue.

Despite the fact that the GDP had diminished by 1 percent in 1993, for the first time in more than twelve years, the country continued to register confidence in Balladur, though his poll ratings were lower at the end of 1993 than in May. Once again, however, a crisis emerged on the student front, as in 1986.

In January, Mitterrand used his address to the press to object to the changes in the old Falloux law authorizing communities to finance without any limit investments by private schools. On January 16, more than a half million people turned out in Paris to demonstrate against the law, which the government had already hastily with-drawn. In March, there were student demonstrations against the government's pro-posal for a new *contrat d'insertion professionelle,* or CIP, intended to increase employ-ment by permitting youths to work at 80 percent of the minimum wage. Lycée students (not the main target—the basic idea was to employ school-leavers) were in-censed and were joined by university students in demonstrations in eighty French cities from March 10 to March 30. The government then withdrew the scheme. Balladur had backed down in the preceding November, after a plan for increased economies and 4,000 dismissals at Air France had caused a strike that paralyzed air-ports for six weeks. Backing down again after the Falloux demonstrations and the

CIP affair diminished his air of authority—rightly or wrongly, he was seen as weak, and his poll ratings went down. The charge of "immobilism" was raised again.[68]

Nevertheless, after indications that the economy was improving (the government's slogan: Things are picking up), Balladur won back approval and rose in the polls for a number of months. Unemployment increased in the autumn, however, and a new rash of scandals shook the government. Communications Minister Alain Carignan, who was also mayor of Grenoble, was forced to resign from the government when implicated in a Grenoble corruption case, and he was arrested in October after he had apparently tried to influence witnesses. Another minister, Gérard Longuet, who was also president of the Parti Républicain, was forced to resign in October after being involved in a different affair.

From fall 1994 to the presidential election in April, the rivalry inside the RPR dominated the government's attention. After Chirac's defeat in 1988 it had been generally agreed that the presence of two candidates on the Right, Chirac and Barre, had in the end detracted from success in the second round. Various schemes for "primaries" were floated in the intervening years, pushed in particular by Pasqua. At first those were seen as a means of avoiding a conflict between an RPR candidate—sure to be Chirac—and a UDF one, conceivably Giscard. But in 1993–1994, as Balladur's popularity soared above that of other politicians of the Right and remained obstinately fifteen points or more higher than Chirac's throughout 1994, Balladur's ambitions were confirmed.

Chirac, however, had no intention of ceding the way to his former protégé. He declared his candidacy in November 1994, in order to give himself momentum. (Balladur did not declare until January 18.) Paris wags amused themselves by remarking that Chirac, who had fashioned his career by "betraying" first the 1974 Gaullist candidate Chaban-Delmas in order to elect Giscard, then Giscard in 1981, was only reaping what he had sown. Chirac seemed to have little chance. In January 1995 Interior Minister Pasqua, not one with a fondness for the losing side, declared for Balladur. In order to establish his right to be president, Chirac had to differentiate himself from Balladur—which meant that he had to run to the left of him.

Chirac still controlled the machinery of the RPR, but Balladur, himself a member of that party, had attracted part of it: not only Pasqua, but also all those whom his shadow Nicolas Sarkozy (also RPR) had recruited, arguing that they could safely abandon Chirac, with the line "Balladur never forgives, Chirac always does"—in other words a risk-free operation. The bulk of Balladur's troops, however, came from the UDF—the CDS had declared in favor of Balladur, as had the Parti Républicain. Twenty-one members of Balladur's government declared for him, although some important UDF figures decided for Chirac—notably Alain Madelin, a strong advocate of free enterprise, Rhône-Alpes regional president Charles Millon, and ultimately, late in the campaign, even Giscard.

Chirac's rhetoric could easily have been mistaken for that of the Left: "France is in trouble. . . . Ultimately, we are at the point of thinking we can do nothing. . . . These renunciations sometimes take on the seductive colors of modernity.

. . . Everything that is not conformist is denounced as unreasonable, irresponsible or insolent. . . . I have come to tell the French that it is time to renounce renunciation."

At the end of January *Libération* could write, "Chirac totally alone." Suddenly, in February 1995, Chirac made a breakthrough in the polls, and Balladur's ratings dropped. Some of this loss was attributable to a major mistake by Pasqua, who up to then had figured as a probable prime minister if Balladur were elected. In December 1994 magistrate Eric Halphen, who had been investigating a case involving dummy receipts of the public housing office in the Paris region, was attacked indirectly when RPR official Didier Schuller accused Halphen's father-in-law of demanding a payoff to help call off his son-in-law. The father-in-law, J.-P. Maréchal, was arrested for extortion amid discussion of pulling Halphen off the case. In early 1995 more facts came out—involving illegal phone taps—and it seemed probable that Maréchal had been set up in order to keep his son-in-law from pursuing a case that might have embarrassed Pasqua in his home department. The director of the investigatory police felt obliged to resign. Pasqua thought he could recover the situation by trumpeting the discovery of economic espionage by the CIA—an affair that the foreign ministry had not wished to dramatize, and that found the Interior and Foreign Ministries contradicting each other. Pasqua's ploy was a bit too obvious.

At the same time, Balladur was proving a poor candidate. An electorate whose chief concerns were the high rate of unemployment and possible descent into lasting poverty had for nearly two years seen in him its best hope. His disclosure of his fortune—which had become obligatory for French politicians—showed that he was a rich man—and served to dramatize his character as a *grand bourgeois.* The conjugation of scandals in his government and shadows thrown on his character cut Balladur's momentum. Chirac had never enjoyed great popularity outside the RPR, but he was a natural and very energetic politician, whereas Balladur was at best an awkward one, slow to understand the importance of getting out of Paris and campaigning, unable to rebound once his popularity began to slide. In the event, Chirac outpointed his rival in the first round on April 23 by 574,000 votes and went on to face Socialist candidate Lionel Jospin.[69]

The PS: A Field of Ruins?

In December 1991 Rocard and Fabius had agreed that the younger man should be first secretary, the older one the party's "virtual candidate" for president. Before the legislative election of 1993, there was some fear that a severe defeat might trigger a settling of accounts between the old Rocardians and the Mitterrandist Left, with a chunk of the PS veering off into the abyss of the totally unelectable Left, like the British Labour party after 1979. Rocard moved to assert his leadership and preempt this possibility with a speech about *"le big bang"* on February 17, 1993. The speech itself was remarkable in Rocard's frankly discounting defeat, saying, "Do not think that they [the French electorate] have any illusions about the Right, but know that if they are thinking of giving it power, that provides the measure of the reproaches they make to us."[70] Its purpose was to put up signposts for the bleak postelection period.

The "big bang" speech was initially interpreted as a sign that Rocard wanted to merge a PS that had grown too weak into a larger whole, to pick up Green and Center votes. It rapidly became apparent that even if that was his medium-term goal, a shoring up of the PS base was a priority.

Some parts of the PS had been looking with interest at the increase in the ecologist vote, which by the early 1990s, despite division into at least two parties, les Verts, led by Antoine Waechter, and Génération Ecologie, headed by Brice Lalonde, was rapidly growing. In 1990 the main Socialist thrust was somehow to co-opt this vote—which would reach nearly 15 percent for the two parties together in the 1992 regional elections. After 1992 the Socialists sought alliances, which were rejected. The Verts–Génération Ecologie alliance fell 12 percent short of its highest polling rating in the first round in March 1993, to 7.6 percent of the vote—but there was no consequent benefit to the PS. The Center gained more National Assembly seats than ever before, and its leaders were given a prominent role in the new Balladur government. There was thus no immediate prospect of gathering much new strength from these quarters, even if Rocard tried. Indeed, just before the election Rocard defined his task thus: "to transform completely our common home, but in no case to destroy it." [71]

Between mid-February and early April 1993 the Rocardian forces became increasingly doubtful whether Fabius could be kept even in a nominal position as PS first secretary. It was suggested before the elections that he step down and become leader of the PS group in the National Assembly. Rocard had lost his assembly seat in March 1993, whereas Fabius had held on to his, but that did not make much difference. Even before the elections a number of figures in the PS had concluded not only that Fabius had been seriously wounded by the charges in the blood scandal, unfounded or not, but also that he did not have the stuff of a real leader.

At a *comité directeur* meeting on April 3, Fabius was deposed as first secretary and Rocard became party leader, in a confused battle that did little credit to either of them. Rocard was accused of reneging on an agreement brokered by Pierre Mauroy that he and Fabius act in concert; but apparently Fabius's tenacity in holding on to his position as long as possible excited increased opposition to him. As always, the followers of Lionel Jospin (who had declared his withdrawal from politics) were anti-Fabius, but so was the Gauche Nouvelle group of Julien Dray and Jean-Luc Mélanchon.

Rocard's takeover met with much initial criticism: as a "putsch" (Fabiusian Paul Quilès), "night of the long knives" (Jean Poperen), "pronunciamento" (Jack Lang). Jean-Pierre Chevènement, who with his friends had planned to leave the party in any case after the elections and set up their Mouvement des Citoyens, announced at that point that he was leaving the party.[72]

Rocard proposed to galvanize and reorganize the PS. He had described it in his "big bang" speech as "a closed society attached to its rites, with its little factional quarrels or struggles, claiming to offer to the outside world a monolithic discourse,

[but] for which any disagreement is a drama, every deviation a sacrilege—and [which] only accepts allies in submission." After considering opposition to Rocard, the Fabiusians, having lost the support of the Pas-de-Calais federation, the strongest in the PS, decided to cooperate and accept Rocard's game, for the time being at least. But the gulf between the Rocardians and the Fabius Mitterrandists—and some Mitterrandists who had followed Jospin—had not closed. The ideas of the Fabius faction were little different from those of the Rocardians—but talk about ideology in the PS of the 1990s was infinitely less important than membership in the right clan. Former interior minister Paul Quilès, a hard-line Fabiusian, had said bitterly after Rocard's coup that Rocard was not even "un homme de gauche"—he meant that as the ultimate insult—but it was a stock insult, no more meaningful than "son of a bitch."[73] Rocard had taken over the party, but his power in it was slight and depended on success, with a first electoral test in the European elections of June 1994.

Rocard failed that test. The PS had never done well in European elections; when Fabius headed the list in 1989 he was criticized for getting only 23.5 percent of the vote. In 1994, after its 17.8 percent score in the 1993 elections, the PS could hardly hope to do well. Rocard nevertheless decided in 1993 that he had to head the list in June 1994, rather than put in a symbolic figure (as the RPR/UDF did in 1994 with Toulouse mayor Dominique Baudis, not a figure of the first rank). Rocard reasoned that a defeat would be ascribed to him in any case.[74] When he made the decision, he knew that he would probably have to reckon with the new Mouvement des Citoyens headed by Chevènement, which would take a certain percentage of the Left vote strongly opposed to Maastricht. He had not reckoned on the emergence of a reconditioned MRG under the leadership of Bernard Tapie.

Tapie was perhaps François Mitterrand's favorite scoundrel, whom he continued to support even when scandals accumulated around him. In 1994 his once-flourishing businesses were failing, and he was about to be declared bankrupt. He had already been indicted in two cities for misuse of company funds and would soon face four more indictments. In July, after the elections, the police would search his luxurious house and confiscate his furniture for payment of debt. He was, however, still a deputy from Marseilles, owner of the local football team Olympique, and extraordinarily popular in his city, where he hoped to be elected mayor in 1995. He had faced down and defeated Le Pen in Marseilles and had been twice a minister in Bérégovoy's government, having resigned when indicted and later returned to office.

Mitterrand encouraged Tapie to run for the European Parliament, did nothing to dissuade former PS minister of European affairs Catherine Lalumière from taking third position on Tapie's list, and allowed rumors to escape that he looked favorably on Tapie's effort. Mitterrand's entourage now admits that pushing Tapie was a deliberate tactic on the president's part, risk free, as he saw it, because Tapie's highest ambition was to become mayor of Marseilles. Mitterrand may not have guessed how well Tapie would do, but his tactic was to have someone with popular appeal use the themes of the Left, plus Europe, to hang on to an electorate that Rocard seemed to be losing. If Rocard were badly damaged by this tactic, Mitterrand could contain his sorrow. As the president saw it, Rocard's policies had reduced the PS to a party of state employees and cadres, and a popular vote that once had favored the PS looked as if it might not just go briefly to Le Pen or the RPR but be captured by or split by them.[75] Tapie campaigned on a pro-Europe line, but his most extraordinary domestic slogan was a promise to make unemployment illegal. Rocard did not mobilize his electorate; Tapie did. The election results were a shocker: Rocard's ticket gleaned just 14.49 percent of the vote, whereas Tapie had 12 percent.

As postelection surveys showed, Tapie was supported by a larger percentage of men between eighteen and thirty-four than Rocard (he did more than twice as well in that category) and by women eighteen to twenty-four. Tapie did better than Rocard among employees, workers, the unemployed, and students. He also did better than Le Pen in all these categories. Half of Tapie's voters had voted PS in March 1993.[76]

Rocard had campaigned on a slogan of "Europe, yes, but socially responsible" *(solidaire);* the "yes, but" failed to carry conviction. His campaign was badly organized, and although he had expected to gain votes by imposing a ticket split evenly between men and women, he was not pleased by the list of candidates he finally adopted in order to achieve factional balance, and his speeches were not convincing. Rocard, said his friend Guy Carcassonne, is incapable of making a good speech if he is not entirely convinced of what he's saying.[77] This is a considerable handicap for a politician, and goes some way to justify Mitterrand's disdain for Rocard's talents.

Rocard attempted to put a good face on his defeat, but a week after the election the PS national council met, and a Mitterrandist coalition, only in part Fabiusian, demanded and received Rocard's resignation. He was replaced by Henri Emmanuelli, who immediately adopted a more leftist line. Rocard was no longer the future Socialist candidate for the presidency; he was merely another defeated politician.

Rocard admitted in retrospect that probably his real mistake had been to take over the party. "I thought to rehabilitate the PS," he said, "but it was the wrong tactic." Carcassonne thought Rocard had little choice but to take over the party and then had two choices—to reassemble the Socialists, which meant compromises, or to renew the party, at the risk of splitting it, knowing that at best half of it would follow him. In the event, he tried to do both, and lost at both ends.[78]

Serge Halimi wrote about the Tapie vote:

> In a despairing France, haunted by fear of losing status, this apparently ruined businessman had as his principal virtue that of being pursued by the authorities, scorned by the elites, and wanting to make unemployment illegal. . . . To see nothing in this "program" but "demagogy" means forgetting a deep aspiration of the *peuple de gauche:* that the primacy of political will should take precedence over theories of impotence.

A more sober assessment, not essentially different, was given by George Ross, who wrote of

> Rocard's hope-deflating technocratic managerialism. [He had] apparently come to believe by the later 1980s that managing the margins for maneuver allowed by globaliza-

tion and a sluggish international economy, and preaching that there were no other alternatives, was a formula for success. This betrayed a basic misunderstanding of the historic role of the Left, which had always traded on hope for change as well as competence. Rocard's political line actively discouraged optimism in the name of realism, at a moment when the world itself gave fewer and fewer reasons for hope, particularly to the "people of the Left."[79]

Tapie's legal troubles deepened rapidly after his performance in the European elections. In any case, he was not a Socialist but had joined the MRG, rebaptized merely as "Radical," and later, Parti Radical-Socialiste (PRS). Rocard was no longer a possible candidate for the presidential elections of April 1995. The remaining popular figure was not in Paris—his popularity derived in part from the fact that he had spent the past ten years in Brussels: European Commission president Jacques Delors.

Delors and Rocard had enjoyed roughly equal popularity for a number of years, well above that of other Socialist figures except Mitterrand. But Delors's poll ratings remained ten points or more above Rocard's during the period after Rocard took over as first secretary of the PS (when Rocard's ratings went down) and of course far above them after Rocard's loss in the European elections and ejection from his party post.

By summer 1994 Delors thus appeared to be the Socialist party's sole hope of winning the presidency in 1995, and the party desperately wanted him to run. Here was an apparent paradox. Under Henri Emmanuelli, the party had taken a turn to the left, which was emphasized at a special congress held in November in the northern industrial town of Liévin. But Delors, though a member of the Mitterrandist faction who had joined the PS in 1972, was regarded by many Socialists as an outsider. Had he not been the brains behind Jacques Chaban-Delmas when he was Pompidou's prime minister in 1969–1972? Was he not a devout Catholic, practically a Christian Democrat? Emmanuelli, immediately after the Liévin congress, published an article in which he declared: "To my knowledge, Jacques Delors is neither a candidate to become first secretary of the Socialist party nor to define its doctrine." Here was a warning: The Socialists would welcome a successful Delors candidacy, but would not accept his ideas.[80]

Mitterrand, who had no "dauphin" left by 1994, favored Delors but had doubts whether he would run. He twice sent his political counselor Maurice Benassayag up to Brussels to persuade Delors to run, but confided cynically to him, "He not only has a chance to win, he has a very good chance to win—which is the reason he won't run!"[81]

Delors had just put in ten difficult years as president of the European Commission, was nearly seventy, and was still suffering from the sciatica that had been afflicting him in recent years. On December 11, Delors announced that he would not be a candidate. Some of his reasons were apparently personal, one of them being that he did not want to affect the future career of his daughter, Martine Aubry, one of the rising stars of the PS, afterwards mentioned as a possible prime minister had Jospin won. The major reason he gave was the difficulty of creating a working majority (if he won and then dissolved the National Assembly, as he would have had to do). A Socialist-Centrist ticket would probably have suited Delors, and he did sound out the Centrists, notably Jacques Barrot and Pierre Méhaignerie. Their view was that they would do well to stay with Balladur (then seen as a winner), and adherence to Delors was electorally too risky.[82] But any alliance with the Centrists would have been more difficult for Delors to manage than the abortive opening to the Center in 1988 would have been for Mitterrand.

After Delors had said no, there was no obvious Socialist presidential candidate. Whereas polls testing the popularity of candidates had given Delors 65 percent a few days earlier, no one did better in late December than Jack Lang's 31 percent. Lang, however, was unpopular with the Jospin faction. His major asset was his claim that if he ran, "Radical" would not present Tapie. On December 14 a court order to liquidate Tapie's assets also made him ineligible for election for five years. Rocard formally announced on December 13 that he would not be a candidate. In a December 17 meeting he referred to the PS as "a field of ruins."[83]

On January 4, Lionel Jospin announced his candidacy (which he had decided on before Christmas, informing both Mitterrand and Emmanuelli). There followed a confused period in which the various Socialist leaders sought to inherit what power would be left in the party after what everyone considered a hopeless election. Fabius declared on January 15 that he was not in a position to run (since the contaminated blood affair still hung over him), whereas Emmanuelli and Lang both declared their candidatures. Fabius did not want Lang and, after failing to find another viable candidate he liked, backed Emmanuelli, and Lang withdrew. The choice of a candidate was made by a hastily organized internal primary of all party members on February 4. They elected delegates who met on the following day for a formal nomination. Seventy-three percent of the members of the now much reduced PS (103,000 adherents) voted; 66 percent cast their ballots for Jospin.

In a poll on six possible Socialist candidates in late December 1994, Jospin had come in fourth, behind Lang, Martine Aubry, and Rocard. Now he seemed like Fortinbras in the fifth act of *Hamlet*, the only claimant left alive on a stage littered with corpses. With the momentum given him by the strong Socialist vote of confidence, he mounted a vigorous campaign. Jospin is not a charismatic figure and has always appeared rather rigid, but he projected an aura of conviction and deep personal honesty, which contrasted with the recent record of François Mitterrand. He had risen in the PS as one of Mitterrand's favorites, but had resented the preference the president gave to Fabius. Some of the difference between the two men was personal, but there remained on Jospin's part a dislike of the way with which Fabius had adapted so easily from the left-wing rhetoric of 1979 to the cool moderation of 1983 and after.

Jospin was a Mitterrandist, but he had marked his differences with his old chief. In the statement he made at the Liévin congress, he went further than any other Socialist leader in criticizing the ethics of the Mitterrand period: "The profligacy of some of the friends of the Socialist government, the personal failings of some of our own people, not immediately denounced, an insufficiently rigorous style of power and an astonishing indulgence for persons who have been compromised have tarnished our collective image."[84]

Mitterrand cannot have cared much for this criticism. He reportedly never had forgiven Jospin for opposing Fabius in 1988 and in 1990. But Jospin did not want his active support and, after paying Mitterrand a visit during the campaign on April 3, declared, "Any candidate, even if he is a friend of the president, even if he shares—as I do—a certain number of ideas and values in common—has no business asking for the president's support." And he continued to claim a "right of inventory" on the record of fourteen years of Mitterrand's power.

Jospin had never made a formal alliance with Rocard, but over the years his ideas had approached those of the other leader. He had become a Socialist whom Delors could support with enthusiasm, and Rocard, with considerable conviction. The Emmanuelli leadership, in contrast, regarded him with suspicion—not entirely for partisan reasons.

In the first round of the elections Chirac had to win against Balladur to be in the second round. He became a "new Chirac," overtaking Balladur by passing him on his left, denouncing those who looked to the experts for everything, making five (very general) promises: Give everyone in France his place and his chance in society, set the vital forces in France to serve employment, build real solidarity, give back to the French the mastery of their own destiny, guarantee the republican order. Said Jospin, "He's hiding the man of the Right he has always been behind a thick fog."[85]

There had been concern on the part of the Left that the two top runners would both be Rightists, as in 1969. To the general surprise, Jospin topped the poll with 23 percent. Chirac had to rally the Balladur voters to him, which of course meant steering further right; he had polled only 20.47 percent of the first-round vote. When the second round was over, Jospin had put up a good fight, better than anyone had expected, but Chirac won with a convincing 52.63 percent, with majorities in all age groups except those thirty-five to forty-eight (the so-called Mitterrand generation). Postelection polls showed that the personality of the candidate counted for a good deal, and whereas 39 percent of respondents accorded Chirac the stature of a chief of state, only 5 percent did so for Jospin. Finally and perhaps most important, 55 percent of respondents had concluded that the overall balance of Mitterrand's fourteen years was negative.[86]

The votes of the first round were also significant. Le Pen had his best score ever: 15 percent. Philippe de Villiers, who with an anti-Maastricht message on the Right had equaled Tapie on the Left in the 1994 European elections, failed to break through and had only 4.74 percent. The veteran Trotskyite candidate Arlette Laguiller did better than any other of that stripe in the past, with 5.3 percent. The ecologist candidate Dominique Voynet saw the once-rising Green vote fall back to where it had been in the two previous presidential elections, barely over 3 percent. And the new head of the Communist party, Robert Hue, unable to convince voters that he and his party had changed despite the retirement of Georges Marchais, took only 8.64 percent.

Various conclusions may be drawn from these votes. De Villiers's failure suggested that the right wing of the UDF that he represented, mostly rural and elderly, could not mount a real challenge to the pro-European majority of the party. The good Trotskyite score reflected continuing anger on the part of those inclined toward the far left at Socialist policies since 1983.

The cases of the Greens and the National Front are more interesting, since each had seemed in 1992 able to take nearly a sixth of the electorate. But the ecologists had begun to run downhill in 1993, did worse in 1994, and failed utterly in 1995. The attraction of their cause had diminished as unemployment became the dominant concern of all electorates, and their credit as a fresh, apolitical force was badly shattered by the infighting that increasingly marked them.[87]

The National Front's Hold on the Voters

If 1995 showed that the Greens had worn badly, the National Front had confirmed its strength. In the 1994 European elections it had done less well than in 1989, and some observers thought that its influence had crested.

But in the first round of the 1995 presidential elections, Jean-Marie Le Pen made his best score, with 15 percent of the vote. The National Front is a party with extreme-right-wing leaders, but with a sociological profile not typical of French right-wing parties. In 1995, 46 percent of Le Pen's voters were workers or employees—a higher percentage than any other candidate (34 percent for Communist Robert Hue, 31 for Jospin, 26 for Chirac). Although it lost some voters in the departments of the Mediterranean littoral, its area of early strength, the FN has made broad advances (between 25 and 30 percent) in some of the devastated industrial towns in the French rust belt, the departments hard hit by the restructuring of industry in the north and east in the 1970s and 1980s.

To Le Pen's constant themes of the dangers of immigrants and the proliferation of crime were added new inflections of the traditional values theme, based on denunciation of corruption, which by 1995 could be seen to be no monopoly of the Socialist party. Le Pen drew 27 percent of the worker vote, more than any other candidate. Fewer members of the middle classes voted for him than in 1988, when he had shocked the nation with 14.5 percent, but many more workers and unemployed.

Le Pen's highest scores came, however, in the two Alsatian departments (25.83 percent in Bas-Rhin and 24.8 in Haut-Rhin). If those statistics had come from neighboring Germany, they would have rung alarm bells everywhere. In Alsace, which is not depressed economically, the FN vote is something of a puzzle. The best explanation is that aside from resentment at the presence of a poorly integrated Turkish immigrant population in some areas, the problem is cultural. Alsatian conservatism and particularism have responded to Le Pen's traditionalist discourse. "In an Alsace that has doubts on its identity and is looking for its place 'at the junction of two great European countries,' the dizziness of the quest for identity has sought a perch in a mythical national identity reviewed and corrected by Jean-Marie Le Pen."[88]

In the first round of municipal elections in June 1995 the National Front received more than 10 percent of the vote in 108 cities with more than 30,000 inhabitants. In the second round, it won the mayor's office in the cities of Toulon, Orange, and Marignane, and a dissident from the FN was elected mayor of Nice. Political scientist Pascal Perrineau wrote, "For the first time in its history, an extreme rightist movement has sunk real popular roots."[89] Overall, crime and the immigration question rate much higher in the concerns of National Front voters than those of other parties. Unemployment rates higher still, but that is a general concern—it was the combination of these themes in a single program that apparently drew new voters to Le Pen.

François Mitterrand's gamble on splitting the Right has thus turned against the Left as well. With its simultaneous appeal to disgruntled youth, workers, and part of the middle classes, the FN has some resemblance to Fascist movements before World War II. Up to now, however, the FN has largely kept to an electoral and parliamentary strategy.

Polls have shown up to 40 percent of the population not ill content to have Le Pen in some way as their spokesman on crime and on the immigrant question. However, the number of those who have indicated a bad opinion of the National Front in monthly queries dropped below 75 percent only twice—and then briefly—between 1988 and 1995; the variations in the number of good opinions of the FN come rather from rallies by the undecideds—who in the election month of April 1995 were tallied at 6 percent.[90] We thus have an apparent contradiction indicated by polling and electoral data—a large number of French voters disgusted and disillusioned with both Left and Right, a large number who reject a movement that they consider unacceptable. Nevertheless, this disgust with parties that have failed to reduce unemployment and are mined by corruption has left the National Front as the great protest party, supported by voters coming from traditional Left and Right.

The PCF, formerly the great protest party, saw its score in the 1995 presidentials improve over the disaster of 1988 (8.7 versus 6.8 percent). However, the improvement resulted from the more sympathetic image of the candidate, new secretary-general Robert Hue, who picked up votes in areas where the Communists cannot win the more-significant local elections, whereas the party's vote in its old areas of strength fell off. In the years between 1978 and 1995 the PCF has lost the youth vote: In 1978 the PCF had 28 percent of young people eighteen to twenty-four, and 26 percent in the twenty-five-to-thirty-four-year-old group. In 1995 those figures were 6 and 10 percent. One great obstacle for the old PCF was its devotion to the Soviet Union (which paradoxically coexisted with a fierce French nationalism). The National Front does not have that handicap.

The Post-Mitterrand Political Scene

By running to the left of Balladur, Jacques Chirac had contrived to fulfill his life's ambition of winning the presidency. The electorate preferred Chirac to the Socialist candidate in part because Jospin was an unfamiliar face, in part because, despite

Jospin's personal probity, the PS was thoroughly discredited. Chirac, however, entered office with no great capital of credit, and the blunders of his first year diminished this slender stock, so that his poll ratings compare poorly with Mitterrand's at his lowest.

A certain sense of entitlement now exists at most levels of French society that co-exists uneasily and confusedly with the sensation that France cannot long afford the cost of its welfare state. The Chirac government lacks the authority to resolve this contradiction. The Socialists heightened the sense of entitlement, then disappointed it in multiple ways without ever explaining to the country (or to themselves) the causes of their action.

After the revolutions of 1989 the French Socialists (and their fellows elsewhere) asked themselves whether the collapse of socialism in eastern Europe had any relevance for social democracy. In the narrow sense, the answer is no—the kind of tactics pursued in the east bloc had no counterpart in western Europe. But in a wider sense, the notion that the attempt to improve society on a large scale by state action leads to a "socio-economic and political order that is feasible and viable, more efficient than and morally superior to capitalism" had been dealt a heavy blow, probably a fatal one. "The Left today must face questions . . . how to make capitalism work for the benefit of the least advantaged, the vulnerable and the excluded; how to tame the destructive effects of markets; how to attain more social justice in the face of the declining reach of the state."[91] That those questions were relevant for the Right was amply demonstrated by the upset election of 1997, which put the interrogation again to the Left.

7

Successes, Failures, Question Marks

The Serendip Effect

The scandals and frustrations of the final years of the Mitterrand period are by no means the whole story of the fourteen-year presidency. In 1986 the Socialists had asked the country to renew its confidence in them on the basis of the laws they had passed and their record as administrators. The voters' judgment on the administrative record of 1981–1983 was harsh, although their view of much of the legislation enacted in 1981–1986 was favorable.[1] After two years, the voters changed their minds and voted to renew Mitterrand's lease on the Elysée, then stopped just short of giving the Socialist party a new legislative majority.

The list of laws passed and administrative actions taken does not sum up all the transformations in France that came about as a direct or indirect result of the Socialist victory in 1981. The Socialists had thought of themselves as the architects of change. With the retrospect of only a few years it is possible to see them instead as its agents, generating change here, eliciting it elsewhere, often without deliberate intent or preconceived plan.

In 1976 the Gaullist politician and writer Alain Peyrefitte described the role of the unexpected and unintentional in the history of France: "In the strange country of Serendip, everything happens backwards. You find what you were not looking for; you never find what you are looking for. . . . The Serendip effect is the daily bread of our history. It affects all the regimes that France has given itself—they have all achieved the opposite of what they sought."[2]

The Socialists had no cause to love Gaullist politician Peyrefitte but might nevertheless admit some resemblance between the Serendip effect and the course of events after 1981. A striking example of an indirect result of Mitterrand's election is the conversion of the French Right from Gaullist *dirigisme* to free enterprise, provoked to a considerable degree by its need to find a doctrine totally distinguishable from *dirigiste* socialism.

The second great unintentional change after 1981 was that in the Socialists themselves. Their program, combining certain socialist measures and left-Keynesianism, was thrown off balance by bad timing and mistaken estimates. What followed, after 1983, was a Socialist retreat from ideology. The Socialists of 1981 had seemed more firmly ideological than they really were, in part because they were persuaded that all their ideas were logically interconnected.

Reflation (with socially beneficent effects) would aid a centrally controlled economy to expand and vanquish unemployment. The link connecting reflation, nationalization, and socialist ideas in general was shattered when reflation failed and the "commanding heights of the economy" turned out to command only the necessity of assuming new fiscal burdens. The cure for debt and inflation had to be found in an austerity that kept growth low while unemployment was rising.

As intoxication with their rhetoric evaporated into a disabused hangover, French Socialists came to realize that new and nonideological policies were necessary. They had fallen into an error Stanley Hoffmann has described as "typical of Liberals (be they reformist democrats or social democrats): a belief that all good things must come together," a mind-set that sees no reason why obtaining social justice by higher corporate taxation might be incompatible with a desired rise in profits and investments.[3]

Once the Socialists recognized the incompatibility of economically necessary policies and their ideology, they faced the choice of falling back on the interior lines of bunker mentality or advancing into the unexplored country of pragmatism. Under Mitterrand's leadership, most of the party found it possible to understand that some of its goals might be contradicted by others.

Some of their original goals were reached; other results were at least in part unintentional. The results of ambitious Socialist legislation on decentralization, nationalization, labor relations, audiovisual communications, the administration of justice, and other areas remain to be considered.

Institutional Change

The constitution of the Fifth Republic had been legitimized not only by the referendum that ratified it but still more by its success in providing stable government. At the end of the 1970s the new institutions were generally accepted by a country almost equally divided between Left and Right. Nevertheless, the system still seemed blocked and endangered by the seeming impossibility of electing a president and a legislature of the Left. The elections of 1981 took care of that problem, and Mitterrand declared at the beginning of his first term that he would "exercise the full powers granted him by the constitution, neither more nor less."[4]

One institution created by the constitution of 1958 posed a special problem for the Socialists. This was the Constitutional Council, a body intended by the founders of the Fifth Republic as an executive instrument to check the powers of a potentially assertive legislature. Its chief purpose was to provide a constitutional body to clarify the distinction between laws and regulations. The constitution defined certain areas where only the parliament could pass statutes, mentioning but not defining other areas with "a regulatory character" (Article 37:2) where the government could rule by decree. The Constitutional Council's task was to determine whether such decrees were in fact "regulatory." The council was also supposed to review disputed elections and annul them where fraud or other irregularities were discovered and to watch over the regularity of the presidential election.

The other key text governing the council's powers (Article 61) allowed it to verify the constitutionality of laws prior to their promulgation. Originally, only the president, prime minister, and the presidents of the National Assembly and Senate possessed the power of referring legislation to the council—which they used so sparingly that between 1959 and 1974 only twenty-nine cases were sent to it. The original intent of this provision was once again to act as a check on the parliament. The authors of the constitution had no wish to create a court undertaking judicial review, with the extensive scope and powers of the U.S. Supreme Court.[5]

In 1974 President Giscard had been searching for liberal social or institutional measures, which he hoped would attract moderates on the Left to back his programs. In this spirit, he sponsored a constitutional amendment allowing the Constitutional Council's examination of a bill to be invoked by a petition signed by sixty deputies or senators. The suspicious Left parties voted against the amendment. Believing that the voters would soon entrust the government to them, they saw in the amendment only the strengthening of a nonlegislative power wielded by a body of conservative magistrates.

The idea of judicial control over the legislature was in any case foreign to the national tradition. The Constitutional Council had only the slightest precedent in French constitutional history—a Constitutional Committee instituted by the Fourth Republic. It had little power and met only once. The German and Austrian Bundesgerichtshöfe and the Italian Corte Costituzionale were little known or regarded in France, whereas the better-known U.S. Supreme Court inspired distrust. The French spoke of a "government by judges," a phrase coined in an influential 1921 book on the U.S. Supreme Court by Edouard Lambert, which examined the record of the Supreme Court and concluded that judicial review resulted in a reactionary "government by judges."[6] The phrase also recalled the *parlements* of the old regime, swiftly abolished by the Revolution in 1789.

The warnings against a government by judges therefore came naturally to the Left, although the Left opposition did make some use of the new constitutional provision, referring sixty laws to the council in 1974–1981.[7] But when the Left won both the presidency and a National Assembly majority in 1981, conservatives realized that the council was the only constitutional weapon left in their arsenal. Its nine members had all been appointed by their side: by past presidents of the Republic, the National Assembly, and the Senate. Each of them named three members, who sat for a term of nine years.

The council proved a considerable obstacle to the smooth passage of legislation by the overwhelmingly powerful Left majority. In January 1982 it blocked the nationalization law, on the grounds that although nationalizations were acceptable on principle (they were even mentioned in the constitution), the formula for compensation was not just. The opposition and the conservative press were overjoyed at this blow to the Left. A redrafted law was presented to the National Assembly ten days after the council's decision and pushed through to go to the Senate and the council two days later, but the cost of nationalizations had been increased by 30 percent. The total delay was only one month, and Socialist complaints about the extra cost must be weighed against their own insistence on 100 percent nationalization. The real Socialist objection concerned the frustration of the popular will by an unelected court. The council's decision celebrated the rights of property. It was based on the Declaration of the Rights of Man of 1789, which together with the preamble to the 1946 constitution figured as a preamble to the constitution of 1958. These preambles had been recognized in a 1971 decision as an integral part of the 1958 document. The council's decision concerning property rights thus had the additional effect of reaffirming the declaration as a French Bill of Rights, guaranteeing the rights of the individual as well as of property.

Sixty-six laws were appealed during the life of the 1981 legislature, and the council declared thirty-four to be at least in part unconstitutional. Many of these judgments concerned loosely drafted legislation. Even though the council had to give a judgment within a month after its opinion had been requested, government procedures were delayed and the government was frequently infuriated by adverse council decisions forcing redrafting. Given the speed with which the government was presenting legislation, it seems likely that the council forced the improvement of many texts, and Socialist measures were rarely rejected in toto. However, since the council ruled adversely on twice as many cases referred to it in 1981–1986 as it did during the seven years of Giscard's presidency, its conservative bias remained evident.

The most important government bill that was really frustrated by the council was the 1984 law limiting the concentration of ownership of the press. Commonly referred to as the Hersant law, the bill (despite theoretical merits) had been pushed by Prime Minister Mauroy and the Socialist party in a highly partisan manner (see Chapter 2). The council rendered the Solomonic decision that the law was constitutional but could not be applied retroactively—thus leaving the Hersant press empire intact.

In September 1986 the conservative government of Jacques Chirac brought in a new law replacing the High Authority for Audio-Visual Communication with a new one, the Conseil National des Communications et des Libertés (National Council for Communication and Liberties, CNCL). The council struck down two key articles in the bill that it judged insufficiently protective of pluralism. In other 1986 decisions unwelcome to the Chirac government, the council placed difficulties in the way of the prime minister's plan to legislate extensively by decrees authorized by general framework laws, *lois d'habilitation,* demanding that such laws be more specific.

(Article 38 of the constitution provides for such *lois d'habilitation,* which specify the area in which decrees—*ordonnances*—are legally valid.) In January 1987 the council objected to an amendment fixing work hours inserted into a general law on social affairs, on the grounds that it exceeded the inherent limits of the right to amendment. The conservatives were outraged, in a mirror image of Socialist fury when the council had found against them. The conservative presidents of the Senate and the National Assembly protested the decision as an arrogation of new power and "an attack on national sovereignty embodied in the parliament."[8]

Thus both Left and Right found cause for frustration at delays to or blockage of their legislation by nine magistrates not elected by the people. Because or in spite of that, the Constitutional Council emerged from the double alternation in power of 1981–1988 with increased authority and prestige. An August 1986 poll found that 59 percent of respondents thought the powers of the council a good thing, with higher percentages among Socialists and adherents of the RPR and UDF.[9]

None of the council's decisions in 1988–1995 was as controversial as were those that had alternately infuriated Left and Right in the previous seven years. In May 1991 the council rejected a clause in a reformed statute of the island region of Corsica that spoke of "the existence of a Corsican people." There had already been much controversy over the phrase, it being difficult for the very centralist French to admit that any part of the French people is different from any other part—even when the fact is obvious. The amended language carefully qualified the Corsicans as *"une composante du peuple français."*

In 1993 the council ruled out some clauses of the Pasqua immigration and nationality laws, and in June 1994 in an action designed to heighten the salience of controversial legislation, National Assembly president Philippe Séguin appealed to the council to verify the constitutionality of laws on organ donations—which was done.

On the advice of Robert Badinter, council president from 1986 to 1995, Mitterrand proposed a constitutional amendment whereby litigants in the ordinary or administrative court system would have been able to challenge trial-related legislation "on the grounds that it had violated their fundamental rights." The challenge could rise to the council only if either the Council of State or the Cour de Cassation had decided that it was serious. Passed by the National Assembly in 1990, it failed to find entire approval by the Senate. Badinter's idea was to use it only for issues that had a constitutional interest; no "frivolous" counts would have been allowed.[10] Had the amendment passed, it would have given the council "a formal link to the judicial system and individual litigants, and its status as *the* guarantor of rights and liberties would have been consolidated."[11]

The council has confirmed its importance—but has not become a "government by judges." (Indeed, its members are not necessarily even jurists, as are the justices of the U.S. Supreme Court, although a majority of the council is made up of lawyers or law professors.) The council has emerged as a check on the power of the legislature, but still more on that of the executive, drafter of the vast majority of bills.

The current council president, former foreign minister Roland Dumas, was nominated in 1995 to replace Robert Badinter just before Mitterrand left office. Although the political balance will change over the years, the council's legitimacy is now well established; the Socialists have been the opponents and then the partisans of the council; as have the conservatives. The council has thus proved its nonpartisan worth. Here, as in other areas, the arrival in power of the Left did not create change by deliberate intent—but did serve to precipitate it.[12]

The Electronic Media—A Real Revolution

In the early years of the Fifth Republic an American or Briton who watched news programs on French television or listened to the French radio might easily have concluded from their content and tone that the electronic media in France were closer to Soviet than to American or British standards for coverage and freedom. France abolished censorship of the written press in 1881. The electronic media had no such freedom after a government monopoly in radio broadcasting was established in November 1945, and the Radiodiffusion Télévision Française agency (set up in 1959) was placed under the authority of the Minister of Information, who appointed the directors of radio and television networks. No private radio stations were permitted. The *radios périphériques*, Radio-Télédiffusion Luxemburg (RTL), Europe 1, Radio Monte Carlo—commercial stations with their headquarters outside France —were in turn indirectly controlled by state participation in much of their capitalization.

General de Gaulle in particular paid close attention to the content of TV news, frequently firing off complaints to his information minister. Georges Pompidou, who referred to television journalists as "the voice of France" (i.e., *his* France), approved of the existing system, and Prime Minister Jacques Chaban-Delmas's attempts to relax state control were reversed by his successor Pierre Messmer. In 1974, Giscard reorganized the unitary radio and TV, but the government still appointed the heads of all agencies, and the state monopoly remained. Government intervention diminished somewhat; however, a TV reporter has related as typical that during the 1978 elections a story he had prepared on quarrels within the conservative camp was killed, although a similar story about the Left was broadcast. Nor was he ever allowed to report on the allegations that the Central African president/emperor Bokassa had presented diamonds to Giscard.[13]

By the early 1980s, there were 20.5 million television sets in France and 47 million radios. Television had become the principal source of news and entertainment. Radio, restricted to a few stations, could satisfy the demand neither for a wide variety of musical fare nor for much cultural variety of any sort. Pirate radio stations sprang up, but were immediately repressed by the police.

Mitterrand entered office having promised to remove state controls over radio broadcasting, with the result that 850 local stations sprang up instantly in Paris and other cities. The Mauroy government decided to create a new High Authority of Audio-Visual Communication, which would guarantee the independence of broadcasting from government interference. The High Authority became effective in July 1982. Its most conspicuous function was to name the heads of radio and television networks. Though modeled in some ways after the American Federal Communications Commission (FCC), the High Authority possessed neither the FCC's technical responsibilities of licensing (sharing its responsibility with the state) nor the budget and personnel to monitor the airwaves. The result was immediate confusion, as stations proliferated on the FM band. No transmitter was supposed to exceed 500 watts, but the High Authority found it hard to stop them—some Paris stations tested out at 20 or 25 kilowatts. In December 1984, when the High Authority tried to crack down on the popular Paris rock station NRJ for this reason, NRJ was able to bring thousands of young protesters into the streets.

Although the Socialist government wished to free the airwaves, its ideological prudery on commercial radio forbade the new stations from selling advertising. Prime Minister Mauroy was particularly insistent on this point, and Mitterrand easily yielded.[14] This policy of "hang your clothes on a hickory limb, but don't go near the water" was naturally not very effective. Disguised publicity instantly appeared, and again the High Authority found it possible to intervene only in the more flagrant cases. Finally, in a press conference in April 1984, Mitterrand conceded that numerous stations needed to accept advertising in order to exist.[15]

Before the High Authority had been established, the new government had removed the directors of the three television channels, the general news editors, and the chief editors of political news desks. All were replaced by loyal Socialists or persons thought close to the government. The nine members of the High Authority itself were named in groups: three, including the authority's president, by the president of the Republic, three by the president of the National Assembly, three by the president of the Senate. Six of the nine were thus named by the Socialists.

Michèle Cotta, the able and experienced journalist selected to head the new body, has told how Mitterrand sounded her out on the job, saying that he would not interfere, but asking one thing, "that the office of president not be attacked. Would your sense of professional ethics keep you from doing this?" She replied that there would doubtless be conflicts, although she would not look for them, but she thought that at some point she would come in conflict either with him or his government. "And if I go too far?"[16]

Here was the difficulty: The Socialist government wished to free the media and at the same time expected kindness from it. Although Pierre Mauroy won respect from the High Authority for not protesting often-critical coverage, that was far from true of other ministers or figures in the Socialist party, who kept the phone lines to the High Authority humming.

In 1984, the much respected and very independent Pierre Desgraupes, head of television channel Antenne 2, was obliged to retire on grounds of age. The new prime minister Laurent Fabius told Cotta that he and Mitterrand had "our candidate" to take over A2. Bristling at this direct interference, Cotta asked who Fabius's candidate was and then blurted out: "Bad luck. He's not mine." The government's candidate, Jean-Claude Héberlé, was nevertheless appointed. One account of the affair has Mitterrand telling Cotta, "I created you to resist me, naturally, but only up to a certain point!"[17] The High Authority had been shown vulnerable to government wishes, and its reputation never entirely recovered from the Héberlé affair.

The government's desire to secure more influence in the affairs of television was again apparent in 1984–1985, when new commercial channels were finally licensed. A commercial movie channel, Canal Plus, was authorized and launched in fall 1984, after negotiations where the Elysée played a major role and the High Authority was not consulted.[18] Although the network was nominally independent, nearly half of its stock was held by the large government-owned advertising agency Havas, whose chairman, the president's friend André Rousselot, was also the organizer of Canal Plus. The channel, which uses a scrambled signal with decoders, took off slowly. By late 1985, however, it had gained over a million subscribers, and continued thereafter to be a great commercial success.

The French producers of television programs (and the defenders of French culture in general) take alarm at the massive importation of American television shows, exported inexpensively because their production costs have already been met in the giant North American market. The purely French industry cannot hope to compete if confined to the area of 55 million French, plus some 6.5 million Francophone Belgians and Swiss. Expansion to a European market is thus a necessity if French production is not to be driven back entirely to talk shows, movies, and special programs, the latter two increasingly financed by the state. European television companies are intensely conscious that if they do not create a European network for programs and news, the Americans will do it for them.

The decision to advance into pay television had already been taken in principle with Canal Plus, and once the radio stations were allowed to take advertising there was no logical justification for blocking private television. The conservative opposition had never done anything in its twenty-three years of Gaullist power to disestablish state control over television. But once converted to free enterprise, the conservatives intended to set up and control private networks after the expected victory in 1986. Mitterrand and the French Left had always defended publicly owned television as superior to the commercial system dominant in the United States, which they found distasteful, and to the chaotic mix of public and low-quality private television in Italy. But political logic outweighed distaste, and Mitterrand decided that he must make a virtue of necessity. He would demonstrate that the Socialists believed in free enterprise—and establish private TV ownership friendly to the PS.

The three existing television networks drew revenues from limited advertising and funds from the television tax paid by all set owners. The problem was that there was just so much money available in France for advertising, and the government was under pressure from the written media not to sop up too much of it. A 1985 report on the problem recommended establishment of one additional national private network, with a charter limiting the amount of permissible advertising per hour. Mitterrand nevertheless decided to create two private networks to cover most of France by late 1986, one with a general program for a mass audience, the other mainly musical, aimed at young people. Less than a year remained for the Socialist government if it wished to be midwife to the birth of private television in France.

The candidate favored to organize the private fifth network, baptized La Cinq, was the Compagnie Luxembourgeoise de Télédiffusion (CLT). Although the CLT was ready in principle to meet the French government's specifications, the Fabius government suspected it of dragging out negotiations until a new conservative government was installed in Paris. Wishing to entrust friends with a television channel that might favor the Socialists after their 1986 defeat, Mitterrand decided in October 1985 to give the contract to the pro-Socialist capitalist Jérôme Seydoux and his Compagnie des Chargeurs Réunis. But since Seydoux had neither sufficient capital nor the technical staff to proceed alone, another entrepreneur was brought in, with a 40 percent interest, in the person of the Italian television magnate Silvio Berlusconi.

Berlusconi was then not so widely known internationally as he later became, but he had a bad reputation in French television and cultural circles. He had risen rapidly in the Italian television world after the state monopoly on television was lifted, evading the ban on national networks by organizing the countrywide simultaneous transmission of prerecorded programs. Most of them were the American situation comedies and shoot-em-ups that French intellectuals deeply deplored. Nicknamed "Sua Emmittenza" by the Italian press, Berlusconi had so flooded the Italian entertainment market that the Italian motion picture industry was near death, having lost half its public within five years.[19]

Fears were immediately expressed for the French industry, already heavily subsidized by the state in order to keep it alive. But if La Cinq were to go into production by early 1986, Berlusconi was the necessary man.

A howl went up in French cultural circles (and particularly those on the Left) when it became known that the contract negotiated by Berlusconi granted very easy conditions for presenting original French productions and in setting minimum quotas for French and European programs (as opposed to American ones). The quantity of permissible advertising spots (restricted to the beginning and the end of programs in French television) was unclear, and many wondered whether private television in France would begin to resemble the chopped-up late-night movies on American television. Mitterrand had disappointed his own camp by choosing the politically opportune solution at the expense of Socialist ideas.

Jacques Chirac revoked the contract for La Cinq, as he had promised to do when he came to power. Exit Seydoux—but not Berlusconi, who became a partner in a new consortium for La Cinq, together with French press lord Robert Hersant. In the event, the channel was to prove unprofitable, and it disappeared in 1991.

After March 1986 the victorious Right pursued plans to privatize one or more of the existing state channels. After much debate, it was decided that Channel 1, TF1, was to be put up for sale. Culture Minister Léotard speedily announced plans to replace the High Authority by a new organization, the CNCL.[20] The Right had criticized the lack of independence shown by the High Authority, with special reference to the nomination of Héberlé. The CNCL was presented as an improvement on the old institution. Whereas the High Authority had possessed a very small staff and an annual budget of 12 million francs, the CNCL had 223 employees and a 150-million-franc budget. It could authorize frequencies, choose licensees, and designate the heads of the public channels. The idea was to create a jurisdiction on the lines of the American FCC. The CNCL had, however, less authority and a much smaller staff (the FCC has 1,300 employees). Whereas the High Authority's nine members had been nominated in groups of three by the presidents of the Republic, the National Assembly, and the Senate, the CNCL's thirteen members were chosen in such a way that Mitterrand's appointees formed a minority of two.

A major issue hovering over the new dispensation was the concentration of power in the press and electronic media. The leading candidate to take over a privatized TF1 was not Hersant (who contented himself with a share of la Cinq) but big industrialist Jean-Luc Lagardère (Matra), who also controlled Hachette, France's biggest editorial chain, and was the owner of the radio network Europe 1. The CNCL decided instead for a consortium headed by cement and prefabricated housing tycoon Francis Bouygues. New restrictions imposed by the Constitutional Council limited concentration of ownership of TV networks, radio, and the press.[21]

The CNCL nevertheless failed to convince the country that it was accomplishing its mission. After Mitterrand criticized it in a September 1987 interview as "unworthy of respect," a poll found that although nearly half of respondents did not agree with him, only 24 percent believed that the CNCL was doing a good job.[22] Charges by a magistrate that CNCL member and academician Michel Droit had intervened to grant a license to a right-wing radio station in Paris did nothing for the CNCL's reputation.

Once reelected, Mitterrand did not seek to renationalize TF1. After some time-consuming negotiation, he replaced the CNCL with a new regulatory institution, again with nine members. The new communications commission, the third in eight years, was called the High Audio-Visual Council (CSA). It had extended powers—and many problems to solve. TF1 showed itself the star of the new firmament, and the two public channels, Antenne 2 and FR3 (France 2 and France 3), soon registered larger and larger deficits.

Continuing financing problems and the presence of cable channels and TV satellites complicate the overall television scene. In 1996, there were three public channels, FR2, FR3, and La Cinquième (renumbered from La Sept, since there are no longer seven channels). This last transmits during the day and in the evening gives way to a French-German cultural channel called Arte. Private channels are TFI, Canal Plus (coded), and M6, a channel largely dedicated to music and sitcoms.

Despite ambitious plans in the early 1980s, cable television in France has not caught on. In late 1996 the estimate of subscribers for the whole country was only

1.4 million households.[23] There are, however, a number of private satellite channels with small subscriptions. CNN, Euronews (a new CNN competitor), the BBC, one Francophone Belgian channel, and RTL (Luxembourg) are also available by satellite.

With large resources from advertising, TF1 has over 40 percent of the viewership. Antenne 2 and FR3 (FR2 and FR3) could not be financed only from the *redevance* (user fee) but also lost advertising revenue. The state was obliged to bail out both and to cut staffs.[24]

In her memoirs of her presidency of the High Authority, Michèle Cotta summed it up: "Whoever is in power, the audiovisual structure is only the facade of ideological structure. Behind the changes made by politicians is one fact: an irresistible mistrust of audiovisual power, an irresistible desire to 'take things in hand.'"[25] Certainly neither the Socialists, for all their talk about "areas of freedom," nor the conservatives, with their new talk of *libéralisme,* resisted that need.

Nevertheless, despite early hesitations on financing and a too-evident desire to free the media and still maintain some control, the Socialist government brought a freedom to the electronic media that the press had achieved 100 years earlier. Under Socialist and conservative governments, TV and radio journalism is now more independent than ever before. The news director of a network can refuse a minister's request for TV time. Stories that displease the government are broadcast, and if it is not yet unthinkable that a network chief, a news bureau head, or a journalist can be fired for lèse majesté, it is much harder to do so and may become impossible. The proliferation of hundreds of small radio stations has been largely positive. The intellectuals complain that the new dispensation responds too easily to the ratings game, and that French television too much resembles American—not just because a large number of American programs are shown. (The number of hours of transmission per day has tripled since 1983—not counting satellite.) Unfortunately, a great deal of television automatically means a great deal of bad television. However, despite the contradictions, uncertainties, and failures of its media policy, the Socialist government elected in 1981 could in retrospect be proud of achieving at least one real revolution in French life, one that daily touches the lives of almost all the French.

The Auroux Laws

Decentralization and the liberation of the audiovisual media must be reckoned the two great reforms of 1981–1986. Another much-discussed reform was the enactment of the Auroux laws of 1982 on labor rights. Bitterly attacked by the Right when first presented in the National Assembly, they have turned out to be less than revolutionary. These laws provided for obligatory firm-level bargaining; systematized the arrangements for committees dealing with health, safety, and working conditions; and defined workers' rights and provided in particular for new shop-level "rights of expression." ("Collectivism," said the RPR leader Bernard Pons.)

The overall intent was to strengthen workers' rights and provide stronger incentives to engage in collective bargaining at the lower levels rather than on an industry-wide level. Continuing dissension among the three main union confederations and the decline in French union strength in a period of industrial restructuring contributed to altering the effect expected of these laws. They did not strengthen the union movement; they simplified the task of management in dealing locally with its workers. "The Auroux industrial relations reforms of 1982–1983 in France affected the strength and role of trade unions very differently because they were put in place during a period of historic union weakness than had they been introduced ten years earlier. As a result, the actual results have differed from the expectations of the Socialist government that put them in place."[26]

Profound changes took place in the structure of employment in the 1980s. Mining, synthetic textiles, and steel production declined steeply. A million industrial jobs disappeared in 1973–1984, whereas between 1967 and 1984, 2.7 million jobs were created in the tertiary sector. The number of salaried workers in enterprises employing 500 or more workers (those most likely to be unionized) dropped between 1972–1984 and increased in the smallest enterprises employing fewer than 50 workers. The French union movement had never been strong when compared to organized labor in most developed European countries. At its height in the 1970s it made up only 20 to 25 percent of the workforce. (The unions exaggerate their strength, so that exact statistics are not available even to experts.) One plausible estimate of the rate of unionization in late 1985 put it at 15 percent of the workforce (counting teachers' unions and independent and autonomous unions), down from about 20 percent ten years earlier.[27] By 1990, the comparable figures were 8 to 10 percent, and by the mid-1990s probably less.[28]

A further weakening of the union movement came in 1992, with a schism in the powerful Fédération d'Education Nationale (FEN), leading to the exclusion of the secondary school and physical education teachers unions (SNES and SNEP), with about a third of the FEN's 300,000 membership.

Before 1981 the Socialists talked a great deal of *autogestion,* or self-management. Once elected, they did nothing to further it. There were a number of reasons for this. In the first place, there was no real agreement on what self-management might mean: Both the Rocardians and the CERES, who agreed on almost nothing, had favored something with this name. In the later 1970s the Communist party and CGT also picked up the idea, to which they had previously been opposed. The CGT's version would have been Communist control. Chris Howell argued that although Socialist leaders (i.e., the dominant Mitterrand group) probably never took *autogestion* seriously, the fact that its focus was more on the worker than the union and "emphasized self-transformation through daily struggle in the workplace" favored one of the implicit logics (the successful one) within the Auroux reforms, by which labor regulation centered on the firm, and employers and workers bargained at the firm, not the branch level.[29]

Thus if the Socialist party hoped to increase both the rights of workers and the power of trade unions, it succeeded in the former but not the latter task. By the end of Mitterrand's first term it had become apparent that the traditional tripartite labor scene had not changed but that the union confederations were weaker. Those changes should not be seen only in the context of "union busting." "The French Socialist party's most important contribution to the 'modernization' of France has been the creation of a system of industrial relations with a structural bias toward co-operation rather than conflict," wrote Howell. The national union organizations are left as "semi-public organizations who lobby the government, legitimize government initiatives and support spontaneous strikes."[30] (This last function became particularly evident after Mitterrand had left office, in the great wave of strikes in November-December 1995, largely by public-sector workers.)[31]

The Auroux laws were not irrelevant, but their consequences were not what the Socialists intended. They "have had a lasting effect upon labor regulation and have brought about fundamental changes in the role, locus, and nature of collective bargaining in France and in the organizational resources of labor."[32] In other words, the Auroux laws were still another illustration of the Serendip effect.

Education

After the monster demonstrations against the Savary law of June 1984 (see Chapter 2), Savary's successor Jean-Pierre Chevènement had succeeded in quieting the excitement by a return to the three R's and a redirection of policy toward greater educational opportunity. The minister's proclaimed goal that 80 percent of students should have passed the baccalaureate by the year 2000 was not primarily oriented toward the academic but rather the professional lycée—that is, technical training. Studies commissioned by the Education Ministry had convinced him that by the year 2000 the need for unqualified workers would have disappeared—and if France was to maintain and strengthen its industrial position, workers must be trained for higher technologies. Chevènement created the new professional baccalaureate degree, which was to include long training periods in firms and factories. However, the archetypical left-Jacobin Chevènement spent little time coordinating this idea with the business world; he merely announced and explained it.

The next education minister, the conservative René Monory, adopted and furthered this policy, which pleased a large number of families and students. Previously, the lycées, with a policy of "orienting" students to one or another of the tracks presented, had in practice limited the number of students who could pursue higher secondary education. Many had taken refuge in private schools, which was one major reason why the perceived threat to private education posed by the Savary law had caused such disturbance. The new 80 percent goal opened up places in the lycée.

What it did not do was expand the facilities, a problem that faced Monory's successor Lionel Jospin. Mitterrand had not made as many promises in his 1988 campaign as in 1981, but a prominent one was to make education "the national priority." In four years as minister Jospin was able to raise the education budget from 199 to 263 billion francs a year—and that was still insufficient. Jospin's first effort was to improve the pay and status of teachers, and after devoting much effort to explanation and coordination, he succeeded not only in raising salaries but also in giving primary-school teachers the same status as those for secondary and higher education. Jospin reconfirmed the commitment to the goal of 80 percent of students taking the baccalaureate examinations and pushed other reforms of primary schools and creation of university-level training institutes to train both schoolteachers and professors of more generalized subjects.

Although the professional baccalaureate was a response to a real need, the prestige of the older academic *bac* led larger and larger numbers of students to flood into the lycées once the obstacles had been removed. Between 1985 and 1989, the number of lycée students increased by 320,000. The number of those in the final year of the lycée (including professional lycées), which had been only 36 percent of the total age class in 1985, rose to 42 percent in 1987 and 54.5 percent in 1990.

The immediate result was a physical overcrowding and an increased class size that not only was uncomfortable but also threatened the quality of education. The student protests of 1990 (see Chapter 6) were the direct result. A government that had already greatly increased the education budget for teachers was now compelled by street action to put another 4 billion francs into the budget.

From increased lycée enrollment followed swelling university numbers, in a country where passing the *bac* is the only condition for admittance to tuition-free universities. (There is a small registration fee, and when students do not live at home, food and lodging are of course an expense.) In 1994, there were 485,000 more university students than in 1980, for a total of 1,285,000.[33] Part of this increase, of course, was caused by the multiplier effect of students motivated to continue their studies both because they could not find jobs and because they hoped increased qualification would help. When they found on graduating that diplomas did not equal jobs, they were naturally the more bitter.

Jospin had been poorly rewarded for his efforts by students acutely conscious of the defects of their system and thus inclined to see the glass half empty—or lower still. If lycée students (now at least as likely to take to the streets in protest as their university elders) were reasonably satisfied with their teachers (56 percent somewhat satisfied, 18 percent very happy), only 17 percent were happy with their schools' physical plant, and 40 percent were dissatisfied or completely dissatisfied.[34] Finally, in a system where "for parents, professors, and students an examination where no one fails is an examination without value," there is naturally a large quotient who fail, drop out—and have still less chance of a job than their fellows.[35]

The educational system has thus been the victim of its ambitions. An ever larger student body faces a static job market, and the laudable objective of training young people longer and better for an economy that will demand higher qualifications has collided, for the moment at least, with an economy that is not producing enough to need these more qualified graduates.

The policies followed in the 1980s and early 1990s, however mixed their success, have considerably democratized French education. Although 47 percent of the students in law, science, and letters have fathers who are upper- or middle-level executives, and only 15 percent have fathers who are workers, in the university system in general 58 percent of students have fathers (and 69 percent mothers) who did not have an university education. However, certain universities, particularly those in Paris and other major cities, have student bodies coming from the upper-middle classes, whereas children of the lower-middle class and workers are disproportionately found in the newer universities of smaller urban centers.[36]

When Bérégovoy became prime minister in March 1992, Jospin was dropped from the government (less because he had failed as minister than because Mitterrand had not forgiven him his political independence) and replaced by Jack Lang, who also kept his old job of culture minister. Lang was able to put an end to an old problem when in June 1992 he signed an agreement with the secretary-general of the Catholic teaching association on the state of financial commitment to parochial schools. But Lang had no better luck than Jospin with the students. In March he was forced to drop further projects for university and lycée reform first drafted under Jospin after student protests. Students again took to the streets in 1994 to protest a Balladur plan for lower wages for jobs for youth—and the government had to back off.

The *Grandes Ecoles*

The French educational system differs from others in that whereas other countries turn out elite graduates from the top schools and faculties, France has in the *grandes écoles* an entirely separate system that forms its elites. In the late 1980s there were some 52,000 students in these elite establishments, where entry demands special preparatory courses after the baccalaureate or at least some university work. Finishing a *grande école* no longer means that the graduate is instantly snapped up on graduation, but he or she is assured of an excellent job within a few months at the worst. There are famous schools like the Ecole Nationale d'Administration (ENA) whose 5,000-plus graduates, called *énarques,* almost literally run the country; the Ecole Polytechnique, the oldest and formerly the most prestigious, founded during the French Revolution; the Ecole Centrale, for top-flight engineers and civil servants; the Ecole Normale Supérieur, another French Revolutionary institution. But there are dozens of other *grandes écoles,* for engineers of all sorts and specialties, agronomists, physicists, chemists, and so on. After high-level preparation, the candidate must pass a stiff entry examination.

Because the *grande école* system was so conspicuously a meritocracy tilted to the children of the upper classes who received adequate preparation to pass the entrance examinations, the Left government tried to alleviate the system by allowing lateral entry into ENA for candidates with government experience. But only a small number of slots were offered, and the scheme finally broke down. ENA graduates were originally supposed to be the trained administrators needed to run the country. The top forty in an ENA class have a choice, according to their ranking, of entry into one or another of the *grands corps,* the peak of the French bureaucracy: the Inspection des Finances, Cour des Comptes, Conseil d'Etat, Corps des Préfets, and diplomatic corps. Lower-ranking graduates become civil administrators in less prestigious jobs. But the high-flyers are often taken very young into ministerial staffs, later offered ministerial posts themselves, and often are encouraged to run for office. Among the eight prime ministers of 1981–1996, four have been ENA graduates, as were many of their ministerial colleagues and a large proportion of their staffs. The Socialists did nothing that could change this kind of near monopoly on administrative and political power by a narrow range of men and women with the same kind of training. The *énarques* are impressive, but as a general once said of them, shaking his head, "They know everything—but that's all they know."

Decentralization

Decentralization, declared *"la grande affaire du septennat"* by François Mitterrand, was a reform carried out by the Socialists, not a socialist reform. Since the early nineteenth century a centralization begun by the monarchy and systematized by the Jacobins and Napoleon had come under regular attack. By the 1960s, centralization was seen as an obstacle both to economic growth and to democratic participation. Shades of opinion from Gaullist technocrats to PSU leftists could agree that local communities should have more voice in their own economies and development. But the *notables* of the provincial establishment were deeply suspicious of changes in a system affording them comfortable arrangements with the central power and had always blocked innovation.

In 1971 Interior Minister Raymond Marcellin tried voluntary mergers to reduce the number of the 36,000 communes, the smallest units of territorial administration. Only 2,000 mergers took place. In 1982, half of the French population lived in the 800 communes that had towns of 5,000 or more people, whereas 80 percent of the communes had fewer than 2,000 inhabitants. Of the 32,417 mayors of these tiny jurisdictions, 68 percent presided over communes of fewer than 500 inhabitants.[37]

Each *commune* had an elected council, which in turn elected the mayor. Collectively, they were responsible for basic services such as garbage collection, sanitation, maintenance of tertiary roads, problems of housing, parks, and libraries. The mayor was subject to the authority of the prefect and responsible for making known and enforcing legislation. Mayors of very small towns, often part-time officials quite unable to cope with all the laws, regulations, and circulars streaming out of Paris, inevitably deferred to the prefect and his services. The mayors of medium-sized and larger towns, however, resented the need to ask for government approval on local matters such as zoning and building permits. In the larger towns mayors came to a tacit understanding with cooperative prefects, who did not care to frustrate men who were often also senators or deputies to the National Assembly. By the 1970s, the prefect would customarily guarantee a delay of no more than two weeks on local requests by the mayor.[38] Meanwhile, mayors of small places were frequently grateful to the prefect for taking from them the responsibility to veto popular but costly projects.

The prefects were highly trained and high-powered officials appointed by the minister of interior and were usually graduates of ENA. They were the executives of the ninety-six *départements* of metropolitan France and coordinators of all national services emanating from the various central ministries. Prefects also presided over the twenty-two regions created in 1972; public establishments only for economic planning, the regions possessed no legal personality. Restless under Gaullist power, the Left had sought a means to give localities more autonomy in the areas of housing, public transport, and education. The Common Program of 1972 had advocated most of the decentralizing measures enacted into law a decade later.[39] The *Projet socialiste* of 1980 breathlessly described decentralization as "one of the most powerful levers of the break with capitalism, which will allow citizens to take direct part in the immense enterprise of social transformation." Many on the Right as well desired decentralization, although more soberly. A bill drafted under Giscard's interior minister Christian Bonnet was discussed in the Senate in 1980–1981 but did not become law.[40]

In the formation of the Socialist government Gaston Defferre made it plain that he wished to have the portfolios of both interior and decentralization. The latter activity was to be his contribution to the history of the *septennat,* an achievement paralleling his framework law of 1956 that had prepared the way for decolonization. Defferre was in a hurry—the possibility that delay might allow opposition both outside the majority and within it to delay and weaken his bill was only too evident in the prior history of decentralization. He chose to enact irreversible principles first and let details follow. In the lengthy parliamentary debate over decentralization the opposition introduced more than 4,000 amendments, opposed Defferre's priorities, and warned of financial difficulties to come.

Defferre's first step was meant to be irrevocable. The law of March 2, 1982, suppressed all *tutelles* or controls over local authorities and replaced them by partial controls administered by tribunals. The title "prefect" was abolished and replaced by *commissaires de la République.* (But those titleholders were still addressed as "*Monsieur le Préfet*" and rebaptized prefects by the Chirac government in 1986.) The prefect's executive powers over the department were transferred to the president of the departmental *conseil général.* In the next step, a more complicated one that took place between 1983 and 1985, some responsibilities (and resources or financing) were transferred from the state to lower levels. In all, 33 laws and 219 decentralization decrees (and a large number of circulars, many of them very long) were issued between 1982 and 1985.

As the Right voted en masse against the early laws, even though it did not fundamentally oppose decentralization, the Socialists can claim credit for bringing about this long-delayed evolution. When cantonal and then municipal elections showed a swing away from the Left, however, the Left rapidly discovered that the Right would profit more from it. In 1995, the Right controlled all but 75 of 95 *conseils généraux,* 20 of the 22 regions, and 61.5 percent of municipal counselors. The Left had a small majority in the number of cities over 30,000 inhabitants that it held: 129 over 118. (These figures result from the poor scores by the Left in the cantonal and regional elections of 1992 and its somewhat better performance in the 1995 municipal elections.)[41]

The important questions on decentralization concerned its scope and purpose—what levels of administration would be decentralized, what means would be used, how drastic would it be. Above all, would it genuinely attack a widely perceived problem—that of a society too tightly and inefficiently controlled by a central bureaucracy? Would it advance democratic participation as well as economic growth?

In its 1977 proposals for the revision of the Common Program, the PS had upheld and praised the existence of all 36,000 communes, while calling for the abolition of the office of the prefect. By so doing, the Socialists signaled unwillingness to attack the interests of the local *notables,* an appreciable percentage of whom were themselves Socialists. In 1981, other potential obstacles were avoided: communes, departments, and regions were all treated as equals, with no level having any power over the others. The question of the *cumul des mandats*—the simultaneous holding of political offices at different levels—was postponed until later.

From the viewpoint of the American citizen of a federal state, the reform was relatively modest. Decisions on zoning and land use have been transferred to local mayors. But education (under local control even in centralized Britain) remains a state monopoly—except that the localities now have the dubious privilege of school maintenance and transport. The police, as one might expect, remain national.

On the commune level the new dispensation has confirmed and systematized a long-term evolution toward autonomy for big-city mayors, has given more scope to energetic mayors of medium-sized and small towns, and presented both opportunities and problems for mayors of tiny communes. The prefects retain an important role as coordinators of national services, especially vis-à-vis the mayors of small communes. The prefect is no longer the executive officer of the department. A president of the *conseil général* is now responsible for presenting its budget and chairing the departmental assembly. The *conseillers généraux* elect the president, who acting together with his *bureau* of four to ten vice presidents, plus an often sizable staff, has become a real departmental executive. Finally, the region has become a major player, with regional representatives *(conseillers régionaux)* directly elected for the first time, although from a departmental list.

Block grants *(dotations budgetaires)* from the national budget help to pay for the responsibilities the state has transferred to a lower level. Other taxes, such as annual automobile registration fees and drivers' licenses, have also been transferred to the *collectivités locales.* An important local levy is the business tax *(taxe professionelle),* introduced by Chirac in his first prime ministership, denounced but retained by both Mitterrand and then Chirac. Since the tax brings in about 45 percent of local revenue (82 billion francs in 1986), finding a replacement for it has been difficult.

Many of the French believe that France cannot afford four levels of government—national, communal, departmental, and regional (with EU regulations and financial contributions figuring as a fifth level). In any case the responsibilities of these various levels overlap confusingly. Didier Borotra, senator-mayor of Biarritz, who has been vice president of the Aquitaine regional council and vice president of the Pyrénées-Atlantiques departmental council, pointed out that a mayor could not easily represent his town alone, because of *financements croisés,* that is, the multiple levels of financing by the state, the region, the department, the city, and the EU, which are necessary for a variety of projects. If a mayor is present at one or more of these levels as an official of the department or region, he is in far better shape to negotiate financing for projects that interest his town.[42]

Another example of the problems of overlap was described by city officials in the southern city of Montauban. A European framework law *(loi cadre)* requires severer regulation than did the old French ones on pollution created by the local incinerator. New filters and other equipment had to be installed by a certain date to bring things up to the level prescribed by the EU. Initial coordination with the prefect on improving the local incinerator raised the idea that Montauban's incinerator could be enlarged to take care of the household garbage of surrounding communes in order to make the incinerator affordable. Montauban, however, did not want to be "the area's garbage can," whether or not its incinerator was efficient. The question (still unresolved at the time of the interview) will not be resolved by prefectoral fiat as it once might have, but only by compromise. The city and surrounding area deal with the prefect who deals with the Ministry of Health, which pays a part of the bill—but so does the EU.[43]

The region is in many ways the most interesting of the newly manumitted *collectivités locales,* but also the most problematic, pitting regionalists against "departmentalists." One such departmentalist, Jacques Douffiagues, who when interviewed in 1985 was still mayor of Orléans and president of the *conseil général* of his department, feared that regional "barons" (he named powerful conservative politicians in western France) would be only too happy to create "feudalities" in their regions to widen their power base. Douffiagues's preference lay with a clear distinction of powers for the different territorial levels; he doubted that France needed regions. He saw questions involving roads and schools as problems of restricted geographic areas, with the region as a rather artificial construct, not very useful on the economic level. Where the power did not exist on the local level to cope with an economic problem, why, he asked, should one refer it to a medium-level authority, not the national one? Douffiagues and Jacobins like him also remain suspicious of the pretensions of regions that have or "claim to have" a local language. One can sense the enduring apprehension of French centralizers that the state will be weakened if centralized conformity is relaxed.[44]

Although the powers of the regions are equal, some possess a historic identity. Douffiagues's Orléans is situated in a composite region colorlessly named the Center, and no one is geographically a "Centriste." But for the 200 years since the Revolution abolished the old provinces the French have continued to identify themselves with the names of many of the old provinces that are the new regions—as

Auvergnats, Bretons, Bourguignons, Lorrains, Alsatiens, Picards, and so on. The Jacobins fear that national unity will suffer from revived particularisms; proponents of the region dismiss that as scare tactics.

By the early 1990s, the regions had gained more prestige and were viewed, somewhat cautiously, as the administrative level most likely to develop new projects—not surprising, since that is their function. In 1993, 60 percent of respondents in a large sampling of opinion believed that decentralization should go further, and 70 percent of respondents said the region was the administrative-political jurisdiction of the future (20 percent favored departments).[45]

The regions are very unequal in population and wealth. The Ile de France, with more than 10 million inhabitants, is more populous than all but six U.S. states. Only Rhône-Alpes, with its 5 million, comes near to matching it, although even little Limousin, with 737,000 inhabitants the least populous region, has more people than six U.S. states. Whereas the departments are burdened with multiple responsibilities, the regions—still seen as centers for economic development—have greater potential scope. They have relatively little money: The 1988 budget of the Ile de France region was roughly 6 billion francs. That is more comparable to the budget of a very rich American county than to that of a large state. The other mainland regions together had budgets totaling 25.7 billion. U.S. and French local expenditures on education are of course not comparable—an American county may spend from a quarter to three-quarters of its revenue on education, whereas the personnel expenses of the French system are entirely borne by the national government. The Ile de France region, responsible in education for technical training only, plus construction and maintenance of its secondary schools, budgeted 362 million francs for its lycées in 1986.[46] The main expense of a regional budget is investment; 65 percent of the Ile de France's expenses go for transportation: the suburban lines (RER), buses, subways, and so on. Though Jacobins continue to worry over the danger of an enlarged bureaucracy, that has been successfully avoided—the Ile de France by 1987 had only 400 employees.

Regionalists contend that the possibilities of imaginative investment are already creating new visions. The new ability of regional authorities to discuss and undertake initiatives with their colleagues across national frontiers is one notable advantage of decentralization. All of France's neighbors—Belgium, West Germany, Switzerland, Italy, and Spain—are now themselves either federal or decentralized. The regions may also play an important role in the post-1992 Europe of disappearing frontiers. The Nord–Pas-de-Calais looks to the Walloon region of Belgium and, especially with the cross-channel tunnel, to closer economic ties to England. Midi-Pyrénées looks to its Spanish neighbor, Provence–Côte-d'Azur to Lombardy and Piedmont. The planned development zones cut across frontiers. Regions can also look to more distant partners—French regions are cooperating with Bavaria and Baden-Wurttemberg, with their high tech industries, while the Ile de France was involved in the French-sponsored projects for the Cairo subway.

The state has the predominant role in education, but the regions may introduce auxiliary programs. The Nord–Pas-de-Calais region, for instance, pioneered in introducing computers in its schools before the state program took shape. The overall advantage of decentralization lies in the increased scope it gives to initiative. It reduces the red tape involved when local communities wish to repair buildings, conserve natural resources, or increase cultural opportunities. It encourages the regions to invest in infrastructure and seek out new economic opportunities, again without the drag a central bureaucracy puts on initiative, and permits *collectivités* at all levels to seek out and take up small-scale initiatives to fill needs the state might not recognize or would disdain.

The wave of corruption scandals that became increasingly notorious after 1991 brought accusations that decentralization had favored corruption. Decentralization gave increased powers to elected officials at lower levels, especially municipal, because they could give out building permits. The controls supposedly built into the law did not function well, and the regional *chambres de comptes* did not reach full function until 1987–1988. Another aspect of increased latitude for corruption was the decreased powers of prefects, who became unable to block construction projects, but were supposed to determine within two months whether a given project needed to be investigated by a tribunal. Christian Sautter, who in 1991–1993 was prefect of Paris and Ile de France, noted that he had only three or four officials to check on all the acts of the Paris city government! He remarked that in some local situations, there was often no will to check at all.[47]

A necessary corollary to decentralization was limitation on the *cumul des mandats,* the French tradition whereby a politician could, as in the extreme case of Jean Lecanuet, be at once mayor of Rouen, president of the *conseil général* of the Seine-Maritime department, regional counselor (i.e., regional deputy) of the Upper Normandy region, senator, and deputy to the European Parliament. Until March 1986 more than 90 percent of French senators and more than 80 percent of French deputies held at least two offices. The "deputy and mayor" or "senator and mayor" was able to intercede for his constituents at the national level with an effectiveness mere local officials could not attain. Deputies and senators are dependent for research and much office work on the joint services provided by the staff of their parliamentary groups. Their office space is exiguous and shared with a single secretary. Their mayor's offices in French town halls give them far more scope to confer with constituents and handle business of many kinds.

French politicians continued to hold their jobs as mayors of major cities even when elevated to the highest levels. While serving as prime minister, Jacques Chaban-Delmas, Pierre Mauroy, and Jacques Chirac remained mayors respectively of Bordeaux, Lille, and Paris, and after becoming prime minister in 1995, Alain Juppé sought and was elected to Chaban's succession as mayor of Bordeaux. Chirac, as president, did have to step down as mayor of Paris. However, in 1997 new prime minister Lionel Jospin promised to end the *cumul* entirely.

The law on the *cumul* adopted in December 1985 limited the system without abolishing it. It allowed a politician to hold only two important offices. The office of deputy or senator is incompatible with more than one other office—European deputy, regional or departmental counselor, Paris city councilor, or mayor of a town of more than 20,000 inhabitants. (Only 386 mayors were affected, but in 1991, 48.6 of parliamentarians were mayors.) One person may not be president of both a *conseil général* in his or her department and of the regional council of the region. However, a politician may run for a third office, and if elected choose which one to renounce. Most mayors of large cities have preferred to give up their seats in regional councils (or less commonly, departmental ones) rather than their seats in parliament. The result will swell the ranks of younger or local politicians holding office in these councils. (The aftermath of the 1988 legislative elections saw the first big wave of resignations from departmental or regional offices by newly elected or reelected deputies.)[48] There is, however, an accessory *cumul:* presidents of local organizations, such as the important organizations that exercise certain interjurisdictional powers beyond the old city borders, called *communautés urbaines,* or *syndicats intercommunaux,* are not included in the law.[49]

There are new trends. In June 1994 a poll reflected the increasingly common opinion among constituents that a mayor should not have a *cumul.* Sixty-seven percent thought the mayor should have no other office but should concentrate on communal responsibilities; of the 30 percent of other respondents expressing an opinion, 74 percent thought the mayor should be a deputy, 67 percent a *conseiller général.* The survey also showed that mayors enjoy more confidence than other elected officials: 73 percent said they had considerable confidence in their mayors, against 64 percent expressing confidence in regional counselors, 60 percent in *conseillers généraux,* and only 47 percent in deputies.[50]

Mayors, much better paid than they used to be, now find they can exert influence in the departmental assembly, either by themselves or through their deputies. These councils are no longer dominated by deputies and senators. In 1994, only twenty-three deputies and twenty-four senators were presidents of departmental councils—which is to say that forty-eight council presidents (of a total of ninety-five departments) exercised power outside the ambit of national politics. In 1990, this figure was 20 percent higher.[51]

At least on the communal and departmental levels, French decentralization has not so much created local self-government as transferred administrative responsibilities. The French political scientist and decentralization expert Yves Mény wrote:

> The quintessential characteristic of decentralization . . . is less "democratization" than the utilization of the "authoritarian executive" model which now totally dominates French institutions. The model has two variants—the mayoral and the prefectoral—at the local level. The mayoral variant has now been extended to *départements* and regions, turning their executives into genuine local "bosses."[52]

Thus the "democratization" in this reform lies essentially in the efficiency of having services provided at a level less remote from the people than the central government. Certainly it is likely now that public opinion will be better heard and even listened to on questions of zoning and town planning, cultural services, and the creation of new schools. Local mayors can no longer duck behind the authority of the prefect, using him as an excuse for not taking responsibility. One may, however, legitimately doubt whether much "democratization" is possible in departmental rather than the state control of a variety of social and health services (much the largest and most expensive of relocated tasks), or in administration of commercial and fishing ports. Decentralization may facilitate popular discussion on these questions, but much of the debate will unfortunately center on whether and how to increase benefits in an economy that is not getting richer—in other words on a limited set of hard and frequently unpleasant choices. It is undoubtedly healthy for the national state to delegate and so rid itself of many of these responsibilities. The changes are considerable, long-needed, and promising—but something less than revolutionary.[53]

8

The Economics of
Socialism and Un-Socialism

Analysis of the economic record of the years 1981–1995 poses numerous questions. What exactly were the economic policies of 1981, what were their long-term results, and did they handicap or advance the French economy? How severe were the constraints that induced Mitterrand to abandon the economic program of 1981, and did he have a choice? Did the decisions of 1983 determine the economic course of the next twelve years (and beyond), or were there turning points later on and roads not taken? Finally, to what degree did the policy of the *franc fort* (strong franc) and the Maastricht convergence criteria contribute to *exclusion*[1] and the ascending unemployment that more than ever trouble France?

The Decisions of 1981

There is no argument whether the Socialists made mistakes in 1981–1983; they admit they did. A larger question is the severity of the structural problems in the economy the Socialists inherited and intended to change. In the 1970s the Socialists had blamed the crisis almost entirely on the policies of Raymond Barre and denied its structural and international nature. Once in office, they were obliged to face these factors, which the Right in its turn happily overlooked when damning them.

The French economy had grown rapidly in the 1960s, thanks to initially low labor costs—which rose rapidly at the end of the decade. Although oil was cheap until 1973, the fact that France imported a larger share of its energy than other European countries placed it at a disadvantage (later alleviated by a heavy investment in nuclear power begun under Giscard). Inflation was consistently high, obliging France to have recourse to frequent devaluations. The French industrial export product was characteristically standard, medium-level technology. Before the 1960s its markets were found in less-developed countries. During the 1970s, when some of the oil-producing countries were at the height of their boom, France was a major supplier. But when those countries ran short of cash (or as in the case of Iraq, went to war), then France's exports dropped off, except for armaments.

The French economy at the beginning of 1981 was clearly in trouble, with unemployment running at 1.7 million. The Socialists had bold plans for the economy: Their new and different economic and social system would control "the commanding heights of the economy," promote democracy on the factory floor, and make the economic system more dynamic. The Left proclaimed its will to break with a timid, pusillanimous rentier capitalism, break up industrial feudalities, and give new courage and design to the central administration.[2]

Since the Socialist economists saw weak domestic demand and ill-adjusted investment as the great problems of the French economy, nationalization and reflation of the economy went together, the two scissor blades of their attempt to attack, change, and improve it. The Left in power sought to recover the virtuous circle of growth, whose means were economic reflation, including an acceptance of budgetary deficit, increase of domestic consumption, job growth, increased competitiveness, and a positive balance of trade. What the Socialists got in the next three years was a vicious circle of indebtedness, a larger budget deficit, increasingly unprofitable industry, a loss of competitiveness, underinvestment, a need to borrow both domestically and abroad, foreign trade deficit, devaluation, and increased unemployment.[3]

What happened? The first great mistake was an error in timing—which was a Socialist mistake only in that it was a mistaken application of left-Keynesianism. All the economic think tanks had predicted strong economic growth in late 1981 or early 1982, based on an assumed American takeoff. That takeoff did not arrive until the second or third quarter of 1983. The second mistake was to suppose that the increased purchasing power pumped into the economy by reflationary methods would be absorbed by French production. Instead, the trade deficit soared. Whereas it had been 101 billion francs in 1980, it rose to 104.7 in 1981, and to 150.1 billion in 1982.[4]

Fresh buying power did increase imports, but exports dropped—the result of both high prices caused by an overvalued franc and the influx of highly competitive Japanese and other non-European products into German and other European markets. The French automobile industry in particular suffered a rapid loss of export markets, as its products lost the ability to compete with the Japanese cars imported freely into the smaller European countries with no automobile industry of their own.[5]

Another fundamental Socialist mistake was to suppose that there was a magic wand effect in nationalization—that a change in control from private to public hands would suddenly remedy the problems of French industry. French industry did not possess sectors where it was dominant in the world market—unlike West Germany or Japan. For example, the five largest sectors of the Japanese economy made up 50 percent of Japan's positive balance of trade in the mid-1980s, whereas for France the top five sectors with a positive balance composed only 11 percent of French trade—and two of those were agricultural.[6]

The conditions of the early 1970s left their imprint on the economic analysis developed by Mitterrand's advisers—an analysis left over from the 1972 PS-PCF Common Program of Government. In part because Mitterrand's plans for political competition required the Socialists to keep to a leftist line close to the Communists in order to seduce the PCF electorate, they had done little to rethink the new economic conditions of the world after the 1974 oil shock. (To be fair, the economists of the ruling Right had no very clear idea of the new situation either.)

France had done remarkably well in the Thirty Glorious Years. The sudden rise in oil prices in 1974 broke this momentum, but the immediate effect of higher fuel costs and inflation (stagflation) were only the first signs of profound changes in the world economy, changes that for France would shake the foundations of the prosperity it had built. These changes, wrote Christian Stoffaës, were as follows:

- Slowdown in the traditional markets that had brought growth since 1945: construction, public works, household equipment including automobiles; all areas approached saturation where replacement often demanded better quality.
- Overcapacity in some previously dynamic sectors: Facing markets growing hardly or at all, the big industries of the expansionary period fought to preserve their market share, the more bitterly because in extrapolating from the past they had overinvested. Here French industries such as steel, ship building, and chemicals were badly hurt by international competition.
- Competition from the new industrial countries, especially in Southeast Asia, but also in Latin America, hurt sectors employing less-qualified workers, such as textiles, leather goods, assembly of electronic goods.
- Development of industrial specialization in the developed countries. As the world economy became increasingly integrated, with transport and communications costs falling and transfer of production easier, specialization based on experience and large-scale production created concentrations favoring the most efficient producers. In this changed world economy the giant U.S. economy lost a large share of its automobile market to Japanese imports, Japanese consumer electronics conquered the world, and only East Asian shipbuilding became profitable.
- New technologies proliferated, especially in microelectronics, telecommunications, and automation. The field of biotechnology exploded.[7]

The effects of the overall crisis for French industry in the period 1974–1990 are striking: The average annual growth was only 1 percent (with remarkable fluctuations: –5.9 percent in 1975, the year of Chirac's failed reflation, –2 percent in 1981, but +8 percent in 1986–1988). A million and a half industrial jobs were lost in this period, circa one-third of the industrial workforce. Textiles and clothing alone accounted for 33 percent of this job loss, the steel industry for another 6 percent.[8]

After 1981, a weakened French industrial sector could not dominate markets, which in any case were frequently declining. France's problems were further complicated by a franc that was overvalued by 10 to 15 percent in 1981. French products, in competition with others of equal or higher quality, were particularly price sensitive. The industries that the Left was nationalizing were not the engines of a powerful and productive economy, rendered antisocial by selfish or short-sighted private ownership. They were instead almost all loss making and would require large amounts of capital to redress their balances.

Nationalization

Nationalizations did not give the French Socialist government "the commanding heights of the economy," did little to promote democracy in the enterprise, and did not make the economic system more dynamic in the hoped-for manner. This ambitious and radical program did have important effects, however. What were they?

The cost of nationalization was not high: 39 billion francs, plus the interest paid on the bonds issued former shareholders during the time most of the industries were held by the state. Since the privatizations of 1986–1987 and 1993–1995 brought in 200 billion francs, a former Elysée official could observe wryly in 1996: "We bought cheap and sold dear. Of course, that wasn't the original idea."[9]

Five conglomerates were nationalized in 1982: Saint-Gobain (glass, plastics), Péchiney (aluminum), the Compagnie Générale d'Electricité (CGE), Thomson-Brandt (electronics), Rhône-Poulenc (chemicals), thirty-nine savings banks, and two investment banks. Dassault (aircraft) and Matra (defense industries) were nationalized at 51 percent, and Usinor and Sacilor (steel) were nationalized in 1981 at 95 percent by consolidation of the loans the Giscard government had previously given them when bailing them out. The newly nationalized sector made up 20 percent of the gross turnover of French industrial production and, together with the older nationalizations of 1945–1946, employed 24 percent of the industrial labor force.

State control did permit a certain useful rationalization of nationalized industry, where acquisitions had been made without too much logic. For example, CGE was given all branches of telecommunication, whereas Thomson, losing some elements, was given consumer and defense electronics. These changes were generally judged a success. However, the efforts of Jean-Pierre Chevènement as minister of research, then of industry as well, were resented by firm officials, and he eventually was obliged to surrender the combined portfolio. Increasingly, the state's philosophy was that state control and administration were separate spheres.

In 1981, only CGE and Saint-Gobain were making a profit; in 1982 only CGE, and the combined losses of the nationalized firms added up to more than 9 billion francs in 1982, but only 1.5 billion in 1983, and by 1984—thanks largely to Rhône-Poulenc—the sector was in the black by 2.639 billion francs.[10] In 1981–1985 state grants to industry alone amounted to 49 billion francs (during that time losses amounted to 67 billion francs) and nearly 40 billion more in grants in 1987–1990. In 1986–1990, all nationalized firms were profitable (Renault in 1987, Usinor-

Sacilor in 1988). The nationalized industrial firms then wished to buy or buy into competing firms, but the state was unable to furnish sufficient capital.

Since nationalized firms could not find private capital, a number of devices were used to bring in what the economist Elie Cohen terms "fake capital." In 1983, a law inspired by Delors allowed nationalized companies to sell stock without voting rights. The use of this technique grew rapidly, and in 1986 it brought in more than the state subsidies. It was, however, necessary to provide a large dividend, which made them expensive. In Mitterrand's second *septennat* a new scheme was developed that involved creating and selling off branches of the mother firm to raise capital. Mitterrand's 1988 "ni-ni" promise, neither more nationalization nor more privatization, was interfering with the necessary process of raising capital. Finally, in April 1991, it became possible to open 49 percent of a firm's capital to foreign buyers.[11] By that time, of course, the original policy of nationalization was a thin wisp of itself, and the Right, returning in 1993, began immediately to privatize extensively, renewing its 1986 promise deferred in 1987.

Total privatizations from 1986 to 1995 brought in U.S.$34.1 billion—$16.2 billion in 1994 and 1995.[12] Privatization, like nationalization, took place for political rather than economic reasons, although budgetary reasons may be added.[13]

Nationalization had waved no magic wand—but the nationalized firms had been nursed back from near disaster into profitability. A Right that was now neoliberal had no desire to retain a large public sector, even when large parts of it had been originally nationalized by its patron saint Charles de Gaulle. The Socialists were no longer sufficiently convinced of the importance of nationalization to raise much fuss—even if they had possessed the strength after 1993 to do so. In fifteen years, the issue had become almost irrelevant.

Monetary Policy

If nationalization descended from its early policy eminence to appear only a species of nursemaid for ailing industry, monetary policy became a major theme of Mitterrand's two terms. It presented itself first in May 1981, as devaluation of the franc came in question, later and more lastingly under the slightly different guise of the policy of the strong franc (*franc fort*) and its beneficial or detrimental effects on the economy.

In 1981 the new French government faced two alternate choices if it wished its economic policy to be consistent. It could continue the Barre government's economic policy, sticking to the idea of a strong franc and refusing devaluation, keep economic borders open, stay in step with economic partners to attempt to improve profitability, de-index wages, and keep control of inflation.

The alternative would have fitted better with the announced policies of the incoming government: Undertake competitive devaluation, attempt to renew dynamism in industry through investment and thus gradually reconquer the domestic market, selectively close off economic borders at the risk of de facto secession from the EC, and undertake a bold industrial policy with a clear set of priorities.

The new government instead refused devaluation and new tariff barriers but stepped out of phase with economic partners and nationalized large parts of industry, but its priorities were never clear.[14] Mitterrand did not wish to devalue immediately after he became president for political reasons—he believed it would be seen as a sign of weakness.

Could the government have devalued in June 1981 after the elections, when it was politically strongest? Should it have done so? Perhaps that would have been the most appropriate moment, and one argument runs that failure to devalue sharply in 1981 condemned France to "a series of insufficient devaluations coupled with a tighter, contractionary fiscal and monetary policy that, in turn, contributed to a deceleration in inflation, a sustained period of low growth, and an increase in unemployment [which] set the course for the remainder of the Mitterrand presidency."[15]

The dangers of the immediate devaluation advocated by a number of people in 1981 were, however, great. Sufficient devaluation of a franc overvalued by perhaps 15 percent and rising might well not have been possible within the European Monetary System, since Germany probably would not have agreed. (German policy in 1980–1981 was that the French-German currency difference should not exceed the accumulated inflation differential since the EMS went into effect in March 1979, which was 7.1 percent.) Devaluation therefore probably meant leaving the EMS and floating the franc—with selective closing of economic borders. In the past, such devaluations had sparked inflation—already running at nearly 14 percent. Leaving the EMS and some aspects of the EC would, on the part of a new and radical Socialist government, have set the other West European states (and certainly Reagan's United States) against France—and would have compromised and perhaps ruled out the relationship with West Germany that Mitterrand would soon pursue.

The energy bill would have shot up. (Much of it was paid in dollars, whose value was already rising steeply.) The exchange rate in May 1981 stood at 5.34 francs to the dollar; at the end of 1982 the rate was 7 francs to the dollar, and in 1984, 10 to the dollar before sinking again. France's trade deficit with the petroleum-producing countries in 1981 was 62 billion francs; its overall energy bill was 177.8 billion francs in 1982.[16] It was already clear in 1981 that a large devaluation against the dollar would constitute a major addition to the burdens on France; early devaluation would have made it heavier.

Refusal to devalue was not mere stubbornness. Having watched as successive devaluations provoked inflation, followed by the need to devalue again, French economists had by the mid-1970s decided that the German example of strong currency was superior to their own past practice or that of Britain or Italy. Since inflation in early 1981 was nearly 14 percent, a new Socialist government had excellent reasons not to incur still more inflation.[17]

The devaluation vetoed in spring 1981 had become inescapable in October 1981, as the balance of trade deteriorated and the money that social policy was pumping into the economy fled to foreign imports. By September it was becoming clear that the international recovery that experts had predicted had not arrived. The government was still making optimistic noises. Mitterrand asserted in September and again in December 1981 that the economy was picking up.

Economics Minister Delors had little control over a Mitterrand favorite who was nominally his junior, Budget Minister Laurent Fabius, and as they disagreed on policy, they went off in different directions. Fabius's 1982 budget contained an increase of 25 percent over the previous year and presupposed growth of 3.2 percent (in fact, it was 2.3 percent). "Ministries were positively encouraged to increase their budgets," says Elie Cohen. The immediate result was a new speculative attack on the franc. Delors, together with the governor of the Bank of France and the director of the Treasury, decided immediately that devaluation was necessary.[18]

The effect of the devaluation was slight, in part because in negotiating with the Germans and Dutch Delors had been unable to achieve the 12 to 15 percent devaluation he wanted; he had to settle for an effective devaluation of 8.5 percent against the mark. Delors also wished to reduce expenditures and freeze other proposed rises, but he was opposed by the other members of the Council of Ministers and had to settle for a freeze of 15 billion francs of expenditures—from a total budget of 800 billion francs.[19]

In the following months, as the trade deficit increased and speculation against the franc picked up once more, Mauroy's economists warned that another devaluation would be necessary sometime in 1982. This time it must be accompanied by an austerity package. Mitterrand agreed in principle but insisted on waiting until after the elaborate G-7 meeting to be held in Versailles in early June.

When Mauroy finally caught the president by the arm as the last gala luncheon at Versailles was ending, he demanded and finally obtained the green light. The austerity package of June 1982, euphemistically entitled *"rigueur,"* included wage and price controls, cuts in expenditures, and tightening of credit through higher interest rates. In a press conference three days after Versailles, Mitterrand spoke of obstacles encountered and the need to control the budget and social security expenses. He avoided mentioning either the words *rigueur* or *devaluation,* and press and public did not at first understand clearly just how far the government was about to go in turning its back on the policies of the preceding thirteen months. That was Mitterrand's intention.

The franc was devalued by 10 percent (5.5 percent devaluation of the franc, 4.25 percent revaluation of the mark and guilder). To obtain his concessions, Delors briefed the other EC finance ministers on the forthcoming austerity measures; he was obliged also to pledge continuing austerity.

The austerity package was agreed on in a ministerial discussion the next day, with Mitterrand increasing wage and price controls from the original plan of three months to four. When the Council of Ministers met a few days later to review the plan as a whole, it was violently attacked by Jean-Pierre Chevènement, newly named industry minister.

The "other policy" advocated by Chevènement, Bérégovoy, Fabius, and others had already surfaced by the time of the second devaluation. In the early months of 1983 Mitterrand was under siege, bombarded by memoranda on economics from his staff and Mauroy's and from advocates of the "other policy."[20]

Mitterrand was briefly convinced that the "other policy" was the way out of France's difficulties and was then reconverted to the need for austerity, remaining in the EMS, and fully participating in the EC (see the discussion of the political aspects of this in Chapter 2). All commentators agree that this decision made in March 1983 was the fundamental economic choice of Mitterrand's two terms. From it followed not only the *franc fort* policy pursued by Delors, then Bérégovoy, and all ministers of economics in the remainder of Mitterrand's time and the Juppé government of 1995–1997, but also the decision to emphasize and redynamize European policy.

The Socialists had always understood that the French economy had to operate within the general constraints of the European capitalist economy; the argument essentially was how many of these constraints (the EMS, open EC trading borders, the promises on austerity already made to the Germans to achieve the first two devaluations) had to be observed. The logic of Chevènement's and others' "Albanian solution" of raising tariff barriers was of course not really Albanian: The French economy could not sustain autarky, and no one wanted it at the expense of penury, nor could it be sustained in a democratic system. The "other policy" was aimed at a *temporary* exit from the EMS (for most of its advocates), and for *temporary* resistance to the Treaty of Rome through tariff barriers, where necessary; its nationalist advocates were assuming that France's trading partners and allies (and the international markets) would acquiesce in any policy Paris adopted. The scheme's advocates lost out because Mitterrand was ultimately convinced by Mauroy, Delors, and the Elysée-Matignon economists that its chances for success were questionable and its potential for catastrophic failure very real.

The decision made in March 1983 was more important even than the decision for *rigueur* in 1982 because it was a final recognition by François Mitterrand that socialism in one Common Market country was impossible. France could not escape from the integrated, capitalist European market.

The argument has been made that the shift from one policy to another was not simply a matter of external constraints but a deliberate political choice that could have turned out otherwise. The deliberate choice was, however, not abandonment of the "early commitments to reflation, employment, and redistributive spending in favor of such eminently conservative goals as price stability, external balance, fiscal and monetary restraint, and a strong currency," even though that is what happened.[21] The choice was to abandon a course that in the best judgment of those in authority was unsustainable. Mauroy, for example, had no desire to retreat from socialism; he simply saw the risk as too frightening. The difference between Mauroy and Chevènement was less political than ideological: For the latter, the success of his variety of socialism was worth taking any risk, and ideology more than analysis convinced him that the risk would succeed. Could it have succeeded? No one will ever know, but those who declined the risk had powerful arguments.

The policies begun in 1983 and continued thereafter have come under increased attack since 1994. The going phrase for them in France is *la pensée unique,* the received wisdom—that is, the contrary of wisdom. These policies resulted, according to Yale political economist David Cameron, "in a decade-long commitment to an overvalued currency, austerity, low growth, and high and rising unemployment."[22] Cameron's argument began with the decisions taken in 1981, but the thrust of the attack on the *pensée unique* in France in the mid-1990s was on the policies of Mitterrand's second term, linking the *franc fort* with the policy of a common currency and a monetary union.

The initial policies of 1981–1983 may have been responsible for the long-term low growth that has afflicted France. One analysis suggests that by mistakenly identifying 1981 (instead of 1983–1984) as the year when the world economy would pick up speed, French policy stumbled and failed to catch up and did not do so until three years later, in 1987.[23] Reflation produced growth in 1981–1983, and austerity braked it, whereas other European countries were in recession early in the decade and recovered later.

The policies exemplified by Fabius's inflated 1982 budget were unsustainable; regardless of which monetary policy was adopted, France would have had to swallow a large dose of austerity. Employment would have declined, as it did in fact for the next five years. Whether a different policy would have tilted the curve upward sooner and permanently cannot be known—but it seems doubtful, given the structural difficulties of the French economy. It is by no means clear that France ever had a real opportunity to escape the constraints that forced departure from the early Socialist policies.

De-indexation of industrial wages in 1983 was a major victory in the battle against inflation, which fell from 14 percent for 1981 to 4.7 percent in 1985. However, it meant that living standards for salaried workers declined, and the loss in buying power was even greater for the middle-middle class and well-paid salaried employees. French industrial production grew only 12.3 percent between 1980 and 1992, against 10.9 percent in Italy, 14.4 percent in the UK, 21.7 percent in West Germany—with 31.1 percent in the United States and 43.6 percent in Japan.[24] However, it should be noted that in 1992 the per capita share of GDP for France was greater than that of all EC countries except Denmark, West Germany, and Luxembourg—and 28 percent higher than that of the United Kingdom.[25]

The precedent for austerity and commitment to the strong franc was set in 1983–1984 and that commitment continued without alteration during the whole period discussed in this book. After the decisions of 1983 and the restructuring of 1984–1985, there followed the growth period of 1987–1989, until in late 1990 the economy began to falter again. Did the *franc fort* in itself inevitably produce low growth and high unemployment, or should the problems of the 1990s be ascribed to rigid adherence to it in the conditions posed by German unification and the downturn of the 1990s? An economy that was much stronger in 1990 than it had been in 1981–1983 could have taken more distance from German monetary policy than

Bérégovoy did take. As it was, Bérégovoy stubbornly resisted any suggestion that the franc might put some distance between itself and the mark.

The policy Bérégovoy adopted in 1984 when he became minister of economy and finance was defined as "competitive disinflation"—a term opposed to the competitive devaluation pursued by France in the 1960s and 1970s. Its central premise was the intimate link between the search for a balanced economy and the search for growth and job creation. Competitive disinflation and the stability of the franc thus were supposed to go together to create growth and jobs. Low inflation was necessary for France to be competitive and to sell French products at home and abroad. More exports and fewer imports meant more business growth, hence jobs.

A strong franc would promote disinflation, aid buying power, and also draw in foreign capital. Mastery of public finances would reduce interest rates and favor investment, and the tax receipts generated by growth would go toward future expenses (reinforcing growth) instead of financing interest payments. Finally, mastery of the balance of trade, one of the conditions for foreign confidence in the French economy, would keep the franc strong and interest rates down.[26]

Competitive disinflation might have worked, in the QED manner laid out by its advocates, except for the effects of German unification. Unification had involved exchange at one-to-one of small savings held in East German marks, then an enormous transfer of money from western to eastern Germany to pay for new infrastructure and social expenses. The result was an inflation rate that reached 4.5 percent in July 1991—a horrendous height for the inflation-shy Germans and especially for the Bundesbank. The German government declined to pay for most of the new expenses by raising taxes. Borrowing in turn caused interest rates to rise, and as German interest rates rose, the pressure on the franc to follow suit rose with them. Here the pressures of German unification joined the pressures implied by the idea of monetary unification: If there was to be a common currency, the existing currencies had to march together toward that goal, but if Germany was to pay for unification by borrowing, then its associates were going to have to pay too by accepting high interest rates.

However, if France wished to keep a franc as strong and perhaps stronger than the mark, then it had to accept those interest rates. Some authors have claimed that in early 1990 the Germans proposed a revaluation of the mark, which would have permitted lower interest rates and perhaps avoided the EMS crises of autumn 1992 and summer 1993.[27] Hervé Hannoun, Bérégovoy's chief aide at this period, has denied that there was any such démarche, adding, however, that had there been one, Bérégovoy would have rejected it. Apparently there was some informal consultation among experts on this question. The refusal even to consider such an idea is now faulted (often in retrospect) under the *pensée unique* label by many economists as a cause of French difficulties from late 1991 until late in the decade. At the time, Bérégovoy and the majority of French economic advisers were convinced that France would benefit from German import demand once Kohl put through the one-to-one exchange of East German marks with West.[28]

Although the economic recovery of 1987–1989 began to sour at the end of 1990, it was not until the end of 1991 or even the summer of 1992 that recognition of a new recession became general. That summer was marked by the June Danish referendum refusing the Maastricht treaty, the return of 10 percent unemployment, and in the black third week of September by the storm of speculation that drove the pound and the lira out of the EMS. The week ended with the French referendum on Maastricht, with its hairline margin of approval. Although the German government successfully pushed the Bundesbank to rally and save the franc from speculators, Spain, Ireland, and Portugal were obliged to resume currency controls.

Early that summer Michel Sapin, Bérégovoy's successor as economics minister, took soundings with his Dutch counterpart and other finance ministers to see whether EMS members other than Germany might in concert lower their interest rates. There was some interest, but the Dutch declined—they apparently had a secret agreement with the Germans tying the guilder to a 1 percent range with the mark.[29] Apparently there were no further attempts of this sort in 1992–1993, during the life of the Bérégovoy government.

The franc again came under violent attack in late July 1993. The result was a European decision to widen the bands of the EMS from 2.25 percent to 15 percent. But Prime Minister Balladur decided not to take advantage of this latitude, and interest rates remained high.

Successive French governments had thus concluded that they had no choice but to keep close to the mark. As time went on, the *franc fort* was justified and defended as necessary for the pursuit of European integration. For Bérégovoy, however, it was an end in itself, a matter of pride. The common currency plan had been worked out by the Delors committee, composed of central bankers, without participation by Bérégovoy. He had preferred an idea advanced by the British, John Major's "hard écu." Mitterrand would have none of it. He told Bérégovoy: "No reversal of alliances! Germany is our ally. The British are aligned with the United States!"[30] Mitterrand was long skeptical of the idea of a European central bank but had concluded that France would have more influence on a central bank than it would have without such an instrument. If France waited for the British, he believed, it would wait a long time—progress must be made by cooperating closely with the Germans.[31]

The figure of Pierre Bérégovoy is one of the most puzzling of the Mitterrand period. As secretary-general of the Elysée and minister for social affairs, Bérégovoy had argued for the "other policy." When he became minister for the economy and finance in July 1984 he experienced a conversion, and thereafter remained consistent—he became Monsieur *franc fort*. Yet he continued to give interviews deep into the 1980s in which he regretted the choice made in March 1983.[32] The inconsistency might be explained by mere nostalgia for a choice once open to which there was no returning—except that new opportunities to loosen the constraints of the *franc fort* appeared in 1990 (under very different circumstances from those of the early 1980s). Bérégovoy's stubborn adherence to the *franc fort* did not affect his staunch socialism. He told himself that he was defending the little man by fighting inflation. But his deflationary policy also cut down on investment, and thus on growth. Mitterrand remarked in 1990: "Why does he [Bérégovoy] let himself be swallowed up by those people at Finance? When I see him, he's very much on the Left. When he writes to me, he's worse than Raymond Barre."[33]

In 1991 when the president dropped Rocard, Cresson was supposed to push for more of the social policy Rocard allegedly had neglected. Bérégovoy (still in charge of economics and finance) argued that there was no money for that.

Cresson had wanted to establish a sort of French imitation of the Japanese MITI, taking the powerful Treasury department away from the minister of economy and finances, and putting it under the Industry Ministry, to which foreign trade would be added. When weighing choices for Rocard's successor, Mitterrand is supposed to have said: "[Bérégovoy] is the prisoner of the technocrats at the Finance Ministry, and if he were named, he'd act just like Rocard."[34] Yet Mitterrand not only kept Bérégovoy but gave him the "MITI"—supervision of Economy, Finance, Budget, Industry, and Foreign Trade. He was more powerful than ever.

In 1988, France had accepted the lifting of currency controls as part of the logic of efforts toward European union. Bérégovoy had agreed that this should be done, on condition that national taxes on savings be harmonized. Otherwise, Bérégovoy argued, there could be massive capital flight toward low-taxation countries. French currency controls at that time had the advantage of at least slowing down speculation and giving authorities more time to react. Mitterrand was not much interested in this technical question, but agreed—refusing, however, to make tax harmonization a conditio sine qua non, as Bérégovoy very much wanted. Kohl agreed—but after he had introduced a 10 percent withholding tax on dividends in January 1989, he found it very unpopular. Meanwhile the EC Commission was preparing a proposition on a general 15 percent withholding tax. Britain and Luxembourg, which had light taxes on such savings, objected violently. Four months later Kohl switched economics ministers and gave the post to CSU leader Theo Waigel. The conservative opposition to the tax won out, as Waigel insisted on dropping it—without consulting Paris. The French were furious and considered that Kohl had betrayed them.

Later, the 15 percent withholding tax proposition was quietly dropped. All currency controls were lifted as of January 1, 1990. Since there would be no protective tax harmonization, Bérégovoy felt obliged to cut taxes on profits from stocks, bonds, insurance policies, and mutual funds. In December 1989 he introduced legislation instituting tax-free funds for short-term fixed-interest instruments, the *sicav monétaire*. These tax-free mutual funds rapidly became so popular—particularly since the *franc fort* kept interest rates high—that at their height in 1991 a trillion francs were invested in them. In the meantime, ordinary taxpayers saw their taxes going up to pay for social security, unemployment costs, and so on.[35]

Mitterrand was thus complaining that Rocard was not pushing social policies (some, at least, precluded by Bérégovoy's opposition), grumbling that Bérégovoy talked left but advocated policies on the right, yet still confirmed Bérégovoy in the

Cresson government as the most powerful minister, and then made him prime minister after Cresson. Bérégovoy saw his *franc fort* become tied to a Europe that to a growing number of people meant tight money, growing unemployment—and profits for the rich. The effects of his policy were less and less socialist, and he felt this keenly, but blamed it on his president—to whom he nonetheless remained loyal.

Mitterrand and Bérégovoy had adopted policies that led to results they deplored but found ineluctable. For the president, the goal to value above all others was European integration, and if the monetary and tax policies one might have to accept were regrettable, they had by definition to be worth the price. (It is not clear how well Mitterrand understood the chain of cause and effect in economic decisions; his close aide Hubert Védrine has said that Mitterrand saw "no link between the defense of the franc and the economic crisis.")[36]

Bérégovoy was immensely proud of his strong franc. Meeting with the aged Antoine Pinay, conservative symbol of the (momentarily) strong franc in the Fourth Republic, Bérégovoy asked, "Do you know that they call me the 'Pinay of the Left'?"[37] He very much did not want his strong franc to be incompatible with the defense of the little man—except that it was. He knew that his policy of competitive disinflation discouraged investment, which led to rising unemployment, but saw that as a short-term problem—one continually prolonged, however.

If Mitterrand's top priority had not been the close association with Germany to build Europe, he might not have gone along so readily with the *franc fort*—which for Bérégovoy was an end in itself. But Europe came to mean a package containing high interest rates and fiscal relief for big capital. Neither Mitterrand nor Bérégovoy had wanted this—nor did either of them wish squarely to face the facts that their conjoined efforts had produced.

In the days before he committed suicide, Bérégovoy became increasingly critical of the policies he had followed. Listening to a TV interview with Simone Veil, Balladur's new minister of social affairs, who reproached the Socialists for the increase of inequality and noted that the Left had favored incomes stemming from capital over those deriving from labor, Bérégovoy is supposed to have commented, "If I had done something other than this Maastricht mess, we wouldn't be there now!"[38] And talking to a Socialist senator four days before his suicide, Bérégovoy said, "I sacrificed everything to the construction of Europe because I believed in it, also because my president asked for it." The clear inference drawn was that it had been a mistake.[39]

Unemployment

French unemployment worsened steadily between 1981 and late 1987, then fell somewhat between then and the end of 1990, whereupon it rose again until it exceeded 12 percent. In early 1981, when Mitterrand had declared the unemployment rate intolerable, it had been 7.2 percent. The French labor force in 1982 numbered

21.5 million people. It declined in 1984–1985, then rose again to hit a peak in 1990 of 22.27 million, descending again to 21.8 million in 1993. Those figures mask remarkable changes in the composition of employment. In 1982 there were 1.7 million French farm jobs (down from 5 million in 1954), and 1.2 million in 1990.[40]

The industrial workforce lost half a million jobs between 1975 and 1982, and as many again by 1990. In coal mining and steel alone, 100,000 jobs were lost. The textile, clothing, and leather working sectors added another 160,000 to the job deficit. The tertiary sector grew, however, gaining nearly 2 million jobs between 1982 and 1990.

At the end of 1993, overall unemployment stood at 3.2 million people. INSEE statistics demonstrate that unemployment in France has been heavily concentrated among young men and, even more, young women in the fifteen-to-twenty-four-year-old category. Until the end of the 1980s, unemployment was higher for those over fifty than for the twenty-five to forty-nine year olds. Since then it has consistently been lower—the over-fifty-year-olds have increasingly dropped out of the workforce.[41]

Young men and to a lesser degree young women must frequently wait several years before finding a stable job, passing through unemployment, training, part-time jobs, and so on, whereas older workers—once they lose their jobs—are often unemployable. Better-qualified job seekers, where they do not find jobs they actively want, have an incentive to take lower-level work when offered—making things worse for the level of qualification just below them.

How do these unemployment figures compare with those of France's neighbors? In the decade 1971–1980 average French unemployment ran 1.6 percent ahead of West Germany's and 0.3 percent ahead of Great Britain. In the next decade, the figures for France were 2.2 percent higher than for Germany and 0.3 percent lower than for Britain. From 1991 on, French unemployment was slightly higher than in previous decades compared to German, and considerably higher than the British rate.[42]

High youth unemployment is a special problem for the unqualified, many of them school dropouts, and for young Maghrébins, for whom the unemployment rate is approximately 40 percent.[43] Nevertheless, two-thirds of those unemployed have a certificate of some sort, all the way up to the baccalaureate. Young persons with a *bac* plus two years have a 13 percent unemployment rate. In part, unemployment for those who have had some or considerable education is due to the lowering of standards for diplomas. (According to Elie Cohen, a new catchall university diploma, the AES, *administration économique et sociale*—is not good enough to make you an economist and no good for the humanities either.)[44]

Still another problem has been long-term unemployment, in the spring of 1993 affecting more than a million people (35.6 percent of those unemployed). Two-thirds of those unemployed for more than one year in 1993 were between twenty-five and forty-nine years old, one third of them described as qualified workers—that is, with skills in their past jobs.

These statistics configure France's social problem: late entry into the workforce for a third of the young population, with obviously greater worries for the poorly educated and non-Europeans, and the inability of underskilled older men (and to a lesser degree, women) to find jobs once they have lost them.

Throughout the period discussed, different governments made extensive and expensive efforts to correct and reverse unemployment, with too little effect. (Expenses for employment rose to nearly 4 percent of GDP in 1993—unemployment payments making up 45 percent of that sum.)[45]

When growth slowed during the late 1970s, the Barre government had begun to encourage early retirement. In 1981–1982 the retirement age in practice was lowered below the new legal floor of sixty. The thirty-nine-hour workweek (paid at forty hours), the fifth week of paid vacations, and reduction of the maximum workweek were simultaneously social measures and attempts to create more jobs. From 1981 to 1983, the number of early retirees went from 330,000 to around 700,000.

From 1982 to 1985 priorities changed, with more emphasis on the fight against inflation and in favor of industrial restructuring, with more attention to labor costs and less rigid working schedules. The year 1983 saw the creation of *travail d'utilité collective* (TUC) contracts, temporary work programs that "employed" 330,000 in 1985. In those years the government (and the opposition) came to realize that unemployment was a long-term problem, that reducing the workweek or other partial solutions would not solve it, and that rigorous macroeconomic policies would be necessary. The restructuring of 1984–1985 (which cost several hundred thousand jobs) were part of this effort.

During the first cohabitation, when Social Affairs Minister Philippe Séguin frankly admitted that much of unemployment was incompressible, the policy was to reduce the obligations of enterprises, thus lessening labor costs, but there were no real innovations. In January 1987 the government dropped the regulation for administrative authorization of layoffs (ironically, introduced by Chirac in 1975).

Although about 800,000 jobs were created in 1987–1990, unemployment dropped by much less. In 1989 firms were relieved of the burden of social payments for the first new person hired, and another measure exempted employers of apprentices almost entirely. In 1990–1993 a million people were employed on "employment-solidarity" contracts. Launched in 1990 to succeed the TUC program, these part-time contracts were meant to aid the jobless in finding employment.[46] In 1992 the government again tried to stimulate hiring by reducing the social costs of wages for poorly qualified workers and added another program for the long-term unemployed. But as the economy grew worse, so did unemployment. In 1993–1994 the Balladur government again lowered certain charges involving social costs for employers. One of the measures attempted was the *contrat d'insertion professionelle* (CIP), allowing lower wages for very young workers, which provoked student demonstrations and was promptly dropped.[47]

Jacques Lesourne's study of the policies attempted over the years to combat unemployment concluded that various responsible ministers beat the bush in all possible directions, "replacing older workers who could then be called retirees by younger ones, putting the unemployed in training to cut down the statistics, providing carrots to firms to induce them to recruit, creating poorly paid public jobs, creating training programs—often praiseworthy initiatives, but following one after another in a frequently chaotic manner."[48] In January 1997, twenty months after the conservatives had taken over the Elysée as well as the Matignon, unemployment was at new heights. The greatest single failure of Socialist government was inability to improve the unemployment situation—and conservative government did not do better.

Inequality

Another one of the main themes of the Socialists in 1981 was the reduction of social inequalities in a country where they were generally reckoned the highest among developed countries. The Socialists had spoken in the 1970s of reducing discrepancies in wages and moving toward equal pay for equal work among men and women. Those goals clashed with the need to combat the crisis and restore the health of the French economy, and were not met. Continually increasing unemployment was, of course, the worst inequality of all.

The differential between the lowest and highest salary deciles (average worker and employee salaries versus average executive salaries) diminished in the early 1980s, in 1984 standing at 2.91, and then rose to 3 in 1990, and in 1993 to 3.07.[49] Between 1984 and 1992 wage differentials varied from 13 percent less for women than for men in the lowest decile of annual salaries to 32 percent in the highest—and in that eight-year period the discrepancies actually increased slightly.[50] The least-favored workers benefited most, as the government repeatedly raised the minimum wage (SMIC) and later introduced the *revenu minimum d'insertion* (RMI).

The nature of inequality changed markedly between 1980 and 1990. In 1979–1980, 54 percent of households at the lowest income levels were composed of retired persons; a decade later the figure had dropped to 7 percent. People above the age of seventy-five and living alone were, however, often still in poverty. The largest category in the list of most-disadvantaged households was the household headed by an unemployed person—30 percent (33 percent where women were concerned). Poverty (defined as having less than 50 percent of the average revenue) had not increased but had become more visible. Young jobless persons begging in the streets or the métro stood out, whereas the elderly destitute had not.[51]

Unemployment remained the worst curse of the French economy. Although the unqualified and the young (especially when unqualified) were hardest hit, by the 1990s the sensation of insecurity had spread even to those unlikely to be affected, concerned for themselves and still more for their children—a malaise extending far beyond the 12-plus percent of the actually unemployed.

Although a notable percentage of the poor and unemployed drifted away from the Left (both Communist and Socialist voters) and sought political solace in the nostrums of the National Front, the Socialists did not suffer greatly from the loss of worker votes in 1986 and recouped in the 1988 election. By 1992, however, and still more in 1993, the Socialists were losing workers' votes. In a poll of early June 1993 investigating major motives for the stunning Socialist defeat, the rise of unemployment was seen as a major reproach by 77 percent of respondents—and by 69 percent of respondents declaring themselves Socialists. The growth of poverty and social exclusion lagged far behind that as a reason for rejection, at 42 percent for all respondents, and 43 percent for Socialists.[52]

Another conspicuous and much resented inequality was the ability of the more wealthy to avoid taxes by buying tax-free securities (the *sicav monétaire*), while the ordinary wage earner was being taxed heavily. This inequality followed directly from the *franc fort* and the need to keep investors from chasing higher interest rates abroad. Did other policies associated with the *franc fort,* competitive disinflation, and the provisions of the Maastricht treaty also raise unemployment and exclusion? Two economists argued in 1993 that a 30 percent increase in French competitiveness (an unacceptable goal for France's neighbors) would decrease unemployment by only 3 percent. France had increased productivity, but not employment, whereas investment had not increased enough. The implication here is that the problems of the French economy were deeply structural, and a change in the policy on the franc and interest rates might have made a difference only at the margin.[53]

Socialist Capitalism

One of the surprises in Socialist economic management was modernization of French financial institutions. In 1983 a second stock market for new companies appeared, and in 1985 a financial futures market, innovations one might have expected from conservatives. To everyone's amazement, the Paris Bourse had never been so prosperous as under the Socialists in 1985, and Economics Minister Bérégovoy basked in the approval of the financial community. After the 1988 presidential elections, when Bérégovoy was reappointed to the post in the Rocard government, *Le Monde*'s cartoonist Plantu could wickedly portray brokers downing celebratory champagne on the stock market steps while muttering, "Just suppose Chirac had been elected . . . "

The stock market was reformed with the abolition of brokers' monopolies, the Commission des Opérations de Bourse was reformed to give it a closer resemblance to the U.S. Securities and Exchange Commission, currency controls were lifted, and the Bank of France became independent. Beyond that, a mythology of "them-us" dissolved. The pre-1981 Socialists had a long list of dirty words, including *profit, capitalists,* even *business.* Curiously enough, though nationalization was unsuccessful in alleviating unemployment, it convinced the Left that profit was necessary and the entrepreneur a positive figure. The Left even had its own business hero, Bernard Tapie, a onetime singer turned businessman, then politician, who specialized in takeovers that (ostensibly) became profitable.

Public confidence in business leaders went from 44 percent in 1981 to 56 percent in 1985, and business was no longer seen automatically as the exploiter—instead it created much-needed jobs.[54] In 1985, 62 percent of respondents said they had considerable confidence in private enterprise, with only 19 percent declaring they did not. However, when the economy turned down again after 1990, confidence in business leaders dropped again—although not precipitously.

One of the goals of the Right's privatization in 1986 (and again in 1993) was the creation of "people's capitalism," explicitly copied from Margaret Thatcher's Britain, with the idea that a nation of shareholders would be a nation supporting business, not socialism. The number of shareholders did increase, from 2 million before privatization to more than 6 million by 1987, but it is not clear that this meant that 6 million private individuals, let alone families, actually owned stocks. There was, however, no interest in promoting extensive shareholder democracy, and little information was sent out to shareholders.[55] All these privatizations, which undid the nationalizations carried out by de Gaulle in 1944–1945 and then by the Socialists, would have been impossible in the them-us climate that obtained before 1981—the conservatives never considered them, the Left would not have permitted them. Old-fashioned socialism had thus made itself obsolete. Neoliberal capitalism had yet to prove itself.

9

Foreign Policy: 1981–1995

The Shaping of Mitterrand's Socialist Foreign Policy

In 1981, France and the outside world wished to know how the newly elected president would handle relations with the Soviet Union. They waited to see what his defense policies would be, whether he would follow the policies established by his predecessors on Europe, whether he would follow Socialist rhetoric and some of his own in devoting great attention to the Third World—and how he would establish his own and France's Socialist position vis-à-vis the great powers, upholding that essential of the Gaullist vision, France's "rank."

Charles de Gaulle had defined French foreign policy in the 1960s. His security policies had come to be generally accepted (with considerable variation in interpretation and sincerity). All agreed that France should preserve its independent nuclear deterrent; all but the Communists agreed that France should remain within the Atlantic alliance but outside the NATO military structure. Beneath this general agreement, however, lay differences of approach that posed many questions.

Late into the Giscard years orthodox Gaullists were still very influential in the foreign affairs bureaucracy. They treated "as heresy any rapprochement with the United States, any attempt to warm up relations with Israel, any overly systematic cooperation in Europe, any strategic vocabulary that questioned the postulates of dissuasion '*tous azimuts*' [in all directions]." President Giscard, no foreign affairs expert, had innovative ideas in Western European affairs but never rethought the whole complex of Gaullist foreign and security policy. He retained in particular a fascination with the Gaullist legacy of France's "special relationship" with the Soviet Union.[1]

In its most ambitious form, the special relationship had suggested that an independent France, which had escaped from the force field of bipolar East-West tension, could play a unique role as arbiter between the USSR and both Western and

Eastern Europe. When Soviet troops entered Prague in August 1968 de Gaulle immediately realized that his hopes of melting the frozen blocs of the Cold War had ended.[2] Eight months after the blighting of the Prague Spring, de Gaulle left office, and Gaullist foreign policy, often flexible in the hands of its creator, was passed on to overreverent adepts. They were willing to make adjustments—arrangements with NATO softening the harshness of the 1966 break (already begun under de Gaulle with the Lemnitzer-Ailleret agreements) and even the admission of Great Britain into the European Community. Nevertheless, the spirit of Gaullism stalked the corridors of the Quai d'Orsay during the next two administrations, and its liturgies continued to be intoned in Giscard's Elysée.

A Gaullist theory hypothesized a so-called triangular relationship based on French Communist obedience to Moscow. The theory argued that since Moscow thought the French Socialist party unreliable, the Soviets would ultimately command the PCF to break its alliance with the PS rather than aid in defeating a conservative regime friendly to the USSR.[3]

In 1980 Giscard could thus believe he had good reason to maintain the special relationship with the Soviet Union. When in late December 1979 Soviet troops moved into Afghanistan, the United States reacted strongly and requested support from its allies. Giscard refused to join in imposing economic sanctions. Leonid Brezhnev sent him word that the invasion had been forced on him by hard-liners in the Kremlin and asked for help in reinforcing his position and lessening international tension. Giscard rose to the bait, believing that he alone among Western leaders could resolve the Afghan situation. Against the advice of his staff, Giscard flew off to meet Brezhnev in Warsaw in mid-May.

The trip ended badly. Giscard was gulled by Brezhnev into announcing to his colleagues at the June economic summit in Venice the good news of a Soviet promise to pull troops out of Afghanistan—a movement that turned out to be a rotation and ultimately an increase in forces.[4] François Mitterrand described Giscard bearing Brezhnev's message to the other European leaders as "a little telegraph boy." Mitterrand was a master of the biting phrase, but this particular sarcasm had a lasting echo, proving that he had touched a new sentiment in the French people—one unsuspected by Giscard. By the late 1970s faith in the special relationship had worn thin and suspicion of the Soviet Union had grown steadily, on part of both the Right and the Left. Mitterrand's election thus coincided with a change in French attitudes toward the Soviet Union. A lately converted president and Socialist party arrived in office convinced that a France really menaced by the Soviet Union needed to keep its own nuclear deterrent, but form a closer tie with its Western allies.

Mitterrand wrote his close diplomatic collaborator Hubert Védrine:

Had personal views and precise intentions on all of the great subjects of the moment. They were simple: First, kill in the egg any eventual ostracism by the international establishment of the first president of the Left elected by universal suffrage, impose himself [as a major figure], be as firm as possible with the USSR, without breaking contact, show himself the friend of the United States without being tightly bound, try to work for economic progress in Europe and North-South solidarity . . . care more for the defense of the Rights of Man, make France respected everywhere, make it play a larger role in function of the relations of power, and for the rest, act according to the circumstances.[5]

No one in the Elysée or elsewhere foresaw that the hallmark of the new president's time in office would be thoroughgoing cooperation with Germany and a strong emphasis on European unity.

Foreign policy in the Fifth Republic is the president's policy. A French president is constrained to some extent by the policy of his predecessors; he must cast a wary eye on public opinion, but to a degree quite unknown in the United States, the president is free to determine the directions and shape the details of policy, ordinarily with little parliamentary consultation or fear of interference. The policy choices made by François Mitterrand are central to the history of his domestic administration, but the actions and attitudes of his prime ministers, ministers, aides, party associates and opponents also crowd the stage. In the foreign policy area, the president was nearly alone, save for a few aides and extras.

Even the two periods of cohabitation were not complete exceptions to this rule. In 1986–1988, the ruling RPR-UDF coalition had no large foreign policy differences with Mitterrand, and Jacques Chirac did not wish publicly to undermine presidential privileges in foreign and defense questions. This *domaine réservé,* unmentioned in the constitution, had been firmly enshrined in practice by de Gaulle. Chirac therefore nibbled at the edges of foreign policy and associated himself with Mitterrand whenever he could (sometimes claiming sole credit for joint decisions). During 1986, the Quai d'Orsay cut down drastically on the number of telegrams from French embassies relayed to the Elysée, until the president's entourage leaked this and the cutback slackened, though it did not cease until it became apparent that Mitterrand was likely to win the 1988 elections. Mitterrand thus lost control of details in some foreign policy areas, but was by no means ousted from his former role.[6]

In the second cohabitation, 1993–1995, a politically and physically enfeebled president still upheld his privileges. Prime Minister Balladur tried to play a larger role than he could sustain, but he was outmaneuvered by Mitterrand, working with Foreign Minister Alain Juppé, the close associate of Balladur's RPR rival Jacques Chirac. The power struggle was thus an internal one inside the new conservative government, not between the conservatives and Mitterrand. Thus although the president was obliged to share power with a foreign minister not of his choice, his precedence and powers were respected, the more easily because there were no fundamental policy disagreements.

European Policy

When François Mitterrand took office in 1981 his views on foreign policy and those of his party had undergone a number of changes from their pacifist and antinuclear positions of a decade earlier. A convinced European since the days of the Fourth Republic, Mitterrand was obliged to repel several leftist attempts to influence PS foreign policy in the early days of 1971–1973. He kept the PS in a Socialist International thought by leftist militants to be hopelessly reformist and pro-NATO, and fought off proposals to take France out of the Atlantic alliance and the European Community. Mitterrand did make other gestures pleasing to left-wing sentiment in the PS. He tried—in vain—to organize a French-led group of Mediterranean Socialist parties within the Socialist International, which would approve alliances with Communist parties. At every opportunity, he denounced the iniquities of multinational business.

In those years many Socialists feared the United States more than the Soviet Union; Mitterrand worried in 1974 that if he were elected, the United States might try to destabilize him in the way Henry Kissinger had tried to destabilize Salvador Allende. At the same time, Mitterrand had no love for the Soviets, who in turn missed opportunities to cultivate him. Their ostentatious preference for Giscard (repeated in the 1981 election) was a constant affront.

From 1975 on, neutralist and anti-NATO tendencies in the PS diminished, and after their 1977 rift with the Communists, the Socialists were more open to the winds of anticommunism that were beginning to sweep over the intellectual Left. On the urging of then international affairs secretary Robert Pontillon and Mitterrand's friend Charles Hernu, the party expert on defense, the PS drafted a statement in November 1977 singling out the Soviet Union as the only power to use military force in Europe (against its own allies) since World War II. After the Communists had preceded the Socialists in accepting the French nuclear deterrent, the PS finally decided in January 1978 to support maintenance of French nuclear forces—though with some reservations.[7] Mitterrand, still profoundly uneasy about nuclear weapons, led from behind in proselytizing for them, telling Hernu, "Go ahead—convince the party and then I will support you."[8]

American power seemed on the wane after the Vietnam disaster, whereas Soviet power became more assertive in Africa and in the missile buildup. Mitterrand's thinking on the Soviet threat began to change. His ideas on this question in 1977–1979 were not, however, influenced by parallel ideas developed by Helmut Schmidt. Mitterrand-Schmidt relations were chilly—the PS leader resented the chancellor's obvious preference for Giscard, although Mitterrand became friendly with Willy Brandt.

Once elected, Mitterrand met Helmut Schmidt as an equal and realized that he could get on very well with him. Willy Brandt, now head of the Social Democratic Party (SPD), was embittered to find Mitterrand preferring Schmidt to him. Their falling out brought about a failure of communications between the PS and the German Social Democratic party, at a time when the German socialists were moving away from NATO orthodoxy and the French closer to Atlantic loyalty. At their first meeting, three days after Mitterrand took office, Schmidt asked for Mitterrand's support for his position (increasingly questioned in the SPD) favoring the stationing in Germany of Pershings and cruise missiles (a question on which Giscard had wavered). In order to solidify his position with the German leader, Mitterrand agreed immediately.[9]

Socialist foreign policy experts (along with the rest of the French foreign policy establishment) had, since the collapse of de Gaulle's efforts to move West Germany away from its U.S. ties, taken it for granted that German loyalty to NATO was absolute and unalterable. The idea that the West Germans might be drifting from their Atlantic moorings came only slowly to them—and alarmed them deeply.[10]

Gaullist foreign policy since the mid-1960s had operated on the unspoken premise that since West Germany was utterly loyal to the United States, France could afford to dance out of line, remaining loyal to the Atlantic alliance but in its own independent and idiosyncratic way. In the early 1980s the prospect of a possibly neutralist West Germany appeared as a new nightmare to the French. Voices on both the Left and the Right cried out in alarm—every indication that Germany might be "drifting toward neutralism" was scrutinized. Raymond Aron remarked in a 1982 interview: "Today the French are not afraid of German militarism; they are afraid of German pacifism"—by which he meant the threat of neutralism.[11]

With this fear of "German drift," Mitterrand had a powerful motive to move closer to the Federal Republic on security questions, an area sketched out in the Franco-German treaty of 1963. The treaty had originally called for frequent French-German consultations on strategy and tactics to "harmonize their doctrines," exchange personnel, and so on. Strong American objections joined doubts in Konrad Adenauer's Christian Democratic Union (CDU). The Bundestag in ratifying the treaty added a preamble that reaffirmed German loyalty to NATO in such a way that nothing came of the harmonization idea.

In the 1970s, as the United States appeared weaker and less resolute in the wake of the Vietnam war and a then-confident Soviet Union proclaimed that "the correlation of forces" (i.e., the power balance) had shifted in its favor, the Soviets began to deploy a large number of medium-range SS-20 rockets aimed at European cities. Since Soviet long-range rockets already possessed the capability of destroying Europe, the new weapons appeared to be a means of political-diplomatic blackmail. Helmut Schmidt was the first to call for a U.S. response in deploying new weapons in Europe. In 1979 the NATO Council called for a "two-track decision," whereby the major NATO nations would deploy new American Pershing rockets and cruise missiles unless the Soviets agreed to reverse their SS-20 deployment.

Schmidt had found the Carter administration hesitant on making this decision. He was already enraged by Jimmy Carter's reversal of the decision to manufacture the neutron bomb, after Schmidt had publicly agreed to it at great political cost. Finally, Schmidt had been greatly upset by indications that the Americans would not fully defend German territory in case of war. While quite cognizant that the United States, however untrustworthy he feared it might be, remained the bulwark of German defense, Schmidt was now eager to seek a new security relationship with France. He discussed some of this with Giscard, who was interested but unwilling to advance such a relationship before a presidential election that he expected to give him another seven years in office.

Mitterrand had originally thought that Giscard had been too close to the Germans, particularly to Schmidt. He did not desire what he termed a Paris-Bonn axis, and his associates thought that France would do better to improve relations with Britain. But the first Franco-British summit in early September 1981 disappointed them. Mitterrand's aide Jacques Attali noted: "The British want to profit from the changes in Europe, to put an end to twenty years of French-German predominance in Europe. Nothing brings us close to them."[12]

In October 1981 during a visit by Schmidt to Latché, Mitterrand's country home, Mitterrand took the initiative in talking of relaunching French-German security cooperation. He spoke of the necessity of what he termed a privileged friendship between the two countries, describing it as the only way not to be the plaything of the United States or the USSR.[13]

When Schmidt was forced out of office in October 1982 by a change in coalition politics, Mitterrand met almost immediately with the new conservative chancellor, Helmut Kohl. They rapidly found it possible to get on well together. Within the limits of French independence from NATO and German commitment to it, the two leaders agreed to implement the defense clauses of the long-dormant 1963 Franco-German treaty.[14] A Franco-German Commission on Security and Defense was set up to coordinate an exchange of views on security policy, with frequent meetings of defense ministers and staffs.

The best demonstration of French determination to hold West Germany in the tight embrace of the alliance was Mitterrand's trip to Bonn in January 1983 to address the Bundestag, shortly before West German elections. A French Socialist president whose own country took an independent stance in the alliance was ignoring the views of German Socialists and urging German conservatives to accept the stationing of Pershing II and cruise missiles. Mitterrand's speech cemented his new relationship with Kohl and won approbation from Washington, which had needed reassurance about this socialist president.

Mitterrand's Bundestag speech stressed French support for German dependence on U.S. nuclear firepower (a tacit support hitherto well cloaked in Gaullist rhetoric), but it also demonstrated his conviction that France should draw closer to Germany, both politically and militarily. The political rapprochement was relatively simple. Giscard's relations with Schmidt had already been the best between French and German leaders since the de Gaulle–Adenauer partnership and had lasted longer. The crown jewel of their relationship was the European Monetary System—and Mitterrand's decision in March 1983 that France could not afford to leave the EMS was indeed more political than economic. The semiannual summits between French and German leaders and ministers and frequent meetings among high officials stipulated in the Franco-German treaty of 1963 had kept Franco-German relations alive even in periods of chilly relations. Now they became an engine to improve bilateral relations.

Rapprochement in security policy was more complicated. France could not furnish more than a supplementary nuclear guarantee to the Federal Republic. If the United States declined to risk Chicago to protect Hamburg, would the French risk Paris, and if so, would their forces—even if firmly committed—suffice to deter? Quarterly meetings of the Franco-German defense commission instituted in 1982 encountered two basic obstacles. The West Germans were not really interested in a French nuclear guarantee (never actually offered) but in an increase in French conventional commitment to the defense of Europe. The French did not intend to increase their conventional forces and gave priority to their nuclear forces, the factor distinguishing them from other West European continental powers. Neither were they ready to share their nuclear trigger with the Germans, and despite much talk, they would not declare officially that France's defense frontier lay on the Elbe rather than on the Rhine. Defense cooperation nevertheless moved steadily forward into the mid-1980s.

France and Europe

Throughout his political career, François Mitterrand's most persistent and consistent belief was that France had to pursue its engagement in a larger European unity. His concept of Europe had limitations; never a Jean Monnet–style federalist, he was always attentive to the claims of his country's nationalist tradition. He was skeptical of a Europe that might be too closely bound to the United States. As a minister in the Mendès-France government in 1954, he had agreed with the vote against the European Defense Community because he thought it would "give the keys of European defense to the generals in the Pentagon." He said in 1974 that Europe would "be socialist or would not be," and explaining this phrase in 1977 wrote: "Washington continues to be the capital of Europe. Only a socialist Europe, daring to create itself, will build its independence.[15] He repeated this line in 1980. Here he was echoing the line of Jean-Pierre Chevènement's CERES (but he had fought Chevènement and others to keep the PS from opposing the European Community).

By March 1983 Mitterrand was a long way from the balancing act he had engaged in during the 1970s. Now he was forced to make a fundamental choice. Should he, if he wished to pursue the policies of 1981–1982, take France out of the European Monetary System, devalue the franc, perhaps raise tariff borders, and hope that all would work out? If not, he would have to submit to German conditions and pursue the austerity that had been called only a parenthesis. There can have been little doubt in his mind that he was surrendering much of his original program under constraint, but he feared that the "other policy" would fail, taking with it the fortunes of his presidency and his place in history. Mitterrand chose to avoid the risk, and in doing so he made Europe the major focus of his ambitions. At no moment can he have believed that this Europe would be socialist.

For the moment, Mitterrand was opting for German aid in a devaluation/reevaluation, and a large EC loan. Community Europe in spring 1983 was at a standstill, victim of what was termed "Eurosclerosis." Forward motion was blocked by a series of quarrels, the most important of which was British insistence since 1980 on an EC refund of what Margaret Thatcher considered Britain's double contribution to the EC. (Britain thought its payments to the EC of a tax on agricultural products purchased from Commonwealth countries should be considered as a part of its regular EC payments; the rest of the EC disagreed.) This disagreement, Margaret Thatcher's refrain "I want my money back," had by itself paralyzed European Council meetings, although other problems included milk prices, the entry of the Iberian countries, the need to increase community resources, et cetera. Lengthy, futile discussion of these problems rendered European Councils throughout 1982 nearly sterile. Bargaining over the refund check for Britain continued at the European Council Stuttgart meeting in 1983, and again in December, where the Athens meeting failed even to agree on the final communiqué.

France chaired the European Council for the first half of 1984, and Mitterrand resolved to seize the opportunity to restart the European engine. He began with an intensive round of visits or invitations. Nevertheless the March 1984 council meeting in Brussels yielded only an agreement on milk, and Thatcher remained intransigent on her demands. She had, however, united the other European countries against Britain.

The next European Council meeting took place in late June at the palace of Fontainebleau. Mitterrand was in great need of a success. The PS vote had just dropped precipitously in the European elections, the rally in Paris against his government's education bill had seen an unprecedented number of opponents in the streets, and unemployment and his unpopularity continued to rise.

The entente with Helmut Kohl solidified by Mitterrand's Bundestag speech in January 1983 now stood its first test. Britain and Germany were the only net contributors to the EC budget, and Mrs. Thatcher thought she could use this fact to split the French-German accord. Paris and Bonn had, however, already agreed on a maximum offer to meet British demands. They had sketched out a contingency plan to allow the community to function without the British, using a sort of parallel intergovernmental agreement, should Thatcher refuse the offer. This plan was then carefully leaked to the British government.[16]

Finding that she could not split Germany from France, Mrs. Thatcher finally agreed to a generous compromise. The way was now open for an enlargement of EC resources from the VAT, more work on disciplining agricultural prices, and agreement in principle on Spanish and Portuguese entry into the community. (Paris had been less keen on Iberian entry than Germany because of agricultural competition on wines and citrus fruit.) Nevertheless, Mitterrand hastened to Lisbon and Madrid almost immediately after the council meeting to announce that they would be admitted by January 1, 1986. Germany, still the largest contributor, won greater concessions than France for its farmers, causing Agriculture Minister Rocard to complain in the next Council of Ministers. Finally, the Irish EC representative James Dooge was charged with drawing up a committee report on a new treaty for

European Union. In retrospect, the Fontainebleau meeting not only cleared the EC agenda of the moment, but also opened the way for the Single European Act of 1986 and the Maastricht treaty.

As his European policy took shape, Mitterrand found it useful to change his foreign policy team—keeping Védrine, enlarging the role given his European affairs adviser Elisabeth Guigou, and looking for a new foreign minister. Claude Cheysson had served ably, but his incompatibility of temperament with the president outweighed their general accord on principles. Mitterrand had often had to reproach him for saying out loud what might be true but was highly impolitic.[17] Mitterrand's choice was his intimate Roland Dumas, first named as minister for European affairs and then foreign minister in December 1984. Dumas was to serve in this post until March 1986 and again from 1988 to 1993.

At Fontainebleau Mitterrand and Kohl agreed that Jacques Delors should replace the Luxembourger Gaston Thorn in January 1985 as president of the EC Commission. Mitterrand first suggested Cheysson. (He wanted to open up the post at the Quai for Dumas.) The job was supposed to go to a German, and Kohl told Mitterrand that he proposed to name Kurt Biedenkopf—a CDU rival whom he had outmaneuvered and probably did not want in the Brussels job. Kohl, who liked Delors, told Mitterrand that he was willing to accept a French candidate—if his initials were J. D. Germany's turn would come at the end of Delors's term in January 1989. (Delors was still economics minister, but by late June 1984 it was evident that the Mauroy government would soon come to an end one way or another, and Delors, who had no hope of being the next prime minister, had told Mitterrand that he expected to return to being mayor of Clichy.)[18] In March 1988, Kohl confided to Mitterrand that he wanted Jacques Delors to remain president of the EC Commission, renouncing the idea of pushing a German candidate to replace him.[19]

Once he had been formally selected as the new commission president, Delors looked around for new initiatives. At the Fontainebleau summit Mitterrand had largely cleared away the big clouds hanging over the EC. Delors felt that the way was open to relaunch an EC sorely in need of relaunching. He began with visits to all the EC capitals to see what initiatives leaders might agree to, finding consensus on establishing the single market, which he proposed in his "investiture speech" to the European Parliament.[20]

Mitterrand appointed his old friend Maurice Faure (French foreign minister at the time of the Treaty of Rome in 1957) as French representative on the Dooge Committee, which submitted its report in March 1985. The report, with a large input by Faure, called for an integrated common market, with free circulation of goods and capital, and reinforcement of the EMS ending in a common European currency. The powers of the EC Commission were to be increased, with a greater role for the European Parliament. The unanimous-vote rule, which had prevailed since de Gaulle imposed it in the so-called Luxembourg compromise of 1966, was to be progressively abandoned in favor of majority voting. A common foreign policy with a permanent secretariat was also proposed. (Some of these ideas were adopted in 1985, others in the Maastricht treaty, others are still under debate in 1997.) The Dooge report suggested holding an intergovernmental conference (IGC) to implement these recommendations.

Margaret Thatcher had signed off on Delors's nomination as commission president, but she thought to have some check on him by naming former minister Lord Cockfield as a European commissioner. He would disappoint Thatcher by working closely with Delors and as she saw it, "going native." Cockfield, as Internal Market commissioner, drew up a white paper, a list of nearly 300 specific proposals, accomplishment of which would create the internal market.

The Milan summit of June 1985 accepted the white paper. The British had approved it and made some modest proposals on political cooperation. Bonn preferred the idea of a treaty to show that Europe was moving forward. Mitterrand wished to use all occasions to stay close to the Germans. (As always, the fear that Germany would lose interest in Western Europe and turn toward the East and the Soviet Union was never far from French minds.) But Mitterrand also feared to push forward too fast, lest Britain break the newly attained concord. He suggested instead a Franco-German project for a treaty on European union. Delors advised against it, telling Mitterrand, in reference to de Gaulle's unsuccessful attempts in 1960 to align the Europeans behind France, that it was "a Fouchet plan number three."[21] When Kohl referred to the project before the Milan summit, the other countries were angry, and at Milan it was Italian prime minister Bettino Craxi who took the lead in proposing an IGC to work out a treaty of European union. Great Britain, Denmark, and Greece were opposed but later came around. To mollify them, the words "European union" were dropped and replaced by the innocuous term "Single Act," meaning that it covered a wide variety of proposals.[22]

The Luxembourg summit in December 1985 saw Mitterrand worried that the text of the Single Act drafted by the Luxembourg presidency (according to Delors 95 percent the work of the EC Commission) was too close to Anglo-German ideas, smacking too much of a free enterprise Europe. There was nothing about a common currency or a social policy. He found both Germany and, obviously, Britain too close to American policy.[23]

In the event, the summit was a success. The Single Act decided on in December 1985 aimed at completion by December 31, 1992, of an interior market for the Twelve (since Spain and Portugal would soon accede to full membership). Free circulation of goods, services, people, and capital was to be assured. Mitterrand, only half-pleased, was sufficiently content. The Single Act was signed on February 16–17, 1986, and ratified by all signatories in December of that year.

With Germany for Europe

Inability to achieve a common position with West Germany on the Strategic Defensive Initiative (SDI—to be discussed) was frustrating to Paris because French policy increasingly saw French-German cooperation as a bulwark against what it perceived as U.S. encroachments on sovereignty. In 1984 Helmut Kohl had angled for an invitation to the ceremonies commemorating the fortieth anniversary of the Normandy landings, arguing that Germany had been liberated too. No country showed much enthusiasm for that, and Kohl fell back on the idea of a symbolic French-German commemoration of the holocaust of Verdun. The picture of a giant Kohl and a much smaller Mitterrand hand in hand at Verdun symbolized French-German friendship and determination to turn their backs on a history of enmity.

Gestures such as that by no means meant a lack of tension between Paris and Bonn. France still intended to maintain full sovereignty in its military cooperation with the Federal Republic. (See the discussion of Franco-German defense cooperation and French defense policies.) Paris also wished to renew relations with the great power further to the east.

Mitterrand had carefully maintained correct but formal relations with the Soviets in the first three years of his term in office. In April 1983 France expelled forty-seven Soviet diplomats and other personnel for espionage; the government was giving unprecedented publicity to the kind of action that had before always been carried out quietly (and on a much smaller scale). But Mitterrand continued to believe that once the missile question was settled one way or another, it would be useful to visit the Soviet Union.

Mitterrand had declared in 1981 that he would not change the tenor of French relations with the Soviet Union until progress had been achieved over Afghanistan. He considered, however, that the real obstacle had been the crisis over the deployment of NATO missiles in Germany. He prepared his Moscow trip carefully, among other ways by discussing it in his March 1984 visit to the United States.

He flew to Moscow in June 1984 to meet the moribund Konstantin Chernenko. In the meantime, the question of the Soviet dissident Andrei Sakharov and his wife had become a major issue. Should Mitterrand go while the Sakharovs, who were engaged in a hunger strike, were perhaps being force-fed, perhaps dying? This quickly became a major political issue in a France increasingly critical of Mitterrand's domestic policies. The Elysée stipulated that the president would travel only if Moscow made a statement clarifying the status of the Sakharov couple—eventually accomplished by a Tass announcement.

Much speculation remained whether Mitterrand would raise the Sakharov case with the masters of the Kremlin. When he did so in his speech at a Kremlin banquet, the Soviet leaders pretended not to have heard, but Politburo member Gaidar Aliyev (later president of Azerbaijan) whispered to his neighbor, French Communist leader Charles Fiterman: "It would have been better if Giscard had been reelected." The Soviet press did not print Mitterrand's comments, but *Le Monde,* now increasingly critical of the president, complimented him for having used the same language in Moscow, Paris, and Washington. The Soviets swallowed the provocation, but no very substantive results came from the visit.[24] Mitterrand did meet Politburo member Mikhail Gorbachev, seated next him at the banquet. He asked about the condition of Soviet agriculture. Gorbachev, secretariat member in charge of that area, replied that it was not going well. Mitterrand: "Since when?" Gorbachev shot back: "Since 1917!"[25]

In March 1985 Mitterrand would have the opportunity to meet this different kind of Soviet again, when he decided to attend Chernenko's funeral. From a forty-five-minute discussion with Gorbachev after the funeral Mitterrand drew a favorable impression, rather like Margaret Thatcher's "We can do business with him."

Mitterrand had been more reserved toward the Soviet Union than any of his predecessors in the Fifth Republic, but fundamentally, according to Hubert Védrine, "he was formed by a certain French Russophile tradition going back to the czars and the Third Republic, which maintains that at the two extremities of the European continent France and Russia do not threaten each other and can thus only be interested in agreeing, in the face of potential threats from Central Europe."[26] In late 1989, when the Berlin Wall fell and the world suddenly changed, at least the memory of this tradition flamed up in Mitterrand's mind—and died down again.

In 1986 Gorbachev visited Paris on his first official trip abroad, before meeting Ronald Reagan in Geneva three weeks later. Gorbachev's charm had not yet conquered the French—only 9 percent of respondents in a November 1985 poll had a "relatively good" opinion of the USSR. Having come late to anti-Sovietism, the French were unwilling to switch back—particularly since the warmth of the secretary-general's charm was directed primarily at the United States and at West Germany.

Gorbachev sought to drive a wedge between France and its allies on a subject on which Mitterrand had a decidedly different position from Washington—Ronald Reagan's plan for a strategic defense initiative (SDI). He failed: Mitterrand was far too clever to be caught in that trap and limited himself to expressing the anodyne hope that in Geneva Gorbachev and Reagan would arrive at a compromise.

Kohl in conversations with Mitterrand would talk frankly about his fear that the Germans would not be able to resist the temptation of neutralism, since he expected that sooner or later Gorbachev would make an offer involving neutralization. Only French-German agreement could ward that off. Kohl, Mitterrand, and the Quai d'Orsay braced themselves for such an offer. But one German desideratum was co-decision on nuclear questions, which Mitterrand was totally unwilling to accord.

In February 1987 Gorbachev had come out for the "zero option," abolition of all intermediate nuclear weapons in Europe. Mitterrand favored the idea—as long as it did not include the very small French and British forces. The French accepted the Intermediate-Range Nuclear Forces (INF) treaty initialed in December 1987 with some misgivings, fearing a further proposal that would get rid of all battlefield nuclear weapons and produce another proposal on nuclear-capable aircraft. Such agreements, it was argued, favored the concentration of Warsaw Pact conventional forces and would create a special denuclearized zone, essentially in Germany, thus shifting the risk of nuclear attack to France, the United Kingdom, and the United States. Some thought the INF treaty could also favor neutralism in a Germany no longer so threatened.

Another means of binding Germany to a West-oriented Europe was economic. Mitterrand looked with favor at measures that might give France more power in a European economy increasingly dominated by the D-mark. The paramount idea was an economic and monetary union (EMU), which seemed both to the French advantage and in itself a step forward in integration.

In June 1988 the Hanover European Council meeting commissioned a report to "study and propose concrete stages leading to European economic and monetary union," to be submitted in April 1989. Earlier in the year, as the economies of the EC countries improved and the malaise lifted, Delors and Kohl had discussed next steps on the way to closer European ties. They agreed that if there was to be monetary union, it was necessary to prepare it well in advance. German foreign minister Hans-Dietrich Genscher had circulated a memorandum in late February 1988 on a "European monetary space" and a European central bank. According to Genscher, Kohl was at first doubtful, but was convinced by Delors.[27] Since the scheme meant giving up the deutsche mark, symbol of stability in the Federal Republic from its beginnings, Kohl obviously had good reason to doubt the political feasibility of the idea.

Margaret Thatcher pronounced herself opposed to the idea in advance. Kohl outflanked her at the June 1988 EC summit by proposing an advisory commission to be presided over by Delors and including the presidents of the central banks and three experts. They met monthly in Basel, finally reporting in June 1989 at the Madrid conference.

Bank of France governor Jacques de Larosière and Economics Minister Pierre Bérégovoy favored a lesser solution: creating a European reserve fund, enabling the various central banks to coordinate their monetary policies. Only later would monetary union follow. Mitterrand overruled Bérégovoy and de Larosière in favor of Delors and monetary union.

The Madrid European Council meeting in late June 1989 agreed to start the first phase of integration on July 1, 1990. (Paris had first wanted to start on January 1, convoking an intergovernmental conference [IGC] for the same date, but agreed on the delay because Kohl faced a difficult election in late 1990 and did not want the IGC to meet too soon.) The plan called for an independent and autonomous European System of Central Banks (ESCB) committed to price stability, with a central supervising board and an ESCB Council as its supreme decision-making authority; the latter would be made up of board members and governors of the central banks.

There would be three stages. The first required no new legislation; governments were to commit themselves by July 1, 1990, to begin negotiations in an IGC on a new treaty to amend the Treaty of Rome. All EC currencies were supposed to be in the EMS by then; the powers of the governors of central banks were to be increased, on the German model, and convergence of the economies would have increased. In the second stage, a Central European Bank would be set up, and in the third, a common currency, the basis for economic and monetary union. No dates were set for the second and third stages. Kohl was still unhappy about the political problems inherent on renouncing the deutsche mark, but he agreed that the IGC—"preceded by complete and adequate preparation" would determine the dates of further progress. But Paris in early 1989 looked with concern at a Federal Republic whose extraordinarily strong economy had produced a DM 50 billion trade surplus in the past three years, while the French trade balance had been positive only once.

France was also unhappy as it looked at improving Soviet-German relations. Gorbachev's enormous popularity, evident when he visited West Germany in June 1989, revived old fears that the Federal Republic might settle its differences with the Soviets and turn to the East. Although the French believed in the assurances of European solidarity constantly expressed by the West Germans and understood West German interest in East Germany, they could not help being suspicious of every smile exchanged between Bonn and Moscow. The distinct possibility that an SPD tempted by neutralism might win the 1990 elections also disturbed the French. Alain Minc's much discussed and quoted *La Grande Illusion* still dramatized German drift, warning of "Gorbymania" in a country where even the ecological movement was a bad sign. "Love of nature leads to hatred of the nuclear, that to pacifism and thence to decoupling. And so a democratic civil society by its vitality becomes the best ally of the Soviet Union, the only country without civil society."[28]

France took the presidency of the European Council again in the second half of 1989. No one had yet guessed that the 200th anniversary of the French Revolution would bring its own revolution. But stirrings in Eastern Europe were already evident, and Mitterrand determined to begin a round of visits to that region, which the French had neglected in previous years. In December 1988 he was in Prague, where he invited eight dissidents, including the future president Vaclav Havel, to breakfast at the French embassy. He then visited Bulgaria, and in June 1989, Poland. Ceaucescu's Romania had been ruled out, and there remained one capital to visit. Mitterrand had been invited to visit East Berlin when Erich Honecker came to Paris in January 1988. The visit was to take place in rather different circumstances than originally planned.

The Great Turn

In June 1989 the Chinese government had ended a crisis with reform-bent students encamped in Tiananmen Square by opening fire on them. Statesmen everywhere feared a similar series of events in Eastern Europe, which would end the rapidly warming thaw for years to come. In April, the Polish government had legalized Solidarity, banned since 1981; in June, semi-free elections gave Solidarity 99 of the 100 Senate seats, and on August 19, Solidarity member Tadeusz Mazowiecki was named prime minister.

In mid-July, Mitterrand observed to George Bush, in Paris for the G-7 meeting: "The USSR is ready to accept many things in Poland, but there are limits; otherwise it will be like Budapest in 1956. For a certain length of time we ought not to give the impression that we want to go beyond this limit. There has to be an intermediate stage, because wanting immediately to succeed in Western objectives would lead to failure."[29]

In July 1989 no responsible French or other authority foresaw unification soon or imagined that the USSR might tolerate it. But as the tensions of the summer increased, political experts on both sides of the Atlantic understood that the issue of German unification was about to be posed again—and primarily saw the dangers in it. In the following four months, the U.S. position would increasingly downplay the dangers; the French would continue to emphasize them.[30]

Mitterrand's policy of cooperation with the Federal Republic rested on the conviction that France could not stand alone either economically or politically in a world where other nations were becoming more competitive. If the United States could not ultimately be trusted or expected to remain the guarantor of Europe's security—and in the strength of this suspicion there was no difference between Mitterrand and de Gaulle—then close military cooperation with West Germany and other European states was a necessity.

The corollary to this policy, however, was the conviction that France had a political edge on the Germans—a seat in the UN Security Council, an independent nuclear force, and coresponsibility for Berlin and for the ultimate settlement in Germany. France's political strength, to say nothing of its economic strength, was insufficient for sole hegemony in the European Community, but "shared hegemony" with a West Germany only somewhat larger than France had seemed to guarantee a proud future for France—one that Mitterrand had concluded in 1983 would be denied to an isolated, economically unstable Socialist France on indifferent terms with its neighbors. If Germany were united, however, it would in the future be far stronger than France, perhaps no longer disposed even to work closely with France in the EC. That was no happy thought.

Mitterrand's relations with Helmut Kohl were paramount; he could not equal Margaret Thatcher in overtly and strongly opposing unification. He was clearly unhappy with unification as a presumptive diminution of French power and apprehensive as well of its consequences for European stability. His initial attitude was that Gorbachev would not allow unification, then that it might come slowly, but once he began to suspect that Gorbachev would not or could not stop it, he modified his position—to Thatcher's disgust.

The constants in Mitterrand's approach were to secure Kohl's definitive agreement to a rapid opening of the IGC on monetary union and confirmation of the existing German-Polish border. On these two points, as he saw it, hung future German engagement in the making of Europe—and guarantees against any German revanchism that would set the Soviet Union against Germany, perhaps leading to the ouster of Mikhail Gorbachev by the Soviet military.

Events moved with incredible speed between the Hungarian decision on September 10 for a formal opening of the frontier with Austria, which increased the flow of East German refugees, Gorbachev's "Judas kiss" visit to the fortieth anniversary celebration of the DDR (East Germany), the night of October 9 when State Security troops in Leipzig did not fire on a crowd of 70,000 demonstrators, Honecker's resignation on October 18, and the opening of the Berlin Wall on the night of November 9.[31] Once the wall was down, the idea that unification was a realistic possibility gained strength rapidly among Germans East and West. Before the wall fell, East Germans had not shown that they wished unity—although the conditions for taking polls hardly existed. At the same time, the economic situation in East Germany was worsening, and a new government under the Socialist Unity Party (SED) moderate Hans Modrow soon would have to ask Bonn for help.

On November 17 Modrow called for "a contractual community" between East and West Germany—that did not yet mean a confederation, still less unification. On November 21 Kohl's close adviser Horst Teltschik conferred with Nikolai Portugalov, one of Gorbachev's experts on German affairs. He was amazed to hear the Soviet using new, if careful language: "He could imagine that in the medium term the Soviet Union could give the green light to some sort of German confederation."[32]

Teltschik rapidly agreed with the chancellor that this hint called for an initiative. Kohl had been hissed in Berlin the day after the wall opened, he was behind in the polls for the 1990 election, the word "confederation" was already in the air, and others were about to seize the lead, including the Free Democratic Party of his foreign minister Hans-Dietrich Genscher. In great secrecy, Kohl's staff prepared a ten-point program, which he announced to the Bundestag on November 28. He called for joint East-West German economic, environmental, and other commissions that could lead to "confederal structures." No one was advised in advance—not West Germany's allies or even Genscher. Mitterrand was irritated—he was already touchy because Kohl was stalling in setting a date for the IGC.

The most important item in the speech was point three, which read: Expand economic aid to the DDR on a large scale *if* "a fundamental change of the political and economic system is bindingly resolved and irreversibly started." In other words, East Germany might continue for a while as a separate state—but if it wanted to ask for help, it could not remain a socialist one. When Kohl gave the speech he imagined that unification was probably some five years distant. Politically, the speech served its purpose of putting Kohl in the lead. In a telephone conversation with President Bush on the following day, Kohl indicated his hope for free elections in East Germany in late 1990 or early 1991. After reassuring Bush that West Germany would remain in NATO, Kohl noted that "it is an iron law that there is no going it alone in German policy." He told Bush that he had decided to join Mitterrand in backing rapid progress toward a new treaty on EMU.[33] Mitterrand was still pressing him hard to fix a date at the December 8 Strasbourg meeting of the European Council. Three days before the Strasbourg meeting the Federal Chancellery informed the Elysée that it agreed that the IGC should begin in December 1990.[34]

Kohl made the promise formal in Strasbourg, but his staff made it clear that in return Kohl expected the Twelve formally to support eventual unification. The Eleven, with the partial exception of Spain, maintained their reservations on the question of frontiers. Mitterrand raised this again with Kohl the next day, but did not budge him. When Mitterrand brought up the point again in a television interview, Kohl's reaction was to suspect that Paris was using the topic to slow down progress.[35]

Mitterrand's Fears—and Blunders

Mitterrand was particularly concerned that there be no frontier changes in the East. Documents had been distributed at the Bremen CDU congress in September stating that the Oder-Neisse frontier, recognized at the 1975 Helsinki conference, was still subject to change. CSU leader Theo Waigel was already talking about frontier rectifications to the east. According to Mitterrand's adviser on European affairs Elisabeth Guigou, Mitterrand surprised his staff by all sorts of forebodings on what would happen if the idea of German revanchism were posed again and if frontier questions in general were reopened. "At first, some of us were almost intoxicated with joy at what was happening. Mitterrand, however, was more somber, saying that all sorts of ugly nationalism would now break out. His forebodings may have helped to create the idea that he was against all this."[36] Mitterrand expressed the same concerns to Roland Dumas on December 9, after the Strasbourg summit, worrying about "an explosion of territorial claims" in the Soviet bloc, which could lead to armed conflicts.[37]

Before the Strasbourg meeting, Mitterrand had flown to Kiev to meet Mikhail Gorbachev. He had organized this trip to hear from both participants at the Bush-Gorbachev summit in Malta a few days earlier; Bush had briefed his allies on the talks in Brussels on December 4. In Kiev Mitterrand met a Gorbachev who on the previous day in a meeting with West German Foreign Minister Genscher had attacked Kohl's ten-point plan as a "diktat" and emphasized that the DDR must remain an independent state and a member of the Warsaw pact. Gorbachev told Mitterrand how angry he had been with Genscher and repeated to the French president what he had said to him in a telephone conversation a few days earlier: "On the day Germany is unified, a Soviet marshal will be sitting in my chair." Mitterrand said that he did not fear a unified Germany, but the process of unification should be part of all-European politics, not its first priority. Mitterrand then asked whether Gorbachev would like to join him in his visit to East Berlin in late December. Gorbachev did not reply. At some point during the conversation, Mitterrand asked, "What should we do concretely?" He received no reply to that either.[38]

What Gorbachev did not say to Mitterrand when he spoke of reproving Genscher was the way he had ended their talk. When they had almost finished, and speaking in front of the interpreters alone, Gorbachev said, "When the European process has advanced and Soviet–West German ones have also, then we will be able to envisage the future of the German question." Genscher understood that to mean that Soviet opposition to unification was not absolute but dependent on a number of factors—

including German aid to the USSR.[39] Gorbachev was keeping his options open, as he thought, sending different signals to the Germans and the French.

Mitterrand was much criticized after the Kiev trip for apparently seeking a reverse alliance. The available documents do not confirm any démarche of this sort. He did give Gorbachev the opening to play on the French president's very evident desire not to create difficulties for him and consequent inclination to go slow—and the Soviet leader was trying to gain time in which the new DDR leadership could gain control and prolong the life of a separate German state.

The most doubtful gesture Mitterrand made in these weeks was the visit to East Germany—planned since 1988. On November 11 he confirmed to Kohl his plan to visit East Berlin before the year's end—Kohl was unsure whether he himself should go to meet East German head of state Egon Krenz. Ten days later the Elysée announced Mitterrand's visit in the DDR for December 20–22. This date had not been discussed with Bonn, as the Germans had expected; in the meantime Kohl had announced his intention to visit East Berlin after the SED Congress on December 9–10. Kohl had to rework his calendar in order to arrive in East Germany before Mitterrand and was not particularly pleased.[40]

The East German republic was dissolving with incredible speed, as its citizenry showed that they had lost all fear of their former masters. Elysée staffer Caroline de Margerie, sent to Berlin to prepare the visit, reported: "No one knows where the increasingly chaotic transition in the DDR is going, toward what regime, toward what sort of state." Mitterrand phoned her to ask if that meant she advised against his going, but when she said yes, he replied, "We'll see."[41] In his book on French-German relations, published posthumously, Mitterrand wrote merely that he was "curious to learn something of this country where a part of Europe's destiny was being played out"; he also left out the details of his conversations with the East German leaders.[42]

Mitterrand's two days in East Germany demonstrated his fundamental ambiguity regarding unification. As Kohl's aide Teltschik wrote in his diary immediately after Mitterrand's visit: "It's clear that two spirits are fighting in Mitterrand's breast. On the one hand he does not want to stand in the way of the process toward German unity. As he has said several times, he is not afraid of German unity. On the other hand, he is always talking about major hurdles that must be surmounted."[43]

Mitterrand may not have been afraid of unification, but he certainly did not welcome it. Yet his principal objective was to work with Helmut Kohl in building Europe, and if he departed too far from Kohl he could expect no cooperation from the Germans. Thus Mitterrand could tell students at Karl Marx University in Leipzig: "Only free, open, democratic elections will permit exact knowledge of what the Germans want, on both sides. For the moment, there are two states that have a sovereign existence." He added that if the German people opted for unity, "it is not France that will oppose it."[44] Mitterrand was, however, impressed by the intellectuals from the New Forum he met in Leipzig, all of whom were antiunification and for a third way—clearly a temptation for him.[45] Some of the New Forum interlocutors had earlier signed a declaration regretting what they called the premature opening of the Berlin Wall. By mid-December they were no longer representative of East German opinion.

Meeting with the East German leaders, Mitterrand continued to emphasize that the elections (then set for May 6; soon moved up to March 18) would decide, but told his hosts that

> too rapid a course of events carries with it the risk that the order existing in Europe for forty years will collapse and lead to an unstable situation. It is up to the DDR to prove that its forty years of existence as a state represent a durable political reality. He had been told that the majority of the people of the DDR wanted a democratic renewal, but within the present state order.[46]

From his own reception by enthusiastic crowds in Dresden on December 19, however, Kohl had drawn the opposite conclusion, that the East German regime was finished and unification would come.[47] In late December East German public opinion had not yet shifted decisively; the situation changed from week to week. To this extent, there might be some excuse for Mitterrand's ambiguous remarks, calculated to please everybody. But there can be no doubt that the trip was a mistake and Mitterrand did himself no good by making it.

The chancellor was no doubt annoyed with Mitterrand, but his visit in early January to Latché, the president's country house, went reasonably well, although Mitterrand continued to warn Kohl about going too fast and endangering Gorbachev. By mid-January he had changed his mind. The East German regime was weakening daily. On January 15 Mitterrand told a restricted group of ministers that unification was certain, and two days later, visiting Budapest, he said to Reformed Communist Rezsö Nyers, "The USSR no longer has the means to oppose unification." Thus when Margaret Thatcher came to Paris on January 20 to insist that France and Britain work together to slow down unification, he told her that it made no sense to raise objections that would have no effect.[48]

After a conference with Modrow on January 31, Gorbachev announced, "Among the Germans in East and West as well as the four power representatives, there is a certain agreement that German unification has never been doubted by anyone."[49] Ten days later when Kohl went to Moscow, he was able to announce that he and Gorbachev agreed that the German people alone should decide whether or not to form a single state.

Washington and Bonn were agreed that it made no sense to allow the East German situation to degenerate further, or to drag out negotiations with Moscow that might result in something like neutralization of Germany. Moscow had been pressing for Four Power discussions on Germany, to which Kohl expressed violent opposition: "I don't need four midwives!"

To avoid German resentment, James Baker's staff came up with the tactfully named Two Plus Four talks, to begin after the East German elections. Both German states would be participants in talks that would give them a mandate for unity. After considerable maneuvering, this formula was accepted all around.

Mitterrand was nearly indifferent to the maintenance of the unified German state in NATO, the major U.S. concern in these months. He did not see NATO as a continuing guarantee in a postunification world and thought military alliances were losing their raison d'être.[50] What Mitterrand apparently did not see was that even if NATO were rapidly to become irrelevant in the coming years, insistence on united Germany's presence in NATO was the best guarantee against neutralization; a neutralized Germany would have been a doubtful partner in the European Community.

However, Mitterrand continued to insist on a firm guarantee on Poland's western border. He was well aware that Kohl was reticent in giving a guarantee on the Oder-Neisse frontier for domestic political reasons, to keep the expellee constituency quiet and not encourage German right-wing movements. The Oder-Neisse question embittered his relations with Kohl for months; in March Mitterrand received Polish president Wojciech Jaruzelski and Prime Minister Mazowiecki, who had come to Paris to ask for his help with the Germans on the Oder-Neisse question, but who were also asking for a seat at the table in the Two Plus Four process that would resolve the German question. Mitterrand annoyed Kohl by continuing to raise the matter and asking for formal guarantees, even after Kohl had repeatedly assured him that he had no intention of putting the 1945 borders in doubt.

The East German election of March 18 gave the CDU-East a stronger vote than the East SPD and the other groups that were more doubtful on accelerated unification. The tone of the French press changed. The debacle of the PS congress in Rennes in the same week may have contributed to the new critical spirit: Mitterrand could do nothing right. Not only had he foolishly encouraged the doubters in Germany, he had been wrong where Kohl had been right, had been wrong to go to Kiev, had been wrong to go to East Berlin, had not perceived what was so clearly taking shape. Mitterrand had been reelected in 1988, not as the most illustrious of the French (as René Coty said of de Gaulle in 1958), but as the cleverest, the man who could always find a way out of difficulties and dilemmas. After 1990 the president was more and more often thought to be stumbling.

The conflicts in Mitterrand's soul and mind on German unification were very real. But the press was availing itself of its ancient privilege of 20/20 hindsight. In retrospect, the press wished that Mitterrand had, like Bush, been seen to have backed unification from the beginning. If he had done so, he would assuredly have been violently criticized from the beginning by the same press. For Hubert Védrine, Mitterrand's principal mistake was in not explaining his view of the situation to his compatriots. In retrospect, the president understood this clearly—and in managing public opinion far more carefully during the Gulf war, he said repeatedly to his staff, "Oh, if I had only spoken like this during German reunification." But he had seen the situation as too complicated, too hard to explain without creating further problems, and thus took refuge in his familiar pose of ambiguity.[51]

Mitterrand had not made Margaret Thatcher's mistake of noisy, last-ditch, and futile opposition to unification. He had certainly annoyed Kohl—but he had not really damaged their relationship, which continued to be close. But they were not yet agreed on the precise date for the IGC on economic and monetary union, which Kohl still wanted to delay until after the December 1990 Bundestag elections. Kohl was much more interested in giving new form to political Europe. Mitterrand was not—the word *federalism,* present in French dictionaries but not in the French Jacobin, centralist spirit—was suspect to him, and the idea behind it even more.

To Mitterrand's displeasure, Jacques Delors had called for a European federation and a parallel IGC on political Europe. He also asked the Irish presidency of the European Council to call a special summit on the EC and the forthcoming unification. Mitterrand now swung over to the Delors proposal—in form, at least, and together with Kohl on April 18, 1990, sent a letter to the Irish EC presidency proposing parallel IGCs, one on political as well as one on economic union, to launch "a European Union"—employing the name not used for the Single Act. The letter contained only vague language on political resolutions—but did include language on European defense that made Washington uneasy.[52]

At a meeting with George Bush on April 19 at Key Largo, Florida, Mitterrand attempted to assuage American worries. Bush once again tried to explain that if U.S. troops were not in Europe as NATO soldiers, there could in the eyes of the U.S. public and Congress be no political justification for their presence. Mitterrand understood that well enough, but continued to suspect American intent to play the dominant guardian of post–Cold War Europe.

Moscow was still blowing hot and cold on a unified Germany in NATO until July 15, when at a Kohl-Gorbachev meeting in the Caucasian spa of Zheleznovodsk the Soviet leader agreed that unified Germany could decide on its choice of alliances. On October 3, the two Germanys became one. French policy had not much affected this outcome, but neither had it hindered it. Paris's basic decision to approve unification had been taken by the end of January when it became clear that the DDR was no longer viable and that delay was more dangerous than precipitation.

Mitterrand was annoyed that he had mistaken Gorbachev's vehement opposition to German unification for firm determination. "Luckily, I didn't take him at his word and didn't take a position against Germany in NATO!"[53] Nevertheless, he continued to believe that the Soviet leader had to be supported and aided insofar as possible. In mid-April 1990 Mitterrand received Gorbachev's rival Boris Yeltsin, newly elected president of the Russian Supreme Soviet. Yeltsin was rudely treated at the European Parliament in Strasbourg by European Socialist faction president Jean-Pierre Cot and was annoyed by having been received in Paris in the Elysée secretary-general's office before being ushered in to see the president. Both Mitterrand and Bush (who had received Yeltsin the same way) were still intent on upholding Gorbachev.[54]

When the hard-liners of the Soviet Communist party mounted a putsch against Gorbachev on August 19, 1991, Mitterrand was skeptical that it could succeed, according to those who were with him at the Elysée that day. However, because he reproached himself for not having used television enough during the unification crisis, he thought he should address the nation, and he made the mistake of reading the letter he had just received from coup leader Gennadiy Yanayev. The effect was to suggest that he accepted the coup. When his German interpreter Brigitte Stoffaës asked him later why he had read the Yanayev letter on television, he replied, "I don't know; it was a mistake—a bit in scorn."[55]

Regardless of what Mitterrand had meant to convey, he was much criticized and mocked for this mistake. The French public and the world now had a picture of a Mitterrand who had lost his sure touch.

The Maastricht Treaty

As the returned Gorbachev lost control and the USSR began to dissolve in multiple secessions, Western Europe moved closer to the goal toward which Mitterrand had been advancing for several years: the treaty on European Union (EU) prepared throughout 1991 by the two IGCs, now more important than ever in Mitterrand's eyes as the best way to give France an almost equal role with a reunited Germany. Germany was now a nation of 80 million people instead of 63. But West Germany had already been more populous and richer than France. Despite evident German desire to continue working with a strong neighbor, a France that was more conventionally nationalist than post-Hitlerian Germany still found it hard to imagine that its neighbor's increased size and riches, present and potential, would not be an intoxicating potion.

The IGC on monetary union was preceded by a great deal of preparation. Political integration was the obvious counterpart of economic, but although there had been much general discussion of institutional reform of the European Parliament, common foreign and security policy, and other measures to provide coherence for EU administration, it was not until April 1990 that Kohl and Mitterrand actually called for a second IGC, on political union. Four objectives were stated: democratic legitimacy; institutional effectiveness; the unity and coherence of the community across economic, monetary, and political areas; and the definition and implementation of a common foreign and security policy. Other issues were then added, and in June it was decided that the second IGC would run concurrently with the first—both beginning in December 1990. The political IGC involved even more complicated issues than the economic one and had not been as carefully thought out.[56]

The Germans wanted a European Union treaty that would give more power to the European Parliament. These new clauses were to be a counterpart to the monetary measures desired by France to introduce a European currency and a European central bank to bridle the D-mark and the Bundesbank. France wanted to keep political matters in the hands of the European Council, where the representatives of national states would make decisions.

The Maastricht treaty was the product of disagreements half-patched over. It was drafted first by the Luxembourg presidency, then redrafted in the second half of

1991 by the Dutch presidency, whose text undid much of what the Luxembourgers had done and met so many objections that the final draft went back to the original texts. The overall result was a remarkably uninspiring text, an almost unreadable document. "The French wanted a strongly integrated and 'deepened' but confederal Community where France could compensate for its economic weakness by its political and administrative leadership (particularly through EMU). The Germans were firmly federalist, but hesitant—and divided—about EMU."[57]

The French won the argument on EMU, and the Germans had to accept a plan on which they were lukewarm, without any decisive attempt to create political legitimacy for the EU. EMU was scheduled for January 1997 at the best, or definitely January 1999. Economics and Finance Minister Bérégovoy was suspicious of the powers of the future European Central Bank that the Germans demanded and proposed to counterbalance it by giving more power to the council of EU finance ministers—a so-called economic government. The Germans refused, and in a compromise meant to reassure the Germans on the solidity of future economic arrangements, France and Germany agreed to propose "convergence criteria" for the several national economies based on their strength. Overconfident in early 1991 on the strength of the French economy, Bérégovoy agreed, and he himself suggested the most stringent criterion, that public deficits should not exceed 3 percent of GDP (with some wiggle room).[58] (At the time, the French deficit was 1.6 percent of GDP.) Other convergence criteria were as follows: The public debt was not to exceed 60 percent of GDP; inflation rates should not exceed the average rates of the three EU countries with lowest rates by more than 1.5 percent; long-term interest rates should not exceed the average rates of the countries with the lowest inflation by more than 2 percent; exchange rates should have been maintained within the EMS limits for at least two years without devaluation. The convergence criteria were to prove an uncommonly tight corset.

Delors could comfort himself with the thought that a treaty that fell short of his hopes was at least a blueprint for the post–Cold War future; that without one, Europe (and France) would have been much worse off. Mitterrand had consistently opposed Delors on federalist initiatives and had less reason to be discontented. His chief worry was the prospective advent of the Central and East European countries into the EU; he did not want the evolving European Union burdened with the problems of new entrants before its powers and rules had been firmly established in principle and practice.

Here was the dilemma of "widening or deepening," which confronted the EU from the beginning. Mitterrand's solution was a European confederation open to all countries of West and East Europe, which would give some reassuring status to these revived societies, democratic or striving for democracy, along with the older democracies of Western Europe. He first launched this idea in his New Year's address on December 31, 1989. Poorly prepared and unexplained, the idea met little or no enthusiasm. Eighteen months later Mitterrand tried again at a conference of intellectuals and public figures in Prague that he had called for, pretentiously entitled the Assises of Confederation.

Mitterrand's concept was a body that would have some responsibilities for environment, economic cooperation, immigration, culture, and so on. For him they were European questions, which did not concern the United States. Security questions were ruled out.

However, given the insecurities of the Central and East European countries, any body that included Russia but excluded the United States was unacceptable. The Czechs and other Central and Eastern European states saw the idea of confederation as a dead end, an empty contrivance designed to substitute for EU entry; they wanted to get into the EU and also NATO as fast as possible. French efforts to calm their fears were in vain.

Mitterrand compounded the initial mistake of calling the meeting with a speech in which he said that the confederation was necessary because it would take "decades and decades" until those countries could join the EU. Despite much advance warning that his initiative would be poorly received, Mitterrand persisted anyway, commenting afterward that the initiative had perhaps been "premature."[59]

The Maastricht treaty was initialed in December 1991, signed in February 1992, and then had to be ratified by the member states. It hit its first reef on June 2, 1992, when a Danish referendum turned down the treaty by 46,000 votes. Before that, Mitterrand had been playing with the idea of a referendum on the treaty. Polls suggested that passage would be easy. Elisabeth Guigou, now minister for European affairs, argued that after years of "stealth tactics" in building Europe, it was necessary to give the treaty popular legitimacy. Mitterrand agreed. Furthermore, the conservative opposition was divided. The UDF was pro-Europe, much of the RPR against it. If, as already seemed probable, the Right won the next elections, Mitterrand thought it necessary to anchor the Maastricht treaty in a ratification by popular vote. He also had more down-to-earth political reasons: If the Right should split on this question, then the Socialists could only benefit.[60]

Mitterrand set the referendum for September 16, soon after the country returned en masse from summer vacations. Overconfidence prevailed over the summer; only Elisabeth Guigou sounded the alarm. Finally, at the beginning of August, Mitterrand entrusted the campaign both to Guigou and to Jack Lang. In mid-August, polls showed that the noes might have it. The government belatedly went into high gear. The results were very close: 51.05 percent of voters said yes, but they represented the better-educated, more comfortable part of the French electorate. A significant part of the Socialist electorate voted no.[61] The referendum had passed, but Mitterrand had not won a victory.

Yugoslavia

Throughout 1991 the impending collapse of the federated republic of Yugoslavia had thrown its shadow over the IGC discussions on common foreign and security policy. The Europeans were acutely conscious that the first test of the European

Union was to solve this crisis in the Balkans. But it rapidly became apparent that France and Germany had variant views of the situation.

The crisis had been lowering since the Croatian election in April 1990, when the nationalist Franjo Tudjman was elected president of the (still federated) republic. Tudjman's government adopted some of the symbolism of the wartime fascist Ustasha regime (flag, uniforms) and refused minority rights to the 600,000 Serbs of Krajna, a population that had lived in Croatia since the late seventeenth century. In early 1991, the Slovenian parliament invalidated federal laws in that republic, and both Slovenia and Croatia declared their independence on June 25, 1991. When the Yugoslav army under the control of the Serbian nationalist president Slobodan Milosevic attempted to prevent these secessions, fighting broke out.

The initial reaction of the EC Twelve was to use the European Political Cooperation (EPC) consultative mechanism, which they were trying to elevate into a common foreign and security policy, to achieve an early success in preventing what they saw as a civil war. That was the German as well as the French view, shared by the other European nations. Mitterrand and new British prime minister John Major argued that "the territorial integrity of Yugoslavia must take precedence . . . over the aims of Croatian and Slovenian nationalists," whereas Kohl said the EC should continue negotiating with the Yugoslav government and give financial aid—as long as Belgrade did not use force to keep the country together.[62]

Very rapidly after hostilities broke out, the German political parties began to call for recognition of the two new states. The nationally circulated and influential *Frankfurter Allgemeine Zeitung* began a series of editorials and articles arguing that Croatia was democratic, Serbia "hardly European at all," and emphasizing the fact that the peoples of Croatia and Slovenia had voted democratically to secede, whereas the Communist Serbian government had reacted with violence. The fact that both Tudjman and Milosevic were ex-Communists-turned-nationalists was not emphasized, nor was the question of Serbian minority rights in an area where the fascist Ustasha had carried out genocide against Serbs during World War II. Instead, Germans who had benefited from self-determination just the year before were asked whether they could support Communist regimes.

Reactions in France were very different from those in Germany. Faced with the probability that the federation would split, with consequent civil war, Mitterrand thought the Europeans could not do very much. He continued to hope that a unified Yugoslavia could somehow be reconciled to itself—anything was preferable to a split followed by war. In early 1991 Mitterrand began to worry about the German attitude, a view shared by U.S. policymakers. Secretary of State Baker declared in Belgrade on June 22 that "the United States will not recognize the republics that might secede."[63] The most centralized country in Europe and the country that had itself once fought a bloody war against secession thus reacted similarly.

On June 23, 1991, Genscher was the only foreign minister of the Twelve who argued that the imminent demand for recognition of Croatia and Slovenia should be met. When hostilities began, the European Council decided to embargo all military supplies to all territories of Yugoslavia, freeze financial aid, and attempt mediation. Mitterrand was worried not only by the South Slav secessions but also by the reaction of the USSR to a looming Ukrainian secession. He had counted as many as seventeen possible wars that might break out as a result of secessions and disputed frontiers. This fixation on the instability of the new world "order" had grown on Mitterrand since autumn 1989. His minister for European affairs, Elisabeth Guigou, remembered: "He was talking about the Chechens, Inguish, Moldavians, whom most of us had never heard of, and our first reaction was, well, he's an old man, and he's thinking in past categories. But of course he was right."[64]

During the summer of 1991 the EC Twelve attempted several times with short-lived truces to end hostilities in Croatia; the fighting in Slovenia had rapidly ended. In early August France called for the UN Security Council to intervene, but the United States was unwilling to join in. A subsequent French call for the Western European Union (see section "Defense and Security," this chapter) to study sending an intervention force met British opposition. The French would have liked to create a precedent for European action, but without Britain, and since there was no question of German troops, it was an empty gesture.

By the end of the year television coverage of destroyed towns in Croatia seized by the Serbs had created an increasingly powerful public image. What had first been perceived as a civil war was now generally viewed as a war of aggression, with historical references running from Hitler to Saddam. Mitterrand studiedly refused to take sides, saying to his advisers that it was useless to expect the Serb populations of Krajna, where most of the fighting was taking place, to accept Croat domination. He was therefore rapidly described in the press and by political opponents as pro-Serb.

In fact, what Mitterrand cared most about was preserving European cohesion. With the conclusion of the EU treaty in Maastricht rapidly approaching, Europe was showing itself unable to stop a civil war in the Balkans, and the two key European powers, France and Germany, were increasingly at odds on how to handle the crisis.

Kohl and Genscher were under great domestic pressure to recognize the new South Slav states. Equally important, perhaps, was the fact that Genscher had persuaded himself (and perhaps Kohl) that recognition was necessary if there were to be peacekeeping efforts, and indeed that recognition, establishing an international border, would stop the fighting.[65] At the Franco-German summit in Bonn in mid-November, Mitterrand appealed to Kohl to attempt to obtain guarantees for minority rights before any recognition, saying that what was at issue was the cohesion of the Twelve and peace in Europe. Kohl replied, "I know all that, but I am going to be obliged to recognize Croatia all the same." Mitterrand: "Don't do that, it would be a mistake!" Kohl: "No doubt, but the pressure on me is very strong. I can't hold up. My party, my liberal allies, the Church, the press, not to mention 500,000 Croats living in Germany, everybody is pushing."[66]

On December 16, 1991, immediately after the Maastricht treaty meeting, Germany declared that it would move to recognize Croatia and Slovenia on

December 23, unilaterally if necessary. Genscher was apparently angry at France and Britain for seeking a Security Council resolution against Germany; UN secretary-general Javier Perez de Cuellar had regretted that recognition seemed to be coming "too soon, selectively, uncoordinated." Genscher also did not want to accept the conditions levied on Croatia, since they were unlikely to be met. So Germany moved ahead alone.[67]

Mitterrand resigned himself to recognizing the two South Slav states because, as Dumas said in the Council of Ministers, "We can't call the long term future of Europe—Maastricht—into question because of a serious disagreement on a grievous conflict, which will, however, end some day or other."[68] On January 18 the EU recognized the two states.

Mitterrand remained bitter. He had told his Council of Ministers: "The dismantling of empires profits only the United States and Germany, but not Europe," and dining with Kohl in February 1992, he said, "You aren't hegemonic, certainly, but you have a special favoritism for Croatia." Kohl replied merely that the South Slav question must not divide France and Germany too much.[69]

Recognition did not, of course, achieve what the Germans hoped. It deprived the EU of diplomatic flexibility—and set an example for the recognition of Bosnia, which would prove an even more serious problem. German action also set off an international polemic, as foreign press and nations spoke of new "German assertiveness." Surprised by the strength of the reaction, the Germans pulled in their horns, especially as it became evident that their actions had no restraining effect on hostilities. France, by the same token, had increasingly to recognize that Serbian aggression was a real problem—especially when the war spread to Bosnia.

France went on to play the largest role among "peacekeeping" forces in ex-Yugoslavia, from 1992 on, along with Britain and other countries. Since the United States refused to use ground forces in the conflict and in 1993 called for the arms embargo to be lifted and for NATO air strikes to stop Serbian ethnic cleansing, the frustrated Europeans were led to oppose what they saw as an unhelpful and mistaken approach that would put their troops on the ground at risk. Not until 1994—with a French initiative and finally with American cooperation—did it become possible to move toward what became the Dayton accords of 1995.

The South Slav tragedy had shown that the European Union was not sufficiently united to take action against a war in a part of the European continent. One reason was the complexity of the issues; another was the difficulties inherent in military engagement on the ground. Ultimately no outside state considered that it was in its national interest to lose soldiers by engaging them in a serious military action. George Bush's, then Bill Clinton's America refused to send any troops; Germany could not—or thought it could not. France and Britain could send only a few thousand for "peacekeeping."

When Alain Juppé succeeded in January 1994 in getting more U.S. involvement to use air power and diplomatic pressure to lift the siege of Sarajevo, the stage was set for the Dayton accords of 1995 (after Mitterrand had left office). Now acting more or less in unison, the western powers also were able to separate Milosevic from the Bosnian Serbs, and finally to bring all Bosnian parties to the table in Dayton, Ohio, to agree to a still very delicately balanced peace.

Whereas Germans in 1991 had championed the Croats, France in 1992–1994 saw a vociferous public movement favoring the Bosnian Muslims, victims of many Serb atrocities (and no doubt perpetrators of some themselves). Mitterrand resisted this wave of public opinion throughout, since France had no intention of engaging in conflict in the Balkans and would in any case have done so without British, U.S., or any other help. Here as elsewhere Mitterrand was an advocate of realpolitik in a media age in which realpolitik has a very bad press. Was he pro-Serb? It seems rather that he had accepted the existing Yugoslav state and, skeptical as always of new states, saw the flaws in Tudjman's Croatia. More important, perhaps, was his questioning of the viability of any Bosnian state; that emerges clearly from Hubert Védrine's detailed account of his chief's dealings from 1992 to 1994. There was much chatter in Paris in those years about the danger of an Islamic state in Europe, but Mitterrand does not seem to have been much affected by any such fear. Rather, he doubted that a Bosnian state made up of three very different communities could survive politically or economically.

Frictions with the United States

Ronald Reagan had sent Mitterrand an unexpectedly warm letter of congratulation on his election, and the French president replied in the same tone. The relationship was solidified by a visit soon after the election from Reagan's friend Senator Paul Laxalt; Mitterrand invited him to his country home at Latché. Laxalt's impression was favorable. Passing through Paris on his way home he told American Embassy chargé d'affaires Christian Chapman that he would advise Reagan that despite divergent political ideas, he and Mitterrand had in common a sure sense of their identities and of the meaning of their roots, that he was a man one might work with.[70]

In June, Vice President Bush came to Paris. The French government had informed the State Department on the previous day that Communist ministers would be entering the Mauroy government, and Bush wanted to know the reasons for the move. (The visit was not for this purpose, having been scheduled much earlier.) Mitterrand explained that inside the government the Communists would be contained—and would in any case have no influence on foreign policy. Bush was reassured and impressed (though he still thought Mitterrand's tactic "crazy").[71]

The echo of Bush's cordial talks with Mitterrand was disturbed by the almost simultaneous release of a State Department statement announcing the distress of the U.S. government at the entry of four Communist ministers into the government of an allied power. Mitterrand had already been briefed by U.S. Ambassador Arthur Hartmann on the closely held details of U.S.-French military arrangements and confirmed both to Hartmann and Bush his intention to maintain harmonious relations furthering the common goal of European defense. He told Bush that French relations with the Soviet Union would be cooler than under his predecessors—not only because the objective situation called for it, but also because a Left government with Communist participation had a point to prove to its domestic opposition and its allies.[72]

Mitterrand's first contact with George Bush laid the basis for a continuing good relationship. Washington's doubts about a government that included Communist ministers had been allayed, and Mitterrand was able to establish reasonably good relations with Ronald Reagan at the Ottawa G-7 conference in July 1981. At Ottawa, Mitterrand took pains to emphasize his government's anti-Communist credentials by sharing information with the Americans from a high-level Soviet intelligence officer who was collaborating with French intelligence. This agent had intimate knowledge of Soviet scientific and technical espionage in both France and the United States, and his information was much appreciated by U.S. intelligence.

At Ottawa, Reagan invited Mitterrand to the celebration of the 200th anniversary of the British surrender at Yorktown to combined French and American forces. The pleasant symbolism of this event in no way precluded a conflict-ridden future. The fundamental problem in French-American relations was the American attempt to assert leadership with little or no real consultation, first on the question of trade with the Soviet Union, then other questions.

In late 1981, the United States began a series of moves to block the sale of Soviet natural gas to Western Europe. A 3,700-mile pipeline was to begin operation in 1984, using a variety of U.S.-licensed and European-produced machinery and technology. The Reagan administration wished to punish the Soviets for repression in Poland and to deny the Soviets hard currency from gas exports, thus putting pressure on the Soviet economy and forcing it to devote scarce internal resources to its military expenses. Washington argued as well that if the Europeans bought gas from the USSR, they would be vulnerable to blackmail by cutoff of essential fuel supplies if the Soviets so decided.

After beginning by preventing General Electric (GE) from exporting turbine rotors to the Soviet Union, in June 1982 the U.S. government extended the restriction to foreign companies with licenses from GE, including the major French firm Alsthom-Atlantique. The decision was taken against Secretary of State Alexander Haig's advice and behind his back, and according to his successor George Shultz, Reagan was advised in this by Secretary of Defense Caspar Weinberger, CIA director William Casey, and new national security adviser William Clark—the least informed and competent of Reagan's numerous National Security Council (NSC) advisers.[73] Shultz found Clark mendacious and thoroughly out of his depth—his reaction to problems, according to Shultz, was always to choose the hard line.

The British, Germans, Italians, and French all reacted sharply against this unilateral American decision. No formal discussion on it had taken place at the June Versailles G-7 summit or the NATO meeting that followed. The European governments ordered their firms to proceed with the contracts, rejecting U.S. restrictions as a totally unacceptable invasion of their sovereign rights. Secretary of State George

Shultz, who had replaced Haig in June 1982, tried to exert pressure on the hard-liners in the National Security Council and Pentagon. Having ignorantly maneuvered itself into an impossible situation, with even its best European friend Margaret Thatcher strongly backing the other Europeans, the Reagan administration announced the lifting of sanctions in November, "based on substantial agreement with the allies" on East-West trade. That was an imaginary fig leaf, and the Elysée issued a communiqué declaring that although France took note of President Reagan's decision, there had been no consultation. The British foreign minister chimed in, terming the U.S. declaration "a unilateral decision."[74]

At the end of 1982, Mitterrand wrote Ronald Reagan a long letter evoking Franco-American agreement on many subjects, but firmly reminding him that "each of us . . . is thoroughly conscious of the prudence required to conduct relations with the Eastern countries. Each of us is thoroughly conscious of his national interests in this regard, of which he is the best judge and the first guarantor, in respect for the existing procedures for agreements." Reagan returned a conciliatory answer.[75]

Despite this reply, Mitterrand began 1983 very much disabused on the possibility of finding a common position with the Reagan administration on the extent and limitations of alliance policy. Mitterrand saw a United States that considered the Soviet threat to be global and that was attempting to extend the area of responsibility of the Atlantic alliance to the whole world. Preparations for the Williamsburg G-7 summit revealed that the United States wanted to insert into summit declarations language on "global security" that French policy regarded with deep suspicion—opening the door for enlarged American assertions of influence over the other allies. Mitterrand was also wary of language that could validate the Soviet demand to count the French and British nuclear forces in any arrangement on the number of missiles to be maintained in Europe—if and when a settlement was reached on the SS-20 question.[76]

In lengthy and difficult discussions at Williamsburg Mitterrand refused to associate France with the U.S. proposals. A final compromise watered down the U.S. language somewhat and explicitly stated that British and French nuclear forces would not be included in any negotiations. The French attitude was not too different from the views of American academic critics of Reagan foreign policy:

> A globalist "two-camp" view greatly simplified the perception of world affairs, especially in the Third World. . . . Such an attitude reflected a unilateralist American approach, rather than a commitment to a "multilateralist" alliance system and shared values. Perceiving alliances as constraints rather than assets, it mirrored skepticism about the steadfastness and commitment of friends and allies, and it often reflected a sense of moral righteousness.[77]

By November 1983, after the Soviets had refused the compromises the Europeans and Americans demanded, NATO began to deploy Pershing II and cruise missiles in Western Europe. Improved French-American relations permitted a constructive Mitterrand visit to the United States in March 1984. (French fears of U.S. policy may have been exaggerated extrapolations from the remarkably unsubtle tactics of the early Reagan administration—which now trimmed its sails slightly.) The trip was a success in that Mitterrand and Reagan could discuss their common view that the Soviets did not want war—and what that might mean—at a time when Mitterrand was preparing to visit Moscow in June. Mitterrand made a number of U.S. stops, including one to Silicon Valley, which impressed him deeply and triggered more thinking on the need for Europeans to work together on technology.

New tensions arose with Reagan's plan for a Strategic Defense Initiative (SDI)—a space-based missile defense against enemy missiles, conceived in 1983, but not presented to U.S. allies until 1985. Mitterrand's advisers differed in their appreciation of the feasibility of SDI—Jacques Attali thought it a real possibility, while Védrine, charged by his president in 1983 with an examination of its feasibility, concluded that nuclear deterrence had a long future before it. Mitterrand listened to them both. For France, the main point was that *if* SDI were feasible, development by one (and, France hypothesized, inevitably the other) superpower of space-based defense would make French nuclear forces obsolete and demote France into the ranks of ordinary conventional powers.

SDI also dismayed the French because Reagan had begun denouncing the concept of mutual assured destruction (MAD). The French nuclear doctrine on the deterrent force exercised by a weaker nuclear power over a stronger one *(réplique du faible au fort)* enjoyed general domestic support—even among French bishops; denunciation of MAD as immoral undermined that consensus. France did not intend to let French firms accept research contracts on aspects of SDI, as the U.S. administration suggested they might. The Germans, in contrast, were both tempted by the research possibilities and uncertain whether to be firm with the United States; here was a situation that gave rise to considerable tension with the French.

Another problem arose after the 1986 election, when Jacques Chirac became prime minister. French participation in SDI research figured among his electoral promises, and he demanded that Mitterrand agree to them. The president refused, threatening a referendum on the question, which he expected he would win. The subject was dropped.[78]

One result of French opposition to SDI was the counterprogram to SDI—a technological research program proposed by Paris, dubbed EUREKA. It did not succeed in its objective of deterring the Germans from approving German contributions to SDI research and faced initial reticence by European Community officials, who feared EUREKA would conflict with similar EC projects like ESPRIT and RACE (on information and communications technologies). EUREKA did not become a formal EC agency, as originally envisioned, but it was adopted as a structure to coordinate European research in high technology. In EUREKA, as in bilateral Franco-German defense programs, French policy reflected the belief that in high technology and defense France's future could only be assured by European cooperation. EUREKA by 1995 had evolved into a complementary program for the research efforts of nineteen countries. Its principal research fields for the 332 projects it completed since its inception in 1986 have been robotics, lasers, biotechnology, and energy.

Tiers Mondisme: Frustrations in Central America

The general rapprochement of Mitterrand's France with the United States saw one important exception—French Socialist policy on Central America. Socialist *tiers mondisme*—the theory that former European imperialism must be redeemed by special treatment of Third World governments, preferably leftist ones—combined with Gaullist momentum to encourage interest in a French role in the affairs of this region. In August 1981 France issued a joint declaration with Mexico on El Salvador, proclaiming "a state of belligerency" in the area and recognizing the Revolutionary Democratic Front/Farabundo Marti National Liberation Front (FDR/FMLN) insurgents as a "representative political force" ready to assume power. Instantly, the foreign ministers of eleven Latin-American countries protested the Franco-Mexican declaration as "interference in Salvadorian internal affairs."[79]

A more serious problem arose over Nicaragua, where French policy saw in the Reagan administration's ardor against the Sandinistas "the intolerable domination of a superpower over a small country, but also a policy likely to make a bad situation worse and cause upheaval in the entire region."[80] In December 1981 France contracted to supply Nicaragua with U.S.$16 million worth of arms useful for counterinsurgency, notably two used Alouette III helicopters and several thousand air-to-ground rockets. Mitterrand had considerable sympathy for *tiers mondisme*, and his wife, Danielle, still more, but the main advocates of this policy were Foreign Minister Claude Cheysson and Mitterrand adviser Régis Debray.[81] The presence in the Elysée of this former comrade in arms of Che Guevara awoke great suspicion in the White House. The Reagan administration leaked news of the arms sale to the *Washington Post* in January 1982 and then reacted indignantly, dispatching presidential aide Michael Deaver to Paris to protest. Mitterrand found it useful in March 1982 to fly to Washington to smooth relations. He had allowed Cheysson to proceed but was unwilling to stake his relations with Reagan on what he saw as a matter of secondary importance. He agreed not to go beyond the existing contract, and in July the French government announced that no new arms sales were contemplated.[82]

Growing recognition that France could not afford either economically or diplomatically to involve herself deeply in Central America blunted the force of French *tiers mondisme*. U.S. displeasure at arms sales to the Sandinista government—and the Socialists' increasingly disabused views on Sandinista democracy—brought an end to remaining arms deliveries to Nicaragua by midsummer 1983, although some economic aid continued. By September 1984 Foreign Minister Cheysson was telling the San Jose conference of European Community, Central American, and Contadora states that if any French action were requested by the Central Americans, "we will examine it to see if it is possible, but would only act alongside the countries in the region and ordinarily in an international framework."[83]

Tiers mondisme met another test in 1982, when Argentine forces took over the Falkland Islands and a British government preparing to retake them looked for support. Mitterrand immediately telephoned Margaret Thatcher to assure her of French diplomatic support—though he would not break relations with Argentina. Claude Cheysson argued for support for Argentina, saying, according to Jacques Attali, "We've nothing to gain from the English; the whole Third World will be backing the Argentines." Mitterrand replied: "We are the allies of the British, not the Argentines. European solidarity comes ahead of everything." The French government took care to stop delivery of Exocet missiles already sold to Peru, believing that they would go to the Argentines. It also furnished military specifications to the British on the performance of French Mirage and Super-Etandard airplanes that the Argentines possessed.[84] The British victory justified Mitterrand's position by bringing about the collapse of military dictatorship in Argentina. Mrs. Thatcher declared her eternal gratitude for French aid, but the French did not find British memory particularly good.

The GATT Question

Amid the other tensions in French-American relations figured a commercial-cultural problem—the final negotiation of the General Agreement on Tariffs and Trade (GATT) Uruguay Round. The negotiations had begun during cohabitation in 1986, were interminably drawn out through the rest of the 1980s, and did not end until 1994, by which time the Right was again in power. Two issues caused particular difficulty: agriculture and cultural policy.

French agriculture had benefited enormously from the Common Agricultural Policy, which, however, was so expensive for the EC that in 1992 it was reformed, to the distress of French farmers. In November 1992 the Bérégovoy government gave tentative agreement to a compromise on GATT policy called the Blair House accord—which, however, did not meet all French objectives and was severely criticized by the Right. The French farm lobby, especially its most powerful organization, FNSEA, has always been close to the Right and expected to be backed up. The PS has always done poorly among farmers but felt itself obliged nevertheless to defend their interests, especially since the heated discussion on GATT proposals, and particularly the idea of paying to keep land fallow instead of for production, kicked up a noisy debate on basic values, evoking the survival of the ancient civilization based on peasant agriculture that had formed the French nation.

In fact, French agriculture has been transformed in the past thirty-five years. Whereas in 1989 there were 982,000 farms *(exploitations)*, down from 5 million at the beginning of the century, 450,000 of them produced 80 percent of agricultural deliveries, and the 100,000 largest produced more than 40 percent. Cereals and rape seed are planted on very large acreages and are the most profitable part of French agriculture, whereas the still numerous small farms are increasingly in difficulty. In 1988, 560,000 farmers were over fifty, and three-quarters of them had no successor or didn't know who he/she might be; 70 percent of farmers' sons turn away from the profession. At the same time, an [average] French farmer nourished thirty people in 1983; in 1960 only seven.[85]

The success of the farm lobby in appealing to the politicians of the Right and turning the GATT discussion into a cultural question masked the fact that French industry stood to benefit from a successful Uruguay Round. Gérard Longuet, trade minister in the Balladur government and a leading UDF figure, pointed out that France was the world's fourth largest exporter, and needed to conclude the Uruguay Round. Before the 1993 elections the RPR had taken a hard line, but RPR general secretary Alain Juppé changed his tone after he became foreign minister.

The second major issue for France on GATT was cultural. France subsidizes its film and television production with a tax levied on tickets, and there has been general agreement that despite laws that 50 percent of what is shown must be French, the film theaters and television screens are flooded with U.S. products. (No one ever seems to point out that with three commercial and two government channels cumulatively broadcasting well over 100 hours a week, the vast majority of what is shown is necessarily trash, regardless of its origin. The other problem is that American movies—bad, indifferent, or good—seem to appeal to French audiences.)

The GATT negotiations became particularly hectic in the concluding year, 1993—the deadline was December 15. The Balladur government, bargaining hard and threatening to block the whole procedure, got some small concessions from the United States on agriculture. Cultural products remained the sticking point, as the United States refused to compromise. The solution was to exclude audiovisual products from the agreement—to American displeasure. The agreement was finally signed and ratified in mid-December, with agreement on a new World Trade Organization (WTO) replacing GATT.[86]

More of the Same in Africa

Tiers mondisme was a relatively minor problem in French relations with the United States. Africa, however, bulked very large in French concerns. In the Mauroy government the minister-delegate for external relations in charge of cooperation and development (the title for the ministry concerned in the first instance with Africa) was Jean-Pierre Cot. This son of a Popular Front minister was a Rocardian but was well regarded by Mitterrand. Like his chief, Claude Cheysson, he was a believer in a more vigorous French policy toward the Third World and particularly on human rights in Africa. Cot proclaimed that he wanted to "decolonize" and "de-Africanize" his ministry, ideas unwelcome to the Francophone African chiefs of state, France's traditional friends and clients. French foreign aid had largely been directed in the past to their countries in sub-Saharan Africa. Now it was supposed to be enlarged and in part redirected.

Cot's propensity to lecture on human rights proved a handicap with the African presidents, most of whom were running repressive one-party states. Simultaneously with the nomination of Cot, Mitterrand had decided that he would also continue the practice begun by de Gaulle of maintaining an "African cell" directly attached to the Elysée. (Cot had originally hoped the Elysée cell would be abandoned.) Mitterrand selected an old friend, Socialist militant Guy Penne, dean of the Paris dentistry faculty. Penne knew nothing of Africa; his attractiveness to the African presidents who were the real clients of the Elysée African cell was precisely that he had Mitterrand's ear. When Mitterrand added his son Jean-Christophe as Penne's assistant, he gave the African presidents an even stronger signal. After a few months they realized that the Elysée cell was happy to keep up the old personal relations— thereby downgrading the authority of the cooperation ministry.[87] Policy disagreements between Mitterrand and Cot were not great, but since Mitterrand was not ready to change the nature of France's relation with the African leaders, a personalized small staff, ready to drop everything and fly to a meeting in Africa, would always have the advantage over a ministry.

Mitterrand was also realistic, not to say cynical, about France's relations with Africa. His rhetoric was high-minded and idealistic, but the clientilist nature of that relation, established in the de Gaulle years by Jacques Foccart and continuing under Pompidou and Giscard, was a pattern that would have been hard to break. Mitterrand did not try to break it. In any case, there was little room for maneuver, given the dilemma of dealing with authoritarian regimes where stability often took higher priority than human rights. In Africa, foreign aid was entangled in a network of trade, financial, and cultural relations that linked business interests, personal friendships, and the intrigues of French intelligence. All these factors hindered the application of any grand design.

Mitterrand doubted that there were alternative French policies for Africa. According to his aide Hubert Védrine, he believed that if France dumped the reigning dictators, the opposition forces would behave the same way once in power. Before 1989 he also worried that the dictators, if pressured too much, would move closer to the Soviet Union—as some threatened to do. More important still, in Mitterrand's eyes, was the danger that once those regimes were destabilized, ethnic antagonisms more or less well contained by the frontiers dating from colonial times would reemerge.[88]

Mitterrand eventually offered Cot another post; he chose instead to resign in December 1982. He was replaced by Penne's friend Christian Nucci, who got on better than Cot with the African leaders—but was to get into trouble over an affair of corruption and misappropriation of special funds.

Throughout Mitterrand's two terms France continued a policy of military interventions in Africa.[89] Védrine gave a list: in Chad, Operations Manta in 1983 and Epervier in 1986 (about 3,000 troops in all); dispatch of 150 paratroopers to Togo in 1986 after the attempted coup d'état against President Gnassingbé Eyadema, reinforced after disorders in 1990; dispatch of 200 troops in 1990 to the Comoro Republic after the 1989 assassination of President Ahmed Abdallah; 300 troops to Rwanda in 1990–1993; aid in evacuating French citizens from Zaire in 1991 (450 troops); in the same year a deployment to the north of Djibouti after the Afar rebellion and 2,500 men to Somalia as part of Operation Restore Hope; in 1994, evacuation of 1,000 French and other foreigners from Rwanda in April, then 2,500 troops sent to Rwanda in Operation Turquoise from June to August.

Of these, the longest engagement took place in Chad, where French interest was almost entirely strategic: If Libyan intervention succeeded in dominating Chad, the sub-Saharan states would stand open to Colonel Muammar Qadhafi's persuasion and subversion. Libyan forces had been involved in Chadian civil wars since the 1970s. Chadian leader Goukouni Oueddeï, who at one point announced the "fusion" of Chad and Libya, was chased from the capital, N'Djamena, in June 1982 by troops commanded by his rival and former ally Hissène Habré. In June 1983, Goukouni's forces took the offensive, with Libyan aid. Habré appealed for help and France sent supplies, but when Qadhafi committed his air force and more troops, the French were reluctant to move. The U.S. government urged Mitterrand to intervene in northern Chad and dispatched General Vernon Walters to make the case. Mitterrand refused, seeing in northern Chad nothing but desert and a few date palms.[90]

Southern Chad, however, was too close to other African countries, and Paris finally concluded that the Chad "domino" must not fall totally into the Libyan sphere of influence. Mitterrand's words were, "If Niger and the Cameroons crack, that's the end of French influence in Africa."[91]

Operation Manta deployed 3,000 French troops as a trip-wire force on the fifteenth parallel to prevent the Libyans from occupying populous southern Chad and N'Djamena. No French ground troops went into action against the Libyans; Mitterrand sought a diplomatic solution. After much negotiation, Paris and Tripoli announced an agreement on "total and simultaneous evacuation." The French began to depart, but French intelligence reports suggested that the Libyans intended to stay. Mitterrand had agreed to meet Qadhafi in Crete on November 15, 1983, and, despite the reports of deceit, decided to go through with the meeting. Qadhafi began by denying that his troops were still in Chad. Mitterrand told the Libyan leader that if he did not keep his agreement, war would result. Relations between their two countries were possible if Libya respected its promises.[92]

Mitterrand was much criticized on his return for going to meet the Libyan leader, an instigator of terrorism. The Libyans remained in northern Chad; the French withdrew. But in February 1986 when Goukouni's men and the Libyans attacked across the sixteenth parallel, the French bombed a Libyan air base in northern Chad and then introduced a new force, code-named Epervier, with a large contingent of airplanes and 1,200 troops. The trip wire now was the sixteenth parallel—but the French allowed Habré's men to operate north of that line. Mitterrand took care as before to keep French soldiers out of the line of fire.

In 1987 Epervier was reinforced, more anti-tank missiles were supplied to Habré's forces, and between January and April 1987 the Chadian forces defeated the Libyans in several battles, forcing a Libyan retreat up to the Aouzou strip along the Libyan frontier. The rich and powerful Libyans had been defeated by one of the poorest peoples in Africa, although the French aid had, of course, been decisive. The African leaders had been reassured and Habré's position confirmed.

Habré was overthrown in December 1990 by General Idris Déby, quietly encouraged by Paris. Déby too had received some Libyan aid but promised not to dispute the Epervier force in the north, which had been designed to dissuade any Libyan offensive. Habré had also been bitterly criticizing recent French policy in Africa.[93]

Looking back at the Chad intervention, Mitterrand congratulated himself for having handled the situation well and for having rejected American pressure: "The U.S . . . wanted us to liquidate Libya. They wanted us to be their secular arm to finish off Qadhafi instead of them."[94] French policy had triumphed, without France having to make more than a carefully limited military commitment.

In his second term one of Mitterrand's first actions was to forgive the debt owed by African countries to France (and encourage others to forgive Third World debts). A greater change, real or apparent, came after the events of late 1989 brought an end to the Soviet empire. The desire to contain or avoid communism in Africa had been one of French interests in Africa. Another was the web of French investments—and the political weight of individuals interested in them. Still another was the political support of African countries in the United Nations for French positions. More fundamental yet, perhaps, was the belief, which went back to colonialist days, that part of French identity as a great nation rested on the continuation of a Francophone area. As France saw English increasingly becoming the world language, with French the native language only of France, Quebec, and a few million Belgians and Swiss (fewer than 70 million people in all), *francophonie* gained increasing importance in the minds of French elites, with François Mitterrand in the first rank. He even established a state secretariat for *francophonie* in his second term.

The occasion of three decades of African independence led to extensive review in French publications of France's record in Africa, and the verdict was negative. External aid had not produced development, Africa was poorer than ever (and more populous), and African rulers corrupt and undemocratic. Ambassador Stéphane Hessel had produced a report on French aid to Africa at Michel Rocard's request in 1988, but its recommendations were unwelcome in the Elysée: that the *domaine reservé* be abandoned, and that greater emphasis be placed on democracy and less reliance on African presidents.[95]

President Mitterrand's speech at the Franco-African summit at the Breton resort of La Baule in June 1990 thus seemed a new departure. Its advance planning witnessed unusual disagreement in a meeting between the president and his closest advisers. Elysée secretary-general Jean-Louis Bianco, although skeptical on pushing democracy in an uncongenial climate, considered that French policy in Africa was "clientilist, immobilist, and deprived of any vision of economic development." Presented with criticisms of past policies and unwelcome suggestions, Mitterrand grew testy. "All this goes back to one question: should we or should we not stay in Africa? . . . If we leave, I'll tell you what will happen: There are countries totally without resources like Burkina Faso, which interest no one and would be in greater misery. And there are countries with potential, like Gabon, where the United States would be delighted to take our place." Later, after a scene with Bianco in which Mitterrand called him an idiot, the president consented to listen to a program for more-complete development projects and more emphasis on human rights, democracy, pluralism, and the fight against corruption. He still had no belief that much could be done.[96]

At La Baule Mitterrand called for more democracy even while pledging more French aid. He suggested that France would help more where democratic conditions were respected, tempering the message by stressing that each country should proceed at its own rhythm. The African presidents understood. "Once back home, for the most part they worked to organize their permanence in power by a democratic process that they wished to make as artificial as possible."[97]

In the following years there were changes at the top in Benin, Mali, Niger, Madagascar, the Congo, and the Central African Republic, although the transition in several of them was far from smooth. In any event, France was responding to the necessity of change that was already on the way.

Alarming changes of a different sort came in the former Belgian colony of Rwanda, where France had come to play a considerable role. There tensions between the majority Hutu and the minority Tutsi rose to the danger point after the invasion of Rwanda in 1990 by a Tutsi force from Uganda, the children of Rwandan Tutsis who had fled massacres thirty years earlier. They were supported logistically by the Ugandan army, in which they had fought against the former dictator Milton Obote.

The Tutsi Front Patriotique Rwandais (FPR), which also included dissident Hutus, won initial successes against the small and badly organized Force Armée Rwandaise (FAR). Mitterrand thought Rwandan president Juvénal Habyarimana one of the better African leaders. When Habyarimana requested French military aid, Paris sent two parachute companies "to assure the security of French residents" and a training mission to bolster the FAR.

Paris was the more inclined to support the existing Rwandan regime because it was threatened by an outside force over which France had no influence. There was much talk in Paris of Ugandan aggression backed by the United States—a threat to French influence in Africa. Moreover, the leaders of the FPR were painted as totalitarian, para-Communist, in fact, "black Khmers."[98] That was the propaganda of Habyarimana's inner circle, but it seems to have affected some French representatives also. Nonetheless, Paris continued to encourage a multiparty system, and a coalition government came into being in April 1992. But party militias excited by violent anti-Tutsi propaganda committed numerous atrocities. Hundreds of thousands of refugees, almost all Hutus, fled south before the advancing FPR, and crowded Kigali, the Rwandan capital.

The Socialist government, which had backed Habyarimana, was replaced in April 1993 by the Balladur government, less interested in Africa and more in Eastern Europe and Asia. Paris pushed for a negotiated settlement. The Arusha agreement of August 1993 called for repatriation of refugees and integration of the FPR into the Rwandan army, with a 40 percent share of troops and 50 percent of the officer corps. The French withdrew all forces by December 1993, replaced by a small UN force of 2,500 troops.

In April, President Habyarimana and his Burundi colleague Cyprien Ntaryamira were killed by a missile fired at their airplane, which was landing at Kigali. Immediately, a wave of anti-Tutsi genocide (also directed at moderate Hutus) broke out all over the country. The helpless UN observer force was withdrawn on April 21. The FPR army advanced on Kigali, which fell on July 4. As reports of the massacre began to emerge, the UN Security Council reversed itself on May 17 and agreed to send up to 5,500 peacekeeping troops to Rwanda. Estimates of deaths in the ten weeks after the deaths of the two presidents already ran at 200,000 or much higher. However, no Western power was willing to commit forces. The United States had hesitated on the UN resolution, arguing that the parties to the conflict showed no readiness to agree to a cease-fire or even agree to a UN operation. Off balance from the Somali disaster, U.S. policymakers were still hesitant to intervene in Haiti, much closer to home.

On June 15, France declared its willingness to intervene militarily to halt the genocide. Operation Turquoise was authorized on June 22 by a UN resolution, to create a safe zone into which the FPR should not come. Hundreds of thousands of terrified Hutus, many of them complicit in the massacre of other Hutus and Tutsis, were fleeing north, and in July the Red Cross estimated that 2.3 million refugees were in the safe zone and Zaire. An estimated 1 million had been killed in the genocidal madness, more died in the overcrowded camps of cholera. On August 21, French troops withdrew from Rwanda.

As the extent of the tragedy unfolded, the French government was bitterly criticized at home and abroad for its action and inaction. Why had Paris supported the Habyarimana government, in which key elements had before the genocide maintained the "Zero Network" murder squads? Was it not clear that an epidemic of murder that spread so rapidly over the country had been long prepared? Why did Paris take so long to intervene, and was the intervention not a means of aiding the retreat of those Hutus most responsible for the genocide, whose leaders ended in comfortable exile in Zaire or Paris, ready to prepare revenge?

Mitterrand's aide Hubert Védrine defended his chief's record in this affair, arguing that a successful invasion by Tutsis, who made up only 15 percent of the Rwandan population, could lead only to further trouble, and that French policy aimed at the kind of compromise achieved at the Arusha conference. Védrine vehemently rejected the imputation that France deliberately supported a regime that was preparing genocide. Probably that is literally true, in the sense that Paris did not desire the genocide—but it looked the other way both before massacres began on a large scale and afterwards, taking refuge in the formulation that atrocities were being committed on both sides. A sick and enfeebled François Mitterrand wanted both to support Habyarimana and to pretend that nothing was wrong. French policy thus continued to support the Habyarimana government, more or less on automatic pilot, fearing the worst while doing nothing to prevent it. A complete and dispassionate account of this whole tragedy may be long in coming.[99]

In early 1994 the CFA, the common currency of former French colonies, supported by Paris, was devalued by 50 percent. The IMF and the World Bank had for years argued that it was overvalued and that the higher expenses for those in Africa who could afford imported products would be more than compensated by a rise in exports. The African presidents opposed the idea, as did Mitterrand. He was finally convinced in 1992 by IMF director-general Michel Camdessus and Pierre Bérégovoy. The African leaders refused, but in 1993 when Balladur argued that the measure was overdue, they finally acquiesced. The IMF and the World Bank sweetened the pill by allowing more than 10 billion francs in aid, and France canceled 25 billion francs of debt payments over three years and created a special 300-million-franc development fund for urgent social operations.

France's problem in Africa is the generic one attached to any attempt to exert a major foreign influence, in Africa or anywhere else: With influence comes responsibility for the consequences. It is certainly true that a western society cannot impose democracy on a completely different society—even given the will to do so. Mitterrand inherited the complex, corrupt system of postcolonialist influence in Africa built up by de Gaulle and his first two successors. Any attempt to change it rapidly would undoubtedly have been in vain. It is, however, legitimate to wonder whether a consistent policy aiming at small steps forward would not, over fourteen years, have accomplished something more. There was no consistent policy, at least not one consistent with Mitterrand's rhetoric, and the president who had first known Africa when he was minister for Overseas France in the early 1950s may never have changed greatly the views he then conceived—as he did not drop his old African friendships. Jean Audibert, Jean-Pierre Cot's *directeur de cabinet* in 1981–1982 and Mitterrand's African adviser, who replaced Guy Penne in 1986 and served until 1990, said as much in an interview in May 1996, adding that Mitterrand's views on Africa were quite conservative—he believed France must consolidate the structures that existed.[100]

The Middle East

France had long felt that it had special interests in the Middle East. Under the Ancien Régime, French protection was given to the Maronite Christian community in Lebanon, and France intervened in 1860 after a Turkish massacre of Maronites. After World War I France held the mandate for a newly created Lebanese state in which France favored the Maronites, and after Lebanese independence at the end of World War II, cultural ties to Lebanon and the Maronites in particular remained very strong.

Elsewhere in the Middle East, French policy was pro-Arab. Initially friendly to and supportive of the new state of Israel, French policy altered in 1967, when de Gaulle was angered at Israel's refusal to follow his advice not to go to war. A pro-Arab policy then continued under his next two successors. France had also had excellent commercial relations with Iraq, a major customer in the mid-1970s.

In 1981, French policy in the Middle East was initially marked by tension between the pro-Arab sentiment of Cheysson and the Quai and Mitterrand's desire to improve relations with Israel. The president was far more pro-Israel than his predecessors—but firmly in favor of Israeli concessions to the Palestinians that would culminate in a Palestinian state. Immediately after his election, even before he took office, Mitterrand dispatched close collaborators on a round of Arab embassies in Paris to assure them that he was neither anti-Arab nor in any way disposed to confiscate foreign property in France.

Mitterrand's plans for an early visit to Israel were frustrated by the Israeli attack in June 1981 on a French-installed Iraqi nuclear facility, which killed a French technician. The French president finally paid his state visit in March 1982. In a Knesset speech Mitterrand proclaimed Israel's right to live—but spoke also of the rights of the people surrounding Israel. He was coldly rebuffed by Menachem Begin. However, Mitterrand believed Begin's assurances that an Israeli incursion into Lebanon, which was already being mooted would be limited to a forty-kilometer advance. When the Israelis attacked into Lebanon on June 6 and continued on, encircling Beirut, the French president was incensed, declaring, "Begin lied to me!"

A French contingent dispatched in August 1982 to the international force in Beirut to help evacuate Palestine Liberation Organization (PLO) fighters was kept there (like U.S. and other international forces) after the Sabra and Shatila massacres, in which Lebanese Christian militia killed more than 1,000 Palestinian civilians. When Shiite militia artillery batteries fired on French troops, French planes attacked them. In October 1983 the explosion of an Islamic Jihad suicide truck killed 58 French soldiers minutes after a similar attack cost 239 American lives. Mitterrand flew immediately to Beirut and on his return proclaimed that France would remain faithful to its history and its agreements. In early November, having decided that Teheran had ordered the fatal bombing, Mitterrand ordered French intelligence agents to retaliate against Iran by exploding a car bomb against the wall of the Iranian embassy in Beirut. The explosion failed to go off, to the embarrassment of the DGSE. Paris and Washington then agreed on a coordinated bombing attack in mid-November on the barracks of Iranian irregulars and pro-Iranian Shiite militia. At the last minute Reagan changed his mind, and French planes alone carried out the attack, which had only limited success.[101]

In late February 1984 Ronald Reagan cut his losses and withdrew the U.S. force. A month later, Lebanese president Amin Gemayel officially ended the international mission Lebanon had requested in 1982, and two weeks later French troops withdrew in somewhat better order than had the Americans, "with their flags flying and a band playing," wrote U.S. secretary of state George Shultz. "I liked their style."[102] But the retreat from Lebanon was a sign by both countries that they could not afford to exert direct influence on the ground in a part of the world gone mad.

French policy had wanted an independent Lebanon where the Maronites would continue to play a considerable role. By the end of 1983 Mitterrand was obliged to admit that France could not simultaneously affront a hostile Syria with its Lebanese constituency and a hostile Iran manipulating pro-Iranian Lebanese angry with France because of arms contracts with Iraq, even while hoping to continue a policy for Israel that the Israeli government rejected. France would no longer engage or let itself be engaged alone in this wasps' nest. And France must conclude a tacit nonaggression pact with Syria. Mitterrand had written Syrian president Hafiz al-Assad a conciliatory letter to this effect on February 10, recognizing "the historic role of Syria and the Syrian people in the region."[103]

To what degree did French involvement in Lebanon in 1983–1984 bring on the terrorism that afflicted France in 1985–1987? The kidnapping of French (or other) hostages by various terrorist groups was in part motivated by the desire to free terrorists held in Kuwait or in France. Terrorist actions of Middle Eastern origin in Paris in 1985–1986 were similarly intended to pressure the French into releasing prisoners. Paris also believed that Iranian-sponsored terrorism was striking back at France for furnishing arms to Iraq. Nevertheless, the overall context of persistent attacks on the French presence in Lebanon (as with those on the U.S. presence) was the desire of radical, usually Shiite, groups to uproot Western influence in Lebanon and the Middle East in general. Although wishing to maintain a presence that had a long tradition and much sympathy inside France, Mitterrand by the mid-1980s had been almost totally disabused of the real power of France to play a role in Lebanon or to find much sympathy from a Maronite community that had in considerable part decided that it was better to depend on close neighbor Syria, even as a puppet, than retain hope that France (or the United States) could sustain it.

Mitterrand had throughout these vicissitudes attempted to protect Yasser Arafat, believing that if he disappeared, the situation would be worse. French warships escorted the Greek merchant ships that evacuated Arafat and 4,000 of his men from the area where they were encircled in Lebanon, making sure they could be withdrawn to Tunisia. But Mitterrand carefully avoided meeting Arafat personally—although Cheysson did so—and did not receive him until after the Palestinian leader's December 1988 renunciation of terrorism and recognition of Israel's right to exist. After their first meeting in May 1989, Arafat used a phrase suggested to him by Roland Dumas, that the clause in the PLO charter on the destruction of the state of Israel was null and void *(caduque)*.[104] Mitterrand was nevertheless sharply criticized by the French Jewish community.

French Middle East policy in the period 1984–1988 had been much concerned with the question of the French hostages taken in Beirut by the pro-Iranian forces. They were freed under obscure circumstances in 1988, at the time of the presidential election. The Iranians maintained that the counterpart to this action was freedom for a commando arrested in France in 1980 for the attempted assassination of exiled former Iranian prime minister Shapour Bakhtiar. Chirac and Pasqua had allegedly made promises to free them, which they afterwards denied. After a number of false starts, the five members of the Iranian commando were expelled to Iran in July 1990. They had served ten years in prison. In August 1991 Iranian agents assassinated Bakhtiar in his residence in the Paris suburbs.

The Gulf War

Like the United States, France had been far more openhanded toward Iraq than Iran during their war in the 1980s, and Iraq had large unpaid debts with France. But

Saddam Hussein's sudden invasion of Kuwait on August 2, 1990, found French policy unequivocally anti-Iraq. If Saddam had hoped for a split among the Big Five in the UN Security Council, he did not find it—neither from the Soviets nor the French. For France, the oil question was important; it was concerned about Kuwaiti oil and the possibility that Iraq would swiftly control both Saudi and United Arab Emirate oil. The idea that tolerating Saddam's aggression would give the green light to other adventurist powers tempted to rectify some disputed border also counted. Mitterrand thought too that if Saddam really menaced Israel, the Israelis might respond with nuclear arms, and that "any Israeli-Arab nuclear conflict would dig an uncrossable ditch between the Western and the Arab-Islamic worlds, lasting for many years."[105]

On August 9 Mitterrand took counsel with key ministers. Should France send troops to join the Americans and British in Saudi Arabia? The ministers were reluctant to join with the United States, except possibly under the UN banner. Defense Minister Chevènement's position was the most negative. He feared for France's position with the Arab states and did not wish to join the United States. Mitterrand, however, was categorical. The UN, he prophesied, would do nothing on its own; the question was whether France should take its place with the British and Americans. "We are glad to have the Americans in certain circumstances. We are their allies. Not when they uphold Israel unconditionally, [or] bomb Libya, but in the present case, we must be clear in our solidarity. If we must choose, I think we must fight against Saddam Hussein, whatever the consequences may be."[106]

On the same day, Mitterrand announced that France would take part in a blockade against Iraq and reinforce its air and naval forces in the Gulf area. On September 9, after Iraqi troops broke into the residence of the French ambassador in Kuwait, France announced that it was sending troops to Saudi Arabia.

French public opinion at first strongly supported the government's position, but by late September 1990 it began to waver, strongly opposing use of conscripts or reserves in any military action against Iraq. One poll in late September found 83 percent of respondents opposed to military action under any circumstances.[107] Public opinion was facing up to the dangers of a war with possibly heavy casualties. On August 21, after Mitterrand said Saddam had put his opponents in a position that logically would end in war, Chevènement, speaking only "as a high government official," told a journalist that he was very worried about the possibility of an attack on Iraq in the next few days. Arguing for negotiation, he spoke of a conflict that could have "thousands, perhaps tens of thousands of victims." His anonymity did not last long. Chevènement did not, however, offer to resign, and the president did not push him.

Mitterrand had been much criticized for what was seen as his tardy reactions on German unification. Very conscious that he needed public opinion with him if he were to take France into a war, he began by calling a special parliamentary session to approve participation in the embargo and condemn the Iraqi action, and he explained his actions in numerous press conferences. In addition, he took care to draw distinctions between France's role as a good ally and any imputation that France was merely following blindly in the U.S. wake. Some of these distinctions annoyed Washington, as when Mitterrand in a speech before the UN General Assembly on September 24 suggested a linkage between solution of the Kuwait problem and a solution in Palestine—a line used often by Saddam, and therefore unwelcome in Washington, which wanted to finish the Kuwait question before putting any pressure on Israel.

George Bush did not want to quarrel with the French, nor did Mitterrand seek more than the right to show that French policy was independent. Despite continued small frictions caused by Mitterrand's determination to show both his own public opinion and the Arabs that France was trying to avoid war, Mitterrand made it clear in private conversations with Secretary of State Baker and President Bush that France would be with the United States. In late November a poll showed public support for a military solution falling: 57 percent of respondents did not want France to participate in a military conflict with Iraq. Chevènement argued in the Council of Ministers that France should not align itself with the United States. Mitterrand said: "There is a moment when it's necessary to say 'yes' or 'no.' You can't stay in a gray area without giving up the role recognized for our country at the birth of the UN. I take my responsibilities before public opinion . . . even if it's judged negatively by a large part of it."[108]

He continued to work on the political class and public opinion, however, conferring with representatives of the major parties, though not the National Front, which had immediately sided with Iraq, to the confusion of many of its militants. (Le Pen presumably thought that stance could be exploited if there were heavy casualties.) The Communists were also opposed to Mitterrand's policy. But there were many in all parties who expressed doubts.

The French military contribution to the coalition consisted first of sending the aircraft carrier *Clemenceau* to the Red Sea—essentially a gesture. After the United Nations in late November authorized the use of force against Iraq, France sent 11,200 troops to Saudi Arabia. Mitterrand wanted to play a visible role—theoretically independent, actually under U.S. command, but he neither desired nor was able to send a larger force. He could not send draftees without permission of the parliament, which was politically far too risky. Britain with its numerically smaller but more professional army showed up much better than France in the Gulf war.

After more maneuvers, some taken in conjunction with the Soviets, who, though cooperative with the West, were anxious to prevent the defeat of their former protégé, Mitterrand finally concluded by early January that Saddam Hussein would only understand force—as he had suspected all along. When hostilities began, polls showed that the president had brought public opinion along with him: 87 percent felt that France had done everything it could to save the peace. The French had feared terrorist actions and worried about the Moslems in France. In the event, although the Moslems were unhappy, they worried also about reactions against them, and there were no demonstrations or terrorist actions.[109]

Mitterrand had kept Defense Minister Chevènement in his post despite this left-wing Socialist's strong and repeated opposition to the war, judging apparently that in the unstable state of public opinion it was better to keep him within the government and relatively quiet. Once war broke out, Chevènement was seen by the military to be braking, and on January 19 Mitterrand asked for his resignation. By that time, although many Socialists were still uneasy, Mitterrand had won his battle for public opinion. Like George Bush, he had thought it useful if not constitutionally necessary to ask the National Assembly for approval of military action—four days after the U.S. House and Senate had given theirs. The French vote was less close than that in the U.S. Congress—523 votes for the use of armed force, 43 against.

France had hoped, and Mitterrand had publicly suggested, that participation in the Gulf war would win a large role for France in subsequent negotiations on peace in the Middle East. By putting pressure on the Israeli government after the Gulf war, Washington was able to open a dialogue in Madrid with, as Hubert Védrine wrote acidly, "a Soviet copresidency for facade, and a folding seat for the European Union." Ideas that Mitterrand had pushed before they became politically possible were now picked up by U.S. diplomacy, but "the Americans intended to conduct the maneuver alone." Mitterrand and his entourage approved the end, but not the means.[110]

One result of the Gulf war was the final chapter of any pretensions of French responsibility for Lebanon and its Maronite Christians. Mitterrand had concluded that France alone did not have the power to stand against the Syrian intention to make Lebanon a vassal state. At the same time, those Maronites who were anti-Syrian had strong defenders in France, particularly among the leaders of the UDF. When Lebanese presidential election procedures broke down in 1988, the anti-Syrian Christians in East Beirut had rallied around a "transitory military government" set up by General Michel Aoun. In March 1989, Aoun called for a "war of liberation" against Syria. While French officials were trying to open peace dialogues, senior UDF deputy Jean-François Deniau appeared in Beirut and proclaimed France's solidarity with the Christian camp. An angry Mitterrand told the Council of Ministers: "I read that we are supposed to save France's honor. But what does that mean, unless it's a military expedition?" He added that when he had received a delegation of parliamentarians of all parties the preceding week, some of the most excited UDF deputies started to talk about honor and history. "I replied: 'Are you asking for a military expedition?' They stammered, and did not dare answer yes." The president went on to qualify the ideas of his opposition as the dream of a colonial intervention, then evoked the fate of the United States in Vietnam and the Soviet Union in Afghanistan, and concluded, "It's the manner of another century, and France will assuredly not go back to this track."[111]

However, an active French diplomacy still hoped to arrange the withdrawal of Syrian forces from Beirut, where they were blockading the Christian eastern sector. France encouraged a tripartite committee of the Arab League that was supposed to find a political solution. With Syrian forces bombarding East Beirut and Aoun's forces resisting, casualties in the war-battered city were heavy. Mitterrand dispatched an aircraft carrier to Lebanese waters and later other ships—partly in the hope of deterring a Syrian assault on East Beirut, partly to evacuate the thousands of French citizens still resident there. Jacques Chirac and François Léotard flew to Beirut, where they hailed General Aoun's resistance. Aoun responded by demanding that French warships break the Syrian naval blockade. Mitterrand's response was to underline that the French mission was to safeguard, not to fight.

After more negotiations in early autumn 1989 saw Aoun's temporary agreement to the election of a president, Maronite René Moawad was elected—and rapidly assassinated. Another Maronite, Elias Hraoui, was quickly elected. Aoun did not recognize him either, and fighting broke out between two Christian factions in East Beirut.

The end for Aoun came when U.S. need for Syrian presence in the coalition against Iraq in the Gulf crisis opened the way for a Syrian assault on East Beirut on October 13, 1990. Many of Aoun's partisans were killed, whereas the general and some of his officers were given asylum in the French embassy in Beirut. French requests to evacuate Aoun to France met Syrian stonewalling, based in part on the Lebanese claim that the general and his associates had seized U.S.$75 million in government funds.

Mitterrand feared that Syrian special forces would attack the French embassy to seize or kill Aoun. He multiplied requests for U.S. help in negotiating a solution with Syrian president Assad. Only well after the end of the Gulf war, in August 1991, was a compromise achieved. Aoun was secretly removed from the French embassy and granted asylum in France, on condition that he cease all political activity.[112]

Mitterrand had understood since 1983 that France did not have the power to play a major role in Lebanon, but he had had to reckon with the determination of the political opposition and a part of the press, persuaded of the continuity of France's nineteenth- and early-twentieth-century role there. Mitigated support for the intransigent Aoun was designed to avoid a possible massacre of Christians in East Beirut (where they were killing each other) and to relieve the political pressure on Mitterrand. The process took so long that an inordinate amount of French diplomatic attention was focused on it. The denouement demonstrated clearly that Hafiz al-Assad was the master of Lebanon.

The Maghreb

The Maghreb—Morocco, Algeria, and Tunisia—had for centuries been the object of French concern. By the nineteenth century France no longer had to worry about pirate raids on its Mediterranean coasts. The French in their turn encroached on the Maghreb, first with the conquest of Algeria after 1830, later with the takeover of Tunisia and Morocco as protectorates in 1881 and 1911 respectively. Morocco and Tunisia had gained their independence in 1955, but the bitter war between France and the Algerian independence movement led by the Front de Libération Nationale (FLN) lasted from 1955 to 1962. French remained an important language in those countries, the link of their educated elites to the West, its culture and technology.

More than 1 million immigrants moved from the Maghreb states to find work in France between the early 1960s and 1974, when recruitment of foreign labor officially ceased. But France's official relations with the Maghreb states had been anything but smooth. Algeria in particular was suspicious of French claims and potential influence. Under Giscard, policy favored Moroccan claims to the former Spanish Sahara, whereas Algeria backed the independence claim of the Polisario guerrillas. Giscard later attempted reconciliation with Algeria.

François Mitterrand had as a minister in the Fourth Republic favored Tunisian and Moroccan independence (he even resigned from Joseph Laniel's government when it deposed Moroccan Sultan Mohammed V). He had initially opposed any separation of Algeria from France, although after 1958 his views on Algeria had slowly evolved. Nevertheless the socialist Algerian government of Chadli Benjedid saw the election of a French Socialist as a good sign. In Rabat, Hassan II feared that a Socialist government would favor the Polisario and encourage opposition forces in Morocco. A number of leaders in the PS wanted to do just that. Mitterrand intended to keep good relations with both Algeria and Morocco, to the degree possible. He had little sympathy for the Polisario, seeing in its cause only an Algerian-Moroccan quarrel. "Basically, he was not and would never be favorable to the creation of new states, in his eyes centers of instability. Except in one case, because there was no other way: the Palestinian state."[113]

Mitterrand cultivated the Algerian leader, while keeping an even balance with King Hassan II of Morocco. In 1982, France agreed to buy annually 9 million cubic meters of Algerian natural gas, at a price 25 percent above the world market. Mitterrand regarded that as a species of foreign aid, although the Algerians did not wish to see it so described.

Problems in the 1980s with Morocco centered on the human rights question, where there was much to be said about the record of the king's government. Publication of a book by the very left-wing writer Gilles Perrault criticizing Mitterrand's support of the king was taken as a devious maneuver by a suspicious Hassan II, because of Perrault's real or supposed ties to Danielle Mitterrand's foundation France-Libertés. But relations were smoothed over, and the Moroccans released some prominent prisoners.

In 1988 the long rule of the FLN over Algeria was shaken when the government's end to subsidies for basic commodities caused a series of riots, which were savagely repressed by the army, with more than 200 killed. Called upon by the French press and the opposition to criticize the Algerian government, Mitterrand refused. "What are we going to do, call in the Algerian ambassador and tell him that if France were there now, order would be better kept?"[114]

Paris received reports that the uprising, in its origins and denouement, had been at least in part a provocation by hard-line elements of the FLN, who felt threatened by some of Chadli's reform ideas. President Chadli now called for a referendum about instituting a multiparty system and dropping all reference to socialism; it won in February 1989 by 75 percent, and Chadli, reelected in late 1988, seemed strengthened in his policy of reforms. However, a country with extremely high youth unemployment in a young population, with buying power in free fall and increasing awareness of the corruption of FLN power, was ripe for the fundamentalist Islamic demagoguery of a new party, the Front Islamique de Salut (FIS). (When a former prime minister accused his predecessors of having stolen $26 billion—the amount of Algeria's foreign debt—the incumbent prime minister attempted to refute him by saying that the true figure was only $1 billion!)[115]

Legalized in the autumn of 1989, the FIS won 54 percent of the vote in municipal elections in June 1990. President Chadli pressed on, scheduling parliamentary elections for June 1991. Faced with bloody street fighting between FIS supporters and the police, Chadli was forced to postpone the elections and arrest some FIS leaders. However, when the first round of the elections did take place in December 1991, the FIS won 42 percent of the votes and nearly half the seats, and stood to win two-thirds of the seats in the second round. In early January 1992 the army took power, canceling the elections and deposing Chadli, whom they suspected of wanting to compromise. He was replaced by Mohammed Boudiaf, one of the historic leaders of the FLN uprising, who had early broken with the Algerian government and lived for many years in Moroccan exile.

Former French ambassador to Algeria Jean Audibert has said that he thought the elections were badly prepared and thus risky and told Chadli so. Not all the voter cards were distributed, said Audibert—a million were missing. Nearly a million ballots were also either blank or spoiled. With two-thirds of the seats, said Audibert, the FIS could have amended the constitution to create an Islamic republic. In those circumstances, Audibert reported to Paris that he saw no choice other than stopping the second round, but Mitterrand protested, although France did not urge Chadli's resignation. According to Hubert Védrine, Mitterrand wanted to help Chadli until the end, hoping that he could escape from the hard-liners without having to ally himself with the fundamentalists. Thereafter, French policy was silent, because the president thought France would have little if any influence in Algeria or any right to a voice.[116]

The three years after the army's action saw the assassination of Boudiaf, increasing tension and killing in Algeria, and the flight of most of the French nationals in Algeria to escape terrorism. After Algerian independence as many as 60,000 French citizens remained in Algeria. Today the number is well below 1,500, as the French government has insistently recommended to its citizens to leave, and terrorist actions are directed against almost all those of French origin, even inoffensive Trappist monks.[117]

The Algerian situation continues to worry France intensely. Looking at the unstable situation there, France fears that the advent of a fundamentalist government would cause a massive flight of westernized Algerians—whom the French do not wish to welcome but would find hard to turn away, and for whom there would be little economic future in a France with its own serious unemployment problems. Whether or not they support Le Pen, the French today believe that there are too many Maghrébins in France. (A SOFRES poll in December 1994 found 74 percent in complete or general agreement with the statement "There are too many immigrants in France." Only 10 percent strongly disagreed.)[118]

Another problem has been the transfer of terrorist actions by the Algerian fundamentalist Groupe Islamique Armée (GIA) to France, which began before the end of the Mitterrand period in December 1994, when an Air France plane en route for Paris was hijacked at the Algiers airport. The air pirates wanted to fly to Paris, reportedly to crash the plane into the city. Denied permission to fly to Paris, they landed in Marseilles, where a commando recaptured the plane. Other GIA actions in France took place after Chirac became president.

Keenly aware that it had little leverage over the military government in Algeria, having apparently little understanding of its dynamics, and with no influence whatsoever over the fundamentalists, the French government first supported the Algerian government, then moved toward a more evenhanded position. France seems to believe that the government cannot destroy the fundamentalists, nor they the government.[119] Yet France is not well placed to be the mediator.

Defense and Security

The defense policy conducted by François Mitterrand was stamped with many of the contradictions inherited from Charles de Gaulle. French nuclear forces were to defend France alone—a policy France had to give up, gradually and reluctantly. France was to work with Germany (but attempt to maintain its own defense policies). France must continue to be ready to project military power abroad (but not very much of it, or for very long). Above all, France had to be independent of U.S. hegemonic influence (but still be part of the Atlantic alliance). De Gaulle had been largely successful in these policies because no war situation arose, and there was no overseas crisis. Mitterrand kept the Gaullist thrust, but had to modify the details.

Mitterrand was able to follow de Gaulle by returning to the Franco-German defense and security cooperation envisioned in the 1963 Elysée treaty but never implemented. A first step was the creation in 1983 of the Force d'Action Rapide (FAR), intended in part to reinforce French capabilities for prompt action in a European crisis. With its 47,000 men, five divisions, and 220 helicopters, the FAR was also a force that could be dispatched overseas. Critics of the FAR noted that much of the force it would use was already deployed in West Germany, so that it added no new forces but redeployed (and possibly split up) old ones.[120]

The French land forces had been kept on short rations for many years in favor of nuclear expenses. The long-range missiles of the nuclear forces were supposed to guarantee only France—and were in any case insufficient in number to guarantee West Germany, whereas the tactical Pluton missiles, with a 120-kilometer range, would in combat fall in West Germany—or in the case of the Hades missile, scheduled to come into service in 1992, in East Germany. The Germans wanted more conventional forces from France and guarantees against the tactical missiles. If the presence of U.S. missiles on their soil made the Germans nervous even while reassuring them, French short-range missiles merely made them nervous.

In a December 1985 meeting with Mitterrand, Kohl suggested a joint statement concerning consultations on any use of these short-range weapons. Mitterrand agreed, but the resulting declaration in February 1986, carefully phrased, spoke of the president consulting with the chancellor on any use of these weapons "within the limits imposed by the extreme rapidity of such decisions." The German press greeted this nonguarantee with sarcasm.

Programs for joint production of armaments had an uneven record. France decided not to participate in production of a European fighter plane, the Germans until the 1990s showed no great interest in a military observation satellite, and the two countries could not agree on joint tank production. There were, however, agreements on manufacture of antitank and antiaircraft missiles and on an antitank helicopter.[121]

Elements of the French and West German armies also conducted joint exercises from 1985 to 1987. In June 1987 France and the Federal Republic announced plans for a joint brigade to be commanded in succession by a French and a German officer. Because the West German army was entirely committed to NATO and France intended to remain outside the integrated command, a unit of this sort was an institutional anomaly—and symbolic rather than effective, its importance as much political as military.

Beyond symbolic steps, the French government looked for mechanisms to emphasize the European aspects of defense. The vehicle chosen was the Western European Union (WEU), called into existence in 1948 as an anti-German treaty but then used in 1954 as a mechanism to fold a German army into NATO. It had slumbered over the succeeding years, despite an attempt in 1972 by Pompidou's foreign minister Michel Jobert to utilize it. France and West Germany agreed that the WEU should be revived, and after much negotiation with the other five signatories, notably Britain, the seven WEU nations met in Rome in October 1984 to renew the organization. The first resolve was for the signatories to the WEU treaty to harmonize their views on defense, but since the first major issue to come up was how to handle SDI, no harmonization took place.

After the fright given them by the U.S.-Soviet near agreement over their heads in October 1986 at Reykjavik, Paris and Bonn agreed to move WEU forward again, and in October 1987 the WEU formally adopted a platform on European security interests signed by Britain, France, West Germany, Greece, Italy, and the Benelux countries. They pledged closer cooperation on security matters, while carefully emphasizing the importance of European cooperation with the United States under NATO.

At the same time as France was pushing forward on European defense initiatives, Mitterrand was giving equal attention to the bilateral relationship with the Federal Republic. In 1987 Mitterrand began discussion of a joint defense council that would "coordinate decisions and harmonize analyses in the areas of security, defense, research, armaments, and the organization and deployment of joint units," and he invited participation in similar talks by other European nations. The November 1987 Franco-German summit meeting in Karlsruhe formally decided on the creation of this defense council, to meet twice a year to work out ideas for the common defense and security, especially on problems such as weapons interoperability. None of these consultative measures created anything like a genuine parallel structure to NATO— nor did the Germans wish to do so. Like the WEU, the defense council provided a venue for the discussion of common defense interests, but was not an operational body. For Paris, the first priority of these Franco-German actions was to keep German attention firmly fixed on Western Europe, as 1988–1989 saw more and more German enthusiasm for Mikhail Gorbachev.

After the Wall

The events of 1989 undermined all previous defense thinking. "Mitterrand's policies presupposed a world in which the fundamentals remained stable and change was incremental."[122] Suddenly this world had turned upside down. De Gaulle had permanently convinced French policymakers that the Americans would sooner or later leave Europe to itself. Now that the United States was no longer confronted by a strong Soviet Union, that time seemed to have come.

Paris was in no hurry to see the Americans leave quickly, but the moment seemed ripe to assert the importance of the WEU and make it a genuine European security player. In 1990 it was not immediately apparent that NATO would retain a major military role, and as Paris saw Washington scrambling to give NATO a political role, the French suspected a U.S. desire to retain political hegemony without important security guarantees. During the negotiations of spring–early summer 1990, which culminated in the July 15 German-Soviet agreement of Zheleznovodsk, Paris was obliged to downplay its doubts on any new role for NATO for fear of a last-minute German compromise with Gorbachev that would swap unity for neutral status.[123]

Earlier in July, the London NATO declaration had spoken of making nuclear arms "weapons of last resort," an idea that Mitterrand's military aide Admiral Jacques Lanxade had described to him as "devoid of any European perspective on security" and oriented toward "an increase in integrated command."[124] Once Gorbachev agreed that a unified Germany could remain in NATO, Paris was freer to express its suspicion of a new role for NATO.

At the Franco-German summit of September 17–18, 1990, Mitterrand announced that he proposed to pull half of the 48,000 French troops out of Germany. French-German defense planners had been working on a scheme for a mixed army division. These included proposals on continued stationing of French troops in Germany and on German units being stationed in France. The London declaration had also announced plans to create NATO multinational corps, and Paris feared German pressure to include French troops.

Mitterrand then told German TV that he was ready to take as much time as was needed and, asking rhetorically whether Germany needed foreign troops on its soil, suggested that if Germany believed that necessary in the framework of European defense, then a new agreement was needed.[125] Although the annoyance created by Mitterrand's tactics troubled relations, Kohl soon showed himself ready to give the French satisfaction.

The Kohl-Mitterrand joint letter of December 6, 1990, to the president of the European Community on common French-German positions for European Political Union suggested the way out of this dilemma. The two leaders declared that "foreign policy will have a vocation to extend to all areas. It should include a real common security policy that will eventually lead to a common defense." The letter further suggested that the European Political Union establish a "clear organic relation with the WEU." In time the WEU could become part of the political union and work out its common security policy. A mollifying phrase directed at the United States stated, "the Atlantic alliance will be reinforced by the increase in the role and responsibilities of the Europeans."[126]

On February 4, 1991, Foreign Ministers Dumas and Genscher announced a plan to relate the WEU to the EC, which was endorsed by the WEU countries' foreign and defense ministers on February 22. The WEU would become the central vehicle for a future defense policy plan. The U.S. government, fearful that a European defense organization would weaken NATO, sent a letter to the meeting strongly disapproving the concept of changing NATO structures or allowing the WEU to take instructions from the European Council. In mid-May during a visit by Kohl to the United States, the chancellor emphasized that moves to strengthen West European defense did not contradict the fact that NATO remained the cornerstone of the Western alliance. But in late May, when the NATO meeting endorsed the creation of a NATO rapid reaction force, Mitterrand (who had just announced—after many years of French opposition—that France would sign the 1968 nuclear nonproliferation treaty) rejected the idea of France joining the rapid-reaction force and expressed reservations on NATO restructuring.

In early October 1991 the French press echoed official displeasure at the U.S. and German proposal to set up a NATO Coordinating Council (NACC), a mechanism to give former East bloc states some sort of relation with NATO. Once again, French opinion makers (and officials) saw the United States working hard to keep a predominant voice in European affairs.

Tensions on the apparent incompatibility between French and American views on WEU versus NATO had risen so high that at the November 7–8 NATO meeting, when British prime minister John Major emphasized "the primacy of NATO," Mitterrand objected to the "primacy" provision. George Bush, departing from his scripted remarks, said the United States would be "opposed and hostile" to any moves by its allies to bypass NATO or to exclude the United States. Challenging them by saying: "If you want to go your own way, say so. If you don't need us any more, say so," he evoked a unanimous statement of support.[127]

At the Franco-German summit on October 16–17, 1991, Kohl and Mitterrand announced the formation of a 30,000-strong Franco-German corps. Not until the Franco-German summit of La Rochelle in May 1992 were plans ready for a formal announcement: a corps of 35,000, with two German mechanized brigades, the French First Armored Division, and the Franco-German brigade, alternating between French and German command. Its missions were to be defense of Western Europe in the NATO (or WEU) mission; peacekeeping and peacemaking in Eastern Europe or out of area; and humanitarian tasks. This body was called the Eurocorps, to be expandable to other European countries, but not to the United States.

The French assumption of 1989–1990 that NATO would be less important militarily and more intrusive politically was shaken by the demonstrated value of NATO logistical structures in the Gulf war and by the absence of the United States from UN operations in Bosnia. According to a senior French diplomat, by the end of the Bush administration French policymakers began to see that France needed to make some compromise on the importance of NATO, and with the entry on the scene of the Clinton administration the ground was more or less prepared on both sides for a change. The turning point came in January 1993, with a French-German-U.S. agreement on the role of the Eurocorps. It stipulated that the Eurocorps could act under WEU command if NATO was not involved, but where the whole Atlantic alliance was involved, NATO command would apply. The Brussels declaration of January 1994, signed by all NATO states, declared that NATO gave complete support to a common European security and defense identity and eventually to a common European defense "compatible with the Atlantic alliance."[128] U.S. policy had thus met the Europeans (notably the French) at least halfway.

A senior French official underlined the importance of the Bosnian experience in French thinking: France came to see that forces operating under the United Nations alone were not effective without NATO support, and German cooperation—important in any future intervention—became possible as a result of Germany's reconsideration of its responsibilities. In both cases Bosnia acted as a catalyst.[129] This new policy (defined in more detail at the NATO Berlin summit in June 1996) involves the use of NATO lift, or transport, capacity, satellite intelligence, and communications in "combined joint task forces" (CJTF) for operations in which the United States declines to take part.

France's future desires to operate "out of area" may not suit a Federal Republic that has decided that its constitution permits such actions but that is not keen to undertake them. France has more in common militarily with Britain, a country with fewer inhibitions on projecting power than Germany (though more than France has).[130]

Nevertheless, long-term policy choices are unclear. U.S. commitment to a variety of possible interventions present and future remains à la carte, a function of views of the president and Congress, not on U.S. national interest, as in the conventional Cold War NATO scenario, but on approximations to national interest such as humanitarian operations, subject to the judgment of the moment and political controversy. The same à la carte approach will probably apply to the policy choices of many European states—especially Germany. The CJTF concept would then be put to its severest test if France and one or two other nations—but not the rest—wished to intervene somewhere. Of course, such situations have occurred in the past, when American lift capacity was used to transport French troops for what one might call weekend operations in Africa, as in Zaire in 1978. But as the concept of common foreign and security policy faces its tests, it will suffer a blow every time a minority of WEU countries wishes to act and others refrain because they think the crisis unimportant to their national interests. The future of such policy will thus be shaped in large part by the nature of future crises and the response to them.

French Defense Forces

The Gulf war gave rise to much criticism in professional and political circles on the insufficiencies of French armed forces. A French Senate report (drafted by a well-informed but very conservative group) pointed out that the interpenetration of professional soldiers and conscripts in the army, which theoretically numbered 280,000, made it impossible to deploy more than 12,000 infantry in the Gulf war, mostly elite troops who had served abroad in Africa. In comparison, Britain could send out nearly three times as many soldiers from a total of 150,000 under arms. The report stated, "The Gulf crisis revealed that the professional part of the French army is entirely insufficient to conduct a conventional operation of any size against a medium-sized power equipped with European weapons." It added that the air force and the navy would also have had difficulties if the war had continued.[131] The report also underlined that France's very modest lift capacity in 1990–1991 consisted of seventy-six Transall C-160s, twelve Hercules C-130s, and four DC-8s, mostly at the end of their useful lives.

The French military clearly understood that the Gulf war had emphasized the irreplaceable logistical importance of NATO. Policy was slow to follow—Mitterrand in particular continued to emphasize the importance of European institutions and forces. Having decided that NATO's role largely belonged to the past, he did not easily comprehend the lesson of the Gulf war—confirmed in Bosnia—that lift capacity, intelligence capacity, and a long tradition of military cooperation based on unified command were assets too expensive for the WEU to duplicate. The indecision on action in ex-Yugoslavia (and elsewhere) displayed by the Clinton administration until 1994 can only have complicated any revision of Mitterrand's thinking.

France had been spending more on its armed forces than any OECD country other than the United States, 196 billion francs in the peak year of 1991—scheduled under Mitterrand to descend very slowly indeed.[132] The budget had gone for the nuclear strike forces, which in 1994 consisted of 5 nuclear submarines, plus a new one under construction, each capable of firing 16 missiles with six warheads each, 18 Mirage IV airplanes, 15 of which had air-to-ground missiles with a 300-kilometer-plus range, 45 medium-range air-to-ground missiles, 18 missiles in silos at the plateau d'Albion base in southeastern France, and 30 Hades missiles, capable of going 450 kilometers. The Hades missiles were put into permanent reserve by Mitterrand, and Chirac took them out of service, along with the obsolescent Mirage IV and plateau d'Albion missiles.[133] The existing capability of nuclear submarines had made France a credible nuclear power; the submarine-launched missiles, targeted on Soviet cities, constituted a very real ancillary deterrence to any Soviet aggression. But in the post–Cold War era, the French military force was unbalanced. The number of French battle tanks is scheduled to decrease to 650, and combat aircraft (notably the enormously expensive Rafale fighter) to 380, and the navy, with 150 ships of all categories in 1985, was to have only 103 in 2004.[134]

France has continued to assert its military presence abroad, with more than 25,000 troops in various countries in French Africa, the South Pacific, and South America (principally French Guyana, the base for Ariane rocket launches). In the early 1990s, France had peacekeepers in at least seven countries, including 4,800 in ex-Yugoslavia, 1,435 in Cambodia, and 441 in South Lebanon. The cost of these peacekeeping operations alone in 1993 was 7 billion francs, only 1.5 billion of which were reimbursed by the United Nations.[135]

Mitterrand's desire to make more of WEU than the political and financial situation permitted and unwillingness to see in NATO anything other than an obsolescent vehicle for U.S. political dominance retarded French readjustment to the changed security universe after 1989—and the exaggerated fears of the Bush administration on WEU did not help much. The Sénat report of 1991 had strongly suggested that France could not afford to maintain a large army with more than 100,000 conscripts who were unusable for most of the likely operations of the future. It was left for President Jacques Chirac to conclude that France had to give up a hallowed conscription policy enshrined in the revolutionary tradition of "a nation in arms" and turn to the more effective British model of a small, highly trained professional army. Paradoxically, this entry into power of neo-Gaullists permitted a less Gaullist view of security policy, culminating after Mitterrand left office in Jacques Chirac's 1995 decision to move much closer to the NATO command structure.

10

The Meaning of Mitterrand

François Mitterrand enjoyed the longest governing term in France since Napoleon III (who also called himself a socialist). The brief time elapsed since he left office makes it premature to ask What is the meaning of Mitterrand? Yet if no definitive answer is possible, the question is inescapable. Definitive answers can be attempted only when time has shown which initiatives and which policies of 1981–1995 have lasting value, which have advanced, retarded, or damaged the French economy and society. Even then the judgment will always be subjective: History, proudly and realistically, does not call itself a science.

François Mitterrand cared a great deal about history's verdict on him, but little about contemporary criticism. His career ended in a long, melancholy withdrawal in the course of a second cohabitation and a debilitating illness, accompanied by scandals and disturbing admissions about his youth and activities as a minor functionary of the Vichy government. But how much of this contemporary comment is likely to enter into history's judgment? One may distinguish between Mitterrand the man and Mitterrand the president, but his personal qualities influenced not only his actions as president, but also the institutions of government which he found, affected, and left behind him, as well as the Socialist party he built and then nearly destroyed. One needs, therefore, to begin with those personal qualities.

Mitterrand was a profoundly secretive and devious man. Some measure of these qualities is undoubtedly necessary in the successful chief of a democratic state, which demands of its leaders the antithetical attributes of honest openness and political effectiveness. Mitterrand's measure was perhaps too great. An intensive study of his statements over the years leads to the conclusion that nothing that he ever said can be taken at face value—it may be suggestive or indicative, but no more.

In Mitterrand's final years, a number of books published new information on his political attitudes and activities in youth—especially the Vichy period.[1] By 1994, all this might have passed as ancient history (it was already known in some detail by many people) had it not been for a new Vichy link that connected Mitterrand with

René Bousquet. A rising young prefect before the war, Bousquet became an enthusiastic collaborator and in 1942 was named secretary-general of Vichy's police. After the war he was tried and acquitted in 1949, afterwards becoming a businessman and a board member of the influential southern paper *La Depêche du Midi*. Mitterrand apparently did not meet Bousquet until after World War II, but they became friends and Bousquet was Mitterrand's guest in small gatherings at his country home in the Landes, as well as his Paris home, as late as 1983. Mitterrand always maintained that he learned only in 1986 that Bousquet was directly responsible for the notorious roundup of Jews in Paris by French police at the Vélodrome d'Hiver bicycle racing stadium in July 1942. This action was taken in close coordination with the Gestapo, which shipped those arrested to Auschwitz, from which almost none returned. (Bousquet probably did not know that meant certain death, but he would have known that people of all ages would be wrenched from their homes, then shipped off somewhere in cattle cars.)

Even people well disposed to Mitterrand have found his statement of ignorance hard to believe. Mitterrand evidently believed that Bousquet had played a double game that had helped his Resistance work: One of Bousquet's subordinates, Jean-Paul Martin, furnished Mitterrand with false documents and information. In any case, Mitterrand was always extremely loath to criticize Bousquet, and when Bousquet was freshly charged of crimes against humanity in 1991, the president tried to quash the affair. Bousquet was assassinated in 1993 before he could come to trial.

Mitterrand was not suspected of anti-Semitism in this affair—his friendship with and esteem for a large number of Jews refuted any such thought. But it was precisely his well-known cult of friendship that implied that friendship meant more to him than ideology or ideas. The Bousquet affair combined with the revelations on Mitterrand's early convictions to raise the question whether he had ever really been "a man of the Left." A Socialist militant of many years' standing put it this way: "What distinguishes *"les gens de gauche"* from *"les gens de droite"* is that those on the Right think that an old friend is an old friend, period, whereas on the Left they wouldn't react this way, but in virtue of his ideas." She added that the Bousquet business had gone down very badly among militants—Mitterrand could not have failed to know about the Vél d'Hiv and all the rest, which for her meant that he was not an *"homme de gauche."*

In a 1994 interview with his friend Elie Wiesel for a book published under both their names, Mitterrand refused to apologize for his association with Bousquet and again stated that he had not known about Bousquet's anti-Jewish activities. He repeated that Bousquet had been acquitted in 1949, was received everywhere, and was a member of numerous boards, including the *Depêche du Midi*.[2] In other words, for Mitterrand, Bousquet had been a high official, moreover, a prewar and postwar Radical Socialist, a man of great charm, who had covered himself by winking at his associates' aid to the Resistance, and if there were other aspects of Bousquet's work, never mind.

A senior political journalist from *Le Monde* commented privately to me that he doubted that Mitterrand had ever really been on the Left—that his whole career had been hypocrisy and opportunism. This view is almost certainly an overreaction. What the Bousquet affair does seem to prove is that Guy Mollet was right when he said that Mitterrand had only learned to "speak Socialist," that his conversion to socialism was superficial at best, emphasized to serve his ambition. None of these suppositions means that elements of the ideas of social justice that Mitterrand retained from his youth were not at least partly compatible with Socialist ones. Yet what if anything of what Mitterrand ever said and wrote can be taken as basic beliefs? Had he any?

No simple and linear explanation can account for this very complicated man. He was at different times on the extreme Right, a *Pétainiste,* resister, moderate Fourth Republic republican, Socialist—and in each incarnation retained something of the previous ones. Beyond that, as Stanley Hoffmann noted, there is "One certainty: the only cause in which he ever deeply believed was himself."[3]

In this deep narcissism one may perhaps find the clue to the other guiding line in Mitterrand's political life: opposition to de Gaulle. Mitterrand had clashed with de Gaulle when they first met in Algiers in December 1943, but on the Resistance leader Henri Frenay's recommendation, de Gaulle had ultimately backed down on his insistence that Mitterrand subordinate his POW network to that of the general's nephew Michel Cailliau. At the Liberation Mitterrand had been named secretary-general of the provisional government's ministerial Department for Prisoners. As a member of the provisional government, young Mitterrand attended the first Council of Ministers meeting. De Gaulle greeted the others, then turned to him with a cutting, "What, you again?"[4]

Soon after, Frenay was named minister for prisoners, disappointing Mitterrand, who then returned to his MNPGD. At this point, he seems to have swallowed his anger at the way de Gaulle had originally received him and become fascinated with de Gaulle. But a stormy encounter with the general took place in June 1945 when Mitterrand had gone along with a mass protest on the slowness of repatriation of POWs organized by the Communists. Receiving the leaders, de Gaulle violently criticized Mitterrand for disturbance of public order and demanded that agitation stop.

The cutting tone of their two meetings in 1944–1945 seems to have revived Mitterrand's rancor at the way the general had first received him. Toward the end of his life, Mitterrand reminisced at length with his German interpreter Brigitte Stoffaës, who had over the years become a friend, often speaking of de Gaulle and of their first meeting in Algiers. He kept coming back to the idea that de Gaulle had chosen him as commissioner for POWs and then at their next meeting spat out, "What, you again?" which badly hurt his feelings.[5]

Resentment and hurt feelings intermingled with other emotions: Mitterrand has also recorded his admiration of the leader of Free France, remembering that first Council of Ministers: "The conviction he had of being France, of expressing its truth, of incarnating a moment of eternal destiny . . . moved me more than it irritated me."[6] Nevertheless, it seems that resentment won out: the idea that de Gaulle, the most eminent Frenchman of his time, could hold him, François Mitterrand, in contempt was a canker in his mind and a source of unending bitterness.

The Stains of Scandal

Mitterrand's propensity to look the other way when his friends were attacked applied also to his attitude toward corruption—despite his frequent fulminations about "money, which corrupts . . . money, whose rot goes even into the consciences of men."[7] Mitterrand's cult of friendship was a virtue in a private individual—but less so in a public one.

Several scandals centered on Mitterrand's old and close friend Roger-Patrice Pelat, who benefited from his close relation to the president in a number of affairs (see Chapter 6). Jean Montaldo charged that over the years Pelat paid large sums to Mitterrand, first in the form of a dummy retainer as his lawyer (until 1981), with Mitterrand's younger son replacing him thereafter, and then to help President Mitterrand buy property for his mistress of many years and their illegitimate daughter.[8]

In 1988, Pelat was identified as one of several persons who had made profits of several million francs from insider trading when the nationalized French aluminum company Péchiney purchased the U.S. company Triangle-American Can. Pelat died of a heart attack in early 1989, shortly after being indicted. In a television interview aired just before Pelat's death, Mitterrand attempted to defend him, though admitting that he might have been at fault.

Mitterrand also persisted in showing high regard for the shady businessman Bernard Tapie, even after Tapie had repeatedly been indicted. Tapie was briefly a minister in Pierre Bérégovoy's government, then Mitterrand's instrument to derail Michel Rocard in the 1994 European elections. The journalist Laure Adler, whose book on Mitterrand's final year in office is largely favorable to the president, remarked: "As my investigation continued, Mitterrand increasingly appeared to me as a man fascinated by highway robbers, excited by the figures of those opposed to society, more interested in hooligans with a good gift of gab than in competent, well-bred *énarques*." She cited specifically Tapie and Pelat.[9]

Public scandals directly or indirectly affecting Mitterrand go back to the affair of Cooperation Minister Christian Nucci and his aide Yves Chalier in Mitterrand's first term. They were merely rapped on the knuckles for moving money not only into party funds but their own pockets as well. Mitterrand's lax practices grew ever more dangerous, as dubious ways for financing party activities increased in scale with political expenses, even as the volunteer militantism that had once reduced expenses steadily declined. A new breed of crusading magistrates (some of them by no means immune to the delights of public notice) then began to lay bare corruption designed to finance parties and sometimes politicians, with the PS as a particular target. A Socialist party that had lost its raison d'être as the party of social change also lost its moral title as the party of clean hands.

Mitterrand could not have prevented corruption from accompanying power; he could, however, have done far more to discourage it. Instead, he very conspicuously tolerated it. The overall record shows a picture of nepotism, aid to old friends at the public expense, and the encouragement of a general air of laxity. All that is particularly disturbing in a man who always took a high moral tone. Does it make him a hypocrite? If not, does the word have any meaning?

The revelations on the details of his early career and the financial scandals prompted the negative verdicts pronounced on Mitterrand toward the end of his second term. They would have counted for much less if the economy had been flourishing and the multiple malaises of unemployment, crime, and the immigrant question had not preyed on the French. These very real blots on Mitterrand's record will thus probably fade with time.

The President's Achievements

When both Mitterrand's friends and his foes are asked what they consider his principal achievements, they speak largely of actions taken in his first *septennat:* abolition of the death penalty, freeing the airwaves and television, decentralization, ending the indexation of salaries. Some add his extensive building program. Mitterrand cannot be given complete credit for the diminution of the Communist party, which was the victim of larger sociological forces (essentially the decline of the working class) and the stupidity of its own leaders, in almost equal measure. But by adopting the tactics he did, he undoubtedly hastened its decline. Unfortunately, the PCF's role as a protest party was taken by the National Front—which Mitterrand did something to promote.

By his victory in 1981 Mitterrand demonstrated that France could safely choose the alternation of different parties in power, against the old nightmare of "the Communists or us," and the two periods of cohabitation further demonstrated the flexibility of the constitution. When one remembers that the doomsayers in 1986 prophesied that cohabitation would not last six months, and that the Sixth Republic would therefore inevitably follow the Fifth, the progress made in normalization (in the best sense of the word) is remarkable. Despite his complex relation to de Gaulle the man and the historic figure, one of Mitterrand's lasting achievements was the confirmation of de Gaulle's Fifth Republic.

Mitterrand's greatest failure, one so great that, exceptionally, he himself admitted it, was his inability to reduce unemployment and his having to endure the distress of watching it almost double during his time in office. The hope of creating greater equality faded away, and if in the 1990s the elderly are better off, the poor and the disadvantaged are very much present. The French in the late 1990s remain far from even relative equality of earning power and opportunity.

Mitterrand's failure to give a moral example highlighted the low standards of the political class—not just the Socialists. His unwillingness to give an explanation for the retreat from promises he could not keep inflicted lasting damage on the Socialist party. If in post-Mitterrand France politicians are held in contempt—and they are—François Mitterrand bears a heavy load of responsibility for a condition combining moral disarray with despair that the democratic process can produce results—an attitude that is thoroughly subversive of democracy. The responsibility, certainly, is not his alone—more has been asked of government than government can produce, and Mitterrand's successor has followed him in promising more than he can perform. But Mitterrand's fourteen-year reign was in this respect a series of wasted opportunities and wrong turnings.

Mitterrand had been a great critic of the constitution of the Fifth Republic—until he found that it suited him very well. In what was perhaps his most arrogant phrase, he announced that its institutions had been dangerous before him and after him would be dangerous again. Yet his only real attempt to amend the constitution came in 1992, when it was clearly too late to get anything done.

Did Mitterrand therefore only mean first to gain power and then to exercise it? His attempt to institute a French version of socialism was a grand design, but it was undertaken at a time when the winds of free enterprise liberalism were rising and would blow ever harder. Only the methods of a Lenin could have resisted them, and Mitterrand (who lived to see Lenin's construct collapse like a cardboard box in a heavy rain) had neither the means nor the tastes of a Lenin. Many people have reproached him for giving up so easily on socialist ideas, later concluding that he was never at any time a genuine socialist. Mitterrand may or may not have believed deeply in the policies of 1981, but it is beside the point to attack him for possible insincerity. Mauroy, in longevity and sincerity more socialist than he, also advocated the policies that led away from the socialism of 1981, and Mitterrand accepted his advice. The only real question is whether the abandonment was necessary.

Mitterrand can be more justly criticized for having tiptoed away from these early policies, for never really apologizing or explaining why they went wrong. Instead, he turned his attention to his second grand design, the making of a Europe in which France hoped to be first among equals. He persevered in it until the end.

His failures in the economic and social spheres stemmed directly from the two great initiatives just described. The Socialist policies of 1981–1983 did not cut unemployment or lead to lasting equality of wages or conditions of life, and the medicine subsequently adopted to cure the conditions that Dr. Socialism had not healed badly shook the patient.

Mitterrand's European policies were based on the optimistic thinking found in the Cecchini report of 1986: that the Single Act would greatly increase prosperity. For a short time this wager (of which the Maastricht treaty was the logical extension) seemed a winning one, then the economy dropped again, in part because of German unification and high interest rates. In both situations, Mitterrand was caught up in the implications of policies he had desired and backed, with little room to change.

Little room is, however, not the same as no room. Here Mitterrand's constant disinclination to admit mistakes actually reduced his room for maneuver, even as he astonished the French with his capacity for it. Praised with faint damns for his Machiavellian ability, Mitterrand had occasionally seen the limits of such tactics, as when he told an interviewer: "Machiavelli, who spent much time in politics, failed in his own political action. Did he apply his principles wrong? Or did his principles betray him?"[10]

Having lost political momentum and popularity with the (unadmitted) failure of his first major program, Mitterrand had switched to his other major initiative, Europe. But successes in this area (such as the Fontainebleau summit of 1984) did not win him back much popularity, and as early as 1983 he knew the 1986 elections were unwinnable. His tactics after the disaster of the demonstrations over the Savary law in 1984 were all dedicated to losing these elections as well as possible—and having achieved this goal, he launched into cohabitation with the aim of winning the 1988 election. (It is unclear when Mitterrand finally decided to run again, but by late 1985 it was in any case clear that the PS had no other candidate who could win—except Rocard.)

In a very real sense, Mitterrand was preoccupied by political survival as his main objective in domestic politics for at least the period 1984–1988, perhaps earlier still. In foreign and defense policy he had a freer hand and played it—particularly in the continuing rapprochement with West Germany. Furthermore, despite the setbacks in his early economic policy, there were real achievements to be signaled to the electorate: decentralization, Auroux laws, and so on, as well as the need to advertise the fact that the Socialists (particularly after 1983) were showing that they understood how to govern the country. The campaign to play up the role of the entrepreneur and to reach out to the business community was an integral part of this effort to show a new face. Its success is indicated by the fact that the campaign of 1986 was fought by the conservatives almost entirely on the theme of the mistakes of 1981–1983.

Mitterrand wanted a second seven-year term in the Elysée, but aside from his continuing European policy, he had no major themes to present. Furthermore, he involved himself in the tactic of *ouverture* (perhaps assuming that the Socialists could not come close to winning back a parliamentary majority), which led him to choose Rocard as prime minister without any real commitment to Rocard's program. Ironically, he may have been led astray once again by the economic think tanks. In 1981 they had led him to suppose that the economy would boom; in 1987 they were predicting low growth for 1988–1989, and he seems to have thought that Rocard would show up badly and be easily disposed of. Instead, Rocard did well, Mitterrand lost control of the PS when he attempted to impose Fabius on it, and finally the Gulf war delayed his plans to fire Rocard. When he did, it was to commit the mistake of naming Cresson.

The president's reputation as Machiavelli the Magician served him well until late 1989, but thereafter, when rabbits stubbornly refused to come out of the hat, it became a handicap—the Wonder Man who could produce no wonders—as in the reproach that he had mishandled the response to German unification. Suddenly he could do nothing right. A failing economy provided less room for fresh social initiatives. The Maastricht referendum was a Pyrrhic victory; scandal was everywhere. Finally, it is unclear how much his illness cut down on his energies—still lavished on trips and ceremonial functions—and inhibited fresh thinking. The second term can thus be read as a series of reactions and defensive gestures—except with respect to Europe.

Mitterrand has been much reproached for his monarchical style—the 600 nominations to high posts that he arrogated to himself, the delight in staging impressive, if hollow, meetings like the 1982 G-7 Versailles summit, or various occasions collecting celebrated intellectuals French and foreign to reflect the glory of the monarch. His building program was the most ambitious since Napoleon III and was much criticized—for its ambitions, its aesthetic value, and its expense: 22 billion francs for the nine major projects begun under Mitterrand.

The most remarked on of these projects was the glass pyramid conceived by the American architect I. M. Pei for the courtyard of the Louvre. Mitterrand had seen Pei's new East Wing of the National Gallery of Art in a 1980 visit to Washington and was greatly impressed. Critics objected that a modern object was out of place in the Renaissance (and nineteenth-century mock-Renaissance) courtyard, and that the president had commissioned the work without any competition for the contract. In the event, the pyramid came to be much admired, and as it became the central entrance to a much enlarged Louvre, which took over the rue de Rivoli wing long hoarded by the Economics and Finance Ministry, it was seen to be functional as well as handsome. The ministry was banished upriver to a new classical-modern immensity on the quai de Bercy, which Mitterrand (no doubt wishing he had not agreed to competitive contracting for his other buildings) described as a giant toll booth. A functional but unimpressive new opera house on the place de la Bastille was supposed to be more accessible to the masses than Charles Garnier's Napoleon III pile on the place de l'Opéra; it has had both financial and artistic difficulties.

The most ambitious of Mitterrand's projects is the vast new national library, variously dubbed the TGB, for Très Grande Bibliothèque, or simply Bibliothèque de France. The bibliophile Mitterrand thought to leave a final great monument to himself by commissioning a much needed new facility to take the place of the overcrowded Bibliothèque Nationale. Critics immediately pointed out that its four towers shaped like open books would let in too much uncontrolled light for delicate holdings and necessitate very expensive air conditioning into the bargain. There are also worries about the nature of the ground, which is close to the Seine. Apparently these problems have been overcome—in part with wooden lattices on the tower windows. Mitterrand dedicated the still unfinished building in 1994, and it opened for initial use in 1997.

Mitterrand and the PS

François Mitterrand took a Socialist party that had been reduced to 5 percent in the presidential elections of 1969 and made it victorious in 1981 and 1988. But he did that at the expense of fostering an institutionalized factionalism that had served him to take over the party in 1971 and to recruit new members in a wide spectrum of opinion. Once he was elected president, the senior party cadres were needed in the government, and although they found successors, to say nothing of the bumper crop of PS deputies of 1981, the influence of the party and its parliamentary delegation on the president was never great. In part this result followed from the nature of de Gaulle's Fifth Republic, in which the general had never wanted parties to have much influence on him. In this as in so many areas Mitterrand agreed with de Gaulle.

In 1982 when Mitterrand amnestied the rebel generals who had attempted a putsch against de Gaulle in 1961, there was a near revolt against the amnesty law, led by the president's usually faithful follower Pierre Joxe, leader of the PS parliamentary group. The government found it necessary to use the guillotine clause, Article 49:3, to avoid a parliamentary debate and pass the law. In 1983 Socialist parliamentarians added amendments to the Savary law on education that made all compromise impossible and triggered the demonstrations that shook the government, forced Mitterrand to drop the law, and caused Pierre Mauroy's resignation. Otherwise, the Socialist parliamentarians had little influence on their president.

As noted above, Mitterrand could never bring himself to explain to his party why he had dropped the policies of 1981–1983. Socialists were thus left to themselves to reestablish a sense of their party's identity. The process was further complicated by the need to rally around the president in order to hold as many seats as possible in the 1986 legislative elections (and avoid a complete debacle like the one that did occur in 1993). In 1986, so severe a defeat might have forced Mitterrand to resign, wiping out everything he and they had done.

Mitterrand's reelection slogan "France United" suggested that he might welcome a coalition government with elements from the Right. If that was his plan, it collapsed when the CDS Centrists refused to meet his terms, but in the June 1988 parliamentary elections the PS made it abundantly clear that newcomers were not welcome, as party militants complained that they were asked to vote for non-PS candidates supported by the Elysée—and did not comply.

Even before the June election, Laurent Fabius had failed to win the post of PS first secretary. He was clearly Mitterrand's choice, but although the president had made no mystery of it, he did not issue orders. In 1990, still with Mitterrand's backing, Fabius tried and failed again to become first secretary, in the disastrous Rennes congress, which saw the Mitterrandist faction split irretrievably. In both cases Mitterrand had gone too far or not far enough. Despite his disclaimers, he had not really stood aside. Fabius could not win at Rennes, but Mitterrand had prevented the emergence of a new interfactional coalition between the Rocardians and the Jospinists. His dislike of Rocard deepened, and he never really forgave Jospin for opposing his will.

When Fabius did become first secretary in 1992, he won the post by an agreement with Rocard. But whether by design or not, Rocard found himself obliged to take over the party in April 1993, only to be evicted after Mitterrand again interfered by encouraging a Tapie ticket in the 1994 European elections, which resulted in a disastrously low score for the PS ticket led by Rocard.

A large number of Mitterrandists had not wanted to see Fabius heading the party to further his presidential ambition. Many in the party were also lukewarm toward a Rocard candidacy. Because neither Fabius nor Rocard was viable by late 1994, the PS entered the electoral cycle with only one possible candidate—Delors—who then bowed out. Mitterrand had no dauphins and did not seem to care.

Only 11 percent of voters had initially indicated a preference for Jospin as a possible president, but he was able to win 47 percent of the vote in the second round, which despite snide remarks by Mitterrand was not a bad score and suggested that the Socialist party would survive its president. If Mitterrand had never taken over the party, never led it to victory, the Socialists might have been much worse off by 1995. But it cannot be said that in 1995 the PS had much reason to be grateful to Mitterrand, and one of Jospin's strengths was that he had taken a certain distance from his former patron and declared "a right of inventory" on his policies and actions.

By waging an honorable and credible campaign, Jospin won the right to take over the PS from Emmanuelli. For the rest of 1995 and 1996, Jospin seemed to have slipped back into his old dull public persona, and the media gave the PS little credit for renewing itself, even while Chirac and Juppé made egregious blunders and saw their popularity slipping. When Chirac unexpectedly dissolved the National Assembly and called early elections for May–June 1997, the president calculated that he would win despite the inevitable loss of many seats in his overwhelmingly large majority. He hoped to be able to face the difficult questions of European Monetary Union with an election safely behind him. But the Right was more unpopular than Chirac knew, his majority was cut by more than 200 seats, and Chirac was obliged to name Jospin prime minister at the head of a Left coalition in which the PS, with 245 seats, must depend on votes from every other Left party in the assembly (notably the Communists) for a majority.

Jospin pointedly declined to name as ministers any of the most prominent old Mitterrandists (although he selected former top Mitterrand aides Hubert Védrine as his foreign minister and Elisabeth Guigou as justice minister). The new government was distinctly post-Mitterrand—but all of its members owed their careers to the former president.

Mitterrand and Foreign Policy

François Mitterrand devoted an enormous amount of time and energy to foreign policy. Even in his last year as president, when age, illness, and political rejection had sapped his powers, he continued to travel to foreign capitals. Certainly the first two years of his first term saw more concentration on domestic policy, but even in those years he delighted in using the authority bequeathed him by his predecessors to set France's course. The main thrusts of his policy are clear enough. In the early years, he did not greatly restrain the *tiers mondisme* of his foreign minister, Claude Cheysson, except to rein him in when he became too pro-Arab and in the Falklands affair, where Mitterrand sided immediately with Britain as a European partner. After 1983 his *tiers mondisme* was more rhetorical than real—he made the right noises on Africa but basically continued on the lines of the precedent set under de Gaulle: a pattern of paternalism and corruption.

Mitterrand began his presidency by taking a more reserved stand on relations with the Soviet Union than any of his predecessors in the Fifth Republic. There were obvious domestic reasons for this policy—the nominal ally of the Communist party needed to be seen taking his distance from the Soviets. But clearly Mitterrand had understood better than his predecessor Giscard that France's "special relationship" with the Soviets was devalued coinage. Once he had made his and his country's position clear on the deployment of missiles to counter Soviet SS-20s, however, Mitterrand was ready to resume good relations with the Soviets—and he had the good fortune to do this just as Mikhail Gorbachev was about to succeed to the Soviet leadership.

Mitterrand sought from the time he took office to improve relations with the United States and in general appeared more pro-American than his predecessors. He was, however, as convinced as any patented Gaullist that France must constantly beware of U.S. encroachment on French rights, French influence, and French culture. As a moderate deputy in the Fourth Republic, he had opposed the European Defense Community because he believed that it would subject France and the French army to the Pentagon, and this suspicion of the United States carried through his whole career. The statement that Mitterrand was more pro-American than his predecessors could be hedged by citing dozens of cases that show Mitterrand determined to uphold French prerogatives and block what he saw as American pretensions to hegemony.

Then was Mitterrand's foreign policy Gaullism by another name, as Stanley Hoffmann termed it in an essay first published in 1984?[11] Certainly it was *gaullien* in its institutional means; Mitterrand was every bit as jealous of his sole control of foreign and defense affairs as was the general.

Whether Mitterrand's suspicion of the United States was a *gaullien* heritage is a more difficult question. The powerful nationalism motivating Mitterrand and so many of the French is certainly antecedent to de Gaulle. However, de Gaulle turned up a flame that was burning very low after the defeat of 1940. Incarnating French nationalism, he inculcated a new pride of country in his contemporaries and the following generations. His institutions allowed new scope for the ambitions (and resentments) of French national sensibility. Once he had passed that way, much French nationalism had a *gaullien* tone. But essentially Mitterrand was acting as a Frenchman of his cultural background and political generation who would have behaved as he did had he never heard of de Gaulle.

The French Communists and Jean-Marie Le Pen are also nationalist. Where is the difference? It lies in intelligence and flexibility, common to de Gaulle and

Mitterrand. It is in the interest of extreme Left and Right to display absolute intransigence—but not in the interest of a statesman. Mitterrand's wariness toward the United States was rather like de Gaulle's, even though it did not bear the scars left by the general's personal and painful experience with American leaders. Like de Gaulle, Mitterrand was able to still his doubts when a larger end was at stake. Like de Gaulle backing the United States in the Cuban missile crisis, Mitterrand could go before the Bundestag to argue for German acceptance of new American missiles. He sided with U.S. policy in the Gulf crisis of 1990–1991—not without unilateral attempts to settle the matter (in part intended for domestic consumption). In lesser affairs Mitterrand often showed himself a difficult ally—in denying overflight permission to U.S. planes bound for a bombing mission over Tripoli, for example.

Mitterrand could see dangers but no advantages in changing the traditional French reserve on integration with NATO after the end of the Cold War. Here his political opponents—younger men still calling themselves Gaullists—were far more flexible, having understood that NATO had future uses and believing that in the new dispensation Mitterrand had overestimated the dangers. Nevertheless, the Chirac government was true to tradition in staying short of literal integration in NATO.

Mitterrand was much criticized by the press and his opposition for a number of gaffes. He could have avoided meeting Qadhafi in 1983 but ultimately did no harm. Receiving General Jaruzelski at the Elysée in 1985 won him criticism even by his own prime minister, but the judgment Poles made on Jaruzelski after 1989 tends to confirm Mitterrand's view that, despite everything, this Polish general was a patriot, not a Soviet puppet.

Mitterrand's management of the *Rainbow Warrior* affair was also severely criticized. Probably he did not know in advance precisely what his security services were planning. Once the plan failed in the most embarrassing and even criminal way, a president who had become fully complicit sought to last out the flap—and only succeeded in making matters worse.

The most severe criticism of Mitterrand's conduct of foreign affairs came in his second term, when he was accused of dragging his feet on German unification, of conducting a retrograde policy that embarrassed France before its German ally and the world. By 1989, Mitterrand had no friends in the press, and journalists seized on every hesitation and stumble to make points. On the one hand, Mitterrand could have shown more diplomatic dexterity in welcoming a unification that rapidly announced itself as inevitable. On the other, his motives for hesitation were in no way discreditable: in the first instance, determination to pin down Helmut Kohl on the calendar for further progress on European monetary integration, in the second, a very real fear that if not properly managed unification would open the door to all sorts of new territorial demands. In any case, Mitterrand did not compromise his good relations with Kohl, which remained both intact and fruitful through the rest of his term in office.

Mitterrand also provoked much derision when he seemed to be ready to admit the success of the coup against Gorbachev. He handled the matter clumsily—but again no harm was done—except to the president's reputation for sagacity.

Perhaps the most serious mistake made by Mitterrand went largely unnoticed by the press. There were excellent arguments—pressed especially by Elisabeth Guigou (see Chapter 9)—for submitting the Maastricht treaty to ratification by a popular referendum. There were also political arguments of a less excellent nature. But once the referendum was decided upon, Mitterrand seems to have been overconfident. He did not really prepare public opinion and, by setting an early date for the vote, greatly complicated the task. The referendum was nearly lost, and its narrow margin in one of the key countries of the new European Union added to the new Europessimism, which has since reigned.[12]

European integration was the most important aspect of Mitterrand's foreign policy from 1984 on. He did not discover Europe as an alternative to socialism after 1983—his previous commitment to expanding European cooperation is on the record. Nevertheless, European policy gave him new scope where it was denied in domestic policy, and he was not slow to seize the opportunity. The Single European Act was more Jacques Delors's work than Mitterrand's, but Mitterrand backed Delors and approved of most of the emphases of the Single Act (except the federalist implications).

The continuation of the Single Act was the Maastricht treaty—and in its drafting Mitterrand wanted a European monetary union in which France would have more freedom than in a Bundesbank-dominated EMS. He gave lip service to political Europe but successfully opposed federalist ideas favored by Delors and Kohl in order to keep the main political power of the new European Union firmly in the control of the nation-state. He feared that an onward rush toward enlargement would endanger the smaller, better organized Europe of his earlier plans, in which France would play a major role.

Mitterrand's immediate legacy had been Chirac's commitment to Europe, although the costs of strict adherence to the Maastricht convergence criteria for monetary union have depressed investment and encouraged further unemployment. By questioning the policies of that legacy, Mitterrand's Socialist heirs raised further doubts about the future of the European Union. Will it develop into a confederal or even quasi-federal entity, probably along lines unknown to political scientists, or turn into a pathetic, invertebrate monster, all pretense and no power?

There was no Mitterrandism to be handed down after the president left the stage, neither in domestic or foreign affairs. The closest approximation would be a determination to see France's future fixed in a French role in a larger, more united Europe. For many French nationalists, the use of the power of the French state to build a European superstate that could render the state in France obsolete is the ultimate abomination. Mitterrand's own intense nationalism convinced him that France's destiny lay in a European integration that would strengthen France—and that his country had no choice but to work closely with its neighbors, especially Germany. The role in a new Europe Mitterrand designed for his country before 1989 was greater than German unification will allow, but after unification Helmut Kohl's Germany still needs France as a partner. With the second largest European economy, a relatively large population, and a high degree of state organization, France can play a major role in even a much larger European Union.

The impress of Charles de Gaulle on modern France can be seen everywhere—not least in the institutions he left for his successors. Can one say today what Mitterrand's impress was—for good or evil—or was his merely a presidency of unusual duration, without major importance? Here the historian writing so soon after the event must be extremely cautious. Since 1788, only seven or eight American presidents have stood out as major figures. In attempting some such comparison for France, one cannot reasonably include the presidents of the Third and Fourth Republics. In the Fifth Republic de Gaulle stands alone. And Mitterrand?

Unalloyed admiration of Mitterrand is very difficult, and only a few Socialists who wish to remain loyal to their past hopes and beliefs maintain such admiration. The historian who is attempting to be evenhanded must take account of Mitterrand's multiple failings but also remember the large number of major figures who had major flaws. Was Mitterrand then a major figure? Longevity in office certainly does not suffice. The relatively uncontested actions—abrogation of the death penalty, decentralizations—are important enough to give their initiator a considerable place in the history of his country, but in themselves are not of the very highest importance. Only carrying out, or at least initiating some major policy could meet this description. The answer to the question of Mitterrand's historical importance lies in one great piece of unfinished business he initiated—the integration of France into the European Union—and the ultimate success (or failure) of the union itself.

By placing social concerns on at least as high a priority level as economic and monetary union (demonstratively turning away from the policies of Bérégovoy, Balladur, and Juppé), the Jospin government raised new problems with Germany and multiplied the already pressing questions about the future development of the EU. François Mitterrand's heirs have the task of determining the fate of the hopes for that European Union, which Mitterrand left to them. The denouement of their efforts may determine Mitterrand's position in history.

Notes

Chapter 1

1. Pierre Favier and Michel Martin-Roland, *La Décennie Mitterrand*, Vol. 1: *Les Ruptures, 1981–1984*, paperback ed. (Paris: Seuil, 1991), 66. The authors, Agence France Press (AFP) journalists assigned to the Elysée for fourteen years, have produced one of the most important and authoritative works on the Mitterrand presidency, in three volumes with a fourth still to come. Given free access to the Elysée archives, they have cited and often reproduced a large numbers of documents. Where they have indicated a document as their source, I have indicated this in my endnotes.

2. For the SFIO, see Alain Bergounioux and Gérard Grunberg, *Le Long Remords du pouvoir: Le Parti socialiste français 1905–1992* (Paris: Fayard, 1992); Yves Roucaute, *Le Parti socialiste* (Paris: Huisman, 1983); Jacques Kergoat, *Le Parti socialiste* (Paris: Sycomore, 1983); Neill Nugent and David Lowe, *The Left in France* (New York: St. Martin's Press, 1982); R. W. Johnson, *The Long March of the French Left* (New York: St. Martin's Press, 1981); and Jean Touchard, *La Gauche en France depuis 1900* (Paris: Seuil, 1977).

3. On the Mitterrand family, see Pierre Péan, *Une Jeunesse française: François Mitterrand 1934–1947* (Paris: Fayard, 1994), 76.

4. Franz-Olivier Giesbert, *François Mitterrand ou la tentation de l'histoire* (Paris: Seuil, 1977), 21–22, quoting François Mitterrand, *Ma part de vérité* (Paris: Fayard, 1969).

5. See Péan, *Une Jeunesse française;* and Emmanuel Faux, Thomas Legrand, and Gilles Perez, *La Main droite de Dieu: Enquête sur François Mitterrand et l'extreme droite* (Paris: Seuil, 1994).

6. Mitterrand, *Ma part de verité*, 25.

7. Giesbert, *Mitterrand ou la tentation*, 29, 43.

8. De Gaulle referred to Mitterrand along with Gaston Defferre and several other distinguished resisters in *War Memoirs*, Vol. 2, *L'Unité, 1942–1944*, trans. Richard Howard (New York: Simon and Schuster, 1959), 190.

9. Péan, *Une Jeunesse française*, 511–514.

10. Speaking of his POW camp experience, Mitterrand wrote: "At the moment when, around me, faith and religious practice took new root in [their] souls, mine moved away." François Mitterrand, *Mémoires interrompus* (Paris: Odile Jacob, 1996), 18.

11. Franz-Olivier Giesbert, *François Mitterrand, une vie* (Paris: Seuil, 1996), 20.

12. Ibid., 151–158.

13. Ibid., 174.

14. Quoted in Catherine Nay, *Le Noir et le rouge* (Paris: Grasset, 1984), 281.

15. Cf. Albert du Roy and Robert Schneider, *Le Roman de la rose* (Paris: Seuil, 1982), 31.

16. Cf. Philippe Buton, "Les Effectifs du p.c.f. 1920–1984," *Communisme* 7 (1985), 8.

17. Cf. Ronald Tiersky, *French Communism 1920–1972* (New York: Columbia University Press, 1974), 350.

18. Georges Lavau, "The PCF, the State, and the Revolution," in *Communism in Italy and France*, ed. Donald L. M. Blackmer and Sidney Tarrow (Princeton: Princeton University Press, 1975), 95.

19. For Marchais's 1972 speech, see Etienne Fajon, *L'Union est un combat* (Paris: Editions Sociales, 1975), 109–110.

20. Mitterrand, *Ma part de vérité*, 78–79, 71–72.

21. Quoted in Nay, *Le Noir et le rouge*, 314.

22. Ibid., 342.

23. Gilles Martinet, *Cassandra et les tueurs* (Paris: Grasset, 1996), 171–172.

24. See Elie Cohen, "L'Etat socialiste en industrie: Volontarisme politique et changement socio-économique," in *Les Elites socialistes au pouvoir: Les Dirigeants socialistes face à l'Etat 1981–1985*, ed. Pierre Birnbaum (Paris: Presses Universitaires de France, 1985), 223.

25. *Le Nouvel Observateur*, June 21, 1980.

26. Author's interview with Michel Rocard, May 12, 1996.

27. Robert Schneider, *Michel Rocard* (Paris: Stock, 1987), 272.

Chapter 2

1. Cf. Monique Dagnaud and Dominique Mehl, *L'Elite rose* (Paris: Ramsay, 1982), and *Who's Who in France*, 18th ed. (Paris: Laffitte, 1981).

2. Thierry Pfister, *La Vie quotidienne à Matignon au temps de l'Union de la Gauche* (Paris: Hachette, 1985), 221.

3. Quoted in *ADA (Association pour débattre autrement) Bilan de la France* (Paris: Editions de la Table Ronde, 1986), 61.

4. Quoted in *Le Nouvel Observateur*, September 26, 1981.

5. News conference of September 24, 1981, ibid.

6. Pfister, *La Vie quotidienne*, 170–171.

7. The actual figures for France were minus 0.5 percent for GNP, 0.4 percent for exports. Cf. Alain Fonteneau and Pierre-Alain Muet, *La Gauche face à la crise* (Paris: Presses de la Fondation Nationale des Sciences Politiques, 1985), 95–96.

8. Author's interview with Henry Nau, August 1987.

9. Fonteneau and Muet, *La Gauche*, 97–98.

10. Ibid., 97–107.

11. Cf. Peter Hall, *Governing the Economy* (New York: Oxford University Press, 1986), 199.

12. Philippe Bauchard, *La Guerre des deux roses* (Paris: Grasset, 1986), 86.

13. Fonteneau and Muet, *La Gauche*, 127.

14. Author's interview with Pascal Lamy, Mauroy and Delors aide, October 1985.

15. Catherine Nay, *Le Noir et le rouge*, 9.

16. Christian Jelen and Thierry Wolton, *Le Petit Guide de la farce tranquille* (Paris: Albin Michel, 1982), passim.

17. For quotes from the Valence congress, see *Le Monde*, October 25–26 and October 27, 1981. For the continuing echo, see Jean-Marie Colombani, "Faire oublier Valence," *Le Monde*, July 4, 1984.

18. Cf. Alain and Marie-Thérèse Lancelot, *Annuaire de la France politique, Mai 1981–Mai 1983* (Paris: Presses de la Fondation Nationale des Sciences Politiques, 1983), 33–34, 81.

19. Cf. Alain and Marie Thérèse Lancelot, "The Evolution of the French Electorate, 1981–1986," in *The Mitterrand Experiment*, ed. George Ross, Stanley Hoffmann, and Sylvia Malzacher (New York: Oxford University Press, 1987); and Jerôme Jaffré, "De Valéry Giscard d'Estaing à François Mitterrand: France de gauche, vote à gauche," *Pouvoirs* 20 (1982).

20. Pfister, *La Vie quotidienne*, 250–255.

21. Cf. *Quid 1987* (Paris: Laffont, 1986), 696c.

22. Pfister, *La Vie quotidienne*, 255.

23. SOFRES poll in *Le Nouvel Observateur*, August 28, 1982.

24. *Le Nouvel Observateur*, July 24, 1982.

25. Fonteneau and Muet, *La Gauche*, 158.

26. Pierre Mauroy, *À Gauche* (Paris: Albin Michel, 1985), 109.

27. Favier and Martin-Roland, *La Décennie*, 1:514–517.

28. Serge July, *Les Années Mitterrand: Histoire baroque d'une normalisation inachevée* (Paris: Grasset, 1986), 85.

29. Ibid.

30. Cf. Giesbert, *Mitterrand, une vie*, 416; Favier and Martin-Roland *La Décennie*, 1:563–568, 591.

31. Author's interview with Henri Guillaume, May 1985.

32. Favier and Martin-Roland, *La Décennie*, 1:554–555.

33. Bauchard, *La Guerre des deux roses*, 141–150; author's interview with Delors aide Pascal Lamy, March 1986.

34. July, *Les Années Mitterrand*, 96, 99, 107–108.

35. Ibid., 111; Mitterrand's remark that "socialisme à la française" was not his Bible was made at a speech in Figeac on September 27, 1982; quoted here from *Le Nouvel Observateur*, October 2–8, 1982, 21.

36. Quoted in Bauchard, *La Guerre des deux roses*, 162.

37. Raymond Aron, *Mémoires* (Paris: Julliard, 1983), 328.

38. Bergounioux and Grunberg, *Le Long Remords*, 416.

39. Ibid., 428–429.

40. Ibid., 428–429.

41. *Le Programme commun de gouvernement de la gauche, propositions socialistes pour l'actualisation* (Paris: Flammarion, 1978), 58.

42. Jean-Marie Colombani, *Portrait du Président* (Paris: Gallimard, 1985), 82.

43. See note 35, this chapter.

44. On Mitterrand's behavior in early summer 1983, see Bauchard, *La Guerre des deux roses*, 167–176.

45. Cf. Pfister, *La Vie quotidienne*, 300, where the author is clearly expressing Mauroy's ideas.

46. Cf. Bauchard, *La Guerre des deux roses*, 165, quoting a private interview with Mitterrand.

47. Favier and Martin-Roland, *La Décennie*, 1:588–589, citing interviews with Communist leaders conducted in 1989.

48. On Rousselot and the negotiations to buy *France-Soir*, see Favier and Martin-Roland, *La Décennie*, 1:252–253; Jean-Michel Quatrepoint, *Histoire secrète des dossiers noirs de la gauche* (Paris: Alain Moreau, 1986), 23; and Pfister, *La Vie quotidienne*, 133. My information on the *Dauphiné Libéré* affair comes from a February 1986 interview with Grenoble journalist Pierre Frappat.

49. See Alain Savary, *En toute liberté* (Paris: Hachette, 1985), 122, 126.

50. Ibid., 15–17.

51. Cf. the discussion on the pedagogical debate and the Savary law in general by Antoine Prost, "The Educational Maelstrom," in *The Mitterrand Experiment*, ed. Ross, Hoffmann, and Malzacher.

52. *Le Point*, May 21, 1984, quoted in ibid., 233.

53. The text of the bill may be found in Savary, *En toute liberté*, 220ff.; the amendments appear on p. 163.

54. Michel Favier and Michel Martin-Roland, *La Décennie Mitterrand*, Vol. 2: *Les Epreuves 1984–1988*, paperback ed. (Paris: Seuil, 1991), 143.

55. Cf. the detailed account in *Le Monde*, June 26, 1984.

56. Cf. July, *Les Années Mitterrand*, 173.

57. Favier and Martin-Roland, *La Décennie*, 2:178–180.

58. Ibid., 2:170.

59. Pfister, *La Vie quotidienne*, 285–287, 343; and for the details of Mitterrand's dealings with Mauroy July 11–17, 336–354.

60. Cf. Favier and Martin-Roland, *La Décennie*, 2:184–187.

61. Ibid., 2:223.

Chapter 3

1. *Le Monde*, July 4, 1984.

2. See the extensive biographical article on Fabius in *Le Monde*, October 26, 1985, and an interview in which he provided some biographical information, "Le Socialisme et la dynamique de la démocratie, entretien avec Laurent Fabius," *Le Débat* 49, March-April 1988.

3. *Le Monde*, July 19, 1984.

4. Cf. "Le Programme Fabius," *Regards sur l'actualité*, no. 104 (September 1984), 11–14, summarizing Fabius's National Assembly speech of July 24, 1984; also see *Journal officiel*, no. 78 (July 25, 1984) for the National Assembly discussion.

5. Thierry Pfister, *La Vie quotidienne*, 358.

6. Jacques Attali, *La Nouvelle Economie française* (Paris: Flammarion, 1978), 5.

7. Alain Gélédan, ed., *Le Bilan économique des années Mitterrand, 1981–1994* (Paris: Le Monde–Editions, 1994), 54–55.

8. Cited in John Gaffney, *The French Left and the Fifth Republic, The Discourses of Communism and Socialism in Contemporary France* (New York: St. Martin's Press, 1989), 189. Gaffney argues (pp. 184ff.) that modernization was made to fit into a kind of socialist millenarianism, in which socialism was linked with modernization.

9. *Le Monde: Dossiers et Documents*, no. 118 (January 1985).

10. Christian Stoffaës, *La Politique industrielle* (Paris: Le Cours de Droit, 1984), 289.

11. Ibid., 177ff.

12. See the detailed analysis of deindexation in Fonteneau and Muet, *La Gauche*, chap. 5.

13. SOFRES, *L'Etat de l'opinion publique—clés pour 1987* (Paris: Editions du Seuil, 1987), 136–137; Olivier Duhamel and Jerôme Jaffré, "Les Douze Leçons de 1986," ibid., 236.

14. Marie-Noëlle Lienemann and Patrice Finel, "Pour un libéralisme de gauche," *Nouvelle revue socialiste*, September-October 1984, 17–18; Jean-Louis Andréani, "Peut-on être socialiste aujourd'hui?" *Le Monde*, December 6, 1984.

15. *Libération*, May 10, 1984.

16. *Le Monde*, December 22, 1984.

17. See the very detailed account of the New Caledonian imbroglio in Favier and Martin-Roland, *La Décennie*, 2:338–366.

18. See the accounts of the *Rainbow Warrior* affair in *Le Monde, Dossiers et Documents*, "L'Histoire au jour le jour 1974–1985," 214–215, and *Le Monde*, March 19, 1988. The latter reconfirms the military obsession with security. The best-informed account is Favier and Martin-Roland, *La Décennie*, 2:405–440. The authors interviewed thirty-nine persons at the highest level knowledgeable on the affair.

19. Favier and Martin-Roland, *La Décennie*, 2:433.

20. Quoted in J. W. Friend, "A Rose in Any Other Fist Would Smell as Sweet," *French Politics and Society* 4 (December 1985). For a detailed account of the affair, see Jacques Derogy and Jean-Marie Pontaut, *Enquête sur trois secrets d'Etat* (Paris: Laffont, 1986); and Stephen E. Bornstein, "An End to French Exceptionalism? The Lessons of the Greenpeace Affair," *French Politics and Society* 5 (1987). For the Tricot report, see *Le Monde*, August 28, 1985.

21. Favier and Martin-Roland, *La Décennie*, 2:404.

22. Cf. Gérard LeGall, "Sondages, l'état de l'opinion," *Revue politique et parlementaire*, no. 921: 7 (January-February 1986).

23. Quoted in *Le Figaro*, October 14, 1985. Also see Friend, "A Rose in Any Other Fist," and Eric Cahm, "From Greenpeace to Cohabitation," in *Contemporary France, a Review of Interdisciplinary Studies*, ed. Jolyon Howorth and George Ross (London: Frances Pinter, 1987), 9–11.

Chapter 4

1. However, see Denis Jeambar, *Le P.C. dans la maison* (Paris: Calmann-Lévy, 1984), for a rather alarmist view of the question.

2. Pfister, *La Vie quotidienne*, 155–157.

3. Favier and Martin-Roland, *La Décennie*, 2:200–202.

4. See Stéphane Courtois, "Le Succès en trompe-l'oeil du candidat communiste," in *Le Vote de crise: L'Election présidentielle de 1995*, ed. Pascal Perrineau and Colette Ysmal (Paris: Département d'Etudes du *Figaro* et Presses de la Fondation Nationale des Sciences Politiques, 1995), 184.

5. On the PCF, see David S. Bell and Byron Criddle, *The French Communist Party in the Fifth Republic* (Oxford: Clarendon Press, 1994); George Ross, "Party Decline and Changing Party Systems: France and the French Communist Party," *Comparative Politics* 25, no. 1 (1992); and Courtois, "Le Succès en trompe-l'oeil," and Stéphane Courtois, "Le Déclin accentué du Parti Communiste français," in *Le Vote sanction: Les Elections législatives des 21 et 28 mars 1993*, ed. Philippe Habert, Pascal Perrineau, and Colette Ysmal (Paris: Département d'Etudes du *Figaro* et Presses de la Fondation Nationale des Sciences Politiques, 1993).

6. See Favier and Martin-Roland, *La Décennie*, 1:199.

7. Cf. the discussion of statistics on immigration in "Les Immigrés en France," *Le Monde, Dossiers et Documents*, no. 115 (October 1984).

8. Louis Pauwels, "Les Sarrasins en Corrèze," *Figaro Magazine*, May 18, 1985.

9. Perrineau and Ysmal, eds., *Le Vote de crise*, 247.

10. These statistics are drawn from *Quid 1987*, 698, and from "L'Insecurité," *Le Monde, Dossiers et Documents*, no. 122 (May 1985).

11. SOFRES,— *Clés pour 1987*, 222.

12. *Le Monde*, June 21, 1983.

13. "La population étrangère en France par nationalité," *Problèmes économiques*, no. 2,301 (November 25, 1992), using the 1990 census figures.

14. Cf. Michèle Tribalat, *Faire France, une enquête sur les immigrés et leurs enfants* (Paris: La Découverte, 1995), 21.

15. Cf. Jonathan Marcus, *The National Front and French Politics: The Resistible Rise of Jean-Marie Le Pen* (New York: New York University Press, 1995), 77–78.

16. Michèle Tribalat reports that 41 percent of Algerian men and 44 percent of Algerian women entering France as adults were illiterate, whereas 31 percent of Moroccan men and 47 percent of Moroccan women had no schooling. *Faire France*, 23.

17. Cf. ibid., 23–24. Forty-seven percent of Moroccan women and 31 percent of Moroccan men who arrived in France after the age of fifteen had never been to school; the figures for Algerians were 44 and 41 percent respectively.

18. Faux, Legrand, and Perez, *La Main droite de Dieu*, 20–25; and Giesbert, *Mitterrand, une vie*, 512.

19. Author's interview with Mitterrand adviser Maurice Benassayag, May 9, 1996.

20. See Marcus, *The National Front and French Politics*, 143–146.

21. Horizon 2000 Group, Emmanuel Le Roy Ladurie presiding, *Entrer dans le XXIè siècle: Essai sur l'avenir de l'identité française* (Paris: La Découverte, 1990), report, 148.

22. Dominique Schnapper, *La France de l'intégration, sociologie de la nation en 1990* (Paris: Gallimard, 1991), 115–116.

23. Gérard Legall, "La Tentation du populisme," in SOFRES, *L'Etat de l'opinion 1996*, 202.

24. Statistics in the two preceding paragraphs are drawn from Adil Jazouli, "Les Jeunes Beurs dans la société française," in SOFRES, *L'Etat de l'opinion 1995* (Paris: Seuil, 1995), 171–175.

25. Jacques Chirac, *La Lueur de l'espérance* (Paris: La Table Ronde, 1978), quoted in Franz-Olivier Giesbert, *Jacques Chirac* (Paris: Seuil, 1987), 306–307.

26. Jean Boissonat interview with Raymond Barre, *L'Expansion*, September 1978.

27. Giesbert, *Jacques Chirac*, 335.

28. René Rémond, *Les Droites en France* (Paris: Aubier Montaigne, 1982), 317.

29. Pierre Bréchon, Jacques Derville, and Patrick Lecomte, "L'Univers idéoloqique des cadres RPR," *Revue française de science politique* 37 (1987), 677–678.

30. Suzanne Berger, "Liberalism Reborn," in *Contemporary France, 1987*, ed. Howorth and Ross.

31. Friedrich Hayek, *Scientisme et sciences sociales*, trans. Raymond Barre (Paris: Plon, 1953).

32. Bréchon, Derville, and Lecomte, *L'Univers idéologique*, 690–694.

33. Cf. Favier and Martin-Roland, *La Décennie*, 2:368–369. The *Monde* article appeared on September 16, 1983.

Chapter 5

1. Duhamel, Dupoirier, and Jaffré, eds., SOFRES,—*Clés pour 1987*, 136.

2. Ibid., 52.

3. Giesbert, *Jacques Chirac*, (358.

4. Ibid., 361.

5. See Olivier Duhamel and Jerôme Jaffré, "La Découverte de la cohabitation," in SOFRES, *Clés pour 1987*, 51; and Jean-Louis Quermonne, "La Présidence de la République et le système des partis," *Pouvoirs* 41 (1987), 99–104.

6. For one such alarmist version, written immediately after the elections, see the article by Denis Jeambar, "La France sera-t-elle gouvernable?" *Le Point,* March 17, 1986.

7. Favier and Martin-Roland, *La Décennie,* 2:461–463.

8. RPR/UDF pamphlet, *Plateforme pour gouverner ensemble,* January 16, 1986.

9. Cf. SOFRES, *Clés pour 1987,* for polls taken in January and March 1986, 107 and 111.

10. Cf. Alain Lancelot, "Le Brise-lame: Les Elections du 16 mars 1986," *Projet* 199 (May-June 1986); and Georges Lavau, "The Incomplete Victory of the Right," in *Contemporary France,* ed. Howorth and Ross.

11. Cf. Favier and Martin-Roland, *La Décennie,* 2:459–472. The Mitterrand quote appears on p. 472.

12. The account of Chirac's career draws largely on Giesbert, *Jacques Chirac,* much the best book on the RPR leader.

13. Cf. Stanley Hoffmann, "The Odd Couple," *New York Review of Books,* September 25, 1986.

14. Favier and Martin-Roland, *La Décennie,* 2:580–581.

15. Ibid., 2:610–611, and Jean-Marie Colombani and Jean-Yves Lhomeau, *Le Mariage Blanc* (Paris: Grasset, 1986), 141–145; also Giesbert, *Jacques Chirac,* 403–404.

16. Cf. Thierry Pfister, *Dans les coulisses du pouvoir* (Paris: Albin Michel, 1986), 236–240; Favier and Martin-Roland, *La Décennie,* 2:660–661.

17. Giesbert, *Mitterrand, une vie,* 505.

18. Cf. "Privatisations: Un premier bilan," *Problèmes économiques,* no. 2037 (August 26, 1987); and *Le Monde* supplement *Affaires,* May 28, 1988.

19. Author's interview with Pierre Bérégovoy, October 1987; *Le Nouvel Observateur,* April 8–14, 1988.

20. *Le Monde,* August 21, 1986.

21. SOFRES, *L'Etat de l'opinion—clés pour 1988* (Paris: Seuil, 1988).

22. Cf. Giesbert, *Jacques Chirac,* 419–428; *Le Point,* December 1 and December 8, 1986.

23. SOFRES, *Clés pour 1988,* 145.

24. Ibid., 161–163.

25. SOFRES poll of March 20–26, 1987, in ibid., 158.

26. Ibid., 122.

27. "La Popularité des présidents," chart of IFOP results in *Pouvoirs* 41 (1987), 162.

28. Cf. Friend, "A Rose in Any Other Fist."

29. SOFRES, *Clés pour 1987,* 232.

30. Cf. J. W. Friend, "Counting Down to '88: The PS Congress," *French Politics and Society* 5, no. 3 (June 1987).

31. SOFRES poll in *Le Monde,* March 24, 1988. Sixty percent of respondents admired Mitterrand's adaptability.

32. Cf. Favier and Martin-Roland, *La Décennie,* 2:436–437.

33. On indications of last-minute voter sentiment and on exit polling, see Roland Cayrol, "Ce qui a changé dans le paysage politique," *Le Journal des élections,* no. 2 (May 1988), 9–10.

Chapter 6

1. "Lettre à tous les Français," *Le Monde,* April 8–9, 1988.

2. Giesbert, *Mitterrand, une vie,* 552.

3. Martinet, *Cassandre et les tueurs*, 152.

4. Giesbert, *Mitterrand, une vie*, 535–536.

5. Ibid., 538. Pierre Favier and Michel Martin-Roland, *La Décennie Mitterrand*, Vol. 3: *Les Défis (1988–1991)* (Paris: Seuil, 1996), 16–17. Note that Mitterrand used the phrase "lever l'hypothèque Rocard" with at least four of his collaborators. I have somewhat inadequately translated this phrase as "get over the Rocard problem."

6. Favier and Martin-Roland, *La Décennie*, 2:935.

7. Jean-Paul Huchon, *Jours tranquilles à Matignon* (Paris: Grasset, 1993), 182; Favier and Martin-Roland, *La Décennie*, 2:939; author's interview with Rocard aide Guy Carcassonne, May 31, 1995.

8. Favier and Martin-Roland, *La Décennie*, 2:939.

9. Favier and Martin-Roland, *La Décennie*, 3:22.

10. Ibid., 3:32–35; *Le Nouvel Observateur*, May 20–26, 1988.

11. Louis Harris postelectoral poll conducted for *Le Figaro*, dated June 11, 1988. Its results indicated that a majority in all age groups opposed the idea of an RPR/UDF majority—as did a majority in all occupational groups except farmers and artisans. A majority of all age groups and in all occupational groups except workers did not want the PS to have a majority.

12. *Le Monde*, July 1, 1988.

13. *Propositions pour la France*, supplement to *PS Info*, no. 351 (February 13, 1988), 2–3.

14. Cf. Bergounioux and Grunberg, *Le Long Remords*, 349–351.

15. Pascal Perrineau, "Les Cadres du parti socialiste," in SOFRES, *L'Etat de l'opinion 1991* (Paris: Seuil, 1991), 229, 232.

16. Robert Schneider, *Les Dernières Années* (Paris: Seuil, 1994), 58, quotes a conversation Mitterrand had with a leading businessman, indicating that Mitterrand was thinking of fifteen months. Favier and Martin-Roland in *La Décennie*, 3:17, cite presidential confidant Michel Charasse quoting Mitterrand: "That'll hardly last more than six months," although other PS leaders spoke in terms of a longer time.

17. Author's interview with Michel Rocard, May 13, 1996; Anne Sinclair interview with Rocard, February 21, 1993, on the television program *7 sur 7*.

18. Robert Schneider, *La Haine tranquille* (Paris: Seuil, 1992), 108–109.

19. Huchon, *Jours tranquilles*, 35–38, 40, 58.

20. See Pierre Rosanvallon, *La Nouvelle Question sociale: Repenser l'Etat-providence* (Paris: Seuil, 1995), 166–170; also *Le Monde*, March 19, 1993, "1988–1993: Regards sur la législature," section entitled "Inégalités."

21. Author's interview with Michel Rocard, May 13, 1996.

22. Cf. Gélédan, ed. *Le Bilan économique*, 136–137; *Le Monde*, October 27, 1990.

23. See Favier and Martin-Roland, *La Décennie*, 3:141–146. I have also drawn on my interviews with Guy Carcassonne, May 31, 1995, and May 9, 1996. Article 49:3 permits the government to pass a bill without debate unless the assembly passes a no-confidence vote on it. Carcassonne's statistics showed that Mauroy, with a big majority, used Article 49:3 five times in three years, Fabius twice, and Chirac seven times in two years.

24. Elisabeth Dupoirier, "Popularités 1988–1993," in SOFRES, *L'Etat de l'opinion 1996*, 56.

25. Author's interview with Gilles Martinet, October 10, 1994.

26. Michel Rocard, *Un Pays comme le nôtre* (Paris: Seuil, 1989), 140–141, quoted in Bergounioux and Grunberg, *Le Long Remords*, 456.

27. Bergounioux and Grunberg, *Le Long Remords*, 458–459.

28. Schneider, *La Haine*, 169–170.

29. On this see Chris Howell, "The Fetichism of Small Differences: French Socialism Enters the Nineties," *French Politics and Society* 9, no. 1 (winter 1991), 27–29.

30. Schneider, *La Haine*, 176, 170.

31. Ibid., 202.

32. I have drawn for this description of the struggles leading to the Rennes congress and the congress itself on my articles in *French Politics and Society:* "The PS Faces the 1990s," vol. 8, no. 1 (winter 1990), and "Report from Rennes," vol. 8, no. 2 (spring 1990), as well as on Giesbert, *Mitterrand, une vie*, 594–599; Huchon, *Jours tranquilles*, 211, 216.

33. Huchon, *Jours tranquilles*, 10.

34. Cf. Howell, "The Fetichism of Small Differences," 31–32.

35. Telephone interview of May 22, 1996, with Cresson biographer Elisabeth Schemla. Cresson took notes on these conversations with the president, which she showed to Schemla. Also see Elisabeth Schemla, *Edith Cresson: La Femme piégée* (Paris: Flammarion, 1993).

36. SOFRES, *L'Etat de l'opinion 1993*, 232.

37. SOFRES, *L'Etat de l'opinion 1992*, 116.

38. *Le Monde*, February 14, 1989.

39. Yves-Marie Doublet, "L'Argent de l'élection présidentielle," *Pouvoirs* 70, special issue on election finances, 1994, 43n.

40. Favier and Martin-Roland, *La Décennie*, 3:137.

41. Guy Carcassonne, "Du non-droit au droit," *Pouvoirs* 70 (1994), 14.

42. Author's interview with Robert Badinter, June 12, 1995.

43. Author's interview with Guy Carcassonne, June 7, 1995.

44. The details given here are largely drawn from the very detailed and extremely well-informed account in Favier and Martin-Roland, *La Décennie*, 3:307–325. See also Antoine Gaudino, *L'Enquête impossible* (Paris: Albin Michel, 1990).

45. Cf. Favier and Martin-Roland, *La Décennie*, 3:325–327.

46. Ibid., 328.

47. "100 élus dans le collimateur," *Le Point*, June 10, 1995.

48. *L'Express*, November 29, 1990.

49. Michel Massenet, *La transmission administrative du SIDA* (Paris; Albin Michel, 1992); Laurent Greilsamer, "1988–1993: Régards sur la législature," *Le Monde*, 19 March 1993. The French press reported extensively after October 1991 on the contaminated blood scandal. See, for example, *Le Monde*, April 23, 1992, and on the National Assembly inquiry into the scandal, *Le Monde*, February 12, 1993. See also Michel Setbon, "Silence mortel dans la transfusion sanguine," *French Politics and Society* 11, no. 4 (fall 1993); and Anne-Marie Casteret, *L'Affaire du sang* (Paris: La Découverte, 1992).

50. There is a large literature on the corruption question. For the background to the 1990 scandals, see Yves Mény, *La Corruption de la république* (Paris: Fayard, 1992), Ezra Suleiman, "The Politics of Corruption and the Corruption of Politics, *French Politics and Society* 9, no. 1 (winter 1991); the special issue of *French Politics and Society* on corruption in France, vol. 11, no. 4 (fall 1993); *Pouvoirs* 70 (1994); Pierre-Henri Allain, "Quatr'ans d'enquête sur un système vieux de 20 ans," *Libération*, March 2, 1995.

51. Schneider, *Les Dernières Années*, 165–166.

52. Cf. Jean Charlot, "L'Opposition à la veille des élections législatives," in SOFRES, *L'Etat de l'opinion 1993*, especially 35–38.

53. Gélédan, ed., *Le Bilan économique*, 159–162.

54. Jean Montaldo, *Mitterrand et les quarante voleurs* (Paris: Albin Michel, 1994), has the most complete account of Vibrachoc. Montaldo, a journalist on the extreme Right, must be taken with precaution, but seems to have the accurate story on this affair.

55. *Le Monde*, May 4, 1993. The story about Pelat's sons was related to me by retired Socialist leader Gérard Jacquet, a friend of Bérégovoy. Interview of June 14, 1995.

56. See the account given by Giesbert, *Mitterrand, une vie*, 659–665, largely substantiated by other sources.

57. The term was coined by Bergounioux and Grunberg in their 1992 history of the Socialist party, *Le Long Remords*.

58. *Le Point*, May 8–14, 1993.

59. *Le Monde*, November 11, 1992.

60. Author's interview with Maurice Benassayag, May 31, 1995.

61. Author's interview with Monory's chief aide Jean-Dominique Giuliani, June 16, 1995.

62. Schneider, *Les Dernières Années*, 224–225.

63. *Le Monde*, special number on the 1995 presidential election, 11.

64. Cf. Alain Duhamel, "Edouard Balladur, ou le retour de l'autorité," SOFRES, *L'Etat de l'opinion 1994*.

65. Cf. Eric Zemmour, *Balladur, immobile à grands pas* (Paris: Grasset, 1995), 71.

66. For information on the "Pasqua laws," see *Le Monde*, April 19, 1995, August 23 and 24, 1996.

67. SOFRES, *L'Etat de l'opinion 1996*, 199, and *Le Monde*, September 17, 1996.

68. Cf. Didier Witkowski, "Deux Ans de gouvernement Balladur face à l'opinion," SOFRES, *L'Etat de l'opinion 1996*.

69. Cf. Jacques Gerstlé, "La Dynamique sélective d'une campagne décisive," in *Le Vote de crise*, ed. Perrineau and Ysmal, 41–42, and in the same volume, Florence Haegel, "Jacques Chirac: Candidat 'naturel' (et métamorphosé) du RPR?"

70. Official text of Rocard's speech, given at Montlouis-sur-Loire, February 17, 1993. See also extensive newspaper coverage on February 18–19, 1993.

71. *Le Monde*, March 19, 1993.

72. *Le Monde*, April 6, 1993, "Comment Laurent Fabius a perdu la direction du Parti Socialiste." See also "L'histoire secrète d'une prise de pouvoir," *Le Nouvel Observateur*, April 8–14, 1993.

73. *Le Nouvel Observateur*, April 8–14, 1993.

74. Author's interview with Michel Rocard, May 13, 1996.

75. Author's interview with Mitterrand adviser Maurice Benassayag, May 31, 1995.

76. See *Le Monde, Dossiers et Documents*: "9 juin–12 juin 1994: Elections européenes," 64.

77. Author's interview with Guy Carcassonne, June 7, 1995.

78. Author's interview with Michel Rocard, May 13, 1996, and with Guy Carcassonne, June 7, 1995.

79. Serge Halimi, "Cure à la base?" *French Politics and Society* 12, nos. 2–3 (spring-summer 1994), 18; and George Ross, "Rocard . . . Victim of the Left's Lingering Illness?" in the same issue, 21.

80. See Gérard Grunberg, "La Candidature Jospin ou la construction d'un nouveau leadership," in *Le Vote de crise*, ed. Perrineau and Ysmal, 68.

81. Author's interview with Maurice Benassayag, May 31, 1995.

82. Author's interview with Maurice Benassayag, May 31, 1995.

83. Grunberg, "La Candidature Jospin," 69–70.

84. Ibid., 70–71.

85. See "L'Election présidentielle," 23 April–7 May 1995, special number of *Le Monde, Dossiers et Documents*, 13, 9.

86. Ibid., 72–73.

87. Cf. Daniel Boy, "Comment l'écologie est-elle tombée si bas?" in *Le Vote de crise*, ed. Perrineau and Ysmal.

88. Pascal Perrineau, "La Dynamique du vote Le Pen: Le Poids du gaucho-lepénisme," in *Le Vote de crise,* ed. Perrineau and Ysmal, 245–251.

89. Ibid., 248.

90. SOFRES, *L'Etat de l'opinion 1996,* 67.

91. Quoted from a review by Steven Lukes of a biography of Harold Laski, *Financial Times,* September 4–5, 1993.

Chapter 7

1. Cf. Jean-Luc Parodi, "Tout s'est joué trois ans plus tôt," and Pascal Perrineau, "Glissements progressifs de l'idéologie," both in *Mars 1986: La Drôle de Défaite de la gauche*, ed. Elisabeth Dupoirier and Gérard Grunberg (Paris: Presses Universitaires de France, 1986).

2. Alain Peyrefitte, *Le Mal français* (Paris: Plon, 1976), 429–430.

3. Stanley Hoffmann, "Conclusion: Paradoxes and Discontinuities," in *The Mitterrand Experiment*, ed. Ross, Hoffmann, and Malzacher, 345.

4. Interview with *Le Monde*, July 2, 1981.

5. See John T.S. Keeler and Alec Stone, "The Emergence of the Constitutional Council," in *The Mitterrand Experiment*, ed. Ross, Hoffmann, and Malzacher, 162–163.

6. See Alec Stone, *The Birth of Judicial Politics in France: The Constitutional Council in Comparative Perspective* (New York: Oxford University Press, 1992), 39–40, 264, n25.

7. Keeler and Stone, "The Emergence of the Constitutional Council," 164. In 1997 there were constitutional courts in nine of the twelve EU countries. See Louis Favoreu, *Les Cours constitutionnelles* (Paris: Presses Universitaires de France, 1986).

8. *Le Monde*, January 25–26, 1987. See also Guy Carcassonne, "A propos du droit d'amendement: Les Errements du Conseil constitutionnel," *Pouvoirs* 41 (1987). The author, an expert on constitutional law, subjected the council's decisions of late December 1986 and January 1987 to a severe procedural examination. In a paper given at a NYU-Columbia conference in October 1987, he remarked, however, that the criticisms of both Left and Right tend to validate the council's activities.

9. SOFRES, *Clés pour 1987*, 215.

10. Author's interview with Robert Badinter, June 12, 1995.

11. Stone, *Birth of Judicial Politics*, 58–59.

12. I have drawn for this section on ibid., Keeler and Stone, "The Emergence of the Constitutional Council," as well as Louis Favoreu, "Conseil Constitutionnel: Mythes et Realités," *Regards sur l'actualité*, no. 132 (June 1987). See also Louis Favoreu et Loïc Philip, eds., *Les Grandes Décisions du Conseil Constitutionnel*, 4th ed. (Paris: Sirey, 1984).

13. *Le Nouvel Observateur,* January 23, 1987.

14. Favier and Martin-Roland, *La Décennie,* 1:242–243.

15. *Le Monde*, April 5, 1984.

16. Michèle Cotta, *Les Miroirs de Jupiter* (Paris: Fayard, 1986), 16–17.

17. Colombani, *Portrait du Président*, 123.

18. Cf. Quatrepoint, *Histoire secrète des dossiers noirs,* 43.

19. Cf. Roland Cayrol, "L'Audiovisuel dans les années socialistes," *Tocqueville Review* 8 (1986–1987), 303–307.

20. Cf. Cotta, *Les Miroirs*, 197.

21. See Olga Blanc-Uchan, "Communications: Les nouvelles lois," *Regards sur l'actualité,* no. 127 (January 1987), esp. p. 11 on media concentration.

22. *Le Monde*, September 25, 1987.

23. *Le Monde*, December 11, 1996.

24. Yves Achille, *La Télévision publique en quête d'avenir* (Grenoble: Presses Universitaires de Grenoble, 1994), 110–115; François Jost and Gérard Leblanc, *La Télévision française au jour le jour* (Paris: Editions Anthropos, 1994), 130–136.

25. Cotta, *Les Miroirs*, 29.

26. Chris Howell, *Regulating Labor: The State and Industrial Relations Reform in Postwar France* (Princeton: Princeton University Press, 1992), 8.

27. *Le Monde*, November 7, 1985, and March 17, 1986.

28. See Guy Groux and René Mouriaux, "Unions Without Members," in *The Mitterrand Era: Policy Alternatives and Political Mobilization in France*, ed. Anthony Daley (New York: New York University Press, 1996), 176.

29. Chris Howell, "French Socialism and the Transformation of Industrial Relations Since 1981," in *The Mitterrand Era*, ed. Daley, 147–149.

30. Ibid., 152–153.

31. On these strikes see "The 1995 Strikes—Something New or Déjà Vu?" *French Politics and Society* 14, no. 1 (winter 1996).

32. Howell, "Transformation," 156.

33. Catherine Bédarida, "La Déferlante étudiante: Un Jeune français sur quatre à l'université," *Problèmes économiques*, no. 2,410 (February 8, 1995), 5, reprinted from *Le Monde de l'éducation*, October 1994.

34. "L'Explosion scolaire et universitaire," *Le Monde, Dossiers et Documents,* October 1991, citing a poll taken June 30, 1991.

35. I have drawn here on a clear and succinct article by Antoine Prost, "Les Reformes de l'enseignement en France," which appeared in the Japanese magazine *Nichifutsu Bunka* in March 1993. I am grateful to Professor Prost for giving me an offprint of his article.

36. Bédarida, "La Déferlante," 6.

37. Cf. *Quid* 1987, 656c.

38. Author's interview with Yves Guéna, mayor of Perigueux, October 8, 1985.

39. *Le Programme commun de gouvernement de la gauche,* 101–103.

40. I have drawn here on the article by Catherine Grémion, "Decentralization in France, a Historical Perspective," in *The Mitterrand Experiment*, ed. Ross, Hoffmann, and Malzacher.

41. Cf. Perrineau and Ysmal, eds., *Le Vote de crise*, 290.

42. Author's interview with Didier Borotra, September 26, 1994.

43. Author's interview with city officials in Montaubon, September 23, 1994.

44. Interview with Jacques Douffiagues, October 1985.

45. *Les Français et leur région* (Paris: La Documentation Française, Observatoire Interrégional de Politique, 1994), 24.

46. *Washington Post*, May 18, 1986; author's interview with Ile de France regional officials, October 1987.

47. Author's interview with Christian Sautter, May 20, 1996. For a number of articles bearing in one way or another on decentralization and corruption, see the issue of *French Politics and Society* 11, no. 4 (fall 1993) entitled "Politics, Morals, and Corruption in France."

48. Cf. I am heavily indebted for this account to the article by Yves Mény, "Le Cumul des Mandats," *Tocqueville Review* 8, 1986–87.

49. Albert Mabileau, "Le Cumul des Mandats," *Regards sur l'actualité*, no. 169 (March 1991), 20.

50. *Le Courrier des maires* 19, September 22, 1994, based on a June 1994 Infométrie poll of 1,000 persons over eighteen.

51. Perrineau and Ysmal, eds., *Le Vote de crise*, table 7; Stéphane Dion, "Le Cumul des mandats en France," *Toqueville Review* 13, no. 2 (1992), 103.

52. Yves Mény, "The Socialist Decentralization," in *The Mitterrand Experiment*, ed. Ross, Hoffmann, and Malzacher, 260.

53. On decentralization, see especially Vivien A. Schmidt, *Democratizing France: The Political and Administrative History of Decentralization* (Cambridge, UK, and New York: Cambridge University Press, 1990) and "Decentralization, a Revolutionary Reform," in *The French Socialists in Power*, ed. Patrick McCarthy (New York: Greenwood Press, 1987), and Mény, "The Socialist Decentralization" and "Le Cumul des Mandats"; *Cahiers français: La Décentralisation en marche*, special issue 220 (March-April 1985); Mark Kesselman, "The Tranquil Revolution at Clochemerle: Socialist Decentralization in France," in *Socialism, the State, and Public Policy in France,* ed. Philip Cerny and Martin Schain (London: Frances Pinter, 1985); the special number of *Projet* devoted to the subject, entitled "Décentraliser vraiment?" (1994).

Chapter 8

1. *Exclusion* is now in general use in French to include long-term unemployment, homelessness, and any other kind of existence on the margins of society.

2. Paraphrased from Elie Cohen, "L'Etat socialiste en industrie," 219.

3. Paraphrased slightly from ibid., 222–223.

4. Cited from Chantal Euseby, "Le Commerce extérieure français au debut des années 1980," *Profils Economiques* 21 (1986), 69.

5. Fonteneau and Muet, *La Gauche*, 156–158.

6. Cf. Elie Cohen, "L'Etat socialiste en industrie," 224.

7. Adapted slightly from Christian Stoffaës, "La Restructuration industrielle, 1945–1990," in *Entre l'Etat et le marché: L'Economie française des années 1880 à nos jours,* ed. Maurice Lévy-Leboyer and Jean-Claude Casanova (Paris: Gallimard, 1991), 458–459.

8. Statistics from ibid., 459–460.

9. Author's interview with former Elysée official Christian Sautter, May 20, 1996.

10. Fonteneau and Muet, *La Gauche*, 337.

11. Eric Szij, "La Nationalisation a-t-elle été un outil efficace de politique industrielle?" *Regards sur l'actualité* 205 (November 1994), 24–25.

12. *Financial Times,* June 14, 1996.

13. Cf. Eric Szij, "Privatisations: Logique industrielle ou logique budgétaire?" *Regards sur l'actualité* 205 (November 1994); and Harvey Feigenbaum, "France: From Pragmatic to Tactical Privatization," *Business and the Contemporary World* 5, no. 1 (winter 1993).

14. This analysis was made by Elie Cohen, "L'Etat socialiste en industrie," 226.

15. See David R. Cameron, "From Barre to Balladur: Economic Policy in the Era of the EMS," in *Remaking the Hexagon: The New France in the New Europe,* ed. Gregory Flynn (Boulder, Colo.: Westview Press, 1995), 72. Cameron argued, against the conventional wisdom, that steep devaluation, within or without the EMS, was possible in 1981 and perhaps later.

16. Euseby, "Le Commerce extérieure français," 69.

17. Cf. Michael Loriaux, "French Monetary Policy and the Integration of Europe," *French Politics and Society* 8 (summer 1990), 6–7.

18. Favier and Martin-Roland, *La Décennie*, 1:486–488; author's interview with Elie Cohen, May 14, 1996.

19. Favier and Martin-Roland, *La Décennie*, 1:488–490; Cameron, "From Barre to Balladur," 64–65.

20. According to a note in Favier and Martin-Roland, *La Décennie*, 1:553n, the Elysée archives (now in the Archives Nationales) contain more than 700 memoranda on economic and monetary questions that were sent to Mitterrand between March 1982 and March 1983.

21. See David Cameron, "Exchange Rate Politics in France, 1981–1983: The Regime-Defining Choices of the Mitterrand Presidency," in *The Mitterrand Era,* ed. Daley, 56–58.

22. Cameron, "From Barre to Balladur," 148.

23. Author's interview with Elie Cohen, May 14, 1996.

24. Françoise Marnata and Chantal Sarazin, "Bilan économique de la France, 1980–1992," *Regards sur l'actualité* 191 (May 1993), 26.

25. Basic statistics, *OECD Economic Surveys: France 1995* (Paris: OECD, 1995).

26. This is a paraphrase of a memorandum of April 1991 by Bérégovoy's cabinet director Hervé Hannoun, cited in Eric Aeschimann and Pascal Riché, *La Guerre de sept ans: Histoire secrète du franc fort, 1989–1996* (Paris: Calmann-Lévy, 1996), 83.

27. See Jean-Paul Fitoussi, *Le Débat interdit* (Paris: Arlea, 1995); Philippe Bauchard, *Deux ministres trop tranquilles* (Paris: Belfond, 1994); Pascal Riché and Charles Wyplosz, *L'Union monétaire de l'Europe* (Paris: Seuil, 1993).

28. Favier and Martin-Roland, *La Décennie*, 3:278–283. See also Aeschimann and Riché, *La Guerre de sept ans*, 133–141, for a long discussion of this question.

29. Aeschimann and Riché, *La Guerre de sept ans*, 141, on Sapin's soundings.

30. Ibid., 91.

31. Ibid.

32. He said that to me in an interview in October 1987, to Pierre Favier and Michel Roland-Martin in November 1988, and presumably to many others.

33. Aeschimann and Riché, *La Guerre de sept ans*, 57.

34. Favier and Martin-Roland, *La Décennie*, 3:563.

35. Aeschimann and Riché, *La Guerre de sept ans*, 48–52. Also see Hubert Védrine, *Les Mondes de François Mitterrand: A l'Elysée 1981–1995* (Paris: Fayard, 1996).

36. Hubert Védrine, quoted in a March 1996 interview with Aeschimann and Riché, cited in *La Guerre de sept ans*, 172n.

37. Christiane Rimbaud, *Bérégovoy* (Paris: Perrin, 1994), 362.

38. Aeschimann and Riché, *La Guerre de sept ans*, 170.

39. Author's interview with Senator Gérard Delfau, May 22, 1996.

40. See Jacques Lesourne, *Vérités et mensonges sur le chômage* (Paris: Odile Jacob, 1995), 26–29; and Sylvie Dumartin and Magda Tomasini, "Déclin de l'emploi industriel et tertiarisa-

tion accrue, l'emploi par secteur d'activité entre 1982 et 1990," *Economie et Statistique* 261 (1993), 34.

41. According to Anne-Marie Guillemard, "France, Massive Exit Through Unemployment Compensation," in *Time for Retirement*, ed. Martin Kohli et al. (New York: Cambridge University Press, 1991), table 10, by 1991 only 68 percent of men and 44.7 percent of women between the ages of 55 and 59 were still in the workforce, and only 24 percent of men 60–64 and 17.7 percent of women in that age group were still working.

42. *Perspectives économiques de l'OCDE,* cited in *OFCE: L'Economie française 1995* (Paris: La Découverte, 1995), 111.

43. Cf. Tribalat, *Faire France*, 175. Figures are based on a 1992 survey.

44. Lesourne, *Vérités*, 31–33; interview with Elie Cohen, May 14, 1996.

45. Lesourne, *Vérités*, 167.

46. Rosanvallon, *La Nouvelle Question sociale*, 190.

47. Lesourne, *Vérités*, 157–161.

48. Ibid., 172.

49. See Alain Bayet, *Les Salaires de 1991 à 1993 dans le secteur privé et semi-publique* (Paris: INSEE, 1994), table 6.

50. Calculated from the *Annuaire statistique 1993* (Paris: INSEE, 1993), table C.03-14.

51. See Elie Cohen, "Une Pauvreté plus visible," and statistics on ten years of inequality studies, *Le Monde, Dossiers et Documents* 183 (December 1990), 3.

52. SOFRES, *L'Etat de l'opinion 1994*, 79.

53. See Olivier-Jean Blanchard and Pierre-Alain Muet, "Competitiveness Through Disinflation: An Assessment of the French Macroeconomic Strategy," *Economic Policy* 16 (April 1993), 33.

54. Vivien A. Schmidt, *From State to Market? The Transformation of French Business and Government* (New York: Cambridge University Press, 1996), 104; SOFRES: *L'Etat de l'opinion 1987*, 157; SOFRES, *L'Etat de l'opinion 1994*, 230.

55. Schmidt, *From State to Market?* 158.

Chapter 9

1. See Samy Cohen, *La Monarchie nucléaire* (Paris: Hachette, 1986), 92, 114–115.

2. Cf. Jean Lacouture, *De Gaulle*, Vol. 3: *Le Souverain, 1959–1970* (Paris: Seuil, 1986), 547.

3. Cf. Samy Cohen, *La Monarchie Nucléaire*, 127–128; and Julius W. Friend, "Soviet Behavior and National Responses: the Puzzling Case of the French Communist Party," *Studies in Comparative Communism* 15, no. 3 (autumn 1982), 221–231.

4. See Samy Cohen, *La Monarchie Nucléaire*, 128–134.

5. Védrine, *Les Mondes,* 89. Védrine, son of an old Resistance comrade of Mitterrand's, served for fourteen years at the president's elbow—first as the president's diplomatic counselor, then as diplomatic counselor and spokesman, finally as secretary-general of the Elysée. His close association with Mitterrand makes his book on the foreign policies of 1981–1995 extremely important—particularly because Védrine had nearly unparalleled access to the president and to his files and archives. Archival documents will be designated as such in the notes. Pierre Favier and Michel Martin-Roland also had nearly unrestricted access to the Elysée archives. The weekly summary on all events of importance made by the secretary-general (Jean-Louis Bianco and later Védrine himself) is a source of great value, which both of these

writers have used. The three volumes of Jacques Attali's *Verbatim 1981–1986* should be a source of equal value but reveal themselves marred by so many inaccuracies that I have used them sparingly.

6. Cf. Favier and Martin-Roland, *La Décennie*, 2:666–670.

7. Cf. Jacques Huntzinger, "The French Socialist Party and Western Relations," in *The Foreign Policies of West European Socialist Parties*, ed. Werner Feld (New York: Praeger, 1978), 68.

8. Author's interview with former defense minister Charles Hernu, March 1986.

9. Jacques Attali, *Verbatim 1981–1986* (Paris: Fayard, 1993), 1:24–25.

10. Interview with PS international affairs secretary Jacques Huntzinger, March 1985.

11. *Documents* (Paris), no. 4 (1982), interview with Raymond Aron, 34.

12. Attali, *Verbatim*, 1:103.

13. Ibid., 1:24–25.

14. Philip Gordon, "The French-German Security Partnership," in *France-Germany, 1883–1993: The Struggle to Cooperate*, ed. Patrick McCarthy (New York: St. Martin's Press, 1993), 143.

15. François Mitterrand, *L'Abeille et l'architecte* (Paris: Flammarion, 1978), 308–309.

16. Favier and Martin-Roland, *La Décennie*, 2:247–255.

17. Favier and Martin-Roland, *La Décennie*, 1:279–280.

18. Author's interview with Jacques Delors, May 21, 1996.

19. Védrine, *Les Mondes*, 415.

20. Cf. Jacques Delors, *La France par l'Europe* (Paris: Grasset, 1988).

21. Author's interview with Jacques Delors, May 21, 1996.

22. On the details of this, see Favier and Martin-Roland, *La Décennie*, 2: 261–266; Andrew Moravcsik, "Negotiating the Single European Act," in *The New European Community*, ed. Robert O. Keohane and Stanley Hoffmann (Boulder, Colo.: Westview Press, 1991), especially 57–60; and Pierre Gerbet, "Le Rôle du couple franco-allemand dans les Communautés européennes," in *Le Couple franco-allemand en Europe*, ed. Henri Menudier (Asnières: Université de la Sorbonne Nouvelle and Institut Allemand d'Asnières, 1993).

23. Favier and Martin-Roland, *La Décennie*, 2:267–268.

24. Ibid., 2:275–280; Védrine, *Les Mondes*, 263–271.

25. Favier and Martin-Roland, *La Décennie*, 2:280.

26. Védrine, *Les Mondes*, 373–374.

27. Favier and Martin-Roland, *La Décennie*, 3:160–161.

28. Alain Minc, *La Grande Illusion* (Paris: Grasset, 1989), 34–36.

29. Favier and Martin-Roland, *La Décennie*, 3:172, archival document.

30. Cf. Philip Zelikow and Condoleeza Rice, *Germany Unified and Europe Transformed* (Cambridge, Mass.: Harvard University Press, 1995), 64–65.

31. Elizabeth Pond, *Beyond the Wall: Germany's Road to Unification* (Washington, D.C.: Brookings Institution, 1993), 102–127, argued that the real significance of Gorbachev's visit to East Berlin was his at least tacit approval for Honecker's replacement by younger and more flexible SED leaders.

32. Horst Teltschik, *329 Tage: Innenansichten der Einigung*, paperback ed. (Berlin: Siedler Verlag, 1991), 44.

33. Zelikow and Rice, *Germany Unified*, 123.

34. Védrine, *Les Mondes*, 433.

35. Teltschik, *329 Tage*, 76.

36. Author's interview with Elisabeth Guigou, June 16, 1995.

37. Favier and Martin-Roland, *La Décennie* 3:210, from an archival document.

38. Zelikow and Rice, *Germany Unified,* 137, quoting from the Soviet memorandum of conversation on the Kiev meeting. The detail on Gorbachev's foreboding that he might be overthrown by a marshal is confirmed in Favier and Martin-Roland, *La Décennie,* 3:197.

39. Favier and Martin-Roland, *La Décennie,* 3:197, quoting from an interview with Genscher.

40. Teltschik, *329 Tage,* 26, 47.

41. Favier and Martin-Roland, *La Décennie,* 3:217, quoting de Margerie's report.

42. François Mitterrand, *De l'Allemagne, de la France* (Paris: Editions Odile Jacob, 1996), 107.

43. Teltschik, *329 Tage,* 96.

44. Favier and Martin-Roland, *La Décennie,* 3:218.

45. Author's interview with Brigitte Stoffaës, Mitterrand's German interpreter, May 26, 1996.

46. *Le Monde,* May 4, 1996, from the East German notes taken at the meeting.

47. *Der Spiegel,* no. 40 (1996), quoting excerpts from Helmut Kohl, *Ich wollte Deutschlands Einheit* (Berlin: Propylaen Verlag, 1996).

48. Favier and Martin-Roland, *La Décennie,* 3:229.

49. Cited in Konrad H. Jarausch, *The Rush to German Unity* (New York: Oxford University Press, 1994), 108.

50. Védrine, *Les Mondes,* 425; and Favier and Martin-Roland, *La Décennie,* 3:234–235.

51. Védrine, *Les Mondes,* 455–456.

52. Favier and Martin-Roland, *La Décennie,* 3:244–246.

53. Védrine, *Les Mondes,* 495.

54. Ibid., 503.

55. Author's interview with Brigitte Stoffaës, May 21, 1996; also see Védrine, *Les Mondes,* 508–511.

56. See George Ross, *Jacques Delors and European Integration* (New York: Oxford University Press, 1995), 89.

57. Ibid., 192.

58. See Aeschimann and Riché, *La Guerre de sept ans,* 92–93.

59. Author's interview with Mitterrand adviser and advance man in Prague Jean Musitelli, June 13, 1995; also see Védrine, *Les Mondes,* 447–448.

60. Author's interview with Elisabeth Guigou, June 16, 1995. Védrine, *Les Mondes,* 554, is quite frank on Mitterrand's domestic political reasoning.

61. Cf. Olivier Duhamel and Gérard Grunberg, "Referendum: Les dix France," in SOFRES, *L'Etat de l'opinion 1993;* and Védrine, *Les Mondes,* 556–557.

62. I have drawn here and in what follows on the excellent article by Beverly Crawford, "German Foreign Policy and European Political Cooperation: The Diplomatic Recognition of Croatia in 1991," *German Politics and Society* 13, no. 2 (summer 1995). See p. 7 for the quote.

63. Quoted in Védrine, *Les Mondes,* 605–606.

64. See ibid., 606–608; author's interview with Elisabeth Guigou, June 16, 1995.

65. See Gordon, *France, Germany and the Western Alliance,* 55–57.

66. Védrine, *Les Mondes,* 615–616, apparently from notes of the meeting.

67. On these maneuvers, see Védrine, *Les Mondes,* 618; and Crawford, "Diplomatic Recognition of Croatia," 24.

68. Védrine, *Les Mondes,* 620.

69. Ibid., 620–621.

70. Author's interview with Christian Chapman, former deputy chief of mission, U.S. Embassy, Paris, May 1988.

71. Védrine, *Les Mondes*, 172.

72. Favier and Martin-Roland, *La Décennie*, 1:105–106; Védrine, *Les Mondes*, 172; author's interview with Ambassador Arthur Hartmann, May 1988.

73. Cf. George P. Shultz, *Turmoil and Triumph* (New York: Maxwell Macmillan International, 1993), 136.

74. See Védrine, *Les Mondes*, 218–228; and Robert J. Lieber, "International Energy Policy and the Reagan Administration: Avoiding the Next Oil Shock?" in *Eagle Resurgent? The Reagan Era in American Foreign Policy*, ed. Kenneth A. Oye, Robert J. Lieber, and Donald Rothchild (Boston and Toronto: Little, Brown, 1987), 177–180.

75. Védrine, *Les Mondes*, 226–228, quoting from an archival document.

76. Ibid., 229–247.

77. Alexander Dallin and Gail W. Lapidus, "Reagan and the Russians: American Policy Toward the Soviet Union," in *Eagle Resurgent?* ed. Oye, Lieber, and Rothchild, 207–208.

78. Védrine, *Les Mondes*, 367.

79. *Le Monde*, August 30, 1981.

80. Quoted in Marie-Claude Smouts, "La France et le Tiers-Monde, ou comment gagner le sud sans perdre le nord," *Politique etrangère*, no. 2 (1985), 350.

81. See Védrine, *Les Mondes*, 196–198.

82. On Mitterrand's assurances to the Reagan administration on arms sales, see Evan Galbraith, *Ambassador in Paris: The Reagan Years* (Washington, D.C.: Regnery Gateway, 1987), 13–14. See also Eusebio Mujal-Leon, *European Socialism and the Conflict in Central America* (Westport, Conn.: Praeger, 1987).

83. On Cheysson's San Jose speech, see Smouts, "La France et le Tiers-Monde," 351. For PS views by middecade on the Sandinistas, my source is an interview with PS international affairs secretary Jacques Huntzinger, March 1986.

84. Cf. Attali, *Verbatim*, 1:200–201; and Favier and Martin-Roland, *La Décennie*, 1:459–464.

85. Bertrand Hervieu, "Les ruptures du monde agricole," *Regards sur l'actualité*, February 1991, 25.

86. See David Hanley, "France and GATT: The Real Politics of Trade Negotiations," in *France From the Cold War to the New World Order*, ed. Tony Chafer and Brian Jenkins (New York: St. Martins Press, 1996).

87. Author's interview with Jean Audibert, Cot's *directeur de cabinet*, May 17, 1996.

88. Védrine, *Les Mondes*, 340.

89. Ibid., 707–708.

90. Favier and Martin-Roland, *La Décennie*, 1:417–418, archival document.

91. Ibid., 1:419.

92. Favier and Martin-Roland, *La Décennie*, 2:334–335.

93. Favier and Martin-Roland, *La Décennie*, 3:383.

94. Favier and Martin-Roland, *La Décennie*, 2:332.

95. See John A. McKesson, "France and Africa: The Evolving Saga," *French Politics and Society* 11, no. 2 (spring 1993), 56–58.

96. Favier and Martin-Roland, *La Décennie*, 3:377–379, archival document.

97. Ibid., 3:380.

98. Antoine Jouan, "Rwanda 1990–1994: De la transition politique au génocide," Paris, Fondation Médecins sans Frontières, December 1995, xeroxed report.

99. I have drawn here on Claude Wauthier, *Quatre Présidents et l'Afrique* (Paris: Seuil, 1995), and on a report by the Observatoire Permanent de la Coopération Française entitled "La politique de la France au Rwanda (1973–1994), dated August 26, 1994, which cites a very large number of journalists, French and Belgian, and other observers, all highly critical of French behavior and complaisance with the Habyarimana government and its immediate Hutu successor. See also Tony Smith, "Recipe for Disaster?" *French Politics and Society* 14, no. 3 (summer 1996), which argues that the polemicists in no way give French policy credit for coping with a complicated and difficult situation.

100. Author's interview with Ambassador Jean Audibert, May 17, 1996. Audibert was Cot's *directeur de cabinet*, in 1985–1990 Elysée adviser on African affairs, and ambassador to Algeria from 1990 to 1992.

101. Favier and Martin-Roland, *La Décennie*, 2:38–43.

102. Shultz, *Turmoil and Triumph*, 231.

103. See Védrine, *Les Mondes*, 321–322; and for the Mitterrand letter, Favier and Martin-Roland, *La Décennie*, 2:50.

104. Védrine, *Les Mondes*, 325; Favier and Martin-Roland, *La Décennie*, 3:427–428.

105. Védrine, *Les Mondes*, 524–525.

106. Favier and Martin-Roland, *La Décennie*, 3:446, quoting the minutes of the meeting.

107. Pierre Lellouche, "La Crise du Golfe: Premières réactions françaises et américaines (8 août–10 octobre)," SOFRES, *L'Etat de l'opinion 1991*, 94–95.

108. Favier and Martin-Roland, *La Décennie*, 3:467–468, quoting the minutes of the meeting.

109. Cf. Elisabeth Dupoirier, "De la crise à la guerre du Golfe: Un exemple de mobilisation de l'opinion," SOFRES, *L'Etat de l'opinion 1992*.

110. Védrine, *Les Mondes*, 546. Also see Favier and Martin-Roland, *La Décennie*, 3:510, quoting Védrine in a 1992 interview: "Mitterrand had the feeling that the war would reshuffle the cards and that France could be present at the moment of clearing up the Middle East situation. But it was shoved aside by Baker's authoritarianism and Shamir's short-sighted opposition."

111. Favier and Martin-Roland, *La Décennie*, 3:398–400, quoting minutes.

112. Ibid., 3:401–408.

113. Védrine, *Les Mondes*, 332.

114. Favier and Martin-Roland, *La Décennie*, 3:386–387, quoting minutes of the Council of Ministers meeting.

115. Andrew J. Pierre and William B. Quandt, *The Algerian Crisis: Policy Options for the West* (Washington, D.C.: Carnegie Endowment for International Peace, 1996), 12–13.

116. Author's interview with Ambassador Jean Audibert, May 17, 1996; Védrine, *Les Mondes*, 685–686.

117. Pierre and Quandt, *The Algerian Crisis*, 27.

118. SOFRES, *L'Etat de l'opinion 1996*, 173.

119. Pierre and Quandt, *The Algerian Crisis*, 28–30.

120. For a summary on the FAR, see "La Force d'action rapide," *Regards sur l'actualité*, no. 105 (November 1984).

121. For a detailed account of the vicissitudes of French-German armaments cooperation, see Stephen A. Kocs, *Autonomy or Power? The Franco-German Relationship and Europe's Strategic Choices, 1955–1995* (Westport, Conn.: Praeger, 1995), 157–183.

122. Steven Philip Kramer, *Does France Still Count? The French Role in the New Europe* (Westport, Conn., and Washington, D.C.: Prager and CSIS, 1994), 33.

123. Cf. Favier and Martin-Roland, *La Décennie,* 3:48–258.

124. Ibid., 3:56.

125. Cf. Kocs, *Anatomy or Power?* 217–218, and French Embassy Information Bulletin, October 4, 1990.

126. *Le Monde,* December 10, 1990.

127. Cf. Julius W. Friend, "U.S. Policy Toward Franco-German Cooperation, in *France-Germany 1983–1993,* ed. McCarthy.

128. Cf. Kocs, *Autonomy or Power?* 222–223.

129. Bruno Racine, Juppé adviser, head of Foreign Ministry policy planning 1993–1995, speaking at a U.S.-CREST meeting on the lessons of Bosnia, January 13, 1997.

130. Cf. Ronald Tiersky, *The Mitterrand Legacy and the Future of French Security Policy* (Washington, D.C.: Institute for National Strategic Studies, McNair Paper 43, 1995), 44–48.

131. Sénat, Rapport d'information no. 303, for the Foreign Affairs and Defense Commissions, on some lessons of the Gulf War, 97.

132. See François Heisbourg, "La Politique de défense française à l'aube d'un nouveau mandat présidentiel," *Politique étrangère,* spring 1994, 79.

133. Védrine, *Les Mondes,* 739.

134. See Kocs, *Autonomy or Power?* 230.

135. See Heisbourg, "La Politique de défense française," 87.

Chapter 10

1. Péan, *Une Jeunesse française,* Faux, Legrand, and Perez, *La Main droite de Dieu.*

2. François Mitterrand and Elie Wiesel, *Mémoire à deux voix* (Paris: Odile Jacob, 1995), 109.

3. Stanley Hoffmann, in "A Symposium on Mitterrand's Past," *French Politics and Society* 13, no. 1 (winter 1995), 8.

4. Péan, *Une Jeunesse française,* 443.

5. Author's interview with Brigitte Stoffaës, May 24, 1996.

6. François Mitterrand, *La Paille et le grain* (Paris: Flammarion, 1975), quoted in Péan, *Une Jeunesse française,* 443.

7. Speech of June 11, 1971, to the Epinay congress. Cited in François Mitterrand, *Politique 1938–1981* (Paris: Editions Marabout, 1984), 327.

8. Jean Montaldo, *Mitterrand et les quarante voleurs* (Paris: Albin Michel, 1994), 217–218, 220, 250–251.

9. Laure Adler, *L'Année des adieux* (Paris: Flammarion, 1995), 30.

10. Edith Boccara, *Mitterrand en toutes lettres* (Paris: Belfond, 1995), 163, citing an interview of August 16, 1971, in *Le Nouvel Observateur.*

11. First published as "Mitterrand's Foreign Policy, or Gaullism by Any Other Name," *Foreign Affairs* 57 (winter 1984–85), and in a revised form in *The Mitterrand Experiment,* ed. Ross, Hoffmann, and Malzacher.

12. See Laurent Cohen-Tanugi, "Une Oeuvre européenne en quête d'héritier," in *François Mitterrand: 14 ans de pouvoir,* special number of *Le Monde, Dossiers et Documents,* April 1995.

Selected Bibliography

Aeschimann, Eric, and Pascal Riché. *La Guerre de sept ans: Histoire secrète du franc fort 1989–1996*. Paris: Calmann-Lévy, 1996.

Bauchard, Philippe. *Deux ministres trop tranquilles*. Paris: Belfond, 1994.

_____. *La Guerre des deux roses*. Paris: Grasset, 1986.

Bell, David Scott. *The French Socialist Party: The Emergence of a Party of Government*. 2d ed. Oxford: Clarendon Press and New York, Oxford University Press, 1988.

Bell, David S., and Byron Criddle, *The French Communist Party in the Fifth Republic*. Oxford: Clarendon Press, 1994.

Berger, Suzanne. "Liberalism Reborn." In *Contemporary France: A Review of Interdisciplinary Studies, 1987*. Edited by Jolyon Howorth and George Ross. London: Frances Pinter, 1987.

Bergounioux, Alain, and Gérard Grunberg. *Le Long Remords du pouvoir: Le Parti socialiste français, 1905–1992*. Paris: Fayard, 1992.

Birenbaum, Guy. *Le Front national en politique*. Paris: Balland, 1992.

Birnbaum, Pierre, ed. *Les Elites Socialistes au pouvoir: Les Dirigeants socialistes face à l'Etat 1981–1985*. Paris: Presses Universitaires de France, 1985.

Boccara, Edith. *Mitterrand en toutes lettres*. Paris: Belfond, 1995.

Bréchon, Pierre, Jacques Derville, and Patrick Lecomte. *Les Cadres du R.P.R.* Paris: Economica, 1987.

_____. "L'Univers idéologiques des cadres RPR." *Revue française de science politique* 37 (October 1987).

Burrin, Philippe. *La France à l'heure allemande 1940–1944*. Paris: Seuil, 1995.

Cahm, Eric. "From Greenpeace to Cohabitation." In *Contemporary France: A Review of Interdisciplinary Studies*. Edited by Jolyon Howorth and George Ross. London: Frances Pinter, 1987.

Cameron, David. "Exchange Rate Politics in France, 1981–1983: The Regime-Defining Choices of the Mitterrand Presidency." In *The Mitterrand Era: Policy Alternatives and Political Mobilization in France*. Edited by Anthony Daley. New York: New York University Press, 1995.

_____. "From Barre to Balladur: Economic Policy in the Era of the EMS." In *Remaking the Hexagon: The New France in the New Europe*. Edited by Gregory Flynn. Boulder, Colo.: Westview Press, 1995.

Carcassonne, Guy. "Du non-droit au droit." *Pouvoirs* 70 (1994).

Casteret, Anne-Marie. *L'Affaire du sang*. Paris: La Découverte, 1992.

Cayrol, Roland. "L'Audiovisuel dans les années socialistes." *Tocqueville Review* 8 (1986–1987).

Charlot, Jean. "L'Opposition à la veille des élections législatives." In SOFRES. *L'Etat de l'opinion 1993*. Edited by Olivier Duhamel and Jérôme Jaffré. Paris: Seuil, 1993.

Chazal, Claire. *Balladur*. Paris: Flammarion, 1993.

Cohen, Elie. "L'Etat socialiste en industrie: Volontarisme politique et changement socio-économique." In *Les Elites socialistes au pouvoir: Les Dirigeants socialistes face à l'Etat 1981–1985*. Edited by Pierre Birnbaum. Paris: Presses Universitaires de France, 1985.

_____. "Nationalisation: Une bonne leçon de capitalisme." *Problèmes économiques*, no. 1972 (30 April 1986).

Cole, Alastair. *François Mitterrand, a Study in Political Leadership*. London and New York: Routledge, 1994.

Colombani, Jean-Marie. *Portrait du Président*. Paris: Gallimard, 1985.

Colombani, Jean-Marie, and Jean-Yves Lhomeau. *Le Mariage Blanc*. Paris: Grasset, 1986.

Costa-Lascoux, Jacqueline. "Les Lois 'Pasqua': Une Nouvelle Politique d'immigration?" *Regards sur l'Actualité*, no. 199 (March 1994).

Courtois, Stéphane. "Le Déclin accentué du Parti Communiste français." In *Le Vote sanction: Les Elections législatives des 21 et 28 mars 1993*. Edited by Philippe Habert, Pascal Perrineau, and Colette Ysmal. Paris: Département d'Etudes du *Figaro* et Presses de la Fondation Nationale des Sciences Politiques, 1993.

_____. "Le Succes en trompe-l'oeuil." In *Le Vote sanction: Les Elections législatives des 21 et 28 mars 1993*. Edited by Philippe Habert, Pascal Perrineau, and Colette Ysmal. Paris: Département d'Etudes du *Figaro* et Presses de la Fondation Nationale des Sciences Politiques, 1993.

Dainville, Augustin de. *ORA, la résistance de l'armée*. Paris: Lavauzelle, 1974.

Daley, Anthony, ed. *The Mitterrand Era: Policy Alternatives and Political Mobilization in France*. New York: New York University Press, 1995.

Doublet, Yves-Marie. "L'Argent de l'élection présidentielle." *Pouvoirs* 70, special issue on election finances (1994).

_____. "Edouard Balladur, ou le retour de l'autorité." In SOFRES. *L'Etat de l'opinion 1994*. Edited by Olivier Duhamel and Jérôme Jaffré. Paris: Seuil, 1994.

Dupoirier, Elisabeth. "Popularités 1988–1993." In SOFRES. *L'Etat de l'opinion 1996*. Edited by Olivier Duhamel, Jérôme Jaffré, and Philippe Méchet. Paris: Seuil, 1996.

_____. "De la crise à la guerre du Golfe: Un exemple de mobilisation de l'opinion." In SOFRES. *L'Etat de l'opinion 1992*. Edited by Olivier Duhamel and Jérôme Jaffré. Paris: Seuil, 1992.

Dupoirier, Elisabeth, and Gérard Grunberg, eds. *Mars 1986: La Drôle de Défaite de la gauche*. (Paris: Presses Universitaires de France, 1986.

Du Roy, Albert, and Robert Schneider. *Le Roman de la rose*. Paris: Seuil, 1982.

Faux, Emmanuel, Thomas Legrand, and Gilles Perez. *La Main droite de Dieu: Enquête sur François Mitterrand et l'extreme droite*. Paris: Seuil, 1994.

Favier, Pierre, and Michel Martin-Rolland. *La Décennie Mitterrand*. 3 vols. Vols. 1–2: paperback ed. Paris: Seuil, 1991. Vol. 3: Paris: Seuil, 1996.

Fitoussi, Jean-Paul. *Le Débat interdit*. Paris: Arlea, 1995.

Flynn, Gregory, ed. *Remaking the Hexagon: The New France in the New Europe*. Boulder, Colo.: Westview Press, 1995.

Fonteneau, Alain, and Pierre-Alain Muet. *La Gauche face à la crise*. Paris: Presses de la Fondation Nationale des Sciences Politiques, 1985. The slightly updated English translation is *Reflation and Austerity: Economic Policy under Mitterrand.*, Trans. Malcolm Slater. New York: Berg, 1990.

Frenay, Henri. *La Nuit finira*. Paris: Laffont, 1973.

Friend, Julius W. "U.S. Policy Toward Franco-German Cooperation." In *France-Germany 1983–1993: The Struggle to Cooperate*. Edited by Patrick McCarthy. New York: St. Martin's Press, 1993.

_____. "Report from Rennes." *French Politics and Society* 8, no. 2 (spring 1990).

_____. "The PS Faces the 1990s." *French Politics and Society* 8, no. 1 (winter 1990).

Fries, Fabrice. *Les Grands Débats européens*. Paris: Seuil, 1995.

Froment, Pascale. *René Bousquet*. Paris: Stock, 1994.

Gaffney, John. *The French Left and the Fifth Republic: The Discourses of Communism and Socialism in Contemporary France*. New York: St. Martin's Press, 1989.

Gélédan, Alain, ed. *Le Bilan économique des années Mitterrand, 1981–1994*. Paris: Le Monde-Editions, 1994.

Gerstlé, Jacques. "La dynamique sélective d'une campagne décisive." In *Le Vote de crise: L'Election présidentielle de 1995*. Edited by Pascal Perrineau and Colette Ysmal. Paris: Département d'Etudes Politiques du *Figaro* et Presses de la Fondation Nationale des Sciences Politiques, 1995.

Giesbert, Franz-Olivier. *François Mitterrand, une vie*. Paris: Seuil, 1996.

_____. *Jacques Chirac*. Paris: Seuil, 1987.

_____. *François Mitterrand ou la tentation de l'histoire*. Paris: Seuil, 1977.

Glaude, Michel. "Où va la cohésion sociale en France?" *Tocqueville Review* 16, no. 2 (1995).

Gordon, Philip. *France, Germany and the Western Alliance*. Boulder, Colo.: Westview Press, 1995.

Grunberg, Gérard. "La Candidature Jospin ou la construction d'un nouveau leadership." In *Le Vote de crise: L'Election présidentielle de 1995*. Edited by Pascal Perrineau and Colette Ysmal. Paris: Département d'Etudes Politiques du *Figaro* et Presses de la Fondation Nationale des Sciences Politiques, 1995.

Grunberg, Gérard, and Etienne Schweisguth. "The French-German Security Partnership." In *France-Germany, 1883–1993: The Struggle to Cooperate*. Edited by Patrick McCarthy. New York: St. Martin's Press, 1993.

Guisnel, Jean. *Charles Hernu*. Paris: Fayard, 1993.

Habert, Philippe, Pascal Perrineau, and Colette Ysmal, eds. *Le Vote sanction: Les Elections législatives des 21 et 28 mars 1993*. Paris: Département d'Etudes du *Figaro* et Presses de la Fondation Nationale des Sciences Politiques, 1993.

Haegel, Florence. "Jacques Chirac: Candidat 'naturel' et métamorphosé du RPR?" In *Le Vote de crise: L'Election présidentielle de 1995*. Edited by Pascal Perrineau and Colette Ysmal. Paris: Département d'Etudes Politiques du *Figaro* et Presses de la Fondation Nationale des Sciences Politiques, 1995.

Hall, Peter A. *Governing the Economy*. New York: Oxford University Press, 1986.

Hall, Peter A., Jack Hayward, and Howard Machin, eds. *Developments in French Politics*. New York: St. Martin's Press, 1990.

Hoffmann, Stanley. "French Dilemmas and Strategies After the Cold War." In *After the Cold War*. Edited by Stanley Hoffmann, Robert Keohane, and Joseph Nye. Cambridge: Harvard University Press, 1993.

_____. "The Odd Couple." *New York Review of Books*, 25 September 1986.

Hollifield, James F., and George Ross. *Searching for the New France*. New York and London: Routledge, 1991.

Horizon 2000 Group: France, Emmanuel Le Roy Ladurie presiding. *Entrer dans le XXIe siecle: Essai sur l'avenir de l'identité française*. Paris: La Découverte, Documentation française, 1990.

Howell, Chris. *Regulating Labor: The State and Industrial Relations Reform in Postwar France*. Princeton: Princeton University Press, 1992.

_____. "The Fetichism of Small Differences: French Socialism Enters the Nineties." *French Politics and Society* 9, no. 1 (winter 1991).

Howorth, Jolyon, and George Ross, eds. *Contemporary France: A Review of Interdisciplinary Studies*. London: Frances Pinter, 1987.

Huchon, Jean-Paul. *Jours tranquilles à Matignon*. Paris: Grasset, 1993.

July, Serge. *Les Années Mitterrand: Histoire baroque d'une normalisation inachevée*. Paris: Grasset, 1986.

Keeler, John T. S., and Alec Stone. "The Emergence of the Constitutional Court as a Major Actor in the Policy-making Process." In *The Mitterrand Experiment*. Edited by George Ross, Stanley Hoffmann, and Sylvia Malzacher. New York: Oxford University Press, 1987.

Kocs, Stephen A. *Autonomy or Power? The Franco-German Relationship and Europe's Strategic Choices, 1955–1995*. Westport, Conn., and London: Praeger, 1995.

Kramer, Steven Philip. *Does France Still Count?: The French Role in the New Europe*. Washington, D.C.: CSIS, and Westport, Conn.: Praeger, 1994.

Krop, Pascal. *Les Secrets de l'espionnage française*. Paris: Lattes, 1993.

"L'Election présidentielle 23 April–7 May 1995, special issue of *Le Monde, Dossiers et Documents*.

Le Monde, Dossiers et Documents: 9 juin–12 juin 1994, élections européenes.

Lesourne, Jacques. *Vérités et mensonges sur le chômage*. Paris: Odile Jacob, 1995.

Lévy-Leboyer, Maurice, et Jean-Claude Casanova, eds. *Entre l'Etat et le marché: L'Economie française des années 1880 à nos jours*. Paris: Gallimard, 1991.

Loriaux, Michael. *France After Hegemony: International Change and Financial Reform*. Ithaca: Cornell University Press, 1991.

_____. "French Monetary Policy and the Integration of Europe." *French Politics and Society* 8, no. 3 (summer 1990).

Marcus, Jonathan. *The National Front and French Politics: The Resistible Rise of Jean-Marie Le Pen*. New York: New York University Press, 1995.

Marrus, Michael R., and Robert O. Paxton. *Vichy France and the Jews*. New York: Basic Books, 1981.

McCarthy, Patrick, ed. *France-Germany, 1883–1993: The Struggle to Cooperate*. New York: St. Martin's Press, 1993.

Mendras, Henri, and Alistair Cole. *Social Change in Modern France*. Cambridge and New York: Cambridge University Press, 1991. English adaptation of Henri Mendras. *La Seconde Révolution française*. Paris: Gallimard, 1988.

Mentré, Paul. "Chômage, emploi, et élections présidentielles." *Commentaire* 69 (spring 1995).

Menudier, Henri, ed. *Le Couple franco-allemand en Europe*. Asnières: Université de la Sorbonne Nouvelle and Institut Allemand d'Asnières, 1993.

Mény, Yves. *La Corruption de la république*. Paris: Fayard, 1992.

_____. "The Socialist Decentralization." In *The Mitterrand Experiment*. Edited by George Ross, Stanley Hoffmann, and Sylvia Malzacher. New York: Oxford University Press, 1987.

Mitterrand, François. *De l'Allemagne, de la France*. Paris: Odile Jacob, 1996.

_____. *Mémoires interrompus*. Paris: Odile Jacob, 1996.

_____. *L'Abeille et l'architecte*. Paris: Flammarion, 1978.

_____. *Ma part de verité*. Paris: Fayard, 1969.

Mitterrand, François, and Elie Wiesel. *Mémoire à deux voix*. Paris: Odile Jacob, 1995.

Moravcsik, Andrew. "Negotiating the Single European Act." In *The New European Community*. Edited by Robert O. Keohane and Stanley Hoffmann. Boulder, Colo: Westview Press, 1991.

Muet, Pierre-Alain, and Alain Fonteneau. *Reflation and Austerity: Economic Policy under Mitterrand*. Translated by Malcolm Slater. New York and Oxford: Berg, 1990. (Slightly updated translation of *La Gauche face à la crise.*)

Nay, Catherine. *Le Noir et le rouge*. Paris: Grasset, 1984.

Northcutt, Wayne. *Mitterrand: A Political Biography*. New York: Holmes and Meier, 1991.

Paillole, Paul. *Services spéciaux 1935–1945*. Paris: Laffont, 1975.

Paxton, Robert. *Parades and Politics at Vichy: The French Officer Corps Under Marshal Pétain*. Princeton, N.J.: Princeton University Press, 1966.

Péan, Pierre. *Une Jeunesse française: François Mitterrand, 1934–1947*. Paris: Fayard, 1994.

Perrineau, Pascal. "La Dynamique du vote Le Pen. Le poids du 'gaucho-lepenisme.'" In *Le Vote de crise: L'Election présidentielle de 1995*. Edited by Pascal Perrineau and Colette Ysmal. Paris: Département d'Etudes Politiques du *Figaro* et Presses de la Fondation Nationale des Sciences Politiques, 1995.

———. "Les cadres du parti socialiste." In SOFRES, *L'Etat de l'opinion 1991*. Paris: Seuil, 1991.

Perrineau, Pascal, and Colette Ysmal, eds. *Le Vote de crise: L'Election présidentielle de 1995*. Paris: Département d'Etudes Politiques du *Figaro* et Presses de la Fondation Nationale des Sciences Politiques, 1995.

Pfister, Thierry. *La Vie quotidienne à Matignon au temps de l'Union de la Gauche*. Paris: Hachette, 1985.

Pierre, Andrew J., and William B. Quandt. *The Algerian Crisis: Policy Options for the West*. Washington, D.C.: Carnegie Endowment for International Peace, 1996.

Plenel, Edwy. *La Part de l'ombre*. Paris: Gallimard, 1994.

Raymond, Gino, ed. *France During the Socialist Years*. Aldershot: Darmouth, 1994.

Regards sur l'actualité 209–210 (March-April 1995). Paris: La Documentation Française, 1995. Double issue on "Les Grands Débats des années Mitterrand" and "La Chronologie des 2 septennats."

Rémond, René. *Les Droites en France*. Paris: Aubier Montaigne, 1982.

Riché, Pascal, and Charles Wyplosz. *L'Union monétaire de l'Europe*. Paris: Seuil, 1993.

Rimbaud, Christiane. *Bérégovoy*. Paris: Perrin, 1994.

Rosanvallon, Pierre. *La Nouvelle question sociale: Repenser l'état-providence*. Paris: Seuil, 1995.

Ross, George. *Jacques Delors and European Integration*. New York: Oxford University Press, 1995.

——— "Rocard . . . Victim of the Left's Lingering Illness?" *French Politics and Society* 12, nos. 2–3 (spring-summer 1994).

———. "Party Decline and Changing Party Systems: France and the French Communist Party." *Comparative Politics* 25, no. 1 (1992).

Ross, George, Stanley Hoffmann, and Sylvia Malzacher, eds. *The Mitterrand Experiment*. New York: Oxford University Press, 1987.

Rousso, Henry. *The Vichy Syndrome*. Translated by Arthur Goldhammer. Cambridge, Mass., and Cambridge, UK: Harvard University Press, 1991.

Sachs, Jeffrey, and Charles Wyplosz. "The Economic Consequences of President Mitterrand." *Economic Policy* 2 (April 1986).

Safran, William. "Rights and Liberties Under the Mitterrand Presidency: Socialist Innovations and Post-Socialist Revisions." *Contemporary French Civilization* 12 (winter-spring 1988).

Schemla, Elisabeth. *Edith Cresson: La Femme piégée*. Paris: Flammarion, 1993.

Schmidt, Vivien A. *From State to Market? The Transformation of French Business and Government*. New York: Cambridge University Press, 1996.

_____. *Democratizing France: The Political and Administrative History of Decentralization*. Cambridge, UK, and New York: Cambridge University Press, 1990.

_____. "Decentralization, a Revolutionary Reform." In *The French Socialists in Power*. Edited by Patrick McCarthy. New York: Greenwood Press, 1987.

Schnapper, Dominique. *La France de l'intégration: Sociologie de la nation en 1990*. Paris: Gallimard, 1991.

Schneider, Robert. *Les Dernières Années*. Paris: Seuil, 1994.

_____. *La Haine tranquille*. Paris: Seuil, 1992.

_____. *Michel Rocard*. Paris: Stock, 1987.

Seznec, Bruno. *Séguin*. Paris: Grasset, 1994.

SOFRES. *L'Etat de l'opinion 1991*. Edited by Olivier Duhamel and Jérôme Jaffré. Paris: Seuil, 1991.

_____. *L'Etat de l'opinion 1992*. Edited by Olivier Duhamel and Jérôme Jaffré. Paris: Seuil, 1992.

_____. *L'Etat de l'opinion 1993*. Edited by Olivier Duhamel and Jérôme Jaffré. Paris: Seuil, 1993.

_____. *L'Etat de l'opinion 1994*. Edited by Olivier Duhamel and Jérôme Jaffré. Paris: Seuil, 1994.

_____. *L'Etat de l'opinion 1996*. Edited by Olivier Duhamel, Jérôme Jaffré, and Philippe Méchet. Paris: Seuil, 1996.

_____. *L'Etat de l'opinion—clés pour 1987*. Edited by Olivier Duhamel, Elisabeth Dupoirier, and Jérôme Jaffré. Paris: Seuil, 1987.

_____. *L'Etat de l'opinion—-clés pour 1988*. Edited by Olivier Duhamel, Elisabeth Dupoirier, and Jérôme Jaffré. Paris: Seuil, 1988.

Stone, Alec. *The Birth of Judicial Politics in France: The Constitutional Council in Comparative Perspective*. New York: Oxford University Press, 1992.

Suleiman, Ezra. "The Politics of Corruption and the Corruption of Politics. *French Politics and Society* 9, no. 1 (winter 1991).

Szij, Eric. "La nationalisation a-t-elle été un outil efficace de politique industrielle?" *Regards sur l'actualité* 205 (November 1994).

_____. "Privatisations: Logique industrielle ou logique budgétaire?" *Regards sur l'actualité* 205 (November 1994).

Tiersky, Ronald. "The French Left and the Third World." In *The Foreign Policies of the French Left*. Edited by Simon Serfaty. Boulder, Colo.: Westview Press, 1979.

Tribalat, Michèle. *Faire France: Une Grande Enquête sur les immigrés et leurs enfants*. Paris: La Découverte, 1995.

Védrine, Hubert. *Les Mondes de François Mitterrand: À l'Elysée, 1981–1995*. Paris: Fayard, 1996.

Wauthier, Claude. *Quatre Présidents et l'Afrique*. Paris: Seuil, 1995.

Zelikow, Philip, and Condoleeza Rice. *Germany Unified and Europe Transformed: A Study in Statecraft*. Cambridge, Mass.: Harvard University Press, 1995.

Zemmour, Eric. *Balladur, immobile à grands pas*. Paris: Grasset, 1995.

Index

293